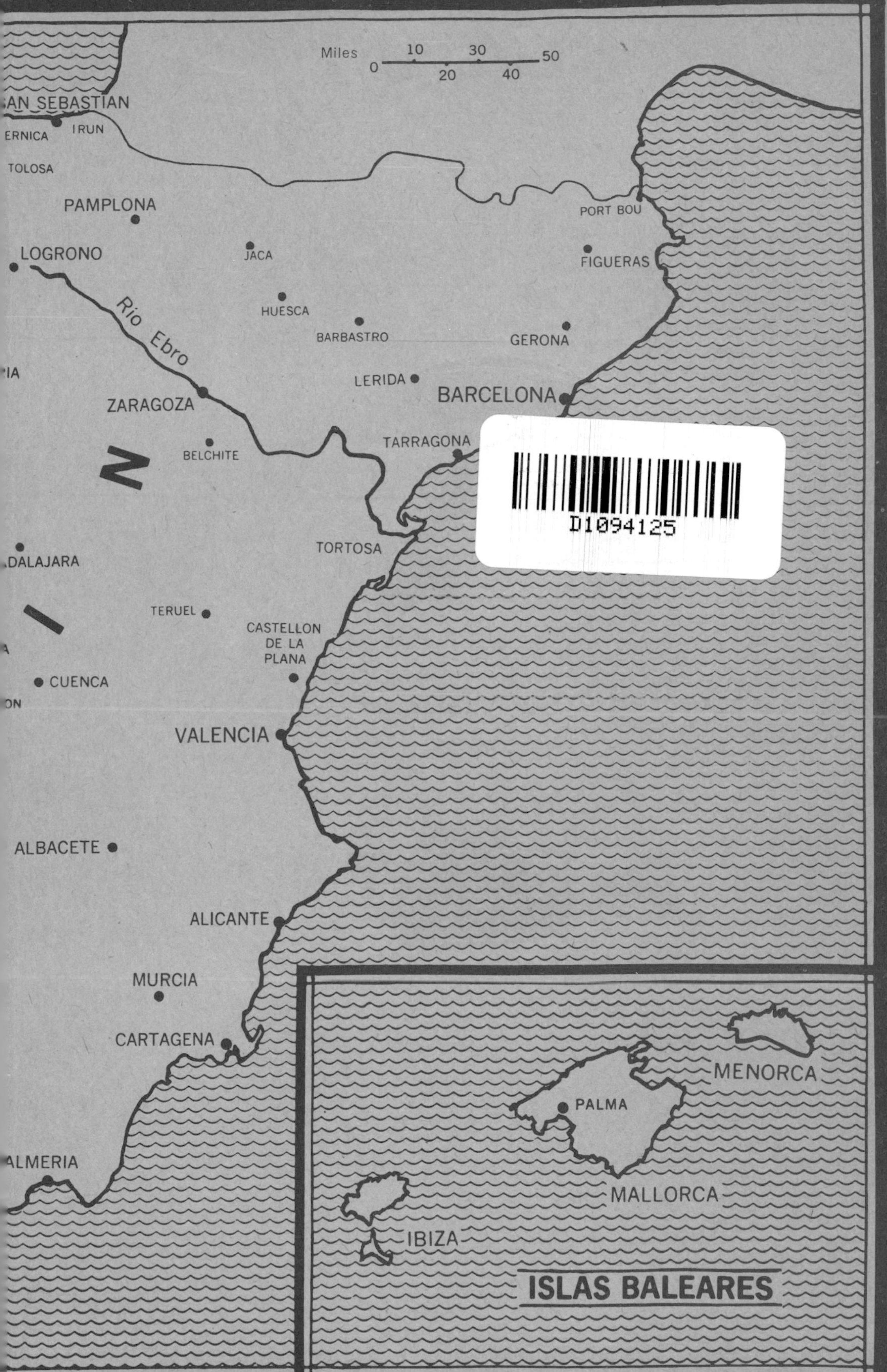
Miles
0
10
20
30
40
50
SAN SEBASTIAN
IRUN
TOLOSA
PAMPLONA
LOGRONO
JACA
HUESCA
BARBASTRO
Rio Ebro
ZARAGOZA
BELCHITE
LERIDA
BARCELONA
TARRAGONA
TORTOSA
PORT BOU
FIGUERAS
GERONA
TERUEL
CASTELLON
DE LA
PLANA
CUENCA
VALENCIA
ALBACETE
ALICANTE
MURCIA
CARTAGENA
ALMERIA
MENORCA
PALMA
MALLORCA
IBIZA
ISLAS BALEARES

ıajor crisis of thi:
nited Spanish Civ'

ıy Unive
ed his B.A.
ıethodist Universit
6 from New York U
ıously taught at Rider Co
rs University, and has be
e theater in both the Unit
d in France.

*ued from front flap)*

sion of how life ought to be. H
wn heroism, sacrifice, passio
passion, they were themselves
vocably changed, and their writing
e soon to change the literary styles
of the entire Western world.
Mr. Benson document
the remarkab

New York University Studies
in Comparative Literature
I

# Writers in Arms

# Writers in Arms

## The Literary Impact of the Spanish Civil War

by Frederick R. Benson

Foreword by Salvador de Madariaga

1967

New York — New York University Press

London — University of London Press Limited

*Library of Congress Catalog Card Number 67–25045* 

*Manufactured in The United States of America*
*Design by Judith Gimple*

# Acknowledgements

Excerpts from W. H. Auden's *Spain,* copyright 1938, and included in the author's *Collected Shorter Poems 1930–1944,* published by Faber and Faber Limited and Random House, Inc., are reprinted by permission of these publishers.

Excerpts from Georges Bernanos' *Les grands cimetières sous la lune,* copyright 1938, are reprinted by permission of Librairie Plon.

Excerpts from Roy Campbell's *Flowering Rifles,* copyright 1939, are reprinted by permission of Curtis Brown Limited.

Quotations from Ernest Hemingway's *For Whom the Bell Tolls,* copyright 1940 by Ernest Hemingway, that appear in this book are protected by copyright and have been reprinted here by special permission of Charles Scribner's Sons, Jonathan Cape Limited, and the trustees of the Ernest Hemingway estate.

Excerpts from Arthur Koestler's *Spanish Testament,* copyright 1937 by Victor Gollancz Limited, are reprinted by permission of A. D. Peters and Company.

Excerpts from C. Day Lewis' *Overtures to Death and Other Poems,* copyright 1938, 1961, are reprinted by permission of the Harold Matson Company, Inc.

Excerpts from Louis Mac Neice's *Autumn Journal,* copyright 1939, are reprinted by permission of Faber and Faber Limited and Random House, Inc.

Permission to translate and quote from André Malraux's *L'espoir,* copyright 1937 by Editions Gallimard, is given by Editions Gallimard, Random House, Inc. (publishers of André Malraux's *Man's Hope,* copyright 1938), and George Routledge and Kegan Paul Limited.

Excerpts from George Orwell's *Homage to Catalonia,* copyright 1952 by Sonia Brownell Orwell, are reprinted by permission of Harcourt, Brace and World, Inc., Martin Secker and Warburg Limited, and the estate of the late George Orwell.

Excerpts from Herbert Reed's *Thirty-five Poems,* copyright 1940 by the author and included in *Collected Poems,* copyright 1966, published by Horizon Press, are reprinted by permission of Faber and Faber Limited and Horizon Press.

Excerpts from Gustav Regler's *The Great Crusade,* copyright 1940 by Longmans, Green and Company Limited, are reprinted by permission of Longmans, Green and Company Limited and David McKay Company, Inc.

Excerpts from Kenneth Rexroth's "Two Poems" in *Salud!,* ed. Alan Calmer, copyright 1938 and included as "Autumn in California" in the author's *In What Hour,* copyright 1940 by Kenneth Rexroth, are reprinted by permission of the author and New Directions Publishing Corporation.

Excerpts from Rex Warner's "The Tourist Looks at Spain" in *Poems for Spain,* eds. Stephen Spender and John Lehmann, copyright 1939, are reprinted by permission of John Lehmann.

# ▸ Foreword

"Flame-like Spain," said Shelley. And Shakespeare speaks of knights "from tawny Spain, lost in the world's debate." English poetical intuition often does penetrate into the innermost being of Spain. "Flame-like" is a wonder. It conveys at once the chief features of the Spanish spirit: it is vertical, spontaneous, immaterial, upward; it is ardent. And even as tongues of fire do, it turns into fire everything it touches.

The civil war set fire to the intellects of Europe, of America, even of the East. The intellectual world forgot that its language is reason. To a lesser degree, it had already happened when the people of Spain rose against Napoleon. The romantic poets of Britain sang the heroism of the men and women of Spain. Southey, Wordsworth, Shelley, wrote moving poems. Canning let the Spaniards down. The pattern of events in our century was similar. There was no lack of poems. There was plenty of heat, indeed, more heat than light. But after the Southeys and the Shelleys, came the Cannings. And they were by no means all English.

What is it that, now and then, sets the intellectual world aflame on a Spanish crisis, usually a civil war? "Now and then" is important. It may stand for "a century" or even more; as in this case. Plains of quiescence always stretch between Spanish volcano and Spanish volcano. What sets the world afire is precisely the contrast between the long quiescent plain and the hot, vertical, upward fire of the volcano.

The world is quiescent by nature, unsteady by circumstance. It longs to stretch into a horizontal peace, as long and as quiescent as it can contrive it. On the soft cushion of reason if possible; on the even softer pillow of doubt, if need be. Provided it can go on half-dozing, half-active, the world is ready to turn a blind eye on many evils. What is the good of . . . ? That is the yardstick. The world is utilitarian. What is the good of . . . ? really means: What are the goods to get out of . . . ? On the basis of this utilitarian attitude (let's not overwork the word *philosophy*) the world manages to traverse many a long stretch of the steppe of quiescence.

After many leagues of time, the world gets dreary. It does reap the benefits of its liberal, objective, empirical, reasonable attitude. It does get a stretch of . . . well, should we call it peace? It does get prosperous. The black patches are discreetly overlooked or kept in the dark. There is a hell of a lot of champagne that gets drunk here or there, and lesser wines too, not to speak of other fiery liquids that help one to do without the real fire of real life inside . . . and yet, the cold, black hearth without fire in the innermost hall of man's being eventually grows bigger and bigger and swallows the whole into its own blackness and emptiness.

Then, lo and behold, the Spanish volcano erupts and sets the skies aflame; and its glow sets alight everybody's eyes. Flame-like Spain. She seemed so lost in the world's debate, and suddenly *c'est du midi que nous vient la lumière.* From that backward nation too! What does "backward" mean anyhow? And why should the forward poets of the forward nations suddenly burst out singing the praises of that straggler in the march of progress—progress, the strange phenomenon that manages at one step to move both forward and to the left?

* * *

"But you forget the world wars, two of them. Aren't they volcanoes also?" Well, no, they weren't. They were deadly crevasses in the plain of peace and of give-and-take; attempts at forcing the issue when the argument of the two opposite reasons had failed, so as to carry the argument on and forward afterwards; but they were not volcanoes, because the stratigraphy of the plain was not in question. Both sides accepted the rules of power and utility. All Cannings, ready to let down anyone whose letting down might have benefited somebody or something, thus enabling a positive answer to be given to the crucial question: "What is the good of . . . ?"

The Spanish volcano is no good to any one, least of all to the Spaniards. When Mussolini, an imitation volcano, in an imitation fiery speech, threatened with exploding if Italian aspirations were not satisfied, Briand, a masterpiece of plainmanship, retorted that he was not impressed, because it was the man who exploded who was bound to suffer the worst effects of an explosion. Spain has suffered terribly from the several eruptions she has undergone in the last and present centuries. But the reason why she underwent them and won by some of them the admiration of so many Euro-American intellectuals was that they amounted to—or were seen as —violent protests against the utilitarian disregard for essentials.

* * *

A Spanish proverb may throw some light on the situation: *Una cosa piensa el bayo y otra cosa el que lo ensilla.* One thing is thinking the bay horse and another thing the groom who is saddling him. Admired and admirers were perhaps less in tune than met the eye; and this might well explain why the intellectuals who admired the Spanish people ranged from communists through liberals to fascists; and also why the dialogues between Spaniards that now and then wove a fleeting net of unity above and across the trenches revealed such an astonishing fraternity between brother enemies.

That so many of the intellectuals who were set afire by the Spanish civil war should have been communists on their way out or actually unfrocked, need surprise no one. The fact is significant of what was going on in those days in the Euro-American brain. The period between the two world wars brings to a head the disintegration of the liberal faith whose prophets had been the Encyclopædists, the Founding Fathers of the United States (including Lincoln), the great English liberals, and the founders of the League of Nations. For many good western minds, this over-optimistic and even smug world had been driven out of the stage by the rival wave of idealism initiated by the great French socialists, and raised to its triumph in the European intellect by the genius of Karl Marx. Many were the European minds who in those days launched themselves in mid-air from the Gladstone-Wilson to the Marx-Lenin trapeze like circus performers; only to find that the Marx-Lenin trapeze was not there. Broken-hearted if not broken-boned, they sought relief and consolation in flame-like Spain.

* * *

Both liberals and socialists-communists were rationalists, while Spain was not. What all but collapsed (it didn't quite) in the thirties was the faith in Goddess Reason. At the time when the liberal system was on the eve of its most spectacular economic victories, many liberals lost courage and faith; and they sought a new faith in Marxism. There it was, gloriously rising in Russia, freeing at last the Russian people from their multisecular serfdom. The whole world hailed that triumph as a new, real dawn, a glorious hope, a reward for those who had believed in reason. And as for world affairs, the League of Nations was at last the blueprint for a World State.

So the two wings of the rationalist world, the liberal and the Marxist, lived on their hopes, nested at last in tangible, visible trees planted in the earth—the Soviet Union, the League of Nations.

The twofold answer was hellish: Stalin. Hitler. Both, mind you, rationalists. Both providing perfectly reasoned out arguments for their animal instincts. Capitalization and the defense of the revolution would justify the murderous Soviet concentration camps; *Lebensraum* for the *Herrenvolk* would justify the murderous concentration camps of Nazidom. Both intellectuals, or aping them, writers of books, clad in the immaculate robes of so-called political so-called philosophy. What sort of a world was this? And could it be said to differ in any way from a lunatic asylum? Readers of *La Condition Humaine* or of *Fiesta* would shake their heads and wonder.

* * *

Those cities in ruins, those trenches soaked in human blood, those cemeteries for not quite dead human beings which were the concentration camps were to act on the Western soul like a spiritual bombardment, and to reduce it to shambles. While the repeated explosions of violence battered that Western soul from the outside, an inner disintegration had already set in. The world had begun the century entering into one of the most dangerous transitions in its history: during the twentieth century, the nations were gradually to vanish as independent, sovereign, political units; and the World Commonwealth was not to be ready to receive them into her wider bosom for many a year to come. The steppe of reason was to lose its bearings. Men were to be deprived of their national frameworks before a human or worldwide framework was ready for them to refer their actions to. The game was fascinating. The stakes high. But where were the rules?

The rules? They would burst out from the bowels of the earth, floating in the molten lava of the Spanish volcano. Let us all go there to save them from the very fire that brings them forth. The rules cannot be evolved in our march to the steppe of reason; they must spring from the innermost levels of the human earth—oh, you can call it spirit, if you wish. I do believe Jung wouldn't mind, though Freud might object. And after all, neither Jung nor Freud is the last word. There is no last word. None. Unless those heroic Spaniards . . .

So, for those noble, disinterested, idealistic, disillusioned intellectuals of the West, flame-like Spain became as the column of fire that led the Jews across the desert, a guiding light. A set of fundamental values was to arise from the Spanish ordeal. The world would no longer be absurd; and we should know not only where we are but where we are going.

* * *

Meanwhile, the Spaniards were thinking quite otherwise. The horse and the groom, remember. What were they thinking? Difficult to say. What were they not thinking? That is not so difficult. They certainly were not thinking of providing an answer for the doubts that tortured the intellectuals, whether of the left or of the right. They were not even thinking in worldwide, human, universal terms. They were beginning again the multisecular duel for a Spain as they saw her, only they did not see the same Spain—hence the strife.

We may be touching here one of the points on which the perspective of the admirers did not tally with that of the admired. The admirers saw Spain as *becoming* something else. The admired saw Spain as *being* something else. You may, of course, argue that becoming means change of being. But if that be so, it only happens in the brain. The Spaniard is. He does not become. And it is just because the issue confronted two different ways of being, neither of which would become, that a civil war broke out.

Its object was to liberate what Spain really is. This struggle occupies the whole history of Spain; just as the liberating of what a man really is occupies all his life. The process has often been altered, twisted, distorted, if at times stimulated, by foreign intervention; for Spain has been invaded a surprising number of times. The civil war was but the last of many such cases of arrested self-discovery under the influence of foreign forces, not always military.

It began early. To go no further back, the influence of the Cluny Order in the eleventh century; the crushing of the Commoners by Charles I (Charles V of Germany) with the consequential economic and political destruction of the free municipal republics of the central-northern parts of Spain, within a horseshoe frontier starting from Santander and taking in the Basques, the Castillians and the northwestern Aragonese, as politically creative a region as any other in Europe at the time; the diversion towards America of the obviously Africa-directed line of Spanish destiny; the absorption of the Austrian dynasty in European wars alien to the destiny of Spain; the French dynasty and its alien, though intelligent and efficient ideas; the Napoleonic invasion followed by an explosion of the Spanish volcano; the extinction of this volcano by the Holy Alliance and by the One Hundred Sons of St. Louis; and last and worst, the civil war, transformed by foreign powers and forces into a battle for their steppe-of-reason ideologies.

For that civil war was not born so and was not meant to be so. For the Spanish people, life is, was, and always shall be a Purgatory. So, why worry? This attitude is often mistaken for fatalism. But there is no fatalism in Spain. What there is amounts to a recognition of the boundaries of man's power over human nature. Active, creative, spirited, the average Spaniard is sceptic about any but a Purgatory view of life.

Then, there come the two extremes: those who insist on life as an orthodox Paradise, quiescent in obedience to the Lord; and those who see life as an anarchist Paradise, free from any discipline but that of man's own self. The two paradise wings will gradually persuade or compel the purgatory center to join in their endeavour to seize Paradise where it lurks hidden in the unrevealed eternity of things. A civil war of flames.

It matters little that a host of utilitarian devils fan the flames on both sides. On the side of the Paradise of obedience to the Lord, the landlords, claiming parentage with the Almighty on the strength of their own might; on the side of the Paradise of anarchy, the political demagogues whose aim it is to climb to power on the back of "the people." This utilitarian element does contribute to the hardening of our civil wars; but could do little without the very essence of the civil war itself, which is a rivalry of flames.

A flame is. It does not become. All those idealistic foreigners, some of whom shed their blood, and some of the best of whom gave their lives, for Spain, were all "becoming." It was the move-on dreaming to be able to help the move-upwards; it was the building-up dreaming to help the burning-out; it was the changing dynamic dreaming to come to the aid of the perennial static; it was the mighty river of Europe endeavouring to quench the fire of flame-like Spain.

Salvador de Madariaga

# Contents

# Political Abbreviations and English Equivalents

| | |
|---|---|
| C.E.D.A. | (Confederación Española de Derechas Autónomas): Catholic Party led by José María Gil Robles; nucleus furnished by Acción Popular, a Roman Catholic political organization |
| C.N.T. | (Confederación Nacional del Trabajo): Anarcho-Syndicalist Trade Union centered in Barcelona |
| F.A.I. | (Federación Anarquista Ibérica): Anarchist secret society composed of extremist elements |
| J.O.N.S. | (Juntas de Ofensiva Nacional-Syndicalista): Fascist organization later amalgamated with the Falange |
| P.O.U.M. | (Partido Obrero de Unificación Marxista): Trotsky-oriented Marxist organization |
| P.S.U.C. | (Partido Socialista Unificado de Cataluña): The United Catalan Socialist-Communist Party, essentially moderate in policy |
| U.G.T. | (Unión General de Trabajadores): Socialist Trade Union centered in Madrid, essentially moderate in policy |
| U.M.E. | (Unión Militar Española): Right-wing officers group |
| U.M.R. | (Unión Militar Republicana): Republican officers group |

# Introduction

The total impact of the Spanish Civil War on Europe and America can never be measured with precision. In retrospect, the passions aroused by the conflict appear disproportionate to any military importance inherent in the struggle. For intensity of emotion, neither the First World War nor the Second World War exacerbated the feelings of people to the extent of those events in Spain from 1936 to 1939. More than any other crisis of the century, the Spanish struggle brought to the surface the incipient political philosophies and humanitarian hopes of an extremely social-conscious generation. For many intellectuals, their great interest in the Spanish conflict was not based on any exalted belief in the importance of the war for the future of mankind, but rather on the realization that something was lacking in their own culture; that the backward, stagnant, and inefficient Spaniard could well compete, in the field of human values, with the efficient, practical, and progressive European. At that time the sociologist Franz Borkenau asserted, "the one seems predestined to last, unmoving, throughout the cataclysms of the surrounding world, and to outlive national usurpers and foreign conquerors; the other, progressive, may progress towards his own destruction."[1]

Hugh Thomas has written that the Spanish Civil War "appeared a 'just war,' as civil wars do to intellectuals, since they lack the apparent vulgarity of [inter]national conflicts."[2] To many antifascists, when all the parties of the left were ostensibly cooperating in the Popular Front, it seemed a moment of hope for a new generation rebellious at its inheritance of a cynical and hypocritical legacy. The democracies—England, France and the United States—had for years been absorbed in an effort to recover from economic disaster, and had shown neither vigor nor resolution in their attempt to contain Hitler and Mussolini. In describing the democratic perspective, Allen Guttman reflects that

> Spain seemed a last chance for a representative government and a pluralistic society in a Europe that had turned with frightening speed toward dictatorship and totalitarianism. At a time when militant Fascism deified the unreasonable, the Spanish Republic seemed to represent the Enlightenment's faith in reason as the faculty by which men govern themselves.[3]

Thus, for many, the defense of the Spanish people was the embodiment of the forces of light struggling against the turbulent onrush of engulfing darkness.

With the perspective provided by the thirty-year interim since the outbreak of hostilities, the historical importance of the Spanish Civil War is clearly discerned. In the political and military history of the twentieth century, the Spanish conflict overshadows other national and international events which occurred between the two world wars. Although its concrete result was a fascist military triumph, it also offered to International Communism, with its discipline, its skillful propaganda machine, and the prestige derived from its defense of a humanitarian cause, the greatest political opportunity since the Soviet Revolution; it converted the concept of a unified front against fascism from a study in Marxist dialectics to a battlefield reality. For the Germans, Italians, and Russians, who undertook to advise, support, and exploit one side or the other, the war in Spain provided the opportunity to experiment with weapons and tactics. Politically, the war helped to delineate the European international situation, although at a tremendous sacrifice in men and ideals.

The Spanish Civil War was a conflict in which the military strategy was easily visualized and the ideological issues, at least on the surface, seemed clearly drawn. Since the area of struggle in

Spain was confined, and the scope of the military action comparatively restrained, the voices of individuals were not submerged, as they were to be in 1939, by the vast machinery of modern warfare. It is not difficult to envision why so many intellectuals found in the outbreak of the conflict that thunderbolt from an increasingly clouding sky, something very like an act both of fulfillment and deliverance. As a result, when literature reflected social and economic problems, as well as the fears engendered by a series of political crises, the war not only served to bring these problems and fears into sharp focus, but became the counteraction that would conceivably contribute to their elimination. It provided writers with the opportunity to base their works on an actual event, an objective situation, which possessed tremendous power as a literary symbol. During the 1930s, an era of incessant social violence, depression, and revolution, climaxed by the Spanish Civil War, these authors felt themselves carried along by history. So traumatic was the impact of this period ending with the Second World War, that it can be said of a great many writers that nothing has happened to them since. If the nineteenth century did not end until 1914, the twentieth did not actually begin until the 1930s. In the democracies, the Spanish conflict ultimately proved to many writers that their political and social theories required closer scrutiny; that a cause which seemed just could nonetheless be corrupted; and that the violence of modern war could not be satisfactorily rationalized in ideological terms. Most intellectuals later conceded that abdication of responsibility by their democratic governments permitted the weak but representative Spanish Republic to be destroyed by fascist aggression; and they generally acknowledged that the defeat of the Loyalists was a major factor in encouraging the fascist dictators to extend their depredations in Europe, thus bringing about the Second World War. Only too late did they come to realize that what was occurring in that tormented country was neither a meaningless fratricidal strife nor a crusade in defense of Christian civilization, but a tragic prologue to the global struggle against international fascism.

Although the political and military history of the Spanish conflict has received considerable attention, less is known about the impact of the war on European and American literature, the importance of which is manifested in those writings dealing with the conflict. From a critical point of view, since 1945 there have been few works that can approach the distinction of the major literary efforts concerned with the Spanish Civil War. Authors of such international prominence as André Malraux, Georges Bernanos, François Mauriac, Jacques Maritain, Antoine de Saint-Exupéry, Louis Aragon, and Paul Eluard in France; George Orwell, W. H. Auden, Stephen Spender, C. Day Lewis, and Herbert Read in England; Ernest Hemingway, John Dos Passos, Theodore Dreiser, and Archibald MacLeish in the United States; and Ilya Ehrenburg and Michael Kol'tsov in Russia, all contributed to the literature of the Spanish Civil War. In South America the Chilean Pablo Neruda and the Peruvian César Vallejo committed their poetry to the Spanish cause. Most of the important writers were antifascist and their central themes were expressed in the context of their democratic traditions. This antifascist thesis was further strengthened by the writers who fled Hitler's Germany and Mussolini's Italy at this time: Gustav Regler, Arthur Koestler, Thomas Mann, Bertolt Brecht, and Ernst Toller from Germany; and Randolfo Pacciardi, Pietro Nenni, Palmero Togliatti, and Luigi Longo from Italy, each of whom later contributed to the literature of the war. In Spain as well, most literary figures, although deploring the extremism in both camps, were sympathetic to the cause of the Republic; few Spanish authors aligned themselves with the insurgents during the period of the conflict.[4] Most Spanish writers and the literary world in general opposed the fascist cause, particularly following the senseless execution in the Nationalist zone of Spain's great poet, Federico García Lorca.

There was in Europe and the United States a small intellectual element on the right which hoped that the demise of the Spanish Republic would be followed by the rebirth of a nationalistic and aristocratic social order; George Santayana and Ezra Pound sympathized with this group. The only intense literary support for the Nationalist cause came from those Roman Catholic writers who saw in Franco's Nuevo Estado a promise of a Christian society in which the menace of communism would be permanently eliminated. Paul Claudel was the leading figure of this group in France, but he was countered by such Catholic intellectuals as Mauriac and Maritain. With the possible exception of

Stefan Andres' short religious novel, *Wir Sind Utopia,* an extremely moving portrayal of conversion and martyrdom, the literary efforts of the Catholic intellectuals were inadequate. The conservative and reactionary responses to the Spanish Civil War failed to produce a major work comparable to several written from a liberal perspective.

Supporters of the right, however, did not monopolize literary ineptitude. Of the considerable output by both sides recounting the war in Spain, much was amateurish and poor even by journalistic standards. The pamphlets, on-the-spot accounts and memoirs which were published shortly after the outbreak of hostilities, made no pretense beyond literary commercialism and are not worthy of serious critical consideration. A large portion of the literature written after the battlelines were drawn and the issues defined consisted of polemics intended to express political ideology. Such writings, often extremist in nature, either distorted or oversimplified the deeper meanings of the conflict. The vast literature on the subject available in books and periodicals was largely topical and evanescent. Much of it was marred by a surfeit of emotion; much was purely sensational; and a large portion of this writing, while passionately committed in sentiment, possessed little literary quality. Few works transcended the clichés of propaganda and found their inspiration in humanistic ideals rather than partisan politics.

The novelist possessed two distinct advantages over writers in other genres when discussing the disparate aspects of the Spanish Civil War. The extreme adaptability of his medium enabled him to cover a wider range than dramatists and writers in other fictional forms and to include within his work such widely diverse phases of the struggle as the siege of the Alcazar, the bombing of civilians in Guernica, the interparty strife in Barcelona, and the defense of Madrid. Thus, the novelist could establish a panoramic view of the war rather than be restricted to the presentation of an isolated theme or event.

Most significantly, the novelist was able to merge his ideas and ideals into the action he portrayed. During this period ideology had become very closely associated with politics in the minds of writers. The response to the conflict by European and American authors was affected by the same social and political forces which strongly influenced the literary movements of the decade. In the democracies there has probably never been a time when organized religion seemed as futile or lacking in reality as it did to many intellectuals when confronted with the human suffering of the depression years; at this same time, historical analyses seemed too remote to provide direction amidst the social protest and upheaval of the 1930s. No other philosophy appeared to fill the void. Political ideology alone seemed to provide a viable solution.

In view of the unique nature of the Spanish struggle, it is understandable that most of its literature is concerned with politics and hence may be termed "political"; in it political ideas play the dominant role and the political milieu is the dominant setting.[5] Because of the close relationship between politics and the literary output of this war, it is difficult to judge the true merit of its product. The measure of effectiveness of a political novelist is his ability to explore ideology, which is necessarily abstract, through the experiences and feelings of his fictional characters. The important works of this genre concerning the Spanish conflict transcended the propaganda tracts of their contemporaries by generating such intense heat that the ideas expounded were endowed with a capacity for stirring the characters into action, while creating the illusion of an independent existence fused within the pattern of the novel. No other novels so well reflect the complexity of the issues involved and the various humanist interpretations of the conflict as those of André Malraux's *L'espoir,* Gustav Regler's *The Great Crusade,* and Ernest Hemingway's *For Whom the Bell Tolls.*

Three other novelists who chose the literary form of the personal narrative to present their experiences in Spain, George Orwell in *Homage to Catalonia,* Arthur Koestler in *Spanish Testament,* and Georges Bernanos in *Les grands cimetières sous la lune,* deserve consideration in a study of the literary impact of the Spanish struggle. The difference between these avowed personal narratives and the fiction of Malraux, Regler, and Hemingway is essentially one of degree rather than kind. The principal distinction between the personal narrative and the novel is the limitation of the former, which restricts its account to the single thread of personal experience, while the novelist may supplement or expand his narrative by an imaginative penetration into the experiences of others. The more autobiographical genre, however, if it is to be worthy of literary attention, must involve considerable selectivity and discrimination in ordering the writer's past experiences. The novelist follows a similar pattern but has greater freedom of selection and arrangement. The heavily autobiographical origins of the Malraux, Regler, and Hemingway war novels are unmistakable, and portions of the Koestler, Bernanos, and Orwell books may be considered in either category. The quality of these latter works provides a meaningful insight into the motivations of those authors who went to Spain, an insight which is not easily discernible in prose fiction. The responses of Orwell, Koestler, and Bernanos to the war, composed against a background of disillusioned hopes and irrevocable commitments, of political treachery, tortured hostages, air raids over placid villages, and mass executions, closely parallel the treatment of the issues by Malraux, Regler, and Hemingway, thus furnishing direct testimony to the importance of the conflict in its own time. These combined works form a history unsurpassed in knowledge of the issues and sensitivity to the sufferings of the Spanish people. Such evidence is extremely valuable in a study of the literary impact of the Spanish Civil War.

At the close of the fighting, the majority of Spanish writers who had aligned themselves with the Republican cause, such as Max Aub, Arturo Barea, Rafael Alberti, and Ramón Sender, were forced into exile and scattered throughout Europe and North and South America. The major theme of these writers was naturally concerned with the Spanish conflict. They had retained their loyalty, but having lost direct contact with their country, these exiles relied on vivid memories for their treatment of the tragedy which they had recently witnessed. Such memories were weighted with the hope and disillusionment accompanying a truly intense experience. So intensely bitter had the struggle been that these authors felt compelled to express a passionately partisan approach to the issues involved. They had participated in one of the most dramatic events of modern times, and it was inevitable that they should testify to their experiences. The martyrdom of their comrades, the poets Antonio Machado and Miguel Hernández, was perhaps the greatest contribution by creative writers in this decade to the spiritual life of Europe.

Inside Spain, since the end of the war, few works of merit

have been published. The reasons for this are conjectural. Government censorship is perhaps a major factor, and possibly the Nationalist vantage point is less propitious for the exercise of the artist's imagination. In the years immediately following the conflict, no significant work concerned with the subject from a Nationalist point of view was produced. Recently, the Falangist author, José María Gironella, attempted to provide the Nationalists with a refutation of the interpretations of the conflict expounded by such Republican authors in exile as Barea, Aub, and Sender, as well as novelists of the stature of Hemingway, Koestler, Malraux, and Bernanos. Gironella's first novel, *Los Cipreses Creen en Dios* (1953), is worthy of consideration as an objective effort to explain the circumstances preceding the military uprising in July, 1936, while at the same time examining the conscience of the Spanish middle class during this period; his second novel, *Un Millión de Muertos* (1961), covering the events of the conflict, however, is little more than a caricature in its biased historical documentation of the three years of the war, accompanied by a tendentious interpretation of the facts involved.

The importance of the Spanish Civil War was diminished by the magnitude of the succeeding holocaust of World War II, but not in the eyes of Spanish authors. Although the immediacy of the Second World War discouraged potential foreign literature dealing with the Spanish struggle which might have been written between 1940 and 1945, this was not so with the native Spanish writers, particularly the Republican authors in exile. The impressive quantity and quality of the product of these authors, fiction as well as nonfiction, exceed all foreign treatment of the conflict and works on the subject published under the Franco regime. If the objectivity desirable in such testimony is lacking, the intensity and vividness embodied by these writers in their works more than justify critical considerations. But because the genuine bellicose fervor found in these works contrasts greatly with the reasonably objective detachment in the writings of the major foreign authors and, more specifically, because of the practical considerations involved in this study, I have chosen to omit a detailed analysis of the response of the Spanish authors to their civil conflict. The quantity of their literary output alone would necessitate a separate critical consideration.[6]

This book is but one contribution to a vast subject. Some day, perhaps, the international literature of the Spanish Civil War will be discussed with a comprehensiveness that will encompass all its various aspects, including detailed analyses of the German, Italian, and Russian contributions, as well as the works of Nationalist-oriented authors. In the interim a selective study of the impact of the conflict on major writers appears especially rewarding. Although monographs on individual authors have appeared, several of which discuss the "Spanish Civil War Period" in the development of the writer, no attempt has been made at a comparative study of the major novels and novelists concerned with the conflict. A study of the characters and their actions in the writings reflecting the events of the war and an analysis of the divergent interpretations of the basic issues involved should provide a penetrating insight into the views of the authors. The primary purpose of this study is to determine how engagement in the Spanish struggle by certain European and American novelists, either as volunteers in Spain or as active supporters of the Republic, affected the attitudes of these writers, which in turn influenced their art.

After surveying and critically evaluating European and American Spanish Civil War literature, I have concentrated on the works of Malraux, Regler, Hemingway, Orwell, Koestler, and Bernanos. These novelists, writing under the immediate impact of the realities of the struggle, show marked differences in attitudes and literary talent. I have endeavored to ascertain the degree to which their works examine the issues which were major factors in the causes and conduct of the war. Their interpretations of the war in a historical perspective, their understanding of the economic aspects of the conflict, their grasp of the political disparities, and their knowledge of the religious factors involved are compared. The objectivity and depth of perception of the individual authors, as well as their doctrinaire commitments, are ascertained.

Other aspects of this study are to determine whether each work agrees with the historical accounts of the conflict and to what extent it presents a realistic view of the action. A consideration of a writer's emphasis on the atrocities, the "pornography of violence," created in the stress and tension of the war, is contrasted with the writer's testimony to the humane qualities of the enemy. The apparently unconscious attempts of Malraux, Regler, Orwell, Bernanos, Koestler, and Hemingway to attribute certain conventional European and American concepts to an alien Spain are contrasted with the facts presented by the historians of the war. It will be seen, however, that philosophically the Spanish Civil War evoked a sympathetic response in all six novelists, primarily for humanistic reasons. Each expressed the feeling that the *whole* man emerged during the Spanish struggle, and the intensification of each author's social and political commitment was secondary to the appeal to the writer's conscience as a man. The impulse behind this more mature war literature was a desire to reveal the immutable truths which emerged from this struggle. Spain was the only place in Europe where fascism had encountered a genuine resistance. Upon the precedent of the Napoleonic era, the Spanish peasants might have risen and halted the fascist advance. But in a technologically-oriented world, with a vastly increased importance for machines and materials over the human spirit, the better equipped forces were certain of victory, and all the bravery and perseverance of the Spanish resistance were no match against them. Thus, this literature portrayed the human suffering, together with instances of great courage, occasioned by the war. Albert Einstein, echoing the sociologist Borkenau, expressed this basic belief: "The only thing in view of the circumstances surrounding our epoch that can keep the hope of better times alive within us is the heroic struggle of the Spanish people for freedom and human dignity."[7]

A study of the literary response to the war offers the opportunity to examine thoroughly the authors' treatment of the issues and the impact of the conflict on the intellectual conscience. The attempt to find in ideology a means of ordering a disjointed world was characteristic of the intellectual approach to the war. The disillusion effected by the betrayals among Republican factions and the eventual defeat of the Loyalist cause produced varying responses among writers. The sensibilities of the six novelists in this study were less fundamentally affected by the violence than many of their contemporaries. Their sensibilities, rather, were modified, but were not entirely shattered and reoriented. Others, however, never fully recovered from the traumatic impact and its accompanying spiritual shell shock. An examination of the reactions of the major novelists who participated in the cause of the Spanish people indicates the influence of that war on subsequent literature, particularly novels written about the Second World War.

The literature of the war in Spain is important because it reflects both the idealism and the subsequent disillusionment of many writers who had envisioned in the struggle of the Spanish people a great cause. No other circumstance is capable of altering the human condition as completely as war. The encounter with violence was to change drastically, not only the attitudes of these writers toward political ideology, but also their philosophy for establishing order in a chaotic world. The results of the encounter are manifest in the literature of World War II which is so obviously apolitical and in which writers seem to have extended beyond disillusionment to a desperate and consuming nihilism. If the writers of World War II cannot in any sense be called disillusioned, it is because they had been divested of their illusions before the great war had ever begun. The Spanish struggle had much to do with the destruction of the political drama of the 1930s, a destruction which left most writers without the direction provided by dogma and ideology when they were confronted by a far more widespread and devastating holocaust.[8] Regarding the earlier conflict, Thomas eulogizes, "The struggle gave birth to a burst of creative energy in many countries . . . which can plausibly be argued as comparable in quality to anything produced in the Second World War. The few real masterpieces that were produced will survive as monuments to those who died."[9]

F.R.B.
Tepoztlan, Mexico
June, 1967

## ▶ NOTES

[1] *The Spanish Cockpit* (London, 1937), p. 300.

[2] *The Spanish Civil War* (New York, 1961), p. 616. Thomas' history is for the most part an impartial account of the war.

[3] *The Wound in the Heart: America and the Spanish Civil War* (New York, 1962), p. 4. Guttmann's study is a comprehensive

analysis of the United States' response to the Spanish Civil War, as is F. Jay Taylor's *The United States and the Spanish Civil War, 1936–1939* (New York, 1956). A comparable account of the British popular reaction is presented in K. W. Watkins' *Britain Divided: The Effect of the Spanish Civil War on British Political Opinion* (London, 1963). New York University Library contains the unpublished M.A. thesis of Janet Siegel, "French Opinion on the Spanish Civil War" (1943), which provides some insight into French public opinion during the years of the actual fighting.

[4] For a detailed study of the impact of the war on European intellectual circles, particularly among Spanish and Italian men of letters, see Aldo Garosci, *Gli intellettuali e la guerra di Spagna* (Turin, 1959).

[5] Irving Howe, *Politics and the Novel* (New York, 1957), pp. 15–24. Howe's study is not specifically concerned with Spanish Civil War literature, but does provide definitive nomenclature in the area of politics and fiction.

[6] Several critical surveys of contemporary Spanish authors, including the Garosci book, have appeared in recent years, and there is currently being undertaken a study of the Spanish Civil War and its treatment by native novelists. The outstanding critical accounts of its influence on Spanish authors have been included in a separate section of the bibliography.

[7] In *The Heart of Spain*, Alvah Bessie, ed. (New York, 1952), p. 422.

[8] See John M. Muste, *Say That We Saw Spain Die* (Seattle, 1966), pp. 10–11.

[9] *Spanish Civil War*, p. 617.

# Writers in Arms

# I

# Writers Take Sides

The Spanish Civil War represented the intellectual as well as the emotional climax of the turbulent 1930s. The clash between the Republican and Nationalist forces served to crystallize the rival ideologies of the time. Spain found itself torn by a desperate struggle, the product of opposing forces which developed out of the long and bitter history of the country. The violent encounter was the result of the basic antipathy between the difficult efforts of liberal intellectuals to move the country in a progressive manner toward a modern twentieth-century social system and the attempts of reactionary elements to retard such changes by allying themselves with international fascism. Whatever the motives which led so many foreign intellectuals to join with the Spanish Republic—to sympathize ideologically, to adopt its cause as their own, to find in its goals a solution to the fundamental problems troubling them and at times to participate physically in the war in Spain—the literary response was overwhelming. A vast majority of the writers in Europe and the United States defined the conflict as a graphic struggle between the defenders and the destroyers of democracy, between the Spanish people and a reactionary group of aristocrats, priests and generals, between constitutional and arbitrary authority, and between freedom and repression.[1] While literary opinion strongly favored the Republic as the legal government of Spain, the Nationalists soon attracted reactionary sympathizers who defended their choice on the grounds that the military revolt had been necessary to save Spain from the threat of communism. More Catholic elements on the right viewed the struggle as one between the Church and a godless Marxism rather than between the fascist and antifascist forces. Thus the Spanish Civil War was transformed into an allegory in which the major social and political philosophies of the time were the chief antagonists.[2] The English social commentators, Robert Graves and Alan Hodge, noted that "never since the French Revolution had there been a foreign question which so divided" intellectual opinion.[3] For these and other reasons, the struggle in Spain became one of the most compelling literary topics of this century.

Never before during this century had writers been so completely involved in a historical event about which they felt moved to express themselves, and which they often supported with their art. Louis MacNeice, the Irish poet whose work had been consciously apolitical, early in the war concluded prophetically:

> Spain would soon denote
>   Our grief, our aspirations;
> Not knowing that our blunt
>   Ideals would find their whetstone, that our spirit
> Would find its frontier on the Spanish front,
>   Its body in a rag-tag army.[4]

The destruction and violence of the war put to the test the ideals and ideologies which had come to be of such importance to writers. The crisis involved fundamental philosophical doctrines which had governed Western democracies for centuries. Authoritarian states were intent on replacing these doctrines with new forms based on the domination by politics of every aspect of life, a hierarchy of races, and the absolute power of the state. In the face of this totalitarian threat, evidenced in Germany and Italy where the new forms of authoritarianism had taken hold, the defense of the democracies to preserve their humanist traditions and to safeguard their citizens nevertheless was at first hesitant and confused. Although most intellectuals after 1940 could agree that fascism at its inception might have been halted in Spain and the Second World War averted, in 1936 the threat of fascism appeared to many less immediate. As a result, factionalism persisted and unified support for the Spanish Republic was hopeless. Only the most perceptive conceived of the ideological nature of the struggle transcending diplomatic maneuvering and partisan issues. Throughout the conflict the choice of factions frequently was based on political or religious commitment rather than a fundamental belief in the necessity for defending a democratic and representative government. Polemics and other writing intended as propaganda confused and distorted the issues involved.

Coterminous with hasty and arbitrary classification was a tendency by writers to oversimplify the causes of the war and to ignore the complex developments which had preceded it. Instead of being viewed as a revolt or civil war waged over peculiarly Spanish problems, with roots inherent in the country's social, political, and religious history, it was transformed by European and American writers—more so as a result of German, Italian and Russian intervention—into a decisive struggle among the rival ideologies of the time: between fascism and democracy, conservatism and liberalism, totalitarianism and a republican form of government, Christianity and communism. Such classifications resulted in both complicating and oversimplifying the issues of the war: the former in the sense of often imposing an alien set of ideologies upon what began as a civil struggle, and the latter by employing familiar terms, which each believed he understood, to clarify complex problems which actually very few fully comprehended.[5] Naturally a certain amount of naïveté and some hypocrisy was inevitable; naïveté on the part of individuals who were unable to distinguish between the ideological contribution they could make and an indiscriminate acceptance of certain political policies; hypocrisy on the part of many statesmen and politicians who professed adherence to a policy of neutrality and nonintervention which they could not reconcile on ideological or even practical grounds.

The effects of the Spanish Civil War on European and American writers were inextricably linked with the political and literary currents that moved strongly through the intellectual life of the decade. Besides determining the ideological future of Spain—and many writers thought it would determine the ideological future of Europe as well—the struggle was seen as a test of the prevailing major political and social theories, providing an opportunity to transform these theories into action.[6] Few writers viewed the character of the Spanish struggle as one determined by a complex of circumstances, some peculiar to Spanish history, others reflections of the political situation in Europe and the United States during the 1930s. The type of ideological war that was waged in Spain was possible only because of the political climate of the time from which could be generated a special brand of idealism predicated on the rights of oppressed people, the justice of foreign intervention on the side of the oppressed, and the right of a people to self-determination. But if the Spanish conflict reflected the prevailing social and political attitudes of the 1930s, it is equally clear that the particular circumstances of the war were possible only in Spain, with its feudal system of landownership, its powerful Church, its decadent aristocracy, its unique susceptibility to anarchism, and its angrily irreconcilable political parties.[7]

Because an understanding of the literature of the Spanish Civil War depends upon a knowledge of the major aspects of the complex and controversial issues involved, some indication of the impact of the war outside Spain is essential. Any attempt at a general survey of the influence of the Spanish conflict on public opinion throughout Europe and the United States must of necessity be simplified by reducing the many diverse currents into a few main streams. It is impossible to present a detailed account of the enormous differences of opinion which existed from 1936 to 1939 in newspapers, periodicals, and the political pamphlets which proliferated during the three-year period. The literary historian seeking to examine the impact of the war on public opinion is forcibly reminded of the futility of accepting surface impressions and interpretations. Understanding depends on recognition of the underlying forces, motives, and tensions. By analyzing the reactions of the major political groups within the democracies to the Spanish conflict, followed by a study of the responses of the German antifascist writers in exile, some indication of the position of the European and American writer in relation to the tide of public opinion may be ascertained.[8]

Despite all its complications, the struggle of the Spanish Republic became for writers of the left symbolic of the struggle against fascism. Spain, in a short time, was transformed into a symbol of hope for all antifascists. It became possible to see in the struggle on the peninsula a true ideological conflict and not just an attempt to seize power by a military junta. As news of the Spanish fighting reached Europe and the United States in the final weeks of July 1936, there were few of these writers who did not feel the necessity for personal involvement. Many believed that the outcome would determine whether the world would remain at peace. For a large proportion the motives that drew these writers into the Spanish conflict were for the most part the same ideals that had originally motivated their earlier entry into radical politics: a humanitarian desire for a world in which poverty, injustice, and misery might be eliminated, combined in varying degrees with a drive for power, a need to participate in a historical movement that would provide for them an identity which they felt unable to achieve as individuals, and an anger and bitterness at the dominant social and political systems of their own countries. The resistance of the Spanish people to the military rebellion during the first few weeks of the war became a symbol for many radical intellectuals, offering the opportunity for an "1848" in the twentieth century; a revolutionary movement—with a greater degree of liberty and justice than was ever believed possible by their cynical contemporaries—had attained victories and offered some hope for success. The conflict thus contained a dual significance: it provided a testing ground for the revolutionary philosophies of the radical writers and also permitted them an outlet for their personal drives. Authors who in the 1920s had analyzed a decaying society, now felt themselves challenged to assist at the birth of a new and better order. Many of these same authors had joined the Writers' Congress and had assisted in labor strikes for similar reasons.[9]

In most cases politics played the decisive role in shaping the reactions of the literary radicals, and when it dominated their perspective of the human element in the struggle, it was at the expense of their art. Very often the writing reflected a tension between their political and humanitarian responses. Authors with anarchist, socialist, and communist commitments in Europe and the United States at the outbreak of hostilities had joined in a literary version of Spain's Popular Front,[10] supporting the cause of the Republic and advocating direct intervention by their own governments. Since most of them had experienced a strong personal interest in the forces involved in the conflict, an important consideration arose in their response to the defects apparent in the Republican government as the war progressed. Equally important was their attitude toward the relationship between the Spanish Republic and the Communist International, especially after the latter had assumed a major position in the social, political, and military decisions of the Loyalist forces.

Not surprisingly, nearly every radical political party and organization became hastily identified with one of the rival Spanish factions. Each political group had its own theory of how best to cope with the military situation. Like their counterparts in Spain, as the war progressed, these writers maintained a loyalty to their political commitments which often influenced their support for the Republic and reflected the interparty strife within the Popular Front. Although dedicated to a political ideology usually advocating some form of economic collectivism, these men who found their cause in the fight of Spanish Republicans were sharply divided regarding the methods and sacrifices necessary to achieve their goals. The writers were not all committed to the same set of ideals, nor were their commitments equally firm. If many of the radicals in Europe and the United States who supported the Loyalists were active members or sympathized with the anarchist, socialist, and communist organizations, others maintained an independent position. Even within the political parties vital fissures occurred.

The anarchists of Spain, the only country where the philosophy took root in a mass movement, saw in the rebellion of the dissident generals the opportunity to establish their version of a syndicalist society, free from the tyranny of state authority which they believed was "the most flagrant, most cynical and most complete denial of humanity."[11] The essence of the anarchist's philosophy is a faith in mankind based on belief in man's dignity and innate desire, given education and the right economic conditions, to help his fellow man. State interference, armies, and property would be superfluous in the anarchist paradise in which the natural instincts towards freedom, justice, intelligence, and fraternity would overcome all thoughts of personal gain, envy, and malice. Thus the Spanish anarchists from their powerful trade union centered in Catalonia viewed the war not as a military or political rebellion, but rather as a social upheaval which could, under their influence, result in the formation of a utopian social structure termed "Comunismo Libertario." The state, demanding obedience and respect for authority, was morally evil, and for these anarchists a policy of immediate and violent action was the only method to introduce the libertarian era. Philosophically, they disagreed with the communists on the necessity of forming a revolutionary government to carry out their plan. Among themselves, the anarchists, writing about the war, disagreed regarding participation in the Popular Front, a policy at complete variance with their previous refusals to participate in any form of organized government. The friction between the anarchists and the communists, the direct reflection of the disputes so many years before between Bakunin and Marx, was inevitable because, according to the Spanish scholar, Salvador de Madariaga, "Anarchy is centrifugal, and denies and defies command; Communism is centripetal and imposes command."[12] Eventually, with their ruthless suppression by the communists, the reservations voiced by the anarchists were shown to be justified.

In America and the rest of Europe anarchists organized aid-for-Spain committees, and a "Sacco-Vanzetti Column" was formed with international volunteers. The anarchist journals published outside of Spain favored the Popular Front and received the contributions of such nonanarchists as Havelock Ellis and Rebecca West in England. The British poet and sympathizer, Herbert Read, in "A Song for the Spanish Anarchists," affirmed his belief in the "natural freedom" necessary for man's survival. In the same poem he expressed his hope for constructive social progress in Spain with the Catalonian anarchists, whose spontaneous opposition to the rebels had been widely credited with saving the Republic during the first weeks of the war:

The golden lemon is not made
  but grows on a green tree:
A strong man and his crystal eyes
  is a man born free.
The oxen pass under the yoke
But a man born free has a path of his own
  and the blind are led at will:

> and a house on the hill.
> And men are men who till the land
> and women are women who weave:
> Fifty men own the lemon grove
> and no man is a slave.[13]

This appeal to man's desire for freedom and the implicit revolutionary message carried in it captures the almost mystical faith in their cause so common to the anarchists. The anarchists themselves, however, lacked the necessary talent to make a major contribution to the literature of the Spanish Civil War, and from one point of view this is extremely regrettable. The analyses of such anarchists as Emma Goldman in party publications in the United States and Vernon Richards in England often proved more informative and perceptive than many of the naïve statements regarding Republican Spain's complete religious freedom and its dedication to capitalism found in the free presses of the democracies.[14] The anarchist writers failed to make a substantial contribution to the literature of the war, and the movement itself in Europe and the United States never rallied popular support in sufficient numbers or influence to affect the course of the conflict. Only in Spain itself, where the conflict between the anarchists and the communists was a vital factor in the internecine strife within the Popular Front and the final defeat of the Loyalists, did the anarchists play a major role in the drama of the Spanish Civil War.

Madariaga's conclusion that within Spain what made the national conflict inevitable "was the Civil War within the Socialist Party"[15] was based on his belief that deep and violent divisions created by the left and right elements in the socialist camp enabled fascism to gain a foothold in Spanish politics. Once the fighting started, the socialists in Spain and the rest of Europe, as well as the United States, expressed their hope that the Spanish Civil War would result in the final attainment of the classless society predicted by Marx and Engels. The question which violently divided the socialist intellectuals outside Spain was not the final goal but the means by which the final goal was to be attained. Neither extreme within the party wished to compromise itself by supporting a communist-dominated Popular Front. From 1936 to 1939 these intellectuals were segmented into several groups: those whose allegiance was to the far left and who placed a truly radical and revolutionary interpretation on the Spanish struggle; a moderate section supporting the Popular Front which was willing to accept the position of alignment with the Stalinists in the face of a common menace; and those socialists who took an independent stand based on their own interpretation of Marxist principles.

Certainly the leading spokesman, in both fiercely attacking the Stalinists and advocating a truly revolutionary approach to the conflict in Spain, was the Russian exile, Leon Trotsky. For Trotsky the correct revolutionary policy in pursuing the struggle was as important as the struggle itself:

> The Spanish proletariat, like the French proletariat, does not want to remain disarmed before Mussolini and Hitler. But to defend themselves against these enemies it is first necessary to crush the enemy in one's own country. . . . To decide on such a measure one must stop crawling on one's knees before the Radical bourgeoisie. A genuine alliance of workers and peasants must be created against the bourgeoisie, including the Radicals. One must have confidence in the strength, initiative and courage of the proletariat. . . . The victory of the people means the end of the People's Front and the beginning of Soviet Spain. The victorious social revolution in Spain will inevitably spread out over the rest of Europe.[16]

Trotsky's essays were published in socialist journals throughout Europe and in the United States where they were especially well received by such noted literary and social commentators as Dwight Macdonald, Sidney Hook, and Philip Rahv, whose *Partisan Review* became a rallying point for anti-Stalinists in the United States.[17] American writers with socialist inclinations who were unable to follow the Trotsky line but found it equally difficult to support a communist-led Popular Front included James T. Farrell, Edmund Wilson, Lionel Trilling, Mary McCarthy, and Joseph Wood Krutch. Their support of the Spanish Republic took the form of protests and petitions critical of Roosevelt's failure to aid the Loyalists and which, with varying intensity throughout the war, demanded repeal of the United States Embargo Act. In France, however, the diffidence felt toward the communists by such socialist-oriented intellectuals as Jean-Richard Bloch, Jean Cassou, and André Chamson rapidly vanished under the growing shadow of Hitler and Mussolini. For at this time, in Paris, Lyons, and in most cities in France, there were incessant street clashes between left and right, between the socialists or communists and fascist groups such as the "Croix de Feu" and "Action Française." A fascist coup often seemed imminent, even in France. Bloch called for the emergence of new left-wing unity in the Spanish cause, and Chamson wrote that Spain was the symbol of liberty in peril and the "prefiguration of our future."[18] In following this reasoning, the more moderate section of the Socialist Party felt that the immediate threat of fascism was sufficient basis for a compromise in its position and advocated joining the Popular Front, a stand which placed them in a dilemma similar to that of the anarchists. Obviously unable to approve of Stalinist repressions, and faced with the impossibility of assuming a policy-making position within the Popular Front because of the power which Soviet aid provided the communists, nevertheless such socialist leaders as Clement Attlee, Pietro Nenni, and Norman Thomas vigorously supported formation of volunteer units for Spain. Thomas attempted to form a volunteer group of American socialists to be called the "Eugene V. Debs Column"; Attlee visited the front lines and the No. 1 Company of the British Battalion of the International Brigades was renamed the "Major Attlee Company"; the Italian Nenni actually commanded a company and fought in the "Garibaldi Battalion" of the Brigades.

On the other hand, a small number of literary figures on the left, more prominent in the United States and England than in the rest of Europe, advocated, if not pacificism, at least support of the concept of "nonintervention" which they felt, if properly enforced, would bring about a Loyalist victory. Although a distinct minority within the socialist camp, this group received encouragement from such internationally famous writers as Aldous Huxley and Theodore Dreiser. Even long-committed pacificists, considerably less uncompromising since Mussolini's invasion of Ethiopia, divided into two groups, with the smaller adhering to a policy which rejected force as a means for halting fascism, while the larger group openly sympathized with the opponents of nonintervention and rather warmly espoused the ideas associated with the Popular Front. The latter rationalized their position by asserting that pacificism was simply not feasible in the light of international affairs existing in 1936. "To remain a pacifist while a democratic government was under attack by the combined forces of fascist dictators was tantamount to being profascist."[19]

The socialist writers in Europe and the United States in general restricted their work to newspaper articles and short essays for magazines in support of the Loyalist cause. Much of their writing reflected the divisions within the party regarding association with the Stalinists. Of their active authors, only John Dos Passos attempted a major literary interpretation of engagement in the Spanish struggle. Dos Passos' *Adventures of a Young Man* (1938) is probably the most bitter novel to emerge from the Spanish conflict. It presents the record of the dismayed proletarian journey of Glenn Spotswood through the world of left-wing politics during the 1930s, culminating in his death in Spain. The book assumes a pro-Loyalist but anti-Stalinist attitude. The hero is not John Dos Passos, but his career and the author's are, symbolically, parallel; the death of the hero in the story apparently signified the severence of Dos Passos' turbulent affiliation with radical politics. Glenn Spotswood joined the Communist Party because, ostensibly, it was fighting for a better social order. He had worked as an organizer of mine workers in Kentucky until he discovered that the party exploited the strikers to enhance its own prestige rather than to aid the miners. Glenn's refusal to conform to the twists and convolutions of the party line had made him a rebel in the eyes of the communist leaders, and their vindictiveness thwarted him in Spain after he joined the International Brigade. Persecuted as a Trotskyite and jailed, he was released, only to be sent on a mission which was practically an unofficial death sentence. Twenty years later, Dos Passos was to comment bitterly on his Spanish experiences:

> Spain torn in pieces by the struggle between believers in all the divergent paths to progress found itself doubly invaded by the bloody Twentieth Century in the form of fascist fanaticism and technology on the one hand and the more organized, more all-pervading fanaticism and technology of the Communist Party, on the other. The liberals were dying under their crossfire. Fascists and communists alike shot the best men first.[20]

The communist position in the Spanish conflict was presented by the Bulgarian, Georgi Dimitrov, then General Secretary of the Comintern, in his address to the Seventh World Congress of the Communist International. He called for the union of all factions in a common front against fascism in Spain, which would include such groups, normally hostile to the communists, as the anarchists and the Basque Catholics.[21] This policy represented a complete reversal of the Stalinist concept that any non-Stalinist position "objectively" aided fascism. At the outbreak of hostilities the Communist Party's antifascist slogans and its Popular Front policy attracted a heterogeneous mixture of radicals and liberals who maintained that interparty quarreling encouraged the fascist nations to increase their aggressive actions and that only a truly "united front" could effectively contain fascism. Early in the war martyrs were provided by the deaths of four promising English communist authors who had volunteered to fight in Spain: Christopher Caudwell, Charles Donnelly, John Cornford, and Ralph Fox. The communist poet, C. Day Lewis, who in his reply to *Authors Take Sides* had described the struggle in Spain as "a battle between light and darkness," in his poem, "The Nabara," sounded the call for all who believed in the rights of man:

> Freedom is more than a word, more than the
>   base coinage
> Of statesmen, the tyrant's dishonoured cheque,
>   or the dreamer's mad
> Inflated currency. She is mortal, we know,
>   and made
> In the image of simple men who have no taste
>   for carnage
> But sooner kill and are killed than see the
>   image betrayed.[22]

If liberty, and even civilization itself, were at stake, and the communists with Soviet support proved themselves indispensable to the defense of the Spanish Republic, then many intellectuals found it difficult to resist the conclusion that the communists were the chief defenders of Western civilization.[23]

The basis of the Stalinist argument was not to be revolutionary, but a liberal campaign in defense of a legal and constitutional state. Communist propaganda which had theretofore treated every bourgeois party as "fascist," now advocated the preservation of the bourgeois parliamentary democracy of the

Spanish Republic. The party emphasized the necessity for the democracies to recognize their treaty obligations to Spain, and in general stressed the legality and constitutionality of the Spanish government. The French intellectuals found nonintervention particularly frustrating since their own government, headed by Léon Blum, had been voted in by a Popular Front movement similar to that which had elected the Republicans in Spain.[24] Throughout Europe and the United States the communists presented the issue as one of democracy versus fascism, the legitimate and democratic government of Spain opposed by a reactionary and fascist dictatorship.

The communist reaction in Europe and the United States was essentially a counterpart of Russia's foreign policy at the outbreak of the Spanish Civil War. In Europe at this time Russia undoubtedly had a genuine fear of Nazi Germany. Rather than risk Russian interests by direct intervention in the form of troops and arms, along with the possibility of France and England misinterpreting such actions, Stalin chose to channel his military assistance covertly. Thus the world learned of the food and basic materials sent to their Spanish comrades by Russian factory workers, but knew nothing of the dispatch to Spain of such communist secret agents as the Italians, Luigi Longo, Vittorio Vidali, and Palmiro Togliatti, the French Jacques Duclos, and the Hungarian Ernö Gerö. Meanwhile the party propagandists, headed by Willi Muenzenberg in Western Europe, were extremely active in linking the cause of the Spanish Republic with the general antifascist crusade, which had begun when Russia adopted the twofold policies of the Popular Front and Collective Security.[25]

Thus the communist influence on intellectuals was exerted through their participation, often undercover, on Popular Front committees and through their propaganda organs. Party writers attempted to avoid all references to the Bolshevik experience or direct Russian military aid to Spain, but chose as propaganda images the heroes of the American and French revolutions. To Louis Fischer, the American journalist, the International Brigades were the "Lafayettes of the modern industrial age," and in other writings he visualized Byron, Kosciusko, and John Reed coming to the aid of the Spanish people.[26] Upton Sinclair wrote in *No Pasarán!*, a hastily prepared novel published by the author himself, "There were not going to be any Lafayettes or Steubens or Kosciuszkos . . . to help the Spanish workers—not if a capitalist State Department and a capitalist Attorney-General could help it."[27] Sinclair's revolutionary onslaught on traditional attitudes and his interpretation of the conflict as an economic struggle creating the "clearest class-alignment in the history of the world" denounced both fascism and capitalism, however, and was incompatible with the moderate communist line. The more subtle French communist writers sought a unified front, not by recalling heroes of the past, but by stressing to the democracies their stake in the Spanish struggle. Paul Eluard, returning to the Communist Party, wrote, "Mais que l'Espagne crie victoire . . . La France aura gagné sa guerre,"[28] and Romain Rolland added, "Au secours de l'Espagne! A notre secours! A votre secours!"[29] This same appeal was directed toward South and Central America by the Chilean Pablo Neruda, in his "España en el Corazón" and by the Peruvian César Vallejo in "España, Aparta de mi cste Cáliz."

The fascist atrocities provided the communists with the propaganda material needed to excite public opinion. Very often much of the public was mesmerized by those tales of horror and perversion, which combined a sensuality and violence amounting to sadism, that revealed more concerning the source than the atrocities themselves. The bombing of civilians in Guernica in 1937 brought a powerful response by the communists in France; Eluard responded with his "La victoire de Guernica" and Pablo Picasso with his famous painting. Picasso, who before the war had shown almost no interest in politics, from July 1936 championed the Republican cause and declared, "The Spanish struggle is the fight of reaction against the people, against freedom."[30] Louis Aragon described the terror perpetrated by Franco's troops in captured villages, while the writer Simone Téry, who had taken a communist position on most questions, provided eyewitness accounts of physical suffering and the massacre at Malaga, where fifty Fiat pursuit planes had again and again strafed refugees fleeing the town.[31]

In retrospect, it is clear that much of the liberal and nonrevolutionary rhetoric disseminated by communist writers was a conscious attempt to persuade the governments of the democracies, particularly England, that the struggle of the Spanish workers was essentially bourgeois in nature. Although the communists presented a moderate line, they did not hesitate to applaud the immoderate and violent suppression of dissent within the Popular Front in Spain. Dolores Ibarruri (la Pasionaria), the communist heroine whom Aragon had described as the symbol of the Spanish proletariat—the embodiment of the principles of Marx, Engels, and Stalin—challengingly demanded that "No measures will ever prove excessive that are taken to purge the proletarian camp of the poisonous growth of Trotskyism," and "The Trotskyists must be exterminated like beasts of prey."[32] The same pseudoliberals who called for a unified front in the defense of democracy against fascism could be fanatical in their charge that the internecine strife in Catalonia was a fascist-inspired revolt by the P.O.U.M. (Trotsky-anarchist-oriented trade union) rather than a suppression by the P.S.U.C. (communist-oriented trade union). From the beginning of the war, minimizing the revolutionary line, communists wrote of the Spanish Communist Party's devotion to middle-class traditions and, as the war continued, the efforts of the truly radical parties to effect a social revolution were squelched. Eventually the conflict between the communists and the anarchists, who were advocating agricultural collectivism of expropriated land, caused a split in the Popular Front, culminating in the violent suppression of the anarchists and Trotskyists in Barcelona in May 1937.[33]

The truly unusual aspect of the situation was the degree to which the democracies were willing to accept the communist position concerning the problem of dissent within the Popular Front. John Gunther, who could not be accused of party leanings, noted that the leaders of the Spanish Republic "were such profound liberals that they believed in free speech even for those who would destroy free speech."[34] Many intellectuals, as a result of communist propaganda, believed that Trotsky was serving the fascist cause, that his followers were doing their utmost to wreck Republican unity in Spain, and that anyone who called attention to the murderous campaign waged by the O.G.P.U. against the anarchists, the P.O.U.M., and even the more radical socialists was doing a disservice to the Loyalist cause. The Barcelona events do not appear to have precipitated any revision of Popular Front support in Europe and the United States, even among the idealists.

George Orwell's magnificent narrative, *Homage to Catalonia*, detailing the communist oppression, was largely ignored in the democracies, and Orwell's experiences in Barcelona had no counterpart among the major French and American writers.[35] The reports of the Barcelona fighting in general were so distorted and contradictory that they could be quietly discounted by those for whom the fascist threat and the need for Republican unity remained the overriding consideration. The activities of the O.G.P.U. might have raised serious doubts about the cause of liberty in communist hands, but the war to be won against fascism was too immediate to permit such examinations.

Stephen Spender, the English poet who broke with the party at the close of the war, attributes much of this dissension to communist subversion within the Popular Front:

> If the Communists had entered into the Popular Front with the same good faith as the Socialists and Liberals, a democratic movement would have extended from the extreme left to the Liberal Center, which would have had the fervor, generosity and imagination of the liberal revolutions of 1848. But the fatality of the Communists was to think only of forming united fronts in order then to seize control of them from within. The diversity of positive energies of many parties was thus inhibited by that party which most loudly and persistently proclaimed its desire for unity.[36]

Finally, although many of the Stalinist writers might have been cynical in their use of liberal traditions, they accurately anticipated the effect these symbols and arguments had on the sensibilities of vast numbers of potential Republican supporters in Europe and the United States. The response toward Spain was essentially a humanitarian impulse, and the sophisticated communist writings displayed an awareness of the implications that a nonrevolutionary line might have for the uncommitted intellectuals of the democracies. The doctrinaire communists, however, such as Alain, Henri Barbusse, Paul Langevin, Paul Nizan, Paul Vaillant-Couturier, and Gabriel Péri in France, Victor Gollancz and Harry Pollitt in England, and Earl Browder and Harry Gannes in the United States, often reduced the war to a simple and one-sided allegory, devoid of human feeling. The talented Louis Aragon, on occasion, seemed able to break with his party obligations sufficiently to produce poetry which reflected a sincere feeling for the plight of the Spanish people. The lines of "Santa Espina," written shortly after the war, reveal a sensitivity not found in the work of his "comrades":

> I remember a tune we used to hear in Spain
> And it made the heart beat faster, and we knew
> Each time as our blood was kindled once again
> Why the blue sky above us was so blue . . .
> But now there is no one left to renew the strain
> The woods are silent, the singers dead in Spain.[37]

But for the others, since their intent was propagandistic, the literary form invariably chosen was the essay which, ultimately, was reduced to the status of polemic.

One other radical group of Republican sympathizers who were centered in the United States saw in the Spanish struggle the evolution of an organic society. Led by such romantics as Waldo Frank and Lewis Mumford, both of whom were influenced by the concept of "social transcendentalism" propounded by Van Wyck Brooks, the movement castigated modern society for its failure to create a more "organic and life-fulfilling world." As admirers of the "profoundly *whole* culture of the Spaniard," Brooks, Frank, and Mumford defended the Spanish Republic. Denouncing England, France, and the United States as "gelded democracies," Frank wrote of "organic" Spain, where the people read Marx without forgetting San Juan de la Cruz, and Einstein without neglecting Cervantes.[38] The attempt of these American writers to see in the Spanish peasant a combination of Emerson and Crèvecoeur is evident in the poetry of Kenneth Rexroth on the Spanish Civil War. The soldiers of the Republic are men who sit up

> All night, talking of trout in the Pyrenees,
> Spinoza, old nights full of riot and sherry,
> Women they might have had or almost had,
> Picasso, Velásquez, relativity.[39]

The Spanish Civil War provided the first violent test, at least for most European and American radicals, of the usefulness of Marxism as a means of ordering experience. If a good many writers had accepted Marxism with some degree of enthusiasm, it was because this ideology offered a means of understanding the disorders of the modern world with confidence that the turmoil had purpose.[40] In addition, Marxism seemed to offer to intellectuals in general, and writers in particular, the opportunity to help direct the course of events and to participate in history. As one might expect, many of the imaginative writers of the decade were acutely conscious of the spreading cracks in the social façade and the hints of impending disaster.

The Marxist myth of history, the vision of the world of the future as an earthly paradise in which the downtrodden would at last rise to claim their rightful heritage, exerted a powerful influence on many writers who rejected the specific program and policies of the Communist International. These writers of the 1930s who embraced the Marxist doctrine or its variants with such fervor were desperate. W. H. Auden wrote that "the struggle in Spain has x-rayed the lies upon which our civilization is built,"[41] and many sympathetic intellectuals noted that the traditional liberal and democratic virtues had been unable to prevent the rise to power of dictators or to avoid a depression of frightening severity, duration, and universality. In turn they were often merciless in their criticism of the failings of the democracies; once converted to Marxism, however, they were ready to tolerate the most flagrant transgressions on individual freedom provided they could be justified as consonant with accepted doctrine.[42] Clearly, the radicals saw the 1930s as a time for action, and when the Spanish political crisis became an armed conflict, the time for such action presented itself.

Today, when political apathy is likely to be construed as artistic dedication, the fervor of these left-wing intellectuals is difficult to comprehend. By 1936 they had lost faith in their countries' liberal and democratic regimes. In such a time of upheaval it is hardly surprising that a good many felt constrained to look for more decisive solutions. Perhaps the scope of this brief survey suggests that their engagement was more than an infatuation with leftist ideologies. The crisis of the Spanish struggle seemed a propitious opportunity to bring their dreams to fruition. The beginning of the war must have seemed to those writers not already totally disillusioned with the Soviet experiment (such as Gide) to offer the first real opportunity for the triumph of the revolution, especially when the people in a number of Spanish cities armed themselves and drove out the rebellious army units. Often the chief attraction to Marxism as a philosophy was the failure of democratic ideals to cope with the fascist trend in Europe. In Marxism these writers sought a freedom, an equality, and fraternity often promised but seldom fulfilled by a liberal democracy. Any doctrine which could explain the chaos as a prelude to a utopian order was destined to have a wide appeal, and socialist thought made its inroads in several areas where liberalism had displayed its vulnerability.

Thus the communists sounded the call to arms for radical authors. The fascist threat during the years of the Spanish conflict made of leftist writers dry tinder for the communist flame. At the Writers' Congress they declared that literature could be created only by those on the side of the people against reaction, fascism, and war. Rex Warner, member of the English Communist Party, reminded intellectuals that within the Spanish struggle:

> It is the aim that is right and the end is freedom.
> In Spain the veil is torn.
> In Spain is Europe. England also is in Spain.
> There the sea recedes and there the mirror is no
> longer blurred.[43]

The independent Thomas Mann, and Granville Hicks, then a dedicated communist, were both able to conclude that it was impossible for an artist not to become involved in the politics of his time, and the concept of "art for art's sake" could produce only sterility. If Thomas Mann could sympathize with the communists in their concern for the fate of the Spanish Republic, so could Archibald MacLeish, Malcolm Cowley, and Edna St. Vincent Millay in the United States; Julian Bell, Ralph Bates, Claud Cockburn, and E. M. Forster in England; and Julien Benda, André Breton, and Roger Martin du Gard in France. These writers did more than lend verbal support to the Republic: they helped compose petitions, organized rallies, contributed money, and some even journeyed to Spain to see for themselves.

Despite the excitement generated by the divergent loyalties during the Spanish Civil War, some writers preferred to remain aloof. T. S. Eliot was speaking for Somerset Maugham, Sean

O'Faolain, H. G. Wells, E. E. Cummings, Robinson Jeffers, and a few others in defense of the "Ivory Tower" when he presented his position on the struggle in Spain by saying, "While I am naturally sympathetic, I still feel convinced that it is best that at least a few men of letters should remain isolated, and take no part in these collective activities." Alec Waugh added in defense of this stand: "The extent of a writer's capacity to detach himself from immediate issues is determined by his individual temperament. But there is an essential difference between the 'Ivory Tower' and a stand-point 'above the battle.' "[44] Literary figures, such as Maxwell Perkins and Sinclair Lewis, chided Hemingway for his preoccupation with the Spanish conflict.[45] Society in the 1930s demanded attention, but a minority of writers and critics alike expressed concern and questioned the moral responsibility of the artist, both to society and to his art.

Many of the right-wing literary factions in Europe and the United States refused to serve as spokesmen for General Franco and, instead, sought the noncommital isolation found in nonsocial literary themes. Although the conservatives were reluctant to champion the "crusade" in Spain, two other groups on the right had no such reticence in their defense of Spain's Nuevo Estado. The right-wing response may be divided into fascist, Catholic, and conservative reactions but, as in left-wing divisions, there was little homogeneity within each group.

The fascists doctrines which exalt nation and race, which demand a centralized and autocratic dictatorship, severe economic and social regimentation, and forcible suppression of opposition, do little to explain the origins of popular support for such a movement.[46] Fascism is better understood as that part of a class struggle in which sections of the bourgeoisie join forces with the old ruling class against what they believe to be a common enemy in the form of a rising socialistic proletariat. Although this alliance between the bourgeoisie and the aristocracy is only a pragmatic and tenuous one, the army usually participates in this common effort and, at least in Spain, served as the cohesive force. But the fascist movements of the 1930s were not cut from whole cloth, and the various fascist parties differed considerably in character and composition. In general, their ideological content was usually less defined than their emotional tone. Fascism is better analyzed in the context of the qualities of its political leaders: Hitler in Germany, Mussolini in Italy, and Primo de Rivera in Spain.[47] Yet the attraction fascism had for many European countries now seems obvious. It received support because of this fear and insecurity, often unjustified but nevertheless real, felt by the middle classes, which caused them to turn to a hybrid "corporate" movement designed either to blend the concepts of nationalism and socialism, or to use the first to control the second. Thus the violent tensions of twentieth-century history can be attributed to either strife between social classes or warfare between nations. In Europe during World War I, "class consciousness was buried beneath an outburst of nationalism that transcended it, but the reasons for the class struggle remained."[48]

In Spain the fascists drew their main strength from the comfortable classes seeking the only new creed which promised to control the anticipated proletarian revolution. The outbreak of the war, however, destroyed any likelihood of fascism in Spain developing along political lines. All the political leaders fell, and in April 1937, Franco combined all groups of a rather diverse movement—not without some resistance—to form a new state party, the Falange Española Tradicionalista y de la JONS, under his absolute dictatorship. In this manner Franco's followers joined with their German and Italian counterparts in opposing the social upheavals caused by the European and American economic collapse of the early 1930s; but in accommodating the Roman Catholic Church they modeled their movement after Mussolini's blackshirts rather than Hitler's supermen.

Various facets of the movement included virulent anti-Semitism, chauvinistic nationalism, and gradual totalitarianism. The Falange Española, originally founded by young José Antonio Primo de Rivera, had denounced the concept of social progress as propounded by the Spanish liberals, and urged "a system of authority, of hierarchy, and of order" in its place.[49] As a reaction against the prevailing democratic disorder in Republican Spain, with its admittedly antimilitaristic and anti-Catholic government, the early Falange maintained they supported "Authority rather than Anarchy, Militarism and Service rather than un-Spanish Anti-Militarism, and, above all, religious feeling rather than laicism and atheism."[50] Thus the Nuevo Estado under Franco later proclaimed itself the totalitarian instrument of national integrity. While under most fascist movements the army was the instrument of the fascist state, in Spain the Falange was never more than an instrument of General Franco's, with the army serving as the dominant force.[51]

Very few of the European and none of the American fascists were sufficiently inspired by the Franco cause to volunteer to fight in Spain. Actual aid given to the Nationalists by foreign fascist volunteers (hardly an appropriate term for the direct intervention by German and Italian troops) was negligible. A fair number of Portuguese fought in the so-called Legión de Viriato, and six hundred Irishmen fought for the Nationalists under "General" O'Duffy; but the motives of the latter for their Spanish adventure were so mixed that it would be unfair to label them as essentially fascist. Many of the Irish considered the trip to Spain as a form of religious crusade, but the majority were casual adventurers. A small group of right-wing Frenchmen served in the Nationalist ranks as the Jeanne d'Arc Bandera, while yet a smaller White Russian company served with the Carlist Requetés along with a few semi-Fascists from Eastern European countries. But none of these volunteers, other than for some notorious blunders by the Gaelic contingent, made a notable contribution to the Franco forces.[52]

As in almost all reactionary accounts throughout Europe and the United States, Lenin was quoted as having predicted that Spain's revolution would follow Russia's. The extremist *English Review* and *American Review* published this interpretation of the cause of the war in Spain. Francis Yeats-Brown, English author of *Lives of a Bengal Lancer,* Pierre Héricourt, and Jean and Jerome Tharaud, French reactionaries, further developed this theme and included their own imaginative versions of Republican atrocities to emphasize the gravity of the communist masterplot. The fascist writers, such as Hilaire Belloc in England and Henri Massis in France, advocated the destruction of the evils of a democratic republic, condemning the political liberty and progressive reforms in Spain, as well as the liberal revolutions in the United States and France, as the illusions of a handful of fanatics. Charles Maurras, leader of the French fascists, visited Saragossa where he was received as a "Head of State" and, along with the younger Robert

Brasillach and Maurice Bardèche of Action Française, crudely attempted to identify support for Franco with that of "Christian dedication," while Florence Farmborough and Robert Sencourt endeavored to make Franco palatable to British taste by presenting him as a "Christian country gentleman."[53] The overall literary quality of this fascist propaganda is depressing, and perhaps it is encouraging to note that they not only failed to produce a single major work, but were unable to support even a moderately successful periodical. Most of the extremist publications, mimeographed on the poorest quality paper, have long since distintegrated or disappeared.

Fascism, however, was not the only political ideology to reject the ideals of a progressive democracy. Although none of the conservative spokesmen in Europe and the United States attempted a full-scale justification of General Franco's Nuevo Estado, several did comment on the politics of the Spanish conflict. Evelyn Waugh, the British author, set the pattern when he replied to the *Authors Take Sides* questionaire, "I am not a Fascist nor shall I become one unless it is the only alternative to Marxism." Thus, conservatives usually confined themselves to a denunciation of the evils of International Communism and its impending takeover of the Spanish Republic. "The significant peculiarity of the Spanish civil war," wrote Lawrence Dennis in *The American Mercury*, "is that it is actually a fight to the finish between Communism and nationalism on Spanish territory."[54] In their failure to discuss the positive achievements of General Franco's rule, both Waugh and Dennis reflect the conservative position throughout the entire war.

Conservative reaction to the Spanish Civil War was inextricably enlisted in support of the policy of nonintervention as practiced by the democracies. The avowed and rather naïve purposes of the policy of nonintervention were to contain the war in Spain, to forestall a general European conflagration as long as possible by dissuading the countries sympathetic to either side from intervening, and to provide a common meeting place for discussions and proposals which might lead to a settlement.[55] In retrospect, it is clear that the policy failed to achieve its purpose. In spite of many transgressions by the Germans, Italians, and Russians, the conservatives continued their support of nonintervention for reasons of their own national security. It was not difficult to convince a public, plainly interested in preserving peace as long as possible, that neutrality was the best deterrent to war. The opposition decried the nonintervention pact as not only discriminatory, but detrimental to democratic interests in the European political theater. The attacks leveled against the isolationist policies of their countries were vigorously expressed by Cassou and Bloch in France and in England by the strong protest of Rex Warner's "Arms in Spain" and Edgell Rickword's scathing satire, "To the Wife of Any Non-Intervention Statesman." Similar sentiments were expressed in a statement issued by 98 American writers, among them Maxwell Anderson, Sherwood Anderson, William Faulkner, Sinclair Lewis, Carl Sandberg, and Thornton Wilder, who declared that the neutrality policy of the United States should not deter private citizens from condemning "the military faction which with its allies is making war upon the legally and democratically elected republican government of Spain."[56] These writers scored conservatives and moderates alike for the unfairness of a policy which obstructed the efforts of the legal government of Spain to purchase arms and supplies to defend itself against rebel attack, while the rebels easily procured supplies needed to push forward their revolt. The governments of the democracies made it convenient for the conservatives to appear as neutrals while actually supporting the Nationalists.

Although George Santayana was permitted to share the hospitality of Mussolini's Italy, he failed to comment at length on Il Duce's Spanish enterprise. However, his brief statement contributes substantially to an understanding of the conservative position. Santayana's opinions, expressed in a personal letter, were the result of the slanted news which reached him in fascist Italy, and should not be regarded as the considered conclusions of an eminent philosopher. But they do indicate why a zealous antidemocrat was inclined to support the military regime of General Franco:

> Since the triumph of Christianity, and again after the Reformation and the English, American and French revolutions, our part of the world has been governed by ideas, by theories, by universalistic sects like the Church, the Free Masons, the Free Trade In-

> dustrial Liberals, and last of all the Bolshies. Such influences are non-natural, non-biological; whereas the agricultural, military, and artistic life of nations is spontaneous, with ambitions that impose morality, but are not imposed by morality of any sort.[57]

To the conservative Santayana, the enemy was more than a liberal, democractic tradition. The enemy was all traditions that attempt to impose their abstract ideals on mankind.

Considering the prominence given to some of the political and social theories of Ezra Pound, one would expect him to be pleased by the establishment in Spain of a "Christian society." Throughout the conflict, however, he contributed little of his talent to the Franco cause, and his statements received even less attention than those of Santayana. But his French hero, Maurras, was eager to approve the fascists' refusal to sever the ideals of patriotism from those of religion, the morality of a lay society from those of the Church. Maurras supported Franco without reservation, and his personal visit to Spain was made long before the French Republic had assumed relations with the rebel military regime. His report on the journey is an enthusiastic, mythologized paean of praise. Pound's English-speaking cohorts, Wyndham Lewis, Evelyn Waugh, and Roy Campbell, also applauded General Franco's treatment of the communist menace and often denounced the pro-Loyalist writers; but Pound himself had little to say about the Spanish Civil War.[58]

The intellectual response of the Roman Catholic Church to the war in Spain was a complex one. It was not an affirmation of Spanish fascism, but rather a fear-motivated emotional acclaim of Franco as a "Christian gentleman" leading a crusade to rid Spain of "communist heretics" and restore the order of the Church. The Catholic attitude, similar to that of the conservatives, was for the most part a denunciation of communism and, surprisingly, in many cases an attempt to present Franco's Movimiento Nacional as a reasonably democratic movement. This latter argument was not particularly convincing and in polls of American Catholic laity, only four out of ten chose to favor the Insurgents; of the remainder, a significant number actually favored the Loyalists.[59] The reaction of Catholic intellectuals to the Spanish Civil War was both a complicated and painful adjustment which in itself deserves an extensive study. It is, moreover, a subject that exposes, through devious channels, the innate problems of an authoritarian church in a pluralistic society.[60]

Although it is impossible to determine the historical relationship of the Roman Catholic Church to the Republican governments in Spain in any detail in this study, it is undeniable that shortly after the Spanish liberals and socialists had joined forces to expel Alphonso XIII, the new Republic drafted a constitution based largely on unseating the Roman Catholic Church from its position of authority in Spain.[61] Pope Pius XI, in turn, warned of the "serious and particularly repugnant error" of separation of Church and State in Spain, "where the Church has always and rightly held the most important and most beneficially active part in legislation, in schools, and in all other private and public institutions."[62] His encyclical proceeded to denounce many of the aims of the Republican constitution and had the effect, perhaps unintentionally, of committing Catholics in many countries to the rebel cause.

It is evident that when the generals and their supporters among the Spanish civilian population revolted in July 1936, the Catholic hierarchy in Spain had good reason for supporting them. Because of the great gulf that separated the rich and poor in Spain, the Church could not remain neutral. On the one side were the poor, the secular working-class movements, and the natural antagonism of the rising middle class and the government toward an extremely self-interested Church. On the other side were the wealthy aristocrats with sufficient funds for the Church to further its aims, a favored position within the government, and what the clergy felt was a vantage point from which to fight secular socialism and godless anarchism. The most powerful elements in the Church chose the latter position, and the Church lost the support of the working classes.[63] Except for the Basque clerical hierarchy, the Spanish prelates were virtually unanimous in supporting the rebels. Among the lower clergy, however, evidence of marked differences of opinion is available.

In the holocaust that followed, all the clergy suffered greatly. Hugh Thomas gives the following estimate of clerical dead: bishops, 12; priests, 5,155; nuns, 183; monks, 2,492; novices, 249. These figures essentially agree with those published in Spain in 1961.[64] The figure of 16,500 clergy murdered was published by *Osserva-*

*tore Romano,* and the Pope officially declared all those priests who had been murdered to be martyrs. Practically every church in Loyalist Spain, with the exception of the cathedrals, was burned or desecrated. Never had the Spanish Church experienced such bloodletting and ruin.

An important exception to these figures of religious persecution involves the Church in the Basque country, which was sympathetic to the Loyalist cause. The Republican affiliation of the Basques, admitted by even fervent supporters of the Nationalists as "the most Christian people in Spain," caused many Catholics to reexamine their loyalties. Early in the conflict two eminent French Catholics, François Mauriac and Jacques Maritain, had issued a pro-Basque manifesto. The destruction of Guernica further strengthened the case of those whom the right-wing French Catholic press had labeled "Chrétiens Rouges." Maritain met the charge of condoning the religious bloodletting by noting that those who killed the poor, "the people of Christ," in the name of religion were as culpable as those who killed priests through hatred of religion. The polemic continued throughout the Spanish conflict, particularly in France. Maurras proclaimed that the Church was the only real International, and in Liège a prayer by the exiled Spanish priests to the Virgin of Pilar appeared: "To You, O Mary, Queen of Peace, we always return, we the faithful sons of Your best-loved Spain, now vilified, outraged, befouled by criminal Bolshevism, deprived by Jewish Marxism, and scorned by savage Communism. We pray You, tears in our eyes, to come to our help, to accord final triumph to the glorious armies of the Liberator and Reconqueror of Spain, the new Pelayo, the Caudillo! Viva Christ the King!"[65]

The bellicose attacks on Spanish "radicalism" and the "antireligious" tendencies of the Republic came mostly from European Catholics, and these often took the form of hate-filled polemics vilifying the anti-Christ. Roy Campbell was in the vanguard of the "great crusade" to expel the heretics whose "dogmatized Utopias" threatened to destroy the religious and social traditions of Catholic Spain:

> The Army of the People of the World,
> The hoarse blaspheming of the godless horde

Against the Cross and Crescent of the Lord
The Cross, our Hammer, and the Quarter Moon
Our Sickle, and Hosanna for our tune![66]

An extended discussion of the hundreds of Catholics who saw in the Loyalists "diabolical, blood-crazed enemies of God" would not prove fruitful, nor did more rational Catholic writers display any particular interest in the theories of Spanish fascism, or for that matter in the theories of Spanish Catholicism. The intensity of the emotional response and the paucity of ideological commitment to the Nuevo Estado are illustrated throughout Catholic fiction dealing with the Spanish Civil War. The number of plays, poems, and stories, with their rather melodramatic plots, is extremely high. However, the most cursory examination would indicate a very low level of literary merit.

Probably the single work from a Catholic point of view which merits critical consideration is Stefan Andres' short novel, *Wir Sind Utopia,* written long after the war. In its one hundred pages is contained an extremely moving statement of religious conversion and martyrdom suffered during the war, a theme common in much of the Catholic fiction treating the conflict. In the tradition of the saints' tales, it presents the experience, symbolically, of Jesus and the crucifixion. The hero, Paco, an excommunicated priest who had lost faith, had served as a seaman for twenty years, and had been conscripted into the Nationalist navy. Captured and held in the monastery where he had once been a young priest, Paco regains his faith and confesses both his fellow-prisoners and his captors. He refuses to kill the Loyalist lieutenant while listening to his confession, thereby jeopardizing his own life and the lives of his two hundred fellow-prisoners. The theme of faith in mankind, despite its imperfections, is recalled by the martyr as he rests in his cell: "Gott liebt die welt, weil sie unvollkommen ist—Wir sind Gottes Utopia, aber eines in Werden!"[67]

Certainly the role of the Church in "internationalizing" the conflict is too great to go unnoticed. But too many Catholics were convinced that simple truths were available, a point of view which does not inspire a very complex art. Even the great French Catholic poet, Paul Claudel, wrote a poorly conceived poem, "Aux Martyrs Espagnols," in which he compared the Spanish Republicans to historical infidels, such as Henry VIII, Nero,

Diocletian, Robespierre, Lenin, Calvin, Voltaire, Renan, Marx, and Judas Iscariot.[68] On the other hand, an awareness of the Spanish Civil War led many Catholics to agonized indecision. They were caught in a painful dilemma; they desired to affirm their Catholicism and at the same time to prove their loyalty to the democratic traditions of their respective countries. Many sophisticated Catholic intellectuals deemed General Franco's "crusade" less than Christian, and they defended their position by indicating that the Pope had never officially issued an authoritative statement in support of the Nationalists; that Miguel de Unamuno, the only Spanish intellectual of international stature who might have been sympathetic to the Nationalists, had denounced the Movimiento Nacional prior to his death; that the people of Spain had lost faith in their priests; and that the Church should not be too closely linked with Franco's "apostles of violence."[69] As the war progressed and the Nationalists instituted a policy of indiscriminate bombing of civilian populations, Maritain iterated the position of many Catholic intellectuals: "Christianity will remake itself by Christian means or it will unmake itself altogether."[70] Although Maritain refused to support the Republic actively, many European Catholic writers found their revulsion to fascism sufficiently powerful to create organizations, such as the French Committee for Civil and Religious Peace in Spain, which numbered among its supporters such esteemed writers as George Duhamel and François Mauriac. José Bergamin, director of the Catholic review, *Cruz y Raya*, early in the conflict championed the cause of the Spanish people—"all the people of every part of our land, knowing themselves, with their tradition and their history, their past and their future clear as never before in the truth of their life and their hopes"—and denigrated the rebel forces which he described as "a handful, a mob of desperate traitors who have had to call in outside help, foreign, barbarous, anti-Spanish, to fight against us, provoking the war which is suicide for them but which they hoped might be suicide for Spain."[71]

The immediacy of the Second World War silenced most of the literary works dealing with the Spanish Civil War which might have been written between 1940 and 1945. For this reason it is in the late 1930s, often while the fighting was still in progress, that the important literature emerging from the conflict is discovered. Despite the accusations of those who see the 1930s as a "Red Decade" of communist domination of political and intellectual life, the majority of writers in Europe and the United States who supported the Loyalist cause were not active members of any political party. Between 1936 and 1939 an overwhelming majority of the intelligentsia—artists, teachers, writers, men and women of all the professions—regarded the Spanish war as a testing ground for war against fascism. The major writers and artists who spoke for the Spanish Loyalists, who raised money for medical aid, or who smuggled themselves into Spain as volunteers, were not consciously furthering party interests, nor was there anything ulterior or sinister in their devotion to the Spanish peasantry. The issues appeared clear-cut; the cause of Spain was the cause of democracy and morality. Sectarian bickerings seemed contemptible in the light of such awesome events, and for more than a few, the nobility of the Spaniards engendered comparable nobility in themselves. The support given the Spanish Republic by such men as George Orwell, André Malraux, Ernest Hemingway, Gustav Regler, and Arthur Koestler, all philosophical humanists and ardent antifascists, despite their diverse political backgrounds, affirmed a belief in the forces of social progress, popular government, freedom of worship, the separation of Church and State, and education for democracy. This creed transcended the pressures exerted by any political affiliations to which these writers were committed at the time. Although many who interpreted the war in Spain as the struggle of a liberal democracy were, to some extent, misled by the degree of Soviet influence, for most of those concerned the Spanish Republic represented a liberal, democratic cause. "Spain . . . symbolized the brightness of the Enlightenment's vision, or, at least, a beacon of hope in a continent darkened by increasingly ominous clouds."[72] It was difficult in the late 1930s not to view the Spanish Civil War as an invasion of Spain by Germany and Italy, and the only natural tendency was to wonder which nation would be the next victim. In essence, most liberals who supported the Spanish Republic did so not because they were influenced by Marxism, but because they believed in the principles of a liberal democracy, and willingly joined with other antifascists in a demonstration of their faith.

W. H. Auden's *Spain* is neither an oversimplification nor a romantic idealization of the war. As a liberal, Auden responded to the attack on those principles which he believed to be inviolate:

> All presented their lives.
> On that arid square, that fragment nipped off from hot
> Africa, soldered so crudely to inventive Europe;
> On that tableland scored by rivers,
> Our thoughts have bodies; the menacing shapes of our
> fever
> Are precise and alive.[73]

In the fascist threat of the 1930s, it seemed that the Dark Ages might return. The war started at a time when the ideals of liberalism—democracy, liberty, justice, fraternity, freedom—catchwords of two hundred years of political activity, seemed to have lost their meaning. Liberals noted that the followers of Franco had resolutely turned against progress, as had men centuries before when they had devised the Inquisition and the auto-da-fé. "Fascism as a 'philosophy' was the apotheosis of unreason, as a way of life it was the denial of rationality, and as a fact of history it was not progress but retrogression."[74] To many, fascism was embodied in the cry of the crippled General Millan Astray—"Muera la Inteligencia!"[75] Liberals were not unaware of the intellectual nihilism implicit in fascism when they supported the Spanish Republic.

Adherents of liberalism were both rational and pragmatic in support of their ideals. They expressed faith in education and law, in constitutional government and legal principles.[76] The Republic's enthusiastic drive toward universal education in Spain was surely one of its most ambitious reform movements, and it gained deserved support among educators throughout Europe and the United States. All liberals extolled the efforts of such men as Marcelino Domingo, Fernando de los Ríos, Salvador de Madariaga, and José Castillejo y Duarte to build schools and raise faculty standards against almost insurmountable obstacles.[77] The Republican objective to provide a minimum education for all Spain's children contrasted with the destruction of Madrid's new university during the Nationalist siege of the city. And the Loyalist publications which appeared during the fighting emphasized this destruction as symbolic of the attitude of fascism toward education. Even when the course of the war developed unfavorably, the Loyalists preserved their confidence in an educational system as a means to make men free. Antoine de Saint-Exupéry, the French novelist and airman, wrote on a visit to the Republican front lines:

> I chanced upon a school that stood on a hill surrounded by a low stone wall some 500 yards behind the trenches. A corporal was teaching botony that day. He was lecturing on the fragile organs of a poppy held in his hands. Out of the surrounding mud, and in spite of the wandering shells that dropped all about, he had drawn like a magnet an audience of stubble-bearded soldiers who squatted tailor-fashion and listened with their chins in their hands to a discourse of which they understood not one word in five. Something within them said: "You are but brutes fresh from your caves. Go along! Catch up with humanity!" And with heavy feet they were hurrying towards enlightenment.[78]

In a discussion of the liberal view of law and constitutionality, it is noteworthy that intellectuals from all segments of society, ranging from communist sympathizers to Catholic moderates, were in agreement as to the constitutionality of the Spanish Republic. Declarations of the legality of the Azaña government ranged from Havelock Ellis' tempered: "While I recognize that there are good men on both sides, I am myself decisively on the side of the legal Government and against Franco and the Fascists," to Ford Maddox Ford's passionate:

> I am unhesitatingly for the existing Spanish Government and against Franco's attempt—on every ground of feeling and reason. In addition, as the merest commonsense, the Government of the Spanish, as of any other nation, should be settled and defined by the inhabitants of that nation. Mr. Franco seeks to establish a government resting on the arms of Moors, Germans, Italians.[79]

Such declarations were essentially apolitical and grounded on broad principles of rights to self-determination and representative government. Although these liberal intellectuals shared in common this respect for law and order with older, more conservative advocates, there was no accord among them on the wisdom of supporting any of the left-wing revolutionary factions. Thus the liberal opposition to the Franco rebellion was essentially based on moral and legal principles, and was definitely not of radical design.

The concept of freedom of the individual was at the core of

the democratic tradition. Accordingly, many viewed the Spanish Civil War as a struggle to liberate the Spanish people from the bondage of an authoritarian and established Church, from a centralized and unrepresentative government, and from the privileged economic power of those whom the state had favored.[80] The tradition of free exchange of ideas had begun in Spain at the Institución Libre de Enseñanza of Giner de los Ríos, and had attained its zenith in the Ateneo under the Spanish Republic.[81] Such concepts of freedom filtered down from the academic institutions to the Spanish peasants. In "The Winds of the People," by the remarkable young poet, Miguel Hernández, the spirit of a people free of the bonds of tyranny, finds meaning in Spain:

I come not from a people of oxen,
my people are they who enthuse
over the lion's leap,
the eagle's rigid swoop,
and the strong charge of the bull
whose pride is in his horns.
Oxen were never bred
on the bleak uplands of Spain.
Who speaks of setting a yoke
on the shoulders of such a race?[82]

All intellectuals were determined to protect free expression and each faction within the liberal camp emphasized that aspect which it valued most. Writers and artists were particularly interested in a climate in which the creative imagination was free to chart its own course. "Poets and poetry," wrote Stephen Spender in his introduction to a collection of pro-Loyalist poems, "have played a considerable part in the Spanish War, because to many people the struggle of the Republicans has seemed a struggle for the conditions without which the writing and reading of poetry are almost impossible."[83] Ernest Hemingway in his address to the Congress of American Writers denounced the situation of the writer under fascism: "There is only one form of government that cannot produce good writers, and that system is fascism." The reason given, typical of the man, is, simply: ". . . Fascism is a lie told by bullies. A writer who will not lie cannot live or work under fascism."[84] To emphasize this thesis, Spender and Hemingway had merely to indicate the contributions of the famous Spanish painters and musicians who supported the Republic: Pablo Picasso, Joan Miró, Luis Quintanilla, and Pablo Casals.

Feelings of equality and fraternity were manifested by the liberal pro-Loyalist supporters during the various humanitarian efforts engendered by the war. Women in the democracies were reminded that under the Republic their Spanish counterparts were given the opportunity to achieve equality, and that Constancia de la Mora, Isabel de Palencia, Margarita Nelkin, and others actively participated in the Spanish government. In the spirit of the International Brigades feelings of equality and fraternity were intensified. The International Brigades fought valiantly, attracting to themselves the adventurous, the idealistic, and sometimes the despairing, from all parts of the world. It was not loyalty to their native land but belief in democracy and hatred of fascism that sent volunteers to the International Brigades. Perhaps never before had such enthusiasm been mobilized, nor had there ever existed such a firm conviction in the rightness of a cause. Since the International Brigades were truly what the name implied, hundreds of writers discovered in their formation just those attributes.[85] The concept of the diversity and the unity embodied by these men is evidenced in much of the literature of the war. Langston Hughes, the American Negro poet, contributed several poems and articles to *Volunteer for Liberty,* the paper of the International Brigades, in which he noted that in Republican Spain there was an absence of racial prejudice: "Folks over here don't treat me / Like white folks used to do."[86] "No man can draw a free breath who does not share with other men a common and disinterested ideal," wrote Saint-Exupéry, then a correspondent for *L'intransigeant* in Spain. "There is no comradeship except through union in the same high effort."[87] On occasion these feelings of brotherhood embraced all of humanity, including the Nationalist soldiers. Romain Rolland, the French communist, momentarily broke from party rhetoric when he called for an affirmation of "the fraternity of all the suffering,"[88] and Saint-Exupéry recorded this curious dialogue in the darkness which bridged the gulf between humans in opposing trenches:

> I can see him as he stood erect, as he rested his strong hands on the low stone and sent forth from his great chest that question of

> questions: "Antonio! What are you fighting for?" . . . "Spain!" "You?" "The bread of our brothers!" And then the amazing: "Good night, friend!" And the response from the other side of the world: "Good night, friend!" And silence.

The true humanist can only ask with compassion, "their words were not the same, but their truths were identical. Why has this high communion never yet prevented men from dying in battle against each other?"[89]

Most of the antifascists confined their sympathies to the Republican cause. On the other hand, most Catholics who grieved for martyred priests and nuns seemed unconcerned about the men and women who died beneath General Franco's bombers. Few men committed to either cause were willing to testify to the humanity of the other. This imperfect impulse toward an international fraternity was articulated largely by Loyalist supporters, but it is not fundamentally different from the humanitarianism that is so much a part of Western humanism. Thus, Roy Campbell, the South African poet who aligned himself with the Franco crusade, could shock many of these intellectuals with the observation:

> The Inquisition in six hundred years
> Pumped not a thousandth of the blood and tears
> As, in some twenty, has the world-reforming,
> Free-thinking, Rational, Cathedral-storming
> Humanitarian, with his brother love. . . .[90]

The Nationalists' acceptance of the concept of total war seemed, to most liberals, a new barbarism and a repudiation of the humanity of man. Although atrocity stories proliferated and there were numerous acts of horror on both sides, the single act of terrorism that most appalled the liberal conscience was the indiscriminate bombardment of cities.[91] Lillian Hellman castigated the Nationalists with the assertion that "Finding the range on a blind woman eating a bowl of soup is a fine job for a man." And Dorothy Parker bitterly echoed this sentiment with the comment, "It was a good job to get those. They were ruthless enemies of fascism."[92] Perhaps nobody wrote so strongly on this subject as the sensitive Saint-Exupéry, who noted that in spite of the suffering accompanying such attacks, the bombardments had the opposite effect intended:

> I do not care a curse for the rules of war and the law of reprisal. As for the military advantage of such a bombardment, I simply cannot grasp it. I have seen housewives disembowled, children mutilated; I have seen the old itinerent market vender sponge from her treasures the brains with which they were splattered. I have seen a janitor's wife douse the sullied pavement with a bucket of water, and I am still unable to understand what part these humble slaughterhouse accidents play in warfare. . . .
>
> Each shell that fell on Madrid fortified something in the town. It persuaded the hesitant neutral to side with the defenders. . . . It was clear to me that a bombardment did not disperse—it unified. Horror causes men to clench their fists, and in horror men join together.[93]

Such unpardonable acts of violence perpetrated against innocent victims horrified liberals and animated vast numbers of potentially political and economic conservatives to support the various committees organized to aid the Spanish Loyalists and to condemn the Franco regime.

Much of the moral support given by literary intellectuals to the Loyalist government was, therefore, generated by intense fear. In a decade of worldwide economic crises, at a time when Nazi Germany had replaced the Weimar Republic and fascist Italy demonstrated the weakness of the League of Nations, the resistance of the Spanish people aroused intellectuals who until then had experienced a feeling of impotence. "It seemed," wrote George Orwell, "the turning of the tide."[94] The Spanish Civil War appeared a last hope, a last opportunity, for the individual to assert himself when confronted with a world in chaos. Most liberals defended the Spanish Loyalists not because they desired a radical social revolution, but because this struggle presented a movement toward, and not away from, humanitarian principles.

The exodus of writers from Hitler's Germany seemed to confirm this attitude. The exile of Gustav Regler, Arthur Koestler, Bertolt Brecht, Thomas Mann, Ludwig Renn, and Ernst Toller suggested, even to the most conservative—that art cannot flourish in a reactionary atmosphere. Further proof was provided earlier in 1933 when millions of books were burned on the campuses of Germany's institutions of learning. In the democracies, intellectuals realized that despite the bravado which attended the burning of the books, the event was a confession of fear—a great fear by the fascists of the printed word and of man's power of perception.

Shortly after the book burning, the leading writers and intellectuals of Germany were forced into exile or suppressed. They had represented a culture that championed reason and spiritual freedom essentially rooted in middle-class Europan society. But, as one speaker at the American Writers' Congress expressed it, fascism was producing a culture detrimental to itself, just as it produced a Popular Front outside the fascist borders.[95] This is revealed in the development of antifascist literature and art produced by these writers who could not live and work under fascism. Among the men who caused German literature to spread beyond German borders, in addition to those exiles previously mentioned, were Heinrich Mann, Max Brod, and Stefan and Arnold Zweig.

Aversion to fascism converted to patriots many of these middle-class writers and convinced them that ethical persuasion alone was insufficient to cope with fascism. In his famous reply to the rector at the University of Bonn, Thomas Mann, like Unamuno, expressed the futility of attempting to still the protest of man against barbarism:

> The mystery of the Word is great; the responsibility for it and its purity is of a symbolic and spiritual kind; it has not only an artistic but also a general ethical meaning; it is responsibility itself, human responsibility quite simply, also the responsibility for one's own people. . . . In the Word is involved the unity of humanity, the wholeness of the human problem, which permits nobody, today less than ever, to separate the intellectual and artistic from the political and social.[96]

Arthur Koestler provides a general outline of the German intellectual's journey into radical politics. The outline includes a middle-class background, inflation of the 1920s and collapse of the bourgeois idyl, poverty and the acquisition of a social conscience, polarization of the pauperized bourgeoisie to the radical right and radical left, introduction of the latter in the early 1930s to the writings of Marx and Engels, and either membership in the Communist Party or sympathy with its philosophy.[97] Many of the

German exiles, usually in France, England, or the United States, sought involvement in the Spanish struggle as rabid antifascists. Of these, most did not complete their journey into radical politics until 1939, which ended with the signing of the Hitler-Stalin Pact.

The years of the Spanish Civil War were active ones in the literary careers of many of these writers. Brecht wrote a play, *Señora Carrara's Rifles,* satirizing the principle of neutrality; and even the venerable Thomas Mann extolled the Republic. As examples of their personal participation in the Spanish cause, it should be noted that Ludwig Renn, celebrated for his pacifist novel *Krieg* based on his World War I experiences, became a commander in the International Brigades, and Gustav Regler, the novelist and critic, was a brigade commissar. Many others, such as Ernst Toller, traveled to Spain personally to view events. Toller, on a visit to the International Brigades at the front, announced: "More and more people in the world recognize the significance of the Spanish war. You—and your fellow volunteers from other lands—were the pioneers. You were the first to bestir the sleep of the world."[98]

Never before in this century had so many authors from different countries written this passionately from a political point of view concerning a historic event; nor had they been this closely identified with a popular movement embracing so many extraliterary functions. Despite all the sincerity and moral integrity that motivated this literature, the frequent lapses in taste make it impossible to commend much of it for more than its historical importance. Such writings reinforce the conviction that good causes do not necessarily produce good literature. Rather than interpret their times, many writers sought to transform them, and to that end partisanship and outright propaganda became integral parts of their literature. This is often the consequence of the generally unhappy relationship between politics and literature.

In one sense the bulk of the literature of the Spanish Civil War is quite discouraging, since many writers who took an interest in Spain were men of more than ordinary talent. Yet few of them actually produced significant expressions of what they learned and felt. In the first advance accounts, once the fighting had started, the tendency was in the direction of pure propaganda. Much of the literature indicates the early hopes of men who could envision no result other than a Loyalist victory; it then recounts the terrible disillusionment of these same men who were trapped in the Loyalist defeat. Polemical in content and inclined to exacerbate rather than explain, such accounts were, in the main, hastily conceived and poorly written tracts designed to arouse and mold public opinion. Most writers had expressed the belief that literature should serve an extraliterary function, a belief common in the early 1930s among literary radicals. The literature of this earlier period had reflected an interest in politics; the political creed which the writers had adopted provided at least part of the stimulus which enabled them to produce a generally commendable literature of social protest. But in the literature of the Spanish Civil War it became clear that when the extraliterary functions were taken to include overt propaganda for a political cause or exhortations to direct action, the results were inferior as literature.

Examining this "political" literature does not preclude considering its success or failure in meeting the more conventional tests of creative writing. More important, the weakness of the term itself may be deceptive. What is involved in a critical study of literature of a political nature is the recognition that the ideas and ideals which create tension and stir characters to action may be politically inspired. A number of authors made the common error, when writing of the Spanish struggle, of failing to create any obstacles whatever for the ideologies they were expounding and thereby eliminated the element of tension from their work.[99] The idea that literature could be a weapon in social revolution apparently meant, to many writers who accepted this premise, that there need be no distinction between literature and propaganda. Much of the writing on the war in Spain, even by the better known authors, is little more than a form of pamphleteering.

The literature of the Spanish Civil War, whether explicitly political or not, is the most informative source of the intellectual climate of the war. Writers regarded the struggle as having a special significance, and the major writings on the war manifest a freedom of perspective not seen in the doctrinaire works of more politically committed authors. Lesser writers committed to the extreme left or extreme right, for the most part, endeavored to make their work entirely orthodox, conforming to the party dogma with regard to ideological questions. The perspective of more independent authors did not necessarily make their accounts of the conflict more accurate or objective, but it did indicate a lesser adherence to a party line. Such writing, free from a doctrinaire point of view, could therefore exhibit a more general concern for the human problems created by the war, although in various ways each author interpreted the war subjectively. It is the best of the writing by novelists during the conflict which supplies the most accurate reflection of the effects of the war on the literary imagination. In writing less involved with political slogans and cant, polemics and dialectics, novelists such as Malraux, Hemingway, Regler, Koestler, Orwell, and Bernanos strove to avoid having their work characterized as Republican propaganda. And in their finest moments these novelists proved themselves nonconformists in form as well as content, persisting, even under the severe pressures of war, in the artist's inviolate right of choice.

As a literary form the novel gave the writer an immediate advantage over the playwright and poet, if only because the novelist had a wider range and was therefore able to depict more fully his situations and characters. By its very nature, the novel requires a scrupulous attention to detail and cannot be hurriedly composed. For this reason, surprisingly few novels have been written about the Spanish struggle. Some writers, among them Upton Sinclair, did manage to rush into print with novels about Spain which were intended to take advantage of the public interest in the violent contemporary event. Fortunately, not many writers had Sinclair's glib ability to concoct, in a few days or weeks, what is called a novel, nor did they, as Sinclair did, possess their own printing presses.

The three outstanding novels to emerge from the Spanish Civil War are André Malraux's *L'espoir,* Gustav Regler's *The Great Crusade,* and Ernest Hemingway's *For Whom the Bell Tolls.* These novelists, whatever their original intention in seeking involvement in the Spanish struggle, demonstrate in their writings that they followed no party line but were engaged essentially as antifascists and as defenders of their humanitarian democratic traditions. Although Malraux and Regler had strong attachments to communism at various periods in their lives before their involvement in the Spanish Civil War, these writers, and Hemingway as well, scrupulously placed their art above politics. Doctrinaire Marxist critics have on occasion classified all three as essentially middle-class liberal intellectuals, with a penchant for social change and all that promised improved conditions for the oppressed and suppressed. Even though Malraux, Regler and Hemingway on several occasions risked their lives for the workers of Spain, these same Marxist critics could conclude that inasmuch as their writings maintained a distinction between life and art, they never truly entered into the revolutionary class struggle.[100] Their zeal in support of the Spanish Republic contained an awareness of political machinations which tempered their enthusiasm, a condition which dogmatic political critics could never tolerate.

The bulk of the literature of the Spanish Civil War takes the form of personal narratives written by those who had witnessed the war. If the number of novels dealing with the conflict is limited, there is an abundance of these memoirs written by war correspondents, diplomats, touring writers, soldiers, and even cabaret dancers.[101] Most of these books were written and published while the war was being fought, although a few appeared during the early years of World War II and some have circulated at wide intervals in more recent years. Most of them were written to take advantage of a temporary market and, as a result, show the effects of this haste. A great many are without literary merit and contain little of historical interest. It is nevertheless true that the best of these personal narratives have their own importance. Such is the case of Georges Bernanos' *Les grands cimetières sous la lune,* Arthur Koestler's *Spanish Testament,* and George Orwell's *Homage to Catalonia.* These personal narratives are the work of professional writers and provide an insight into the motivations of those literary intellectuals who sojourned to Spain. These narratives also provide the most direct testimony of the importance of the Spanish Civil War in its time. Equally important, they reflect directly the various aspects from which most writers viewed the realities of the war.[102]

By limiting this study to the novels and personal narratives of Malraux, Regler, Hemingway, Bernanos, Koestler, and Orwell, various interpretations of the issues involved in the Spanish Civil War may be compared and contrasted. These six writers cannot be classified as a homogeneous group; their politics range from communism and socialism to Catholic conservatism; by nationality they represent the democracies—England, France and the United States—and the German writers in exile; their literary talents and intellectual capacities vary widely. Yet each writer found himself in Spain defending his personal beliefs. Their diverse backgrounds and experiences with the violence of modern warfare created major differences in their interpretations of the events of the war. They arrived in and left Spain at different times and served in different sectors during the conflict. While in Spain their functions ranged from military commander to impartial observer. This heterogeneity establishes comparisons and contrasts with regard to their views on particular issues of the conflict. Yet, in the final analysis, it will be seen that their differences are less obvious than the similarities embodied in their humanism. Despite their contrasts, these six writers were representative of the reaction of the independent intellectual to the Spanish Civil War. Although their interpretations vary, with slight exceptions, the independence of the authors is maintained throughout their writing on the war.

A study of the impact of the Spanish Civil War on the novelist is fortunate in having six writers with the talents of Malraux, Regler, Hemingway, Bernanos, Koestler, and Orwell for research. Their literary careers following the war in Spain are sufficiently well known to afford some indication of the effect of their experience on their artistic conscience. The idealism and subsequent disillusionment embodied in the war caused varying responses among all authors. By examining the reactions of these novelists, some indication of the influence of the Spanish Civil War on later literature, particularly those novels dealing with World War II, should become apparent.

## ▸ NOTES

[1] Of 148 replies received in response to a questionnaire submitted to the major writers in England, *Authors Take Sides* (London, 1937), 127 stated that they favored the Spanish Republic as the legal government and one representative of the people of Spain, 17 preferred to remain neutral, while 5 opposed the Republic in the belief that the Franco revolt would eventually prove beneficial to Spain. Even more unilateral pro-Republic results were obtained

from the questionnaire submitted to American writers, *Writers Take Sides* (New York, 1938).

[2] Hugh D. Ford, *A Poets' War: British Poets and the Spanish Civil War* (Philadelphia, 1965), pp. 20–21.

[3] "The Days of Non-Intervention," *The Long Week-End* (London, 1940), p. 337.

[4] *Autumn Journal* (London, 1939), p. 29.

[5] E. Allison Peers, perceptive English scholar of Spanish politics, in his analysis of the forces involved in the Spanish Civil War, anticipated just such oversimplified "labeling," and as early as 1936 cautioned against the tendency. *The Spanish Tragedy* (London, 1936), pp. 217–23.

[6] Daniel Aaron, *Writers on the Left* (New York, 1961), p. 157. Aaron studies the American intellectuals, but his observations are applicable to the literary reaction throughout America and Europe.

[7] Muste, *Say That We Saw Spain Die*, p. 11.

[8] The order for discussion of these factions is as follows: 1) anarchists, socialists, communists, and other radical writers; 2) literary neutrals and the "Ivory Tower"; 3) fascists, conservatives, and Catholics, the minority voices of reaction; 4) writers in the liberal, democratic tradition; 5) German antifascist writers in exile.

[9] *Ibid.*, p. 25.

[10] Spain's Popular Front consisted of the Republican Left, Republican Union, Left Republican Party of Catalonia, Socialist Party, Communist Party, with the outside support of the Workers Party of Marxist Unity (P.O.U.M.), National Confederation of Labor, and the Iberian Anarchists Federation. Gabriel Jackson, *The Spanish Republic and the Civil War, 1931–1939* (Princeton, N. J., 1965), pp. 184–87.

[11] Michael Bakunin, the founder of European anarchism, quoted in Gerald Brenan, *The Spanish Labyrinth*, 3rd ed. (Cambridge, Eng., 1950), p. 133. Brenan's book contains an excellent analysis of the development of anarchism and anarcho-syndicalism in Spain. J. Peirats, *La CNT en la Revolución Española* (Toulouse, 1951–1953), includes the important anarchist texts for the period of the civil war.

[12] Salvador de Madariaga, *Spain: A Modern History* (New York, 1958), p. 629. Madariaga's book is an authoritative statement on the history of Spain in the twentieth century. The author assumed an active role in the developments described.

[13] Herbert Read, *Thirty-five Poems* (London, 1940), p. 41.

[14] See Guttmann, *Wound in the Heart*, p. 139.

[15] *Spain*, p. 455.

[16] In Felix Morrow, *The Civil War in Spain* (New York, 1936), pp. 63–64. See also Trotsky, *The Lesson of Spain, the Last Warning* (London, 1938).

[17] See Guttmann, *Wound in the Heart*, p. 156.

[18] See Bloch, "Espagne! Espagne!" *Europe* (August 15, 1936), p. 524, and Chamson, *Devenir ce qu'on est* (Paris, 1959), p. 61.

[19] Ford, *Poets' War*, p. 70.

[20] "Spain: Rehearsal for De-

feat," *The Theme is Freedom* (New York, 1956), pp. 114–15.

[21] See Georgi Dimitrov, *Spain and the People's Front* (New York, 1937), and Thomas, *Spanish Civil War,* p. 90. The origins of the European Popular Front movement during the 1930s are discussed in Dante A. Puzzo's *Spain and the Great Powers, 1936–1941* (New York, 1962), pp. 31–33. Puzzo refutes the contention that the Popular Front received its organizational structure and program directly from Moscow.

[22] In *Overtures to Death and Other Poems* (London, 1938), p. 41.

[23] The gains in prestige and membership of the Communist Party in the democracies—England, France, and the United States—during the 1936–1939 period, which can be attributed directly to its policy toward Spain, are detailed in Neal Wood, *Communism and British Intellectuals* (New York, 1959), David Caute, *Communism and the French Intellectuals, 1914–1960* (New York, 1964), and Guttmann, *Wound in the Heart,* respectively.

[24] Blum, the sensitive prime minister, was torn between his pacificism and his desire to assist the Republic. Never had the dilemma of the liberal intellectual in a political situation been greater. British Prime Minister Stanley Baldwin finally convinced him that the threat to peace could be averted only if the major powers would unite in a policy of strict neutrality. James Joll, *Three Intellectuals in Politics* (New York, 1960), pp. 40–41.

[25] See Thomas, *Spanish Civil War,* pp. 214–17. A clear analysis of communist policy during the 1936–1939 period is contained in David Cattell's two studies, *Communism and the Spanish Civil War* (Berkeley, 1955) and *Soviet Diplomacy and the Spanish Civil War* (Berkeley, 1957).

[26] See Guttmann, *Wound in the Heart,* p. 144.

[27] Upton Sinclair, *No Pasarán!* (Pasadena, California, 1937), p. 72.

[28] Paul Eluard, *Poèmes politiques* (Paris, 1948); the first and last lines of a verse of "Vencer juntos."

[29] Quoted in Caute, *Communism and the French Intellectuals,* p. 117.

[30] In R. Penrose, *Picasso: His Life and Work* (London, 1958), p. 283.

[31] Simone Téry, *Front de la liberté: Espagne, 1937–1938* (Paris, 1938).

[32] In Caute, *Communism and the French Intellectuals,* p. 120.

[33] Borkenau, *Spanish Cockpit,* contains an account of the sporadic attempts at agricultural collectivism of expropriated land during the Spanish Civil War.

[34] John Gunther, *Inside Europe* (New York, 1938), p. 169.

[35] André Gide issued a polemic attacking the communists' stand for their repressions in Barcelona, but even the strictly non-communist editorial board of the Popular Front intellectual weekly *Vendredi* refused to publish it, in the interest of "Popular Front mystique." Caute, *Communism and the French Intellectuals,* p. 120. The German emigré, Hans Erich Ka-

minski, in his *Ceux de Barcelone* (Paris, 1938), also protested but went unheeded.

[36] *The God That Failed,* ed. Richard Crossman (New York, 1949), p. 246. Cattell in his detailed study, *Soviet Diplomacy and the Spanish Civil War,* pp. 36–37, confirms Spender's allegations.

[37] Included in Bessie's anthology, *Heart of Spain,* p. 443.

[38] Quoted in Guttmann, *Wound in the Heart,* p. 124. Guttmann's study contains a detailed discussion of this group.

[39] Kenneth Rexroth, "Two Poems," in *Salud!,* ed. Alan Calmer (New York, 1938), p. 30.

[40] Muste, *Say That We Saw Spain Die,* p. 32.

[41] In Thomas, *Spanish Civil War,* p. 222.

[42] Raymond Aron in his book, *The Opium of the Intellectuals* (London, 1957), makes a perceptive analysis of this intellectual phenomenon.

[43] "The Tourist Looks at Spain," *Poems for Spain,* eds. Stephen Spender and John Lehmann (London, 1939), p. 69.

[44] See Eliot's and Waugh's responses to the questionnaire, *Authors Take Sides.*

[45] See Guttmann, *Wound in the Heart,* p. 126. The relationship between literature and politics is treated in more detail in Chap. II of this study.

[46] Recently the first impartial authoritative study of the theory underlying the fascist movement in modern European history was completed by Ernst Nolte, *Three Faces of Fascism* (New York, 1966); Nolte's book concentrates on fascism in France, Italy, and Germany. Together with Stanley G. Payne's *Falange: A History of Spanish Fascism* (Stanford, California, 1961), an excellent, objective treatise on the Spanish brand of fascism, a comprehensive account is now available.

[47] Payne, *Falange,* p. vii.

[48] Payne, *Falange,* p. 1; see also Nolte, *Three Faces of Fascism,* p. 5.

[49] Payne, *Falange,* p. 39. Quoted from a speech by José Antonio Primo de Rivera delivered October 29, 1933, at the Teatro Comedia of Madrid.

[50] José Pemartín Sanjuan, the first historian of the Falange, in his *Los Origenes del Movimiento* (Burgos, 1938), p. 22.

[51] Herbert Matthews, *The Yoke and the Arrows* (New York, 1957), pp. 12–13. Ironically, the displaced José Antonio had once written, "In the last resort, as Spengler puts it, it has always been a platoon of soldiers who have saved civilization."

[52] See Thomas, *Spanish Civil War,* p. 635.

[53] See Francis Yeats-Brown, *European Jungle* (Philadelphia, 1939); Pierre Héricourt, *Pourquoi Franco vaincra* (Paris, 1936); Jean and Jerome Tharaud, *Cruelle Espagne* (Paris, 1937); Florence Farmborough, *Life and People in National Spain* (London, 1938) and Robert Sencourt, *Spain's Ordeal* (London, 1938).

[54] *American Mercury,* XI (February, 1937), 158.

[55] Puzzo, in *Spain and the Great Powers,* devotes over one-third of his study to the complex

origins and eventual repercussions of the international policy of "non-intervention" in the Spanish conflict. His discussion is the basis for the material used here.

[56] *New York Times,* March 1, 1937. Other signers included F. P. Adams, Robert Benchley, Van Wyck Brooks, Erskine Caldwell, John Dewey, John Gunther, Langston Hughes, and Upton Sinclair. In a later statement Maxwell Anderson, Theodore Drieser, and Brooks reiterated their stand that "We can no longer withhold from the recognized government of Spain the right of free access to the American markets under the pretense that this is 'neutrality.'" *New York Times,* March 6, 1938.

[57] Quoted in Guttman, *Wound in the Hearts,* p. 27, and attributed to Santayana in a letter to Robert Shaw dated November 3, 1936.

[58] Se Charles Maurras, *Vers l'Espagne de Franco* (Paris, 1943); Wyndham Lewis, *Count Your Dead; They Are Alive!* (London, 1937); Roy Campbell, "Flowering Rifles," *New Statesman and Nation,* XVII (April 8, 1939); and Evelyn Waugh's reply to *Authors Take Sides.*

[59] Taylor, *United States and the Spanish Civil War,* p. 153.

[60] See Guttmann, *Wound in the Heart,* p. 29 ff., and José M. Sánchez, *Reform and Reaction: The Politico-Religious Background of the Spanish Civil War* (Chapel Hill, N. C., 1962).

[61] Sánchez, *Reform and Reaction,* p. 110. The latent anti-Catholicism in Europe and the United States is inexplicable but cannot be totally disregarded in evaluating the literature of the Spanish conflict.

[62] *Encyclical on Spain . . .* (New York, 1937), pp. 3–4. In a letter to President Roosevelt, American Ambassador to Spain Claude Bowers stated that he was amused at the suggestion of Camille Chautemps, the French Premier, that the Pope was neutral in his feelings: "He is just as neutral as he was in the case of Abyssinia. He is a very loyal Italian always." In Taylor, *United States and the Spanish Civil War,* pp. 143–44.

[63] Sánchez, *Reform and Reaction,* p. 43.

[64] *Spanish Civil War,* p. 173; Antonio Montero Moreno, *Historia de la Persecución Religiosa en España, 1936–1939* (Madrid, 1961), p. 762.

[65] See Thomas, *Spanish Civil War,* pp. 449–51.

[66] *Flowering Rifle* (London, 1939), p. 50.

[67] Stefan Andres, *Wir Sind Utopia* (Berlin, 1943), p. 39.

[68] Verse Preface to [Juan Estelrich], *La persécution religieuse en Espagne* (Paris, 1937).

[69] See Jacques Maritain, *Rebeldes Españoles No Hacen una 'Guerra Santa'* (Paris, 1937).

[70] Jacques Maritain in his Preface to Alfredo Mendizábal's *The Martyrdom of Spain* (New York, 1938), p. 25.

[71] Radio Madrid, September 20, 1936, and included in Bessie, *Heart of Spain,* p. 102.

[72] Guttmann, *Wound in the Heart,* pp. 81–82. This discussion of liberalism and its response to the Spanish conflict is based upon the central theme in Guttmann's study

—that the essential motivation behind the intellectual concern for Spain was a product of a humanitarian liberal tradition.

[73] *Spain* (London, 1937), p. 10. The experience of Auden in Spain (he served briefly as an ambulance driver) is curiously similar to that of Simone Weil. Both (unlike others who visited Spain) were uninformative when they returned, and both provided only nominal support for the Republic after their Spanish sojourn. Simone Weil, who spent some time in Catalonia in August–October 1936, seems to have undergone a religious conversion as the result of her experiences. In a letter to Georges Bernanos she expressed her disillusionment with a struggle which was begun by "famished peasants against landowners and their ecclesiastic accomplices" only to be transformed into "a war between Russia, Germany and Italy." Quoted in *Bulletin de la Société des Amis de Bernanos,* No. 4, June 1950.

[74] Guttmann, *Wound in the Heart,* p. 83.

[75] Millan Astray is reported to have uttered this cry at the University of Salamanca during a speech by Miguel de Unamuno, Spain's leading intellectual and rector of the university. From the beginning of the uprising, Unamuno had clearly demonstrated his distate for the methods of the Nationalists, but he was too old and feeble to take a public position against Franco. In this confrontation with the fanatical general, Unamuno represented the completely civilized man facing the pure nihilist. Unamuno's public declaration in favor of life and civilized values was his last public statement; he died a few weeks later. The account of this incident is recorded by Luis Portillo and is included in Robert Payne's anthology, *The Civil War in Spain* (New York, 1962).

[76] See Guttmann, *Wound in the Heart,* p. 85 ff.

[77] For an account of the educational reforms instituted by the Republic, see Madariaga, *Spain,* pp. 412–13, and Jackson, *Spanish Republic and the Civil War,* pp. 62–65. The construction of schools and the recruitment of teachers under the Republic proceeded at a rate approximately ten times that under the monarchy.

[78] *La terre des hommes* (Paris, 1939), p. 210.

[79] Replies to *Authors Take Sides.*

[80] See Guttmann, *Wound in the Heart,* p. 94 ff.

[81] See Madariaga, *Spain,* pp. 75–84, for a history of the Institución Libre de Enseñanza, and Thomas, *Spanish Civil War,* pp. 22–23, for the influence of this institution on Republican politics.

[82] In *Poems for Spain,* p. 37. Hernández found his inspiration in the fight of his countrymen. He had been a shepherd in the hills taught to read by a priest by examples of sixteenth- and seventeenth-century writings. The outbreak of the war sparked his imagination and resulted in an outburst of poetic activity. Hernández died in Alicante jail shortly after the end of the struggle.

[83] *Ibid.,* p. 7.

[84] Ernest Hemingway, "The Writer and the War," *The Writer*

*in a Changing World,* ed. Henry Hart (New York, 1937), p. 69.

[85] See Alvah Bessie, *Men in Battle* (New York, 1939), p. 181. The history of the American, British and Italian sections of the International Brigades are recorded in Edwin Rolfe's *The Lincoln Battalion* (New York, 1939), William Rust's *Britons in Spain* (London, 1939), and Randolfo Pacciardi's *Il battaglione Garibaldi* (Lugano, 1948), respectively.

[86] In *Volunteer for Liberty,* April 9, 1938.

[87] *Terre des hommes,* p. 204.

[88] Romain Rolland, "Humanité appelle à toi," *Unité,* III (April 1938), 1. This phrase is an echo of Rolland's famous "Declaration of Intellectual Independence" (1919), in which he invited the intellectuals of the world, who had recently disgraced themselves in behalf of narrow nationalism, to write for the "whole of humanity."

[89] *Terre des hommes,* pp. 180–81.

[90] *Flowering Rifle,* p. 55.

[91] Guttmann, *Wound in the Heart,* p. 105.

[92] Lillian Hellman, "Day in Spain," *The New Republic,* XCIV (April 13, 1938), 298, and Dorothy Parker, "Incredible, Fantastic . . . and True," *New Masses,* XXV (November 23, 1937), 16.

[93] *Terre des hommes,* pp. 173–74.

[94] George Orwell, *Homage to Catalonia* (London, 1938), p. 48.

[95] Harry Slochower, "Culture under Nazism," *Writer in a Changing World,* 78. Their Italian antifascist counterparts—Palmiro Togliatti, Carlo Rosselli, Giuseppe Vittorio, Randolfo Pacciardi, Luigi Longo, and Pietro Nenni—while less literary, fought with distinction on the side of the Spanish Republic.

[96] *Ibid.,* p. 80, quoted in the Slochower essay.

[97] See Arthur Koestler in *God That Failed.*

[98] Quoted in Edwin Rolfe, *Lincoln Battalion,* p. 280.

[99] Howe, *Politics and the Novel,* pp. 22–23. A more extensive analysis of the requisites for successful "political literature" will be presented in the chapter following.

[100] The degree to which excellent critics were pushed by the pressure of events is evidenced in separate reviews by Philip Rahv and F. W. Dupee of Malraux's *L'Espoir,* each evaluating the novel as little more than a communist diatribe; less surprisingly, the communist critic Alvah Bessie could refer to Hemingway's *For Whom the Bell Tolls* as a propaganda coup for the fascists.

[101] Janet Riesenfeld, a cabaret dancer, went to Madrid during the fighting and lost her heart to the Loyalists. *Dancer in Madrid* (New York, 1938).

[102] In the succeeding chapters, all quoted material from the Hemingway, Malraux, and Regler war novels and the Koestler, Orwell, and Bernanos personal narratives will be noted simply by a page number in the text. If sources by these authors are from other than the primary works involved in this study, more detailed documentation will be provided.

# ▸ II

# ▸ Political Commitment and the Writer

The civil war, which bloodied the Iberian Peninsula from 1936 to 1939, was more than a historical episode in Europe's onward rush toward self-destruction. It possessed the quality of a great tragedy in which the essential nature of human existence was once again placed on trial. Its crucial position in the intellectual life of a large portion of European and American writers inflamed their passions and impelled them to participate in the struggle. Their decision to commit themselves usually took one of two forms: affiliation with a political organization or individual action. Regardless of the course chosen, it was necessary to determine how best to further their cause. For most it was not difficult to lend their names to partisan groups, and even to participate in demonstrations. But since such support was merely token from an intellectual viewpoint, the writer was forced to decide whether he should dedicate his art, as well as himself, to assist the Republican cause. Such a decision was not an easy one. Authors then had to determine, because of their strong convictions favoring the Loyalist position, how their work on its behalf would be an improvement over the propaganda disseminated by the Popular Front. This question involved the basic relationship between politics and literature, particularly in the context of the 1930s.

The distinction between political literature and propaganda

is extremely complex and involves the writer's ability to distinguish between his social conscience and his obligation to his art. Most writers in the 1930s discovered their social conscience and its implied obligation to their fellowman—Jean-Paul Sartre's idealized "homme libre s'adressant à des hommes libres." Since the economic and social crises early in the decade, the writer's social conscience had been oriented toward politics. When he chose to make this theme prominent in his writing, the merger of art and politics often proved an extremely difficult one. Unless complete fusion was achieved, didacticism and propaganda at the expense of art were the inevitable result. The literature of this period reflected both the constructive and disintegrating phases of contemporary society—processes resulting from social and economic forces of which politics was an important factor.[1] The skillful writer was able to take these abstract ideas, however, and transform them into more than the platform for a political program. In considering the criteria for evaluating this political literature, the qualities under consideration must be the same as those contained in any form of serious literature: to what extent is it an illuminating commentary on life and how ample a moral vision does it suggest?[2]

When Thomas Mann said that "politics is everybody's business," the observation implied that the writer in the 1930s could not retreat to an ivory tower and refuse to participate in the social upheavals of the time. For the exiled Mann, the truly effective writer was of necessity "aware of the unity of the problem for humanity, of the inseparability of mind and politics."[3] During this decade, with the shock of economic collapse and the rise of fascism as dominating factors, the concept of socially-conscious literature proliferated on the literary scene in Europe and the United States. The theme of social protest had existed in literature long before the 1930s, particularly in the naturalism of European and American writing at the close of the nineteenth century and continuing into the twentieth century. But never before had the social protest so involved political considerations. Emile Zola could describe life among the lower strata of Parisian society and Stephen Crane could picture the hopelessness of life on New York's Bowery; but no unified political solution to mitigate the social injustices inflicted on the lower classes appeared in the works of these writers. The social protests of the 1930s, however, for the most part, did exhibit a strong political influence. The events of the decade caused many authors to deny the separability of mind and politics, and to participate in collective action against recognizable forces of barbarism, tyranny, and oppression. The Marxist-oriented critic E. B. Burgum offers one explanation for the drive behind this literary trend:

> Defining democracy with some precision as guaranteeing 'freedom from want' to the masses of mankind, as guaranteeing to each individual the satisfaction of fulfilling his potentialities, their attention as novelists was naturally directed to the common man. And seeing the greatest need there, and there the greatest recognition of the need, the focus of their interest shifted from despair at the muddling of the middle class to hope and trust in the superior sanity and resoluteness of the common man.[4]

Burgum's antibourgeois conclusions are perhaps not so accurate as his observations that out of the midst of a truly catastrophic economic collapse there emerged a group of socially-conscious writers who felt compassion for the deprived throughout the world, and of this group there were many who found in various political ideologies possible solutions to such problems.[5]

The volatile political world of the decade seemed to demand a new and decisive response. The breakdown of the economic system had left millions hungry and jobless. In Italy and Germany, meanwhile, fascist regimes were creating new and menacing armies and navies, and in the Far East a newly modernized Japan was looking toward the Asian mainland for space with which to alleviate the heavy and increasing pressures of overpopulation. It hardly seemed a time for timidity and restraint. And it was not long before the countermeasures proposed by the democracies seemed too tame for many. Given the economic and social conditions in the United States, Western Europe, and the Soviet Union, it is even more understandable that many intellectuals were attracted to communism and to other milder forms of collectivism. They found new villains in the naïve and selfish bourgeoisie (the wealthier classes had long played this role), and new heroes in a proletariat of migrant workers, miners, mill hands, and oppressed Negroes. Many envisioned the solution to all social injustice in a Marxist interpretation of history and society.[6]

With the explosion of the Spanish Civil War in July 1936, all writers whose political sympathies were grounded in these principles found a rallying point, a unifying cause, into which they could channel their feelings. "Spain is no political allegory," noted Archibald MacLeish. "Spain is not . . . a dramatic spectacle in which the conflict of our time is acted out. . . . These battles are not symbols of other battles to be fought elsewhere at some other time. They are the actual war itself. And in that war, that Spanish war on Spanish earth, we, writers who contend for freedom, are ourselves, and whether we wish so or not, engaged."[7] Literary intellectuals were nearly unanimous in siding with the Loyalists, and the Republican cause exerted an extraordinary attraction for many writers who previously had had only the vaguest political beliefs. The motives that attracted these men to the Spanish struggle were for the most part embodied in the same idealism that had led many of them to sympathize with the plight of the lower classes originally. The concept of books used as "barricades to stop fascist bullets" exerted a strong force. Politically, however, these writers differed in the depth and strength of their commitment to the various ideologies of the time. Since the Republican cause was widely felt to be the cause of social justice, those who responded to it believed they were the defenders of Western civilization itself. Intellectuals came to believe that whatever was worth defending had become embodied in the Republican cause. It alone stood for tolerance, compassion, and liberty. Therefore, as writers in the humanitarian tradition, the responsibility to preserve it was unquestionably theirs, and the depths of that sense of responsibility was often evidenced in ringing challenges to the conscience of Western man.

Although the vast majority of the writers in Europe and the United States favored the Loyalists, the question remained to what extent they were willing to support their belief actively. Sympathizing with Republican Spain seemed like saying that one believed in life rather than death; to declare oneself for Franco was to say that one stood for reaction, slavery, or worse. The writer's relationship to his society, however, raised the question of literary responsibility. Assuming that authors might act in some manner to alter social conditions, could they justifiably interrupt their careers to fight in Spain, or give up time from their writing to support their cause at home? To the correspondent Martha Gellhorn, the decision appeared clear:

> A writer must be a man of action now. Action takes time, and time is what we all need most. But a man who has given a year of his life, without heroics or boastfulness, to the war in Spain, or who, in the same way, has given a year of his life to steel strikes, or to the unemployed, or to the problems of racial prejudice, has not lost or wasted time. He is a man who has known where he belonged. If you should survive such action, what you have to say about it afterwards is the truth, it is necessary and real, and it will last.[8]

Most important, should writers channel their talents in support of their political beliefs? At the American Writers' Congress, Granville Hicks harangued those authors who were hesitant to commit their work as well as themselves to the Republican cause:

> No sensitive, alert, broadly sympathetic human being—no artist in short—can remain permanently indifferent to the injustices of our world and to the threat of organized injustice in a fascist world. You cannot stand aloof from the issues today and remain a whole man. There are those, it is true, who became eunuchs willingly for the sake of the Kingdom of Art, but I do not know that they attain it.[9]

Both these questions, with the outbreak of the Spanish Civil War, demanded immediate and conclusive answers.

In his study of *The Writer and Commitment*, John Mander presents an affirmative case for involvement on the part of the writer, not in politics as such, but rather in life. Mander points out that to the ancient Greeks there was no distinction between the political and social spheres, and therefore no illuminating criticism of life was complete that did not contain both social and political implications.[10] Such historical analogies are of value but fail to consider the intellectual climate of the 1930s, infinitely removed from that of classical Athens. The question of political involvement on the part of writers and its effect on their work had occurred to intellectuals long before July 1936. But after that date, with a real fascist enemy in the field and a Popular Front at home that was greatly in need of all the literary support it could get, such issues exerted a critical immediacy.

The question whether literature could be made to serve extraliterary functions, particularly political functions, had been widely and exhaustively discussed, but the alleged antagonism between art and propaganda, between poetry and politics, seemed merely academic to writers facing the realities of 1936. Ultimately there was a question of means and ends, and each author's answer depended on how fervently he believed in the cause of the Spanish Republic, the role each thought he could play in working for victory, and, if affiliated with a political party, on the writer's willingness to submit to party discipline. If some intellectuals had been in doubt about the kind of literature which the social conditions of the times demanded, the outbreak of the Spanish Civil War dispelled any illusions.

Although devotion to a humanitarian cause was the motivating factor in the decision of the majority of these writers to use their art in support of the Popular Front, politically-oriented critics used their influence to convince less socially committed authors. These critics, appealing to the author's conscience, stressed that fascism was intent upon destroying not just the cultural achievements of Spain, but the cultural heritage of all peoples; therefore, as people interested in preserving the culture of the world, writers were obligated to join in the fight against those who would destroy it. Such a communion of dedicated men was the surest way to counter the fascist threat, although speculation on the ideological utopia to follow the fascist defeat was postponed for the sake of unity. The plea for participation in the Popular Front by the young communist poet, Ralph Fox, was grounded in his firm conviction that the only chance of victory for the Loyalist cause was present in a united antifascist front.[11] Granville Hicks reminded authors in the United States, "The united front is being built in America, not formally as in France or Spain, but nevertheless solidly. Nothing in this world can be so important as the expediting and strengthening of that work."[12] Authors were now requested to write, translating the contemporary crisis into emotional terms so as to appeal to the "latent idealism" of the uncommitted. The prewar discussions of artistic integrity had all but disappeared under the pressing demands of the Spanish cause. The primary purpose of writing now, so radical critics contended, was to influence particular groups to unite in the cause of social justice by joining the Popular Front.

The intellectual's decision to commit himself presented two possible courses of action: either he could become affiliated with a political party and act in a "collective" manner, or he could choose to act as an individual. The case against party affiliation was succinctly stated by George Orwell, an independent mind in spite of his socialist protestations, when he noted that the process of literary creation is an extremely personal one demanding complete honesty and a minimum of censorship. Orwell declared that, in retrospect, the literary history of the 1930s would seem to justify the opinion that a writer does well to avoid affiliation with a political party. His refutation of the radical critics is based on a single concept, the necessity for the artist's inviolate "freedom of choice":

> For any writer who accepts or partially accepts the discipline of a political party is sooner or later faced with the alternative: toe the line, or shut up. It is, of course, possible to toe the line and go on writing—after a fashion. Any Marxist can demonstrate with the greatest of ease that "bourgeois" liberty of thought is an illusion. But when he has finished his demonstration there remains the psychological *fact* that without this "bourgeois" liberty the creative powers wither away.[13]

The novelist is more affected by the restrictions imposed by political conformity than writers in other genre. Orwell points out that the atmosphere of orthodoxy is completely ruinous to the novel, which is the most anarchical of all forms of literature, the product of the free mind, of the autonomous individual. It is almost inconceivable that good literature could be produced in an atmosphere where political propaganda was so prevalent and the communist and near-communist critics had such a disproportionately large influence on the literary reviews.[14] But if the dangers of a Marxist interpretation of the function of literature had been realized by politically independent writers such as Orwell, Hemingway, and Bernanos, what of the writers who had political ties and who found themselves committed to a doctrinaire viewpoint?

Politically aligned writers such as Malraux, Regler, and Koestler, with strong Republican sympathies grounded in a conscious humanism, were faced with several alternatives. They could write propaganda which would depict the Loyalist cause as a crusade against whichever faction their political party (in this case the Community Party) had decided to label the enemy at that time. While such a course would practically eliminate the writer's concern over subject matter, since presumably the abstractions would be provided by the party, it would primarily occupy him with political theory and doctrine rather than humanity and his own experience; hence he would be prone to reject anything which did not coincide with the prevailing orthodoxy. The result would be writing that met a certain political standard, but which failed to meet the requirements of good literature.

Two other possibilities which were open to the politically-committed writer resulted in literary sterility. The writer could restrict himself to a narrative treatment of the events of the war. Since in many cases these events were already familiar to the general public, the writer's task would consist of little more than reporting the details to achieve some degree of dramatic unity and emphasis. Such literature made only minimal demands on the writer's creative faculties and could permit, if the writer desired, a complete absence of politics. In contrast to this political estrangement was another possible alternative which faced the writer-as-party-member. He could participate in Popular Front activities, recognize a separation of art and politics, and thereby resist pressure to transform his art into a political instrument. Certain practical considerations discouraged the writer from utilizing his time, but not his art, for political purposes. The writer, as Stephen Spender has observed, ran the risk of drawing too heavily on his credit as a man of letters; that is, in making a contribution to the cause, the writer was counting on his literary reputation to add weight to the faction he supported. The danger here lay in becoming so closely identified with a political group within the Popular Front that too much time would be spent just fulfilling the demands of party leaders for speeches, appearances, and meetings. Eventually the writer would have to choose between literature and politics:

> The impulse to act was not mistaken. But the action we took may not have been of the right kind. It was, for the most part, the half-and-half action of people divided between their artistic and their

> public conscience, and unable to fuse the two. I now think that what I should have done was either throw myself entirely into political action; or, refusing to waste my energies on half-politics, made within my solitary creative work an agonized, violent, bitter statement of the anti-Fascist passion.[15]

The remaining alternative for these politically aligned writers was to use the events which they had experienced in Spain as the raw materials for their writing, but to refrain from placing on their work a veneer of political dogma. In this case the work's content and the emotions resulting from it would be the consequences of the writer's own experience and feeling rather than his desire to meet party specifications. If such a work happened to satisfy certain political standards, it was not because the writer consciously tried to meet these standards. The similarity, while perhaps not wholly accidental, was, nevertheless, not solicited nor completely orthodox. The writer would have reached his conclusions independently although they might correspond in essence at that time with those of a political party. Writers such as Malraux, Koestler, and Regler, either because they wished to preserve their "individualism" as artists or because of a genuine and profound commitment to political principles, wrote books during the Spanish Civil War which for the most part ignored the more rigid demands of the party line on Spain and yet agreed in principle with what the politicians of their party espoused. Along with Orwell, Hemingway, and Bernanos, the imaginations of these writers were stirred by their experiences in Spain, yet remained sufficiently detached from party politics and the propaganda of the Popular Front to create literature which found its inspiration in the human element in the struggle of the Spanish people.

Of the six novelists involved in this study, the extent of their political commitment in 1936 varied from little or no direct affiliation with a political party to active membership within certain political organizations. By examining the political background of each of these authors, some idea of their dedication to the Republican cause and the degree to which their support of the Loyalists was tinged by ulterior political motives may be ascertained. Assuming that their party affiliations influenced their thinking, such influences would be manifested by doctrinaire elements in their writings on the Spanish conflict. Such biographical criticism has obvious disadvantages; but in writing politically motivated as that dealing with the Spanish Civil War, it is possible to evaluate the author's efforts in terms of his avoidance of propaganda and polemic, and in his ability to function primarily as an artist rather than as a political pamphleteer.

Of the six novelists under discussion, Ernest Hemingway may be termed the most apolitical of the group. The Spanish peasant in "The Old Man at the Bridge," who worried about his birds and his cats, said, "I have no politics." From his wound at Fossalta del Piave in World War I to his residence in Madrid's Hotel Florida, Hemingway was almost belligerently nonpolitical. He set down his convictions on the relationship between the writer and politics in the fall of 1934, well before the Spanish conflict:

> A writer can make himself a nice career while he is alive by espousing a political cause, working for it, making a profession of believing in it, and if it wins he will be very well placed. . . . A man can be a Fascist or Communist and if his outfit gets in he can get to be an ambassador, or have a million copies of his books printed by the Government, or any of the other rewards the boys dream about. . . . But none of this will help him as a writer unless he finds something new to add to human knowledge while he is writing.[16]

Hemingway rejected political themes, which he felt were transitory in their relevance, and even in the 1930s, when politics and economics were the chief concerns of the intellectuals in America and Europe, he wrote that "a thousand years makes economics silly and a work of art endures forever, but it is very difficult to do and now it is not fashionable."[17] Such a belief does not imply that Hemingway divorced himself from politics during this period. It merely illustrates his feeling that there was a distinct separation between the artist and the man, and this separation must be maintained or great literature will be sacrificed for histories, economic treatises, political expositions, and interpretations of current social trends.

Carlos Baker emphasizes that Hemingway's views on man in society were determined, in the 1930s, by three major considerations: his experiences during World War I, in which he saw the violence of modern warfare at first hand; his increasing disgust with and hatred of the postwar machinations of European diplomats and dictators in their struggle for power, which he had covered as a newspaper correspondent; and his ingrained belief that the novelist who pontificated on the course of contemporary history would always tend to betray his true artistic purposes.[18] This third factor in the development of Hemingway's views on the writer in politics was most important. To substitute political propaganda for literature seemed to Hemingway an evasion of the serious writer's fundamental obligation to his art, which was

> to write straight honest prose on human beings. First you have to know the subject; then you have to know how to write. Both take a lifetime to learn, and anyone is cheating who takes politics as a way out. It is too easy. All the outs are too easy, and the thing itself is too hard to do.[19]

The utopian world envisioned by the political ideologies of the 1930s did not tempt Hemingway. Perhaps his experience as a foreign correspondent, intimately in touch with political actualities, had released him from such temptation. As early as the 1920s, Hemingway had been on record as antifascist, but such sentiments were not manifest in his novels of the period. In his short story, "Che Ti Dice La Patria," which appeared in 1927, he left no doubt about his contempt for Mussolini and Il Duce's political philosophy. Nor, as Baker notes, was Hemingway an avid supporter of Lenin, Trotsky, or Stalin, although it is more difficult to find literary evidence of his displeasure with the communists than with his violent antifascist sentiments.[20] As a badly wounded veteran of a war which was the outgrowth of conflicting political philosophies, Hemingway was bitter about any talk of "great causes." Throughout the 1920s and early 1930s, he recognized the signs of decadence in European society and the implications inherent in such political decay. But in his novels of the period he refused to confuse his writing career with the work of a political commentator.

When the economic collapse in Europe and the United States reinforced the contention of socially-conscious literary critics on the relationship between literature and social crises and the necessity for the writer's involvement in the political conflicts of his time, Hemingway's novels appeared an incongruity. His literary themes were in another sphere, remote from politics and everyday affairs, in which was found a preoccupation with violence and an impatience with conventional virtues. "It is difficult to imagine," wrote Wyndham Lewis in 1934, "a writer whose mind is more entirely closed to politics than is Hemingway's."[21] Hemingway's cult of the virile and dynamic virtues, his books on bullfighting and big game hunting in Africa during the depression years, seemed only to reinforce Lewis' criticism. Before Hemingway's social conscience could be sufficiently stimulated to manifest itself in his novels, a threat to something as personal as his feelings toward Spain and the Spanish people was necessary.

At the second American Writers' Congress in 1937, one radical critic envisioned the transformation of Hemingway from a nonpolitical writer to one who could wholeheartedly espouse a political cause. With typical politico-literary logic this critic concluded:

> Even if you began as Hemingway began, with a simple emotional desire to transmit experience, to find and convey the truth, if you follow the truth to its logical conclusion, you will end where Hemingway has ended now, in the People's Front.[22]

Such critics recognized that the explosion in Spain had shocked Hemingway into political action, and these same critics who had once been so irritated with the writer's failure to mainfest a social conscience in his novels, were ready now to reverse their evaluation and welcome him as an "écrivain engagé." Philip Young comments that Hemingway's political isolationism was not shattered until the actual fighting began in Spain, which "more than anything else seems to have brought him wholly back to the world."[23]

Hemingway was well acquainted with political developments in Spain. He had followed the Spanish political situation under the monarchy, the establishment of the Republic in 1931, and the reaction during the conservative election victory in 1933. He recognized the faults and virtues of the various political factions contending for control in Spain, but other than being adamantly antifascist, Hemingway refused to take sides in the internal political affairs of the country. By 1936 he was sufficiently knowledgeable to realize the degree of factionalism present in the Spanish Republican government, and the extent to which fascism had influenced the thinking of the reactionary military elements within Spain. Once Italy and Germany had actively entered into the internal affairs of Spain in violation of the nonintervention agreement, Hemingway's old hatred of fascist states and his distrust of the political machinations of European governments furnished justification for his commitment to the Loyalist cause.

The motives behind Hemingway's involvement in the Spanish struggle are contained in a letter which he wrote to Carlos Baker in 1951. In retrospect, Hemingway reflected on his liberal stand:

> There were at least five parties in the Spanish Civil War on the Republican side. I tried to understand and evaluate all five (very difficult) and belonged to none. . . . I had no party but a deep interest in and love for the Republic. . . . In Spain I had, and have, many friends on the other side. I tried to write truly about them, too. Politically, I was always on the side of the Republic from the day it was declared and for a long time before.[24]

With the outbreak of fighting, it was necessary for Hemingway to choose his course of action.

In the early 1930s a wave of hysterical Russia-worship swept through the ranks of English intellectuals, washing many of them into the Communist Party and leaving many more on the brink of it as fellow travelers. The factors which motivated such a reaction were in part feelings of impotence and shame induced by the spectacle of mass unemployment and hunger, and, in part, an extreme reaction to the growing menace of the fascist powers.[25] George Orwell, who must have been unique among the intellectuals of the time in his knowledge of the facts of extreme poverty, was one who refused to succumb to the dialectical-materialist temptations of a Marxist utopia offered by the Communist Party in England.[26] Orwell reflects on his awareness of social problems but his inability to orient himself politically at that time:

> In a peaceful age I might have written ornate or merely descriptive books, and might have remained almost unaware of my political loyalties. As it is I have been forced into becoming a sort of pamphleteer. First I spent five years in an unsuitable profession . . . and then I underwent poverty and the sense of failure. . . .

> But these experiences were not enough to give me an accurate political orientation. . . . By the end of 1935 I had still failed to reach a firm decision.[27]

So as late as 1935 Orwell had avoided committing himself to a particular course, nor had he established a party affiliation.

Orwell's social consciousness did not manifest itself in his writings until 1936. In that year he wrote *The Road to Wigan Pier,* a report on the living conditions of unemployed miners in Lancashire and Yorkshire, and while the book is essentially a straightforward account of what Orwell saw in the mines and the working-class homes he visited, it also contains Orwell's first attempt to put forth his theory of socialism in his writings. When the Spanish conflict began shortly thereafter, it served as a catalyst completing the transformation of Orwell into a political writer:

> The Spanish Civil War and other events in 1936–7 turned the scale and thereafter I knew where I stood. Every line of serious work that I have written since 1936 has been written, directly or indirectly, *against* totalitarianism and *for* democratic socialism, as I understand it.[28]

In 1948 Orwell was able to comment in retrospect on the inevitability of his decision to use his art for political purposes. He noted that the invasion of literature by politics was bound to happen, even if the special problem of totalitarianism had never arisen. The writer's social conscience in a period such as the 1930s, the "awareness of the enormous injustice and misery of the world, and a guilt-stricken feeling that one ought to be doing something about it . . . makes a purely esthetic attitude toward life impossible." But for Orwell the acceptance of political responsibility by the writer did not include a yielding "to orthodoxies and 'party lines,' with all the timidity and dishonesty that that implies."[29] Orwell's own political writings were dictated by his conscience, not in the academic tones of the literary historian, or the cultured accents of the politico-literary dilettante, or the doctrinaire ranting of the party hack; they were the expression of a truly independent socially-conscious idealist sincerely convinced that he had discovered the truth.

Orwell, unlike Hemingway, never rejected politics as a suitable subject for his work:

> It seems to me nonsense, in a period like our own, to think that one can avoid writing of such subjects. Everyone writes of them in one guise or another. It is simply a question of which side one takes and what approach one follows. And the more one is conscious of one's political bias, the more chance one has of acting politically without sacrificing one's esthetic and intellectual integrity.[30]

Although he insisted that authors refuse to be dictated to by a particular political party, Orwell stressed that authors should, nevertheless, not refrain from writing about politics. The important factor must be the ability of the writer to distinguish between his politics, the social commitment, and his art, the aesthetic commitment. To yield subjectively, not only to a party machine, but even to group ideology, is to destroy the creative instinct of the writer.

> I only suggest that we should draw a sharper distinction than we do at present between our political and our literary loyalties, and should recognize that a willingness to *do* certain distasteful but necessary things does not carry with it any obligation to swallow the beliefs that usually go with them. When a writer engages in politics he should do so as a citizen, as a human being, but not *as a writer*. I do not think that he has the right, merely on the score of his sensibilities, to shirk the ordinary dirty work of politics. . . . But whatever else he does in the service of his party, he should never write for it.[31]

Orwell emphasizes the necessity for a writer to keep his creative processes inviolate while he serves a political cause. The writer in England during the 1930s, if he were committed to a particular party, was constantly badgered by political leaders to produce propaganda. Orwell declares that the writer, as a citizen, is able to act resolutely, even violently if need be, in the service of his party. But his writings must always be the "product of the saner self that stands aside, records the things that are done and admits their necessity, but refuses to be deceived as to their true nature."[32]

Orwell's precise political commitment was to "democratic socialism," to the abstract idea rather than to the political party. His concept of democratic socialism included a planned society, democratically governed in the interests of the majority of the people by their elected representatives, with private ownership abolished or greatly restricted. Orwell's suggestions are not so much the voicing of a doctrinaire line but rather an attempt to reform the Socialist Party in England and to improve the generally unsatisfactory state of contemporary socialism. Orwell was not a political theorist, but as a humanist he recognized that the major failure of the Socialist Party to enlist the united support of the working classes was because of its low view of human nature.

> They have never made it clear that the essential aims of socialism are justice and liberty. With their eyes glued to economic facts, they have proceeded on the assumption that man has no soul, and explicitly or implicitly they have set up the goal of a materialistic Utopia.[33]

Orwell's thoughts were always with the workingman and the necessity to gain the support of the labor class to achieve any meaningful change in the social order. His faith in the common man is manifest in *The Road to Wigan Pier,* in which he states that "leaders who offer blood, toil, tears, and sweat always get more out of their followers than those who offer safety and a good time. When it comes to the pinch, human beings are heroic."

Orwell's concept of man as heroic is contained in his writings. His own nature possessed much of this quality and thus influenced his work. His inspiration was found in "a feeling of partisanship, a sense of injustice"; he wrote because "there is some lie I want to expose, some fact to which I want to draw attention, and my initial concern is to get a hearing." But the aesthetic experience never escaped Orwell's consideration. His dedication to prose style often complicated the attempt "to tell the whole truth without violating . . . literary instincts," but the goal has always been "to fuse political purpose and artistic purpose into one whole."[34]

One biographer of André Malraux has noted that the French regard him as "un haut aventurier"—a heroic fugitive from the commonplace and a modern romantic content only when participating in the most dangerous events—and as a writer who has created virile and violent studies of modern man's fate and the tragic heroes who defy it.[35] Inherent in the nature of the man is the existentialist concept of "l'homme engagé," the intellectual obsessed with action who feels that a man must have some form of transcendent reference, something more important than himself, to which he can dedicate himself. "L'engagement" implies a choice which each man must make in his present context, and a willingness to accept full responsibility for his decision. The strength of such men lies in their ability to assume a dominant role in the events of their time.

In an interview for *Time* during the Spanish Civil War Malraux transformed this abstract philosophy into a plea for general action. The ivory tower, he told writers forcefully, was no place for authors who had in democracy a cause for which they should fight. If they lived, he insisted, their writing would be better for the experience gained in the fight; if they died, their deaths would make more living documents than anything they could have written had they remained in their ivory towers.[36] Whether or not a life of action would benefit all writers, there is no doubt that it inspired Malraux, providing him with a subject, a passion for expressing it, and an imaginative intensity.

Malraux's activities in the 1930s shifted with the events of history from his adventures in Asia to the European period of his political writings and experiences. Hitler's ascent to power had awakened many French intellectuals, if not the French government, to the dangers of fascism, and the movement toward the left among these intellectuals was similar to that prevalent in England and the United States. His Asian experiences having introduced him to the revolutionary cause, Malraux plunged into the turmoil of the European political conflict. His work for Gallimard publishers brought him into association with Gide and Rolland, both of whom had traveled to the Soviet Union and aligned themselves with the communists. Malraux became a spokesman for the left. Even at this stage, with the Russians strongly supporting him, Malraux, possibly because of his conception of personal, as well as artistic integrity, could not accept an orthodox party line. Frohock, in his excellent study of Malraux, notes that the 1933 novel, *La condition humaine,* was suspected of Trotskyite "deviationism," and the Russian critic Ilya Ehrenburg reported to his country that Malraux was something of a revolutionary dilettante.[37] Whether or not Malraux was a Communist Party member is shrouded in mystery. Malraux's relation to the Communist Party in France is theorized by Janet Flanner:

> Apparently, Malraux's basic position by this time was what party men today disdainfully call that of a negativist—one who is for something, within limits, because he is totally against something else. Malraux, being a violent anti-Fascist, entered into a mutually pragmatic relationship with the French Party, and was built up as a star literary orator for the Left, despite his bad physical nerves and his unreliability in Marxist dialectic.[38]

Like Gide and Rolland, Malraux visited Moscow several times and was officially invited to attend the Writers' Congress there. Malraux at that time demonstrated his inability to conform to the doctrinaire principles required by party discipline. Although he was greeted with considerable enthusiasm, he retained his independence. He was listed on the program as a "Marxist humanist," and during his address he severely criticized the Soviets for the restraints they had imposed on artistic freedom. He maintained that communism had expressed confidence in man, but the Russians, by deed, had not displayed confidence in their writers. In a note of warning to the Congress, Malraux's philosophical dualism appeared with devastating clarity: "Le marxisme, c'est la conscience du social; la culture, c'est la conscience du psychologique."[39] His audience was displeased, particularly by his insistence that the writer required absolute freedom to practice his art. Malraux contended that the essential freedom for the artist was not liberty to do anything, but liberty to do as he saw fit.[40] His speech before the Congress provoked a heated reply from Karl Radek, and the atmosphere became so acrimonious that finally the Soviet hosts were compelled to call on the venerable Maxim Gorki to reconcile everyone's thesis, including Malraux's. Observations such as these, deliberately formulated at a time when socialist realism was being solemnly consecrated as dogma, demonstrate Malraux's rebellion against any form of political restriction involving his art.

The activity of these years immediately preceding the Spanish Civil War was not limited to discourse in defense of aesthetics. Malraux played an important role in groups organized to fight fascism and anti-Semitism. He signed the antifascist counterblast to Henri Massis' manifesto which had favored Mussolini's Ethiopian adventure undertaken as furthering Western values and Latin civilization. When the Nazi courts convicted Georgi Dimitrov, the Bulgarian communist, for the Reichstag fire, Malraux and Gide traveled to Berlin to plead with Hitler for Dimitrov's release.[41] This was during the period of his defense of Trotsky's right to asylum, and was implicit criticism of Soviet policy which no orthodox communist would have risked.

In 1935 he published *Le temps du mépris* and was seriously engrossed with reconciling the conflict between art and propaganda. Malraux appeared unwilling, as he had the year before, to sacrifice the needs of the artist to the requirements of the revolution. From the theme of this novel it can be assumed that he had reservations about communism; yet his hatred of fascism caused him to align himself with the communists to the extent of actual participation within the party organization. Malraux's association with the communists grew closer during this period, since they appeared to be the most active opponents of the growing menace of the fascist dictatorships.

Despite this close relationship, however, his speeches and articles reveal a liberal mind unable to accept any rigid or dogmatic position. As Malraux's fictional heroes existed in a climate of extreme tensions, in settings remote from French political life, so Malraux was not interested in the mundane and pedestrian tasks required of the normal French communist intellectual. His true allegiance was to a personal cult of action. Of the intellectual motives behind such divided loyalty, the strongest one was probably his notion, paralleling that of Hemingway, of a "virile fraternity." Thus, at the outbreak of the Spanish Civil War, Malraux envisioned participation in a cause which would give back to the intellectual, made sterile by bourgeois egocentricitism, "his fertility," his fundamental sense of *belonging* to a definite time, a definite place, and a specific milieu, without which a meaningful life and true understanding of the self, cannot be achieved. The existentialist aspects of his thought—man is whatever he makes of himself in victory or defeat—eliminated strict fidelity to a single party, but permitted such loyalty to a set of values and the party which might best protect it.

The need for a decision to combine a literary with a political career never occurred to Gustav Regler. His life was a part of the turmoil of history in twentieth-century Germany. At the age of eighteen he had fought and been wounded in World War I, and by the time he was twenty-seven, his editorials in a Nuremburg newspaper were instrumental in sending Julius Streicher, the Nazi anti-Semite, to prison. Regler's early success as a novelist plunged him into German politics during the bloody rioting of the early 1930s, in the midst of Germany's worst depression and most violent political strife. In his autobiography, *The Owl of Minerva,* he describes the conditions at the time in Berlin:

> The city was in a state of fever. Battered and bloodstained corpses were deposited nightly at the doors of the police stations, sometimes bearing the insignia of the Reichsbanner, the Republican private army, sometimes the star of the Communists, sometimes the Swastika, sometimes simply a policeman's number. But there were even more dead bodies that bore no bloodstains and wore no insignia but only the imprint of despair, that pale-green shade which gas imparts to the skins of those who die by it.[42]

Regler does not attempt to justify his decision to join the Communist Party. He knew that living amidst universal poverty and hardship rendered him receptive to a revolutionary creed, and his motives for joining the Communist Party are expressed in his simple declaration that "Things can't go on like this!"

Regler explains that the German government was incapable of relieving the hunger of seven million unemployed and that since organized religion had nothing to offer, "eyes were turned to those who most loudly proclaimed the way to salvation, the Communists and the supporters of Hitler." Regler's participation in the affairs of the Communist Party during this period was restricted to placing propaganda posters about Berlin. But the communists failed to rally the workers, the "Brownshirts" forced them to retreat in violent street fighting, and when Hitler was named the new chancellor, Regler fled to Paris.

It was in Paris that Regler began to work with Willi Muenzenberg, the leading communist propagandist in Western Europe. They collaborated on the *Brown Book,* a documented attack on the Nazi regime in which Regler sought to prove that Dimitrov was not responsible for the Reichstag fire. He also published several short stories during this period, all of which contained an antifascist theme and were used by the communists as another form of propaganda. Regler does not attempt to justify in literary terms his position as a political pamphleteer:

> I belonged to a political party resembling a religious order, in which acceptance and obedience, not speculation, were the first and last requirement. The intellectuals in particular were made to understand that only their talents were required of them, not their thoughts. We were all under the spell of the Russian code, which, discarding the substance of religion, the more rigorously applied its forms.[43]

Regler concedes that some of the more introspective intellectuals experienced great difficulty in submitting to such dogma:

> Most Party-members adapted themselves with resignation to the changing slogans. Others lived a double life, doing what was required, paying lip-service to the pedantic utterances that were supposed to spare us the necessity of thought and keeping our own counsel. We exploded now and then, when an attempt was made to throw too much dust in our eyes. But in general we acquiesced, quick to deceive ourselves with new hopes.[44]

Among Regler's acquaintances at this time were Arthur Koestler, André Malraux, and Ludwig Renn. In this circle dissatisfaction with the communist discipline imposed on intellectuals first began to manifest itself. The elimination of dissenters, often by execution, particularly shocked the idealistic Regler. At this time the Communist Party sent him to Moscow with the intention of possibly placating his growing hostility. In Leningrad, Regler defended Malraux's position when certain elements in the party expressed distrust of the French novelist:

> I answered vigorously, conscious of the mistrust that Malraux's enemies had spread abroad. The question in itself was simple enough. Malraux had never joined the Communist Party, but had

> since 1933 given it all the support his principles allowed. To talk of loyalty or disloyalty was nonsense. . . . the Party should be thankful for sympathisers of his stature, who were worth a dozen Aragons.[45]

Regler was impressed by Russia's ability to provide for the material needs of the people. But the lack of human understanding under the Soviet system, and the deep-rooted fear of spies and informers which inhibited free expression, greatly distressed his liberal sensibilities.

During this same period Regler was invited to attend the Writers' Congress in Moscow and was commissioned by the Communist Party to produce a propaganda film depicting life in the new Russia. Regler's description of the Writers' Congress contains revealing insights into many of its participants, notably Aragon, Toller, Gorki, and Malraux. And it was to Regler that Malraux ironically commented regarding the elderly Gorki's attempt at a reconciliation of all factions at the Congress, "Monsieur est un peu en retard."[46] By now Regler had experienced grave doubts regarding his own position in the communist organization, both as a writer and as a man: "Every propagandist is a schizophrenic. He lives a double life in the maze of his own creating, with no thread of Ariadne to show him the way out, and no Daedalus-wings either."

The following year ended in Regler's complete disillusionment with the communist experiment. "The year 1935 revealed to me a world of hypocrisy which left me crippled in spirit." At a Writers' Congress in Paris sponsored by Malraux and Aragon, with Ilya Ehrenburg, Boris Pasternak, and Isaac Babel representing the Soviet Union, André Gide proclaimed his allegiance to communism. But it was Regler's speech that roused the Congress and caused it to break into singing the "Internationale." Ironically, Regler was reprimanded for this action since the Communist Party at this point was attempting to remain in the background and have such congresses appear to be politically neutral. Immediately thereafter, it became clear to Regler that Stalin's personality dominated the Communist Party and caused suspicion and fear everywhere. Opinions were constantly suppressed through fear of recrimination; often, in order to divert suspicion and secure their own safety, it was expedient to accuse others. "This psychosis, the daily possibility of a lapse into sin, was fostered on the highest level. Any act of kindness was to be viewed with suspicion, and there was no such thing as mercy, so that too was ruled out." Just as Regler was about to break with the Communist Party, news of the military rebellion in Spain arrived.

Regler's disillusionment was complete when the Stalin purges terminated many of his friendships within the organization. On August 15, 1936, with the fall of the Republican-held city of Badajoz, Regler requested an opportunity to participate in the Spanish struggle. The Communist Party no longer assumed a major role in his thoughts; his decision was free of party intrigue. Regler's desire was to fight "against the same evil that had driven me out of Germany." He was not sure what he would find in Spain but anticipated "a peasant people manning the barricades, inspired by nothing but a simple and passionate belief in a form of government." Regler's personal integrity would not permit him to continue in the party's ranks as a propagandist. Nor had he renounced his original purpose in joining the party. Spain seemed to hold the answer.

> Spain was the threatened friend in 1936, after Russia had proved to be the friend fallen into evil ways. Perhaps my decision to turn from Russia to Spain was rendered easier by the fact that to do so was to face more obvious dangers.[47]

Arthur Koestler's political career and affiliation with the Communist Party closely parallels that of Gustav Regler. Although Koestler was of Austrian-Hungarian extraction, after his father's business failure in Budapest in the depression of 1914 and subsequent financial ruin in the Austrian inflation of the early 1920s, Koestler began a career in journalism which found him in Germany during the early 1930s. After two years of reporting in the Near East, he eventually established himself in Berlin, employed by the Ullstein chain of newspapers.[48] Thereafter, Koestler's political commitments followed much the same course as Regler's. Both were involved in the political and social strife of a chaotic and factional Germany preparing for the rise of Hitler.

Koestler joined the Communist Party in Berlin in 1931. His reasons were twofold: devotion to a utopian dream and revolt against a decadent and polluted society.[49] It was as a consequence of his father's financial collapse and his reporting of the poverty prevalent throughout Germany that Koestler developed a social conscience:

> Thus sensitized by a personal conflict, I was ripe for the shock of learning that wheat was burned, fruit artificially spoiled and pigs were drowned in the depression years to keep prices up and enable fat capitalists to chant to the sound of harps, while Europe trembled under the torn boots of hunger-marchers and my father hid his frayed cuffs under the table. The frayed cuffs and drowned pigs blended into one emotional explosion, as the fuse of the archetype was touched off.[50]

To a certain extent this account was typical of the middle classes in central Europe who were ruined by the depression of the late 1920s. Many sought a solution to their economic and social problems through a radical cause, namely, communism.

Koestler recounts in *The God that Failed* the period of intellectual optimism which confirmed his decision to join the communists:

> The stars of that treacherous dawn were Barbusse, Romain Rolland, Gide and Malraux in France; Piscator, Becher, Renn, Brecht, Eisler, Säghers in Germany; Auden, Isherwood, Spender in England; Dos Passos, Upton Sinclair, Steinbeck in the United States. . . . The cultural atmosphere was saturated with Progressive Writers' congresses, experimental theatres, committees for peace and against Fascism, societies for cultural relations with the USSR, Russsian films and avant-garde magazines.[51]

To the young and idealistic Koestler it appeared that the Western world, stricken by the tragedy of World War I, oppressed by inflation, depression, unemployment, and the feeling of despair, was finally attempting a recovery by the only possible solution, radical socialism, and, in its most advanced form, communism. The fear of fascism also served as a stimulus: "The Communists, with the mighty Soviet Union behind them, seemed the only force capable of resisting the onrush of the primitive horde with its swastika totem."

Koestler, like Regler during this period, served the Communist Party as a minor functionary. His position with the Ullstein newspaper syndicate afforded him access to certain diplomatic secrets which he in turn transmitted to the communists. An atmosphere of conspiracy surrounded the organization's internal affairs:

> It was a paradoxical atmosphere—a blend of fraternal comradeship and mutual distrust. Its motto might have been: Love your comrade, but don't trust him an inch . . . nobody seemed to realize the gradual transformation of character and of human relationships which a long Party career infallibly produced.[52]

After his exposure had cost him his position with the newspaper, Koestler became active in a cell as a propagandist and composer of leaflets. The communists directed their propaganda in an attempt to influence the German elections of 1932, but because the communists refused to join with the socialists in opposing the fascists, Hitler's party made substantial gains in the election.

The communist influence on the intellectuals during this period extended to all spheres, including the nonpolitical:

> Lenin had said somewhere that he had learned more about France from Balzac's novels than from all history books put together. Accordingly, Balzac was the greatest of all times, whereas other novelists of the past merely reflected "the distorted values of the decaying society which had produced them."[53]

Communism dictated the concept of "revolutionary dynamism" in art, which in turn was superseded by "socialist realism." Marxist critics glorified the chorus in music and drama as an expression of the collective as opposed to the bourgeois-individualistic approach to the genre.

Koestler notes that the major problems facing the young communist intellectual were not in the area of aesthetics, but in his inability to integrate with the proletarian members of the party. "To have shared the doubtful privilege of a bourgeois education, to be able to see several aspects of a problem and not only one, became a permanent cause of self-reproach. . . . Intellectual self-castration was a small price to pay." It was partly this inability to experience a common bond with the working class which, creating guilt complexes, drove the intellectuals further to devote themselves to the cause.

With the collapse of the leftists during the German elections of 1932, most of the communists, Regler included, fled from Germany. Koestler obtained a Soviet visa and started to tour Russia, where he received the same lavish treatment accorded Regler. Money was advanced to him for unwritten books and, in general, his artist's ego was flattered.[54] The ulterior motives for such treatment did not occur to Koestler until some time after his break with the party. In discussing the reaction of writers and the possible influence of such acceptance of their work, never experienced in their own countries, Koestler writes:

> I do not mean that they have been bribed; we are not concerned here with such crude machinations, but with the dialectics of the unconscious—with that subtle inner voice which whispers that in the capitalist world publishers are sharks who don't care a damn what you write as long as your books sell, whereas your Soviet publishers are the Soviet People, justifiably resentful of any criticism of their free country.[55]

Koestler traveled about Russia for almost a year and witnessed a great deal of poverty and much that did not correspond with the Soviet propaganda depicting Russia as the workers' paradise. Such sights did not appear in Koestler's descriptions of his travels, first, because of a subconscious feeling of gratitude toward the Russian people and, second, because "my Party education had equipped my mind with such elaborate shock-absorbing buffers and elastic defenses that everything seen and heard became automatically transformed to fit the preconceived pattern." The communist rationale, which enabled them to justify the extermination of large numbers of people, numbed Koestler and deadened the impact of the shock to his idealism.

> The necessary lie, the necessary slander; the necessary intimidation of the masses to preserve them from shortsighted errors; the necessary liquidation of opposition groups and hostile classes; the necessary sacrifice of a whole generation in the interest of the next—it may all sound monstrous and yet it was so easy to accept while rolling along the single track of faith.[56]

Koestler's faith was shaken after he returned to Paris and had the opportunity to reflect on his Russian travels and his position in the Communist Party. At a time when he was debating a possible break with the Communist Party, the organization adopted a new policy which served to rekindle Koestler's idealism.

As it did for Regler and Malraux, the shift in communist policy from an emphasis on social revolution to the support of the Popular Front provided Koestler with a reason to renew his support of the party's cause. Thus the antifascist crusade in Spain came at a point when many of the radical intellectuals had become suspicious of Stalin's political machinations and the party's tactics. The events on the peninsula so aroused their humanitarian instincts that often these writers were not fully cognizant of the significance of the purges and Moscow trials of this period. The Popular Front victories in the French and Spanish elections spurred Koestler's enthusiasm and permitted him to disregard many of the failings which had displeased him earlier. But no longer was his doctrinaire allegiance to the Soviets; now he felt the need to direct his efforts toward the fulfillment of his personal ideals:

> In retrospect, one's memories of the Popular Front days are tainted by the ulterior knowledge of the cynical insincerity behind the façade, and of the bitter aftermath. But while it lasted, the Popular Front had a strong emotional appeal and a fervent *mystique* as a mass-movement. For me, it was a second honeymoon with the Party.[57]

Back in Paris, together with Regler, Koestler worked with Willi Muenzenberg. In 1934 and 1935 he assisted the communists in their propaganda campaign during the Reichstag trial and the *Brown Book* period, while working as a free-lance journalist. Later, he was appointed managing editor of the Institut pour l'Etude du Fascisme, an antifascist archive and research center run by the communists. These duties served as an opiate and helped Koestler submerge his dissatisfaction with the communist organization while continuing his fight against fascism. At the outbreak of the Spanish Civil War, however, Koestler was still involved in communist intrigue.

Georges Bernanos, born in Paris in 1888, is the only novelist of the six in this study for whom the appellation "humanist" but not "liberal" is appropriate. His family was essentially middle class with strong nationalist and royalist convictions. He was a student of the Jesuits at the Collège de Vaugirard. While studying law in Paris, Bernanos began his collaboration with right-wing publications and became, like so many Frenchmen of his age and background, a devoted follower of Charles Maurras' nationalist-royalist movement, the Action Française. In these early years Bernanos, with many young intellectuals of his generation, was deeply affected by the Dreyfus case, Maurrassian agitation, the Church-State conflict and, finally, World War I. In the period preceding the First World War, his intense Catholic faith and fervent nationalism drove him to participate in street riots and political demonstrations against the French Republican government, as well as against socialist orators and Freemason meetings. As a demonstrator among the right-wing "camelots du roi," the shock troops of Action Française who were predominantly middle-class Catholic intellectuals, he was in frequent conflict with the police. Arrested several times, he wrote his first published article in the Santé prison.[58]

In 1913, through his affiliation with Action Française, Bernanos was appointed editor of a small nationalist weekly at Rouen. When the First World War erupted, Bernanos, though not fit for service, volunteered. During the course of the war he earned several citations for bravery. After the cessation of hostilities, in order to provide for his growing family, Bernanos accepted a position as inspector with an insurance company. On tours of France's eastern department he wrote short stories and novels. In 1926, following the publication of *Sous le soleil de Satan,* a novel expressing Bernanos' dissatisfaction with postwar France, he rose to fame as the long-awaited, great Catholic novelist of his country. Encouraged by the enthusiastic reception of *Sous le soleil de Satan,* and the acclaim which termed him the Catholic successor to Marcel Proust, Bernanos resigned his position with the insurance company to devote himself to writing.

During this period in France it was fashionable for young right-wing intellectuals to denounce liberal errors, scoff at liberty, equality, and fraternity; joke about progress, look skeptical when human dignity and the right of conscience were spoken of, affirm authoritatively that every plan for international order was an absurd dream, and sneer at the League of Nations.[59] Bernanos' sense of fairness did not permit him to engage in such cynicism and he severed his relations with Action Française. No longer could he believe in the possibility of his country's restoration through adherence to Maurrassian ideals. He recognized the new orientation of the movement: its submission to the interests of the conservative bourgeoisie, and its failure to develop into the elite Bernanos had envisioned. No longer attached to the movement politically, he nevertheless continued to write for its paper and supported his friends during the turbulent period which followed the condemnation of the movement by Rome in 1926. Such actions did not signify scorn or defiance, nor were they intended to do so. They were the result of his deep personal convictions and were intensified by his uncompromising integrity.

Bernanos remained loyal to the monarchist tradition because of his belief that a king could conceivably effect a truce among the many conflicting groups splitting the country.

> Bernanos was then dimly aware of what became a certitude during the Spanish Civil War—that both Maurras and the Church were making grave mistakes: Maurras by alienating definitively the working classes from the ideals of a truly French elite itself linked to the monarchy; the Church by the seemingly realistic calculation that under no circumstances could she lose—that the bourgeoisie, seized by fear before the mounting tide of the revolution, would seek refuge in the arms of the Church.[60]

Such anxieties produced varying responses on the part of the right-wing nationalist-oriented intellectuals in France: the more immediate, instinctive reaction to defend their class against a possible proletarian revolution, and the more aggressive reaction, aimed at creating a counter-movement at once social-minded, nationalistic, and protective of the values of the Church as well as the Church itself. Both such responses culminated in a form of ideological fascism which Bernanos could only reject.

By this time Bernanos was in the forefront, with Claudel and Mauriac, of contemporary Catholic literature in France. Although his reputation grew with the publication of each new novel, the years preceding the Spanish Civil War were difficult ones for the Bernanos family. In 1933 he suffered a grave injury in a motorcycle accident which crippled one leg. For this and other reasons, at the end of 1934 he decided to move with his family to Majorca, where he was living when the Spanish conflict erupted.

Until 1935, it is extremely difficult to assess Bernanos' politics in terms of party affiliation. Like Malraux, he found nothing more distasteful than political maneuvering or the mundane business of parties, programs, and committees. "His domain was, rather, the philosopher's insight and the artist's intuition, the social critic's scorn and wrath, and the prophet's words predicting doom."[61] Even at the beginning of his career, Bernanos seemed less interested in political machinations than in the integrity of the individual; the question of what political system best promoted these values was of secondary importance to him.[62] But the turbulent social questions of the 1930s forced Bernanos to examine the world of politics. At the time Regler and Koestler were expressing doubts about their commitment to communism, Bernanos was renouncing fascism, although such a pronouncement was to cost him many of his oldest friends.

Some critics of Bernanos label him a reactionary on the basis of his early years: his participation among the "camelots du roi," his membership in the Action Française, his admiration for the anti-Semitic Drumont, and his friendly association with Maurras and Daudet. These crtics refer to his earlier writings, his nostalgia for the France of Joan of Arc, and his sharp criticism of modern technologists, and ultra-progressives as indisputable symptoms of his conservative mentality. But certain factors belie such conclusions: Bernanos' emphasis on the human quandary and his concern for the value of the individual, his own intellectual independence, and his desire never to allow his freedom of conscience to be influenced by political considerations are humanist characteristics which refute a reactionary pattern. In addition, his contempt for conformity is savage and his sympathy with man's revolt is associated with an ontological view strikingly at variance with other major Catholic writers. Thus Bernanos did not permit himself to fall into the pattern of the Catholic intellectual, chiefly concerned with Catholic problems and spiritual life. He never lost awareness of his social conscience, continued fighting for causes, never avoided a battle, and accepted the harsh consequences of a series of unpopular opinions, attitudes, and actions. Paralleling Malraux's, Bernanos' predominant consideration was freedom. His keen awareness of the human condition and his compassionate concern for the individual united him with those writers confronted by the menace of fascism.

The nature of the political commitment of these six novelists took various forms, often not clearly indicated. Such commitments, in 1936, ranged from Hemingway's complete negation of politics, Orwell's dedication to a personal form of socialism, Regler's and Koestler's evolving disillusionment with communism, to Malraux's and Bernanos' intellectual idealism which transcended party affiliations. When translated into support for the Spanish Republic, the commitments manifested themselves in several ways: Regler and Malraux, followed shortly by Orwell, journeyed to Spain to fight for their beliefs; Hemingway and Koestler, as journalists, went to Spain to report on the events and to give encouragement to the Loyalists; and, finally, Bernanos, already in Spain at the outbreak of the war, displayed an antipathy for the Insurgents' philosophy and tactics. Yet it is apparent that although these writers, and a great many others, wrote about the Spanish Civil War because of sympathy with the same cause, political beliefs played an important role in the nature of their devotion to the cause and its eventual manifestation in terms of action. While these six novelists did not engage in crude and more obvious forms of propaganda, the needs of the Loyalist cause presented them with some very complex problems which merit consideration in a study of their Spanish Civil War literature.

In his encounter with the violence of the war, the nature of a writer's political involvement was extremely important. At such places as Madrid, Jarama, and the Ebro, where some of the most fiercely contested battles of the war were fought, many authors experienced for the first time the brutal horrors of modern warfare. As they saw the Loyalist ranks depleted, they learned the hard lesson that fighting for a just cause was much like fighting any war. This lesson had a special application in the case of the non-Spaniards, since the Spanish Civil War was a struggle for which they had volunteered. It was a war in which they, as individuals, felt that their efforts were significant, and which challenged their political convictions by affording these authors an opportunity for action. Since the Spanish Civil War had made explicit the conflicts, as well as the hopes, which had long been implicit in the minds of many intellectuals, it was a period of severest testing. By accepting this challenge and going to Spain, writers subjected themselves and their beliefs to the impersonal crucible of war itself.

To a degree, political ideology determined for many writers

their ability to endure the violence and bloodshed and made it comprehensible and acceptable to them. For the more doctrinaire authors, the belief that the killing and destruction of the war in Spain would lead to a new society, provided them with an explanation and justification for the horrors of the struggle. To support the conflict primarily for political reasons meant submerging its meaner aspects in order to emphasize the more positive possibilities. Thus, for less independent authors, the doctrinaire elements tended to convert much of their writing into political treatises, and except for purposes of atrocity propaganda, avoided the grimmer aspects of the war.

It would be quite accurate to state that in the case of the truly dedicated literary intellectuals their commitment to the Loyalist cause was more ethical and moral than political. Hemingway, Orwell, Malraux, Koestler, Regler, and, to some extent, Bernanos, aligned themselves with the Spanish Loyalists because of the belief in a set of ideals which they felt were embodied in the Republican cause and because fascism completely negated these ideals. Such an alignment transcended their party affiliations and freed them from the doctrinaire failings of lesser writers. Since this idealism, tempered by their exposure to the realities of modern warfare, is the constant theme evidenced in their work, it is of great importance in a study of the literary impact of the Spanish Civil War.

In contrast to the idealism of these six writers, however, disillusionment was the inevitable result for those doctrinaire authors whose political affiliations provided the dominant reason for becoming involved in the Spanish conflict. Most of the writing praising the war as a step in the revolution toward the freedom of the working classes was done during the early part of the conflict, when history was thought to be directed toward a Loyalist victory. As the war progressed, however, and the destruction became worse, and the hope of a Loyalist victory faded, the power of political ideology also began to fade. The killings, the destruction, the political intrigue, all might have been tolerated by zealous writers if they had led to improved social conditions in Spain and the satisfaction of a victory for the Republican supporters. But as the war continued, it became increasingly clear that for a variety of reasons the Nationalists would ultimately triumph. For orthodox writers the diminishing power of politics to provide a useful means of ordering the violence followed roughly a chronological course. While literature of almost total disillusionment was produced during most of the war, and after the war some authors were still trying to explain their experience in political terms, it was inevitable that from optimistic inexperience there should follow bitter disappointment. This is a progression which has significance in the history of modern literature. The literature of innocence is clearly related to the optimism of the socially-conscious literature of the early 1930s, the novels, plays, and poems of social protest and political agitation. The literature of experience, dealing with the same war and in some instances the same events, is far distant from the literature of innocence and much closer to the philosophic nihilism found in the literature of World War II.[63]

But for the mature literary intellectuals, however, whose work did not depend on political ideology for inspiration, this pattern did not hold. These writers used the experience of the war as the raw material for their work, and the violence of the experience did not alter their feelings toward the ideals which had prompted them to seek involvement in the Spanish struggle. In their writing, even after the tide of the war had turned in favor of the Nationalists, there is seen less the theme of disillusionment and more the theme of heroism for a just but losing cause. The adherence to such beliefs, in the face of overwhelming adversity, may be the greatest single factor behind the composition of the best literary efforts treating the Spanish Civil War. Such writing admirably translated the feelings of the men participating in the conflict.

Apart from the politics of the situation, perhaps writers like Malraux, Hemingway, Bernanos, and Regler had the advantage of having experienced the violence and the waste and inefficiency of modern warfare before 1936, and thus entered Spain with fewer illusions about the nature of armed conflict. Koestler and Orwell, although not combat veterans, were also more worldly than many of the young idealists whose reasons for defending Spain were essentially nonpolitical. The methods of modern warfare provided a shock to almost all volunteers; few were old enough to remember the First World War, and their formal education could hardly have prepared them for the struggle in which tanks, bombing planes, and other mechanized weapons were to play such a devastating role. Even if the younger writers had some idea of the violence of war, they were often too naïve to understand that military tactics, like those of politics, involved intrigue, betrayal, and a multitude of confusions and compromises which were necessary to make victory possible. One of the reasons for the widespread disillusionment of the younger writers in the Spanish Civil War was the fact that in Spain many of them had their first real encounter with severe military and political discipline and with bureaucratic inefficiency. They soon discovered that wars and revolutions were extremely destructive, that even a just cause could be plagued by inefficient bureaucrats, and that history could fail to move in the direction of progress.[64]

## ▸ NOTES

[1] See Edwin Berry Burgum, *The Novel and the World's Dilemma* (New York, 1947), p. 9.

[2] See Howe, *Politics and the Novel*, p. 24.

[3] In Joseph Freeman, "Toward the Forties," *Writer in a Changing World*, pp. 10–11.

[4] *Novel and the World's Dilemma*, p. 15. Many of these writers were themselves products of a bourgeois background.

[5] Aaron, *Writers on the Left*, and Walter B. Rideout, *The Radical Novel in the United States, 1900–1954* (Cambridge, 1956), provide detailed studies of this literary trend to the left in the United States.

[6] See Muste, *Say That We Saw Spain Die*, p. 9.

[7] "Spain and American Writers," *Writer in a Changing World*, p. 60.

[8] "Writers Fighting in Spain," *Writer in a Changing World*, pp. 67–68.

[9] "The Writer Faces the Future," *Writer in a Changing World*, p. 188.

[10] John Mander, *The Writer and Commitment* (London, 1961), pp. 13–14.

[11] Ralph Fox, *A Writer in Arms* (London, 1937), p. 15. Fox was killed shortly after arriving in Spain to fight with the International Brigades.

[12] "The Writer Faces the Future," *Writer in a Changing World*, p. 185.

[13] George Orwell, "Inside the Whale," *Such, Such Were the Joys* (New York, 1953), p. 187.

[14] *Ibid.*, pp. 187–88.

[15] Stephen Spender, *World Within World* (New York, 1948), p. 184.

[16] "Old Newsman Writes," *Esquire*, III (December 1934), pp.

25–26, quoted in Carlos Baker, *Hemingway: the Writer as Artist,* 2nd ed. (Princeton, N. J., 1963), p. 197. There is no definitive biography of Hemingway at this time although Baker is working on this project. Baker's *Hemingway: the Writer as Artist,* is the most complete single source covering Hemingway's life and work, and is a responsible and often illuminating study. This book and Philip Young's short but provocative *Ernest Hemingway* (New York, 1952), a psychobiographical study of the man and his work, are the main sources for the factual data in this study of Hemingway's politics and his Spanish Civil War experiences.

[17] *Green Hills of Africa* (New York, 1935), p. 109.

[18] *Hemingway: the Writer as Artist,* pp. 198–199.

[19] "Old Newsman Writes," quoted in Baker, *Hemingway: the Writer as Artist,* pp. 199–200.

[20] *Ibid.,* p. 200–201.

[21] Wyndham Lewis, *Men Without Art* (London, 1934), p. 17.

[22] Joseph Freeman, in *Writer in a Changing World,* p. 235.

[23] *Ernest Hemingway,* p. 113.

[24] *Hemingway: The Writer as Artist,* p. 228.

[25] Wood, *Communism and British Intellectuals,* documents this shift to the left by the intellectuals in England.

[26] There are five studies of George Orwell available, each professing to be semibiographical: John Atkins, *George Orwell: a Literary Study* (London, 1954); Laurence Brander, *George Orwell* (London, 1954); Christopher Hollis, *A Study of George Orwell: the Man and his Works* (London, 1956); Henry T. Hopkinson, *George Orwell* (London, 1953); and Sir Richard Rees, *George Orwell, Fugitive from the Camp of Victory* (London, 1961). These are sincere but pedestrian accounts revealing little of the inner nature of the man. In his collection of autobiographical essays, *Such, Such Were the Joys,* Orwell provides an excellent insight into his character and the motivations for much of his work.

[27] *Ibid.,* "Why I Write," p. 7.

[28] *Ibid.,* p. 9.

[29] "Writers and Leviathan," *Such Were the Joys,* pp. 65–66.

[30] "Why I Write," *Such Were the Joys,* p. 9.

[31] "Writers and Leviathan," *Such Were the Joys,* pp. 70–71.

[32] *Ibid.,* p. 72.

[33] Quoted in Rees, *George Orwell, Fugitive from the Camp of Victory,* p. 51.

[34] "Why I Write," *Such Were the Joys,* p. 72.

[35] Janet Flanner, "The Human Condition," *Men and Monuments* (New York, 1957), p. 1. Malraux is the subject of a legend which originated more or less spontaneously. No authorized biographical study of him exists, since he has assumed the attitude that his private life is his own affair, though his books belong to the public. A serious biography of Malraux cannot be written at this time for several reasons. Many of Malraux's early exploits took place in Asia where (even under the best of circumstances) the records would be unavailable. He engaged in lost causes of which only fragmentary

accounts are available, and the nature of his participation was secret. His long association with the French Communist Party does not provide a reliable source of verifiable information. The leading sources of information are listed in the bibliography. In addition to the Flanner article, the studies of Frohock, Blend, and Gannon in English, and Picon, Stephane, Savane, and Mauriac in French, have been most helpful.

[36] *Time* (November 7, 1938), p. 62.

[37] W. M. Frohock, *André Malraux and the Tragic Imagination* (Stanford, California, 1952), p. 7.

[38] "The Human Condition," *Men and Monuments,* p. 36.

[39] André Malraux, "L'art est une conquète," *Commune* (September-October 1934), p. 69. Gustav Regler in his autobiography, *The Owl of Minerva* (New York, 1960), discusses the friction between Malraux and the communist critics at these meetings.

[40] André Malraux, "L'attitude de l'artiste," *Commune* (November 1934), p. 167.

[41] "Never one to be unaware of irony, Malraux has noted that Dimitrov, in his turn, is now condemning innocent people to death." Charles D. Blend, *André Malraux: Tragic Humanist* (Ohio State, 1963), p. 31.

[42] *Owl of Minerva,* p. 143. This autobiography is the only reliable source now available relating incidents of Regler's life during this period. It is the sole authority in the discussion of Regler's politics.

[43] *Ibid.,* p. 168.

[44] *Ibid.,* pp. 168–69.

[45] *Ibid.,* pp. 181–82.

[46] Regler's account of the Writers' Congress and the impact of Malraux's controversial declaration of creative liberty on the delegations is contained in *Owl of Minerva.*

[47] *Ibid.,* p. 271.

[48] Arthur Koestler, *The Invisible Writing* (New York, 1954), 17. This book is the second volume and continuation of his autobiography, *The Arrow in the Blue* (New York, 1952). A biography of Koestler by John Atkins, *Arthur Koestler* (London, 1956), is in factual agreement with the autobiography, repeating much the same material but focusing on Koestler's politics after his break with communism. George Orwell's essay, "Arthur Koestler," *Dickens, Dali and Others* (New York, 1946), also comments on Koestler's literary career after 1939.

[49] Arthur Koestler, *God that Failed,* pp. 15–17. This collection of essays, edited by Richard Crossman, is an attempt to explain why certain intellectuals joined the Communist Party in the 1930s. Contributors to the volume, besides Koestler, include Gide, Spender, Louis Fischer, Ignazio Silone, and Richard Wright.

[50] *Ibid.,* p. 19. Koestler's essay provides an insight into the motives for his political commitment not found in the autobiography or biography. It is used as the primary source for the discussion of his politics.

[51] *Ibid.,* p. 21.

[52] *Ibid.,* pp. 29–30.

[53] *Ibid.,* p. 46.

[54] Koestler's experiences in Russia are described in detail in a section of *The Invisible Writing* which he cynically titles "Utopia."

[55] *God that Failed,* p. 59.

[56] *Ibid.*, p. 61.

[57] *Ibid.*, p. 63.

[58] Although no authoritative biography of Bernanos has been published, there are several essays about him by Albert Beguin, Luc Estang, Gaetan Picon, as well as a longer study by the German Catholic scholar, Urs von Balthasar. An edition of Bernanos' collected letters has been undertaken by Beguin. The only major study of Bernanos in English is Thomas Molnar's *Bernanos: His Political Thought and Prophecy* (New York, 1960). The von Balthasar and Molnar studies are the chief sources of biographical information about Bernanos used here.

[59] See Yves Simon, *The Road to Vichy* (London, 1942), pp. 42–43.

[60] Molnar, *Bernanos*, p. 59.

[61] *Ibid.*, XVI.

[62] Urs von Balthasar, *Le Chrétien Bernanos* (Paris, 1956), p. 502.

[63] See Muste, *Say That We Saw Spain Die*, pp. 28–32, for an expanded analysis of this theme.

[64] *Ibid.*, pp. 32–33.

# ▸ III

# ▸ Writers in Arms

Newspaper accounts of the Spanish Civil War during the early period of the conflict often were inaccurate and incomplete. Reports trickling from Spain into Europe and the United States, instead of enlightening public opinion, tended to polarize it. Hugh Thomas comments on the role of the press in the Spanish struggle:

> Just as the 1850s were the great age of the Ambassador, so were the 1930s the great age of the foreign correspondent. From the end of July onwards, for two and a half years, the greatest names in world journalism were usually to be found south of the Pyrenees. Distinguished writers were hired by news agencies to represent them at the Spanish War. The Spaniards were very conscious of this and were very proud of their fame. The journalists themselves were to write about Spain much that was inevitably inaccurate and much that could be regarded as brilliant reporting. But many journalists deliberately wrote articles which were intended not so much to be commentary or reporting as pamphlets aimed to help one side or the other.[1]

Internationally famous journalists such as Edgar Mowrer, Sefton Delmer, and Herbert Matthews of the British and American press, and George Soria, Louis Delaprée, and Antoine de Saint-Exupéry of France, covered the events of the war. Some distinction must be made between these men, no matter how partisan their reporting, and the Russian correspondents, Ilya Ehrenburg and Michael Kol'tsov. The Russians, though posing as correspondents, were actually secret agents assigned to Spain on Stalin's orders, and no doubt their role in reporting the war was secondary to their undercover operations.

Headlines in the popular press contained such epithets as "fascist warmongers," "Bolsheviks," and "forces of the anti-Christ." Most newspapers devised their own nomenclature to designate each faction, which served to reveal clearly their sympathies. Malcolm Muggeridge, in his review of the 1930s in England, notes:

> The Republican side was commonly designated "the Reds" by sympathisers with General Franco, and "the Loyalists" by its own sympathisers; the Insurgent side was "the Rebels" or "the Fascists" to those who hoped for its defeat, and "the Nationalists" to those who hoped for its victory. Neutral opinion used "Republicans" and "Insurgents." "Junta" for General Franco's side, probably indicated a slight bias in its favor.[2]

Besides the obvious political and religious reasons for the unreliable reporting on the Spanish conflict, certain physical obstacles made it difficult to ascertain exactly what was transpiring in Spain. The principal telephone and cable lines were in Republican territory since the beginning of hostilities, and news from Nationalist-occupied land was usually outdated by the time it reached the democracies. A second factor influencing news from Nationalist-held territory was the generally hostile attitude of the Insurgents toward the foreign press. In contrasting the treatment of foreign journalists by the Loyalists and the Insurgents, it is evident that the Republicans were aware of the considerable influence that favorable press relations could have upon observers throughout the world; thus they spent lavishly on propaganda, which included providing unusually accommodating services for foreign journalists. Nationalists, in contrast, granted few privileges to reporters behind their lines and on several occasions actually expelled journalists whose reports were deemed distortions of fact. In her introduction to Koestler's *Spanish Testament,* the Duchess of Atholl relates the indifference and occasional hostility experienced by conservative journalists who visited Insurgent territory.

In contrast, Arturo Barea, who served as Loyalist censor for foreign correspondents during the siege of Madrid, compiles an excellent picture of the difficulties of the reporters imposed by conditions in the besieged city; at the same time he notes the cooperation extended to these men whenever possible.[3]

The popular press, no matter with which faction it sided, for the most part reached a nadir in terms of objective reporting. Even though in lengthy editorials, articles by special correspondents, and eyewitness accounts, they tried to give the impression of careful analysis and scrupulous documentation, in most instances the length of the documentation merely served to disguise extremely biased journalism. Arthur Koestler gives some indication of the causes for the failure of the press:

> The part played by the Press in the Spanish affair was from the outset a most peculiar one. The rebels refused to allow a single correspondent of any Left-wing or even liberal newspaper into their territory, while correspondents of newspapers with pronouncedly Right-wing views were equally unwelcome on the Government side. Thus a state of affairs was rapidly created whereby, roughly speaking, the Right-wing newspapers had correspondents only on the Franco side, and the Liberal and Left Press only on the Government side. The communiques from the respective headquarters were grossly contradictory, and almost as great were the discrepancies between the telegrams sent by the correspondents on both sides, for whom a drastic censorship, furthermore, made it impossible to send out unbiased messages. (17)

During the struggle, George Orwell expressed his contempt for those "sleek persons in London and Paris who are writing pamphlets. . . . One of the most horrible features of the war is that all the war-propaganda, all the screaming and lies and hatred, comes invariably from people who are not fighting." (65) Orwell's caustic attack on the popular press is well-founded and deserves further elaboration. Several years later, he resumed his castigation of this press:

> Early in life I had noticed that no event is ever correctly reported in a newspaper, but in Spain, for the first time, I saw newspaper reports which did not bear any relation to the facts, not even the relationship which is implied in an ordinary lie. I saw great battles reported where there had been no fighting, and complete

> silence where hundreds of men had been killed. I saw troops who had fought bravely denounced as cowards and traitors, and others who had never seen a shot fired hailed as heroes of imaginary victories.[4]

Orwell's indignation was not reserved exclusively for the propagandists working for the Nationalists. The journalists supporting the Insurgents were limited to describing them as "Christian patriots saving Spain from a Russian dictatorship" and inventing the "presence in Spain of a Russian army," while simultaneously refusing to admit the fact of German and Italian intervention. Koestler calls attention to the almost impossible task of attempting to justify the concept of total war waged by the rebels:

> Badajoz, Toledo, Malaga, Durango, Guernica are bloody milestones on Franco's path. Blunted as are the sensibilities of the world to-day, it has not forgotten these terrible massacres. Franco's propagandists found themselves faced with the thankless task of raising the dead to life and covering the blood they had spilt with printer's ink. (142)

Using techniques developed by fascist Germany and Italy, the Nationalist journalists and pamphleteers created a new trend in modern propaganda: "Here the circumstances are no longer, as in former times, glossed over, touched up, and lightly falsified; the facts themselves are invented." (145) Orwell notes that such propaganda was too fallacious to be taken seriously. But what really incensed him was the discovery that the press supporting the Republic was capable of similar distortions:

> One of the dreariest effects of this war has been to teach me that the Left-wing press is every bit as spurious and dishonest as that of the Right. I do earnestly feel that on our side—the Government side—this war was different from ordinary, imperialistic wars; but from the nature of the war-propaganda you would never have guessed it. The fighting had barely started when the newspapers of the Right and Left dived simultaneously into the same cesspool of abuse. (65)

Bernanos disposes of the French conservative journalists with similar pointed sarcasm:

> Naturally certain French newspapers were of the greatest comfort at these times! When week after week can be seen an increase in Fascist planes, blessed by the Archbishop of Palma, a multiplication of Fascist batteries along the allegedly disarmed coast, and Italian naval officers publicly boasting in cafes of their bombardment of Malaga, it is certainly stimulating to read in one's native language the monotonous diatribes of correspondents squatting in each Pyrenean border station, eyes to the keyhole of every water-closet, scribbling convulsive notes on toilet paper. Never once—not in seven long months—the least mention of Italian or German treachery. (171)

In a cynical attempt to explain at least one of the causes for the poor quality of such journalism, Orwell continues: "It is the same in all wars; the soldiers do the fighting, the journalists do the shouting, and no true patriot ever gets near a front-line trench, except on the briefest of propaganda-tours."(66)[5]

It is chiefly because of this distortion in reporting events in Spain by the news media that the advantages of actually witnessing the conflict become evident. Writers who did not travel to Spain had to rely necessarily on the reports, often unreliable, of participants and observers. No major literary work concerned with the war was written by an author who was not at the scene of the fighting. While participation in a historical event is not necessarily indispensable in writing about it, in the case of the Spanish Civil War it was essential to have access to other than the normal channels of information, as has been well illustrated in Orwell's commentary.

The nature of the personal experiences of Bernanos, Malraux, Koestler, Regler, Orwell, and Hemingway during those war years varied widely and, to an appreciable extent, determined the literary form in which the authors chose to recount them. Where their experiences were essentially isolated and individual, the personal narrative proved a more suitable literary form than the novel. However, the latter enabled the writer to present a panoramic rather than an individualized view of the war. The particular circumstances experienced by the authors while in Spain are reflected in the nature of their writing.

Bernanos' interest in the Spanish struggle was many-sided. He and his family had left southern France in 1934 to reside in

Majorca for reasons of economy and because it was an excellent place to work for a writer with Bernanos' temperament. In addition, according to Molnar, Bernanos had always cherished his Hispanic ancestry:

> He was a Frenchman and immensely, mystically proud of it; but he also belonged to the Latin race, at home near the Mediterranean no matter where and flattered by his Spanish blood and temperament. He felt kinship also with the Spanish quality of religious faith, the total commitment to militancy in Christ's ranks, the all-or-nothing pride of the Spanish soul impregnated with service and sacrifice to God and King.[6]

When the fighting erupted, Bernanos had been living for more than a year in Palma, Majorca, recovering from the aftereffects of a serious motorcycle accident. The rebellion of the dissident generals began in July 1936 and Bernanos remained in Majorca until March 1937. During this time he lived quietly in the home of wealthy Spanish friends in the city of Palma. By an extraordinary combination of circumstances, he was a guest of the Marquis of Zayas, the leader of the Falangists on the island. It was from this vantage point that Bernanos witnessed a separate Spanish struggle, the nature of which was quite different from what was occurring on the mainland.

The military action in the Balearic Islands was minimal. Majorca fell to the Insurgents under General Goded almost immediately after the generals issued their pronunciamiento. The island was under fascist domination throughout the war. In August 1936, a disastrous military campaign was repulsed by the Nationalists with the aid of an Italian expeditionary force. By the end of August 1936, the Spanish Marquis had transferred his power to a fanatical Italian fascist, Arconovaldo Bonaccorsi, who called himself General Count Aldo Rossi. An Italian air fighter squadron which proudly called itself "The Dragons of Death," led by Rossi, prevented Republican air strikes from getting through to the island, and later the base was used by Italian planes for bombing missions over the mainland.[7]

As late as August 1936, Bernanos saw in the rebellious generals a movement to "assure the moral and religious unity of the country." But this mistaken belief was soon dispelled and its awareness completely shattered his earlier confidence. For the ten months of the war during which Bernanos remained in Nationalist-occupied Spain, he witnessed a campaign of terrorism which slowly overpowered the peasant and middle-class communities on the island. He was appalled by the indifference and even, on occasion, consent by the Church to such barbarous acts as the mass arrests and executions of nonpolitical inhabitants of the island.[8] Terrorism became a part of the daily routine which blunted the sensibilities of those who might protest; Christian indignation and horror gave way to weariness and then acceptance:

> These facts were common knowledge—approved by the majority, disapproved by a few, but doubted by no one. Pages would be required to explain how, after an interval, people were no longer revolted by the events. Reason and honor were gradually disavowed, and sensitivity grew torpid, as though stunned. Victims and executioners alike became reconciled in the same drugged fatalism. In point of fact, the civil war only truly frightened me that day I caught myself breathing, almost unconsciously and without nausea, its stale air reeking of blood. (174–75)

Political ideology played no part in Bernanos' outrage over the fascist oppression on the island. His feelings before July 1936 were in sympathy with the young aristocrats of the Falange, of which his eldest son was a member: "In Spain I lived through the pre-revolutionary period, friendly with a small group of young Falangists, who were full of honor and courage, and whose program, though I could not approve of it completely, was nevertheless inspired by a furious sense of social justice." Bernanos stressed that the Italians, under Rossi, methodically attempted to distort the ideals of these young men with the intention of destroying the party and its discipline: "Under the direction of the Italian adventurer Rossi, the Falange was transformed into a kind of auxiliary military police, systematically ordered to perform the army's dirty work, until such a time when its leaders could either be executed or imprisoned under the Franco dictatorship, and its best elements rendered unidentifiable by being merged into the general mass. (114–15) His politics during the reign of terror never really influenced his feelings about the injustice of the situation: "If I have derived any benefit from my experiences in

Spain, I believe it is because I approached them without firmly entrenched preconceptions of any sort." (127)

Although Bernanos' Catholicism and the circumstances of his residence compelled him to remain politically uncommitted while on Majorca, his indignation over the fascists' treatment of the inhabitants must have manifested itself to the community:

> I remained in Majorca as long as I could because there I looked the enemies of my own country in the face. . . . No one could ignore that my son was a lieutenant in the Falange, and that I was often seen at Mass; for some time I had been friendly with insurgent leaders who now were greatly feared. And yet it happened that people I scarcely knew spoke freely to me when the slightest indescretion on my part could cost them their liberty and even their lives. They realized that a Frenchman—a free man—does not permit himself to become a policeman's pawn. But the followers of General Franco never thought of that. (172–73)

Bernanos and his family remained on Majorca, not because they believed that they might serve a useful purpose, but because of a deep sense of solidarity toward these helpless victims of the oppression:

> We held on, my wife and I, not through bravado, nor even with the hope of being useful—there was so little we could do—but rather because of a profound empathy with a group of essentially decent people, whose number increased each day, who had once shared our hopes and dreams and who now foot by foot stood their ground against overwhelming forces. (168–69)

Bernanos emphasizes that those executed were neither belligerents nor inclined toward politics. Rather, they resembled those same peasants he had known in the villages of France: "I repeat simply that these people had neither killed nor hurt anyone. They were familiar peasants, like those you and your father knew and shook hands with, for they greatly resembled those strongly chiselled faces seen in our French villages." (97)

Returning to France in March 1937, Bernanos recognized certain inevitable similarities between his own country and Spain; he knew personally the leaders on both sides of the political conflict who were about to assume the same roles in a similar struggle in France. He believed that his experiences in Majorca had conditioned him to write a message of warning for his own countrymen. Such a warning is the substance of *Les grands cimetières sous la lune*. Bernanos described the reception he received when he returned from Spain with the news of the outrages perpetrated there. First he spoke of the political climate in France:

> It is also necessary to note that after three years living abroad, I returned to France and found my own country so seriously divided against itself that I could hardly recognize it. . . . Political rivalries had degenerated into class hatred in an intolerable atmosphere of mutual distrust. Ce fut le printemps de la Peur! (149–50)

At this time Bernanos thought his message from a well-known Catholic writer, who had never concealed his rightist convictions, would induce his countrymen to unite in the national interest and thus avoid a fratricidal passion similar to that occurring south of the Pyrenees. He addressed himself to the right since he felt that they had been misled and would be amenable to reason:

> I would not blame you for turning your back on these misfortunes which you consider for the most part inevitable. I would nevertheless persuade you to face them for a moment, not in order to retard their course, which may perhaps be unalterable, but to see them truly and clearly. They are not at all what you conceived them to be. They are rather a product of your own fear. I do not speak lightly for I have just witnessed an entire country devoured by a demon of this kind. (109)

Their response to his account of the terrors on Majorca, however, shocked him:

> Italians in Spain? So much the better! Never enough—Germans also? Perfect!—Summary executions? Excellent! No sentimentalism, please!—Can you imagine that an iron worker at the Paris Exposition is paid more than one hundred francs a day! (150–51)

Thus his former friends of the conservative bourgeoisie had chosen fascism, despite their disagreement with its ferocious demagogic acts, as a shield of "respectable men" faced with the demands of the workers. But Bernanos recognized that those dictators thus supported could not be relied upon:

> I doubt that you will be able to truly take advantage of the situation since the Fascists do not appear to serve the interests of your class, at least judging by their practices and precedents. Mussolini and Hitler are what they are, but they are not what you really desire or need. Between us, moreover, they do not care for us very much. I doubt that they would be in sympathy with certain of our social attitudes. (151–52)

The revolution which the French conservatives so feared, according to Bernanos, could not justify a reign of terror by the combined forces of the bourgeoisie, military, and the Church. Such actions lacked the moral basis by which history might one day condone them.

*Les grands cimetières sous la lune* concerns itself with the purges which Bernanos witnessed in Spain. He had seen the unexpected arrival of Italian military units which, in collaboration with the local Falangists, set themselves to the task of purging Majorca. The island was a small world, easily observed, and Bernanos, powerless in his rage and compassion, horrified by a manifestation of evil more inexorable than he had ever known, walked the streets, listened at the cafés, at the barbershops, and to neighbors. The Catholic novelist recorded what he had witnessed. Safeguarding his independence as a writer, he omitted anything which might have cast the least doubt on the integrity of his evidence. He asserted nothing about which he was in any way uncertain, and was scrupulous to implicate only himself. The book was written in the early summer of 1937. The outcome of the war at this time was still in doubt. Although the Loyalists were maintaining their positions throughout most of Spain, Bernanos had been in fascist-occupied territory and the news that reached him certainly was directed toward an approaching Nationalist victory. But the time and the tide of the war had little effect on Bernanos' indignation and the purpose behind his composition of *Les grands cimetières sous la lune.*

*Les grands cimetières sous la lune* covers the ten months, from July 1936 to May 1937, which Bernanos spent in Majorca after the war began. His central theme is an attempt to tell the truth about Majorca, about the civil war, and also about the impending disaster facing his own country at the hands of false elites and dictators. Bernanos' narrative is a work of violent protest against the war and the destruction of ethical values. *Les grand cimetières sous la lune* is marked by a harrowing and emphatic stress on death, mutilation, and moral and physical degeneration. Ultimately the author concerned himself with the failure of the Roman Catholic Church to assume a responsible position. If priests had been killed and abused by certain elements within the Loyalist ranks, Bernanos notes that revenge rather than retribution was inflicted on the nonfascist inhabitants of Majorca. He maintains that there were more peasants executed on the small island than the total number of priests killed in all Spain. Bernanos wrote many years later that the Spanish experience was the most important political experience in his life: "This experience in Spain has perhaps been the most decisive event in my life. I have seen beneath the Spanish 'crusade' and the attempted purification of the peninsula. I had the chance to observe to what depths the totalitarian poison had corrupted the conscience of Catholics and even that of priests."[9] Bernanos reached the conclusion that no justification for the alliance with Franco could be rationalized with the pretext that between two evils, Spanish fascism was the one with which it was possible to come to terms, which one might control. Such a conclusion would only lead to a definitive estrangement of the people from the Church and Christianity.

The reception of *Les grands cimetières sous la lune,* as could be expected, was far from unanimously favorable; there was some enthusiasm from Loyalist supporters and a very indignant response from much of the French right. Those whom the book so vigorously criticized could not forgive him. General Franco, already in control of most of Spain when the book appeared in the late summer of 1937, was the undisputed hero of this French right; the French government which had not dared, even under socialist Prime Minister Léon Blum, to aid the Republicans openly, was soon to send Marshall Pétain as ambassador to Burgos, Nationalist headquarters. The Archbishop of Palma, chief target of Bernanos' attack, denounced the book in a letter to *l'Action Française* as containing false and malicious reports about Spain and ideas which made Bernanos' faith suspect. By September 1938, when this letter was written, Bernanos was no longer in France. In July of that year, with the defeat of the Loyalists imminent, he had left with his family for Brazil, sick, as he wrote, of his country's humiliation and the alarming rise of cynical willingness to let the dictators prevail in Europe.

André Malraux arrived in Spain on July 20, 1936, two days after the military pronunciamiento. According to Louis Fischer, Malraux, while still in France, was instrumental in obtaining tanks for the Loyalists, and early in the conflict he bought aircraft in France, Belgium, and Czechoslovakia, with Republican funds.[10] With the aid of Pierre Cot, French air minister, who defended his position that aid to the Spanish Republic was necessary for the eventual defense of France, Malraux helped supply the Loyalists with a small but courageous air arm.[11]

Many of the pilots, never a part of the hard-core military clique, had remained loyal to the Republic, but their efforts were hampered by airplanes which were in constant need of repair and often obsolete. Malraux purchased planes from abroad and organized an international brigade of the air called Escadre España, including pilots who were recruited abroad.[12] These men disputed the Insurgents' mastery of the air and reinforced Loyalist resistance in August 1936, at a time when otherwise it might have collapsed. They fought bravely, serving as the air arm of the International Brigades. However, as the war continued, the Insurgent air force gained the upper hand, since they possessed new and superior German and Italian aircraft, flown by skilled and highly trained men, the majority of whom later served Hitler and Mussolini in World War II. Álvarez del Vayo, Republican Foreign Secretary, recalled the Axis' intentions:

> Not only the machines, but also the crews of the rebel air arm were for the most part Italian and German. . . . The pressing desire of the two dictators was to obtain the greatest possible number of experienced aviators. The Spanish skies were the traning ground 'par excellence' for the Axis airmen. . . . It is no exaggeration to say that Italy and Germany sent [aviators] to Spain, not merely to dominate the country but also to train men for a future European war.[13]

Malraux's international air squadron was stationed at its own airfield not far from Madrid. From August 1936 to March 1937 Malraux served as titular leader of the Escadre España; the technical chiefs were two pilots who were reserve officers in the

French air force. Half the members of the Escadre were French; the others mostly Americans, English, and German, and Italian antifascists, as well as some white Russians and some reckless pilot mercenaries who were paid 60,000 pesetas a month for risking their lives—a fortune, if they lived to spend it. The first important engagement for Malraux and the Escadre was an August 1936 attack on Franco's forces at Medellín, when they flew low enough to use their pistols. Malraux participated in 65 missions, was wounded on one, and although he possessed no pilot's license, occasionally took over the plane's controls. The squadron also fought at Toledo, Madrid, and Guadalajara. By November 1936, the Escadre was practically destroyed after a gallant battle with Nazi Heinkels over a newly discovered Insurgent airfield near Teruel.[14] The regular Republican air force suffered equally disastrous results, while the Insurgents could claim merely a Pyrrhic victory.

The plight of the underequipped and overworked Republican air force had often necessitated the pilots' flying two missions in a single day and required the organization of ground crews working around the clock to keep the small number of Republican planes airborne. Thus, by this multiplication of the work schedule the Loyalist air force, which at no time consisted of more than 130 first-line planes, was able to battle an enemy almost six times more powerful. When the Loyalist army withdrew from the Talavera front, there was only one pursuit plane in all of Republican Spain to cover their retreat.

In March 1937, after the Escadre España had been rendered ineffective, Malraux crossed the Atlantic in an effort to gain support for the Loyalists and raise money in the United States and Canada for medical supplies. Handicapped by his inability to speak English well, his tour nevertheless was a financial success. Malraux's unlimited energy is demonstrated by the fact that between July 1936 and April 1937 he helped organize the Republican air force, participated in flights as a member of a plane crew and, though wounded, was seated in the highest councils of the Loyalists, made a trip to America to obtain aid for the cause and, in addition, managed to write *L'espoir*. Personifying *l'homme engagé,* Malraux was transforming the philosophy he expressed in *L'espoir* into conscious action: "What is the best thing a man can do with his life? Transform into consciousness the broadest possible experience." (337)

There is an apocryphal tale that when Malraux met Hemingway in Spain, they divided the Spanish Civil War between them. Malraux agreed to write the story of the war from its inception to the Loyalist victory at Guadalajara, and Hemingway agreed to use as his material the subsequent events. From the Loyalist point of view, Malraux appears to have selected the preferable half. Malraux's *L'espoir* follows the chronological development of the Spanish conflict from its beginning to the victory at the battle of Guadalajara in early March 1937. The conception of the novel is panoramic, a series of loosely connected sketches, moving from Madrid to Barcelona, Toledo, then Guadalajara. Many of the episodes are reminiscent of the pages of a combat diary, based on Malraux's personal experiences, with little or no novelistic invention. In his preface to André Viollis' *Indochine S.O.S.*, Malraux expressed his desire for a new form of novel which could combine elements of journalism with fiction. In much of *L'espoir*, Malraux is in effect reporting his own experiences, and this has caused one critic to observe that "the passages on conversations and on fighting in airplanes sound so much more authentic than do the scenes of infantry fighting: conversation and aerial combat were what the combatant Malraux knew best and at first hand."[15]

In Malraux's earlier novels a historical event is used as the background against which the destinies of his characters are developed. In *L'espoir*, however, the events dominate the individual destinies. The characters respond to the situations in which they find themselves, but are never masters of such situations. The causes of the war, the political, social, and economic factors which have contributed to the circumstances, produce the characters in the novel who attempt to adjust themselves in the midst of powerful forces. In many respects *L'espoir* is a work of intensive documentary realism; but in some ways Malraux seems to have distorted, or at least restructured, his narrative in order to illustrate philosophical patterns. Woven into the narrative are many of the theories of the various factions which are engaged in a life and death struggle for the Loyalist cause.

The first portion of *L'espoir*, "L'Illusion Lyrique," describes the early Loyalist victories at Madrid and Barcelona; in the first days of the military uprising the fervor of the citizens enabled them to repulse the dissident officers with little more than courage supported by obsolete arms. Malraux then expounds that enthusiasm alone is too insecure a foundation on which to build an army capable of fighting a protracted war. He uses the anarchists to illustrate the central theme of *L'espoir;* "l'apocalypse" must be organized. The anarchists are depicted as capable of great courage and sacrifice, but more involved as revolutionaries than in planning to win a revolution. When results do not meet their expectations, they are prepared to settle for martyrdom. By definition the anarchist is the complete individualist and entirely incapable of conceiving the necessity for discipline. The communists were the first to realize that the undisciplined horde must be transformed into an army capable of winning the war. The apocalypse must be organized, and Malraux's message is based on the realization that revolution and war cannot be justified merely because they afford an opportunity for intense living and meaningful dying. The concept of "organization," dampening as it is to the revolutionary mystique, becomes the burden of Malraux's mournful song. For Malraux, courage is only a raw material:

> Courage is a thing that *must be organized;* something that lives and dies, which like a rifle, must be kept in condition. Individual courage is no more than the raw material for the courage of an army. Only one man in twenty is really a coward. Two men in twenty are naturally brave. It is necessary for an army to eliminate the first, and to employ the latter two to the best advantage by having them organize and train the remaining seventeen. . . . (150)

This section of *L'espoir* closes with the decline and fall of the Loyalists in the first phase of the struggle, after the loss of Toledo.

In the next portion of the narrative, "Le Manzanares," the communists assume the leadership following the disastrous retreat from Toledo to Madrid. With their organizational abilities, the defense of Madrid is successful and the rebels are forced to withdraw beyond the Manzanares. The Loyalists stall the Insurgent offensive, and in retaliation the civilian population of Madrid is subjected to merciless bombardments. Nevertheless, this second section ends in the excitement of a Loyalist victory.

The last portion, "L'espoir," continues to describe, within

the scope of the book, the decisive victory of the Republicans at Guadalajara. The peasants are shown in a united front fighting with the Republican army. As the novel ends, the final impression is that a Republican victory is possible if the Spanish people are willing to accept discipline and organize themselves into an effective army. Malraux's novel thus introduces the subsidiary theme of the struggle between undisciplined individual heroism and political discipline, between the desire for victory and its organization therefor. It portrays the Western world's final engagement between romantic revolutionary idealism and the newly visible totalitarian policy implicit in the communists' plan to "organize the apocalypse."

Although Malraux, and later Regler and Hemingway, admits that the communists are the most competent organizers and should therefore assume military leadership during the conflict, their novels cannot truly be termed party-line propaganda in any sense. Rather, most of the heroes involved in these novels are fighting for a republic, which embodies many of their personal ideals, and, simultaneously, are fighting against fascism, which seems the antithesis of their beliefs. The concepts of human decency and dignity seem possible only by the defeat of the fascists, and the authors' support of the communist role in the struggle is essentially pragmatic. In Malraux's *L'espoir* the strong figures of Magnin and Hernandez, in Hemingway's *For Whom the Bell Tolls* the idealistic young American Robert Jordan, and in Regler's *The Great Crusade* the German refugee commissar Albert, all realize that to attain a Loyalist victory only the communists possess the force and cohesion necessary to form a winning army. Thus, these men are confronted with a paradox: to win the war they, of necessity, must sacrifice many of their ideals. As expressed by Malraux's communist García: "For me the problem is essentially this: a popular movement, or a revolution, or even a rebellion, can maintain its initial success only by methods in direct opposition to those which provided it with its first victory. Sometimes in opposition even to the sentiments which inspired it originally." (107) Although much of *L'espoir* is concerned with political theory and philosophy, Malraux does offer a realistic explanation of his purpose in defending the Spanish Republic: "As for me, I am not in this uniform because I envision in the

Popular Front the most noble of governments, but rather because I believe such an action will serve to better the lives and living conditions of decent Spanish peasants." (338)

*L'espoir* was published by Gallimard in late 1937. It made an immediate and powerful impression in France, and shortly thereafter, in Great Britain and the United States, where translations were published later in the year. The reading public made a popular success of an intellectual study detailing contemporary history. Part of the popularity may be attributed to the fact that it was the first notable novel about the first modern, mechanized civil war—the first revolution in which the working class used airplanes in its fight. The noted French novelist, Henry de Montherlant, said that "of all the books in the last twenty years it is the one to wish most that one had lived and written."[16]

In 1938 Malraux returned from France to Spain and prepared a motion picture from the last portion of *L'espoir,* hoping to use it to aid the Loyalist cause. The film was produced while the fighting continued. Malraux employed Spanish peasants and soldiers as actors. He overcame countless obstacles in this project. Film had to be flown down from France, flown back to be developed, and flown down again so that Malraux and his colleagues could edit it. In Barcelona, under bombardment, streets and houses used in an unfinished scene would be changed by bombing overnight or would disappear entirely. The film contained scenes of rare beauty and emotion but, by 1939, when it was ready to be released, the Spanish Civil War was nearing its end and France was concerned with its own struggle against Germany. What might have proven a sufficiently moving appeal for France to alter its policies toward the Spanish Republic, ended for Malraux in disappointment.

Arthur Koestler's first trip to Spain after the outbreak of the war was as an undercover agent. The Communist Party arranged for him to sail on August 22, 1936, bound for Lisbon, the only access to Insurgent territory then available. Koestler posed as a reporter for a Hungarian right-wing newspaper, but his actual mission was to collect evidence to prove German and Italian intervention on the Nationalist side. In Lisbon, through fortuitous circumstances, he met with José María Gil Robles, leader of Spain's Confederación Española de Derechas Autonomas, and

Nicolás Franco, the general's brother. Koestler's ruse was a complete success:

> Thirty-six hours after my arrival in Lisbon, I left for Insurgent territory, carrying on me two priceless documents: a Safe-Conduct, describing me as a reliable friend of the National Revolution, signed by Nicolás Franco; and a personal letter of recommendation from Gil Robles to the Commander of the Garrison of Seville, General Queipo de Llano.[17]

The adventure in Seville, though cut short in a dramatic fashion, produced results far beyond his original hopes. In Lisbon, Koestler found ample proof of Portuguese collaboration with the Insurgents and, in Seville, evidence of Nazi intervention was visible everywhere. He ascertained the names of several German pilots, their units, and the types, markings, and approximate number of German aircraft delivered to General Franco. Finally, and what proved most important later, by use of Gil Robles' letter, Koestler obtained an exclusive interview with General Queipo de Llano who, "believing I was on his side, made some highly indiscreet statements referring to foreign aid." Koestler expresses its significance:

> The Civil War had only just entered its second month, and non-intervention was still a carefully maintained fiction; Hitler kept denying that he was sending help to Franco, and Franco denied receiving it. Against this background, the material that I brought back was worth the trouble.[18]

Through Koestler's unfortunate encounter with a reporter for his old newspaper in Berlin, now a Nazi trust, he came under suspicion.[19] By sheer bluff Koestler successfully maneuvered his departure from Seville and drove directly to Gibraltar, one hour before a warrant for his arrest was issued at Insurgent headquarters in the Spanish city.

Returning to Paris and London, Koestler served on the Commission of Inquiry into Alleged Breaches of the Non-Intervention Agreement in Spain. The extent to which the communists had chosen to cooperate within the Popular Front is evidenced by their representation on various committees in which they participated with both liberals and conservatives.[20] Following the hearings by the Committee of Inquiry in London, "which were as successful as a tactical victory in a strategically lost diplomatic battle can be," Koestler returned to Spain on a special assignment which he describes in his autobiography:

> When Franco's insurrection had failed in Madrid, several Right-wing politicians had fled in a hurry, leaving their correspondence files and private archives behind. I was to search these for documents proving that Nazi Germany had taken a direct hand in preparing Franco's rising, and was to bring the material to Paris. The documents were urgently needed as evidence in support of the Spanish Government's case at the League of Nations, and for purposes of international propaganda.[21]

The assignment proved extremely difficult because of the dissension among the political parties in the Republican camp. The jealousies among the various factions forced the Spanish government to conceal many of its activities; the secret shipment of the gold reserves of the Bank of Spain to Russia caused considerable controversy among the Republican leaders.[22] Koestler's mission was accomplished while Madrid was under bombardment, and he left for Valencia following the transfer of the Republican capital to that coastal city during the first week of November 1936. The route from Madrid to the coast was in dispute because of certain anarchist policies, which were opposed to the government transfer, although the fall of Madrid appeared imminent. After a very dangerous drive to Valencia, Koestler and the documents were flown directly to Paris by Malraux's Escadre España.

In December 1936, Koestler began work on a book chronicling his adventures in Spain. Because of the need for sensational propaganda, he permitted the inclusion of various atrocity stories in his book although the authenticity of the documentation was questionable. The French edition of *L'Espagne ensanglantée* went to press in January 1937, and Koestler returned to Spain as a journalist to cover the war from Valencia and Malaga.

Two weeks later Koestler was in a cell in Seville, a prisoner of the same men he had outwitted on his first trip into Insurgent territory. He had departed for Malaga on January 26th; the fascist offensive began on February 4th; Malaga fell on February 8th; and Koestler was arrested on February 9th. Koestler had decided to remain in Malaga at the home of the acting British Consul, Sir Peter Chalmers Mitchell, for two reasons, the first of which proved a disastrous miscalculation. Koestler had felt a "spurious sense of security," since he believed the Insurgent forces would respect the diplomatic immunity afforded him in the sanctuary of the British Consul's home. He could not have been more mistaken. The second reason for staying behind was his desire to be the first foreign journalist in Spain to witness events when the Insurgents captured a town, since General Queipo de Llano had threatened "terrible retribution against the anarchist stronghold."[23]

> I was arrested on February 9, kept for four days "incommunicado" in the prison of Malaga, and was transferred on February 13 to the Central Prison of Seville. I was kept in solitary confinement for three months, and during this period was on hunger strike for twenty-six days. For the first sixty-four days, I was kept "incommunicado" in my cell and not permitted exercise. After that I remained in solitary confinement but was permitted two hours exercise a day in the company of three other prisoners. I was exchanged against a hostage held by the Valencia Government on May 14, after ninety-five days of imprisonment.[24]

During his imprisonment, Koestler was not tortured, but witnessed beatings and executions of other prisoners and, except for the last forty-eight hours, lived in dread of sharing their fate. He was eventually exchanged for the beautiful wife of a Nationalist pilot held in Valencia. This exchange was effected through an extraordinary international campaign organized by the British press, which protested the victimization of a foreign journalist by General Franco's forces, something even Hitler and Mussolini had not dared; Italy and Germany had merely expelled those whom they considered unfriendly:

> I can speak about this extraordinary campaign without appearing to be immodest, for it was in no way connected with my person or merits. The majority of the individuals and organisations who sent telegrams and letters of protest to Franco I did not know, and they had previously not even known my name. Among them were fifty-eight members of the British House of Commons, nearly half of them Conservatives; authors' and journalists' associations; bishops and clergymen; political and cultural organisations of every variety and shape Even the Hungarian Government intervened.[25]

The Nationalists' treatment of Koestler was interpreted by the press as another step in the abolition of intellectual freedom in an explosive Europe. That the innocent victim was a disguised communist was not a consideration. The basis for the support to obtain Koestler's freedom was the fight against a totalitarian threat to civilization, and the fate on one newsman assumed heroic proportions.

Two months after his return to England, Koestler wrote *Dialogue with Death,* which appeared in its earliest edition in the *News Chronicle* as a serialized narrative of his prison experiences. *Spanish Testament,* incorporating *Dialogue with Death* and several chapters from *L'Espagne ensanglantée,* was published in 1938. The work is really a combination of two books, one partial and the other complete. The first portion, excerpted from the earlier propaganda tract, comes closer to informative journalism than possessing any marked literary distinction; its sole justification is that it does provide an absorbing account of the version disseminated by the communists of the causes of the war. However, in all editions published outside England, this has been omitted, and the second portion, *Dialogue with Death,* appears as a self-contained book. This second portion of the book is concerned with Koestler's imprisonment and is important, both for its literary merit, its insight into the human emotions involved in the Spanish struggle, and as the basis for the author's novel, *Darkness at Noon. Spanish Testament* became a Left Book Club choice and had a modest success. It is presently out of print but *Dialogue with Death* has been reissued in England, under that title, in the form in which it was originally written.

In the first section of *Spanish Testament,* Koestler describes his trip to Seville by way of Portugal during the early months of the war. He recounts what he saw in Lisbon and provides a description of his interview with the rebel general Queipo de Llano. There is a serious attempt to depict the atmosphere at rebel headquarters in Seville. Between chapters one and seven of the first section is an unsatisfactory effort to treat the historical causes of the Spanish Civil War, as well as the complex problem of the Spanish Church. Contained in these five chapters is a study of the economic conditions in Spain and the attempts of the Spanish Republic at land reform, public health, and the elimination of illiteracy. He recounts the uprising in the Asturias in 1934 and its cruel suppression by the Moors and Legionnaires. Koestler documents the efforts of the fascists to prepare for the armed rebellion, the close ties of the Spanish and German fascists, as well as a great deal of atrocity material. The machine-gunning of fugitive noncombatants at Malaga and Guernica and the attacks on Republican ambulances and medical units are all continued from *L'Espagne ensanglantée.* The only historical purpose of much of this propaganda is that Koestler is able to expose the unreliability of the official Insurgent statements regarding the proposed communist uprising, which was generally given by the Insurgents as justification for their military insurrection. Thus, this first portion of Koestler's book is good propaganda, poor journalism, and compared with the analyses of such contemporary historians on Spain as Madariaga, Borkenau, and Brenan, is not a serious contribution to an understanding of the more complex issues of the conflict.

*Dialogue with Death* is concerned with observation in a limited field and with self-analysis. It is a fine, sensitive, humane, and objective account of life in a Nationalist prison, as well as an impressive personal revelation on the part of Koestler. The book was written in the late autumn of 1937, immediately after his release from prison, when the events he had experienced were still vivid in his memory. It was based principally on his prison diaries, which he had successfully smuggled out. *Dialogue with Death* is written from the perspective of a man still under the impact of a traumatic experience, and while the Spanish Civil War was still in progress. "The last-mentioned circumstance was responsible for a deliberate underplaying of the spiritual side of the experience, as it would have been frivolous to indulge in introspective reflections while my comrades fought and died in Spain."[26]

Confined to one locale, one line of action, and one dominant character, the personal narrative accumulates great dramatic intensity. The prison scenes are channeled into a concentrated expression of all the horror of war. Koestler's self-analysis during the four months that he occupied the condemned cell in Seville yields a credible portrait of a man thinking or, more important, suffering from the need to reconsider beliefs he once had accepted as truth. Such introspection dramatizes much of the same anxiety felt throughout Europe during the Spanish struggle. Finally, Koestler abandoned the Spanish Civil War, not by choice but because, as a condition of his release, he had been obliged to promise not to return to Spain for the duration of the war, and was therefore under compulsion not to resume his position with the *News Chronicle* and the Spanish News Agency.

Gustav Regler crossed into Spain from France in a small van, bringing with him a printing press for leaflets, a film projector, and some suitable films, all a gift from the International Union of Authors. It was September, 1936, and the sympathetic French border guards deliberately overlooked his passage. After delivering the equipment, Regler found himself in Madrid, without funds, with no knowledge of Spanish, and with no letter of introduction that might assist him in obtaining a useful post. But the exhilarating atmosphere of the city infected him:

> The exciting thing was that my state was exactly the same as that of Madrid itself. Only on this occasion have I known that sense of freedom, a feeling of unconditional escape, of readiness for absolute change; it was the daydream of a whole people. Everything was in readiness for the unexpected, and the unexpected happened. By midday I was guest in a militia-kitchen where they all stood up and sang when they heard that I was a foreign writer come to join them. After our meal they took me to a barracks and gave me a set of blue overalls, and in the evening I went with them to work on the fortifications that were being constructed outside the gateways of the town. We came back singing in the morning.[27]

The impending approach of the enemy remained a constant threat, making life unsafe but at the same time stirring the deepest powers of resistance:

> There was a spirit of intoxication in the people, an infectious eagerness for sacrifice, a hot-blooded unreason and fanatical belief in freedom, which could never lead to the constitution of an orderly State on any early pattern. To judge by their outward aspect, the militiamen might have been pushed out into the streets by the French Revolution, and no doubt many of the acts of violence of the first days of the war had been prompted by unconscious imitations of the "sans-culottes."[28]

Regler proceeded to Albacete, the headquarters of the International Brigades, and offered his services to André Marty, commander of the unit. Marty appointed him special commissar to the international battalions south of Madrid, which had just suffered a severe defeat and were in a state of great confusion. On the journey from Albacete to the front, the German refugee author experienced a feeling of historical prescience in his mission: "We don't write history now, we make it." (54) Regler arrived at the front and immediately became political commissar for "Paul Lukacz," actually the Hungarian writer Mata Zalka, then in command of a unit consisting of French, German, and Italian troops. The men rallied, with Regler's aid, and returned to Madrid to take part in the battle around University City. During this period Regler renewed his friendship with Malraux, whom he had met previously at the Writers' Congress in Moscow, and also became acquainted with Frank Capa, the American photographer.

The hurried preparations for the defense of Madrid are described by Regler:

> Lukacz was poring over his "Baedeker" map. The Battalion doctor, a German named Heilbrun, was searching for beds and an operating table, so as to be "ready." Ludwig Renn, the pedantic writer, was hastily studying Spanish grammar by the light of a shaded candle—an Archimedes whose cogitations were liable to be interrupted at any moment by an irruption of murderous Africans. The French were practising throwing the hand-grenades which the Spanish had contrived for them out of jam-tins, dynamite and a primitive fuse. Less than a mile away were the Moroccans, with German telescopic sights on their rifles. My Italians were organising themselves under Pacciardi's quiet orders.[29]

Russian ships had arrived from Odessa with cargoes of grain, fats, rifles, and field guns, and Mexico had sent arms as well. The civilians and militia were aroused but showed no signs of panic. The spirit of the International Brigades infected the city and, although their number was small, they forced the Insurgents to retreat from University City. Regler singles out the heroes of the valiant defense of Madrid:

> When, in the autumn of 1936, Franco's Moors were on the verge of perpetrating unthinkable atrocities in the naïve, unarmed and daydreaming city of Madrid, they were stopped by those few battalions which were later named the International Brigade. The saviours had no names and will never have any. Their heroes,

very different in character but united in their devotion to the cause of the Spanish Republic, were Paul Lukacz; Hans Beimler and Hans Kahle, the German Communists; the youngster, Alexander Maass, who was the first to make contact with the enemy; Ralph Fox, who was killed, and Ralph Bates, who survived, both British members of the brave Anglo-Saxon formation called the Lincoln Brigade.[30]

For the next several months Regler's war experience was limited to the defense of Madrid. Slogans determined the strategy on both sides—"Madrid será la tumba del fascismo" and "No Pasarán!" were the rallying cries of the Loyalists. The battle lasted through the winter with each side attacking and counterattacking. In February the Moors surprised the French Battalion in a foggy valley of Jarama and annihilated them. The Italian Garibaldi Battalion counterattacked and drove the Moors back, a foretaste of the victory to be achieved by the International Brigades at Guadalajara in March 1937. It was on this front that Regler became friendly with Hemingway and convinced him that his judgment of Italian military ability in *Farewell to Arms* needed reconsideration.

Hemingway brought with him Joris Ivens, the Dutch photographer, who had worked with Regler on his film about Moscow. Ivens was filming *The Spanish Earth,* a propaganda attempt on behalf of the Loyalists for which Hemingway was doing the commentary. Both Regler and Hemingway had previously experienced the unpleasantness of André Marty, who, as the war progressed, became so psychotic that he imagined spies everywhere and ordered the executions of innocent men. Their common dislike of Marty encouraged Regler to confide in Hemingway:

> I told him the inside stories of operations and crises which I had witnessed earlier. I let him know our losses and gave him advance information whenever I could, feeling certain that he really understood what it was all about. I gave him secret material relating to the Party, which he respected, because it was fighting more actively than any other body, although he despised its Martys. He used my material later in *For Whom the Bell Tolls,* and countless readers learned from the brutal interpolations in a work of romantic fiction about things that they would not listen to in

real life. He depicted the spy-disease, that Russian syphilis, in all its shameful, murderously stupid workings, writing with hatred of the huntsman for the poacher.[31]

Regler and Hemingway helped improve the morale of the International Brigade, each in his own way. Morale was an important factor because supplies were low and the anticipated Russian help had not materialized in the quantities anticipated. During these months Regler and Hemingway and Ivens were inseparable. In the end victory in the battle of Guadalajara boosted morale more than any form of propaganda or "commissar psychology" could.

The actual battle of Guadalajara, which to many Loyalists appeared a favorable reversal of the tide, has been described by all the military historians of the conflict, but never more graphically than by Regler in his autobiography. The Italian fascist and Insurgent forces consisted of several divisions, each division with 36 artillery pieces, with a firepower ratio of 12 to 1 compared with that of the International Brigades. Loudspeakers mounted on vans eventually proved more effective than artillery, however. The Loyalists routed the overconfident fascist forces and captured huge quantities of arms and ammunition. What most impressed Regler was that on one section of the front, at Ibarra, the Italian troops on the side of the Insurgents surrendered to their own countrymen in the International Brigades after listening continuously for 72 hours to appeals broadcast to them through loud speakers.[32]

In the early part of the summer of 1937 there was evidence of encouragement in the Loyalists' camp. Spanish reinforcements arrived for Regler's group, now a division, and the new troops were well trained. Although 70 out of every 100 volunteers that had fought to save Madrid in 1936 were now dead, they had been replaced by Spaniards. With these fresh troops and all available equipment, the Brigade, with Regler as one of the staff officers, began the decisive battle at Huesca on June 11, 1937. The International Brigade suffered a disastrous loss the opening day of fighting; a single fascist artillery shell made a direct hit on the staff car in which Commander Lukacz, the division surgeon Werner Heilbrun, and Regler were driving. It was a freakishly unfortunate strike; Lukacz was killed and Regler seriously injured. The next day, during the Insurgent counterattack, an enemy plane spotted Heilbrun's car and he was killed during the strafing. Thus, the three leading figures of the Brigade were eliminated within a period of 24 hours.[33]

With the Loyalist defeat at Huesca, the war of attrition began. Regler remained in a Madrid hospital for four months. When well enough to walk, Prime Minister Negrín sent him to the United States to appeal for funds, a mission similar to that which Malraux had undertaken. Regler's wife accompanied him as the guest of Hemingway. The tour proved successful as a fund-raising venture, but the war was lost. The Russians had begun to withdraw their advisers and supplies. Regler describes these final stages of the conflict:

> A year later, in March 1939, the war in Spain ended with the defeat of the Republicans. The Fascist superiority in numbers and equipment, which had been unavailing at Guadalajara in 1937, triumphed after a winter of starvation. For a year the members of an international commission had been paid salaries to supervise the withdrawal of foreign troops on both sides. The remains of our brigades were shifted aimlessly from one base to another. Sometimes they rebelled and were allowed to take part in a battle. But Franco's Condor Legion kept its artillery always ready for action, while the German generals sat in famous castles making their plans and the Junkers and Messerschmitts made daily sorties. Now they could fly over Barcelona without encountering any opposition. The Spanish sky was theirs, and presently an officer of the Falange appeared in Port Bou, where two and a half years earlier I had smuggled in the printing-press and the film-projector in my van, and raised the hated flag of dictatorship.[34]

Regler had been in Paris when Barcelona fell, and he immediately went to Perpignan to "search for the Brigade and render it my last service as commissar." The description of the refugees crossing the border into an unsympathetic France, and the French border guards herding the Spaniards into a concentration camp consisting of primitive trenches on the sands at Argelès, are all recorded in Regler's autobiography. Not far from this camp, Regler, with the aid of Herbert Matthews, *New York Times* correspondent, found the 75 survivors of the brigade who had been the last to cross the border. The fanatical André Marty was planning the execution of all the survivors he deemed unreliable when Regler, together with a group of Quakers who arrived on the scene with food and clothing, intervened. Regler's final act prior to writing his novel, *The Great Crusade,* in 1940, as the guest of Hemingway at the latter's home in Key West, Florida, occurred in the south of France, near a concentration camp. There he found Spain's fine poet, Antonio Machado, ill and dying of neglect. At Cerbère, risking his own internment, Regler summoned medical aid for the valiant Spaniard.

Gustav Regler's episodic roman à clef, *The Great Crusade,* deals with the combat experiences of the International Brigades. Specifically, it is a novel of the Twelfth International Brigade, with which Regler served throughout the Spanish struggle. The characters in the novel are international—Germans, Frenchmen, Italians—and the novel takes form by following them from the defense of the University City sector of Madrid to the Jarama front, and culminates in the battle of Guadalajara, recounting many of the same incidents, viewed from the ground, that were described in *L'espoir* from the air. *The Great Crusade* concerns the victorious six months of the 1936–1937 campaign during which the International Brigades consistently triumphed, from the defense of Madrid to the total victory over the Italian divisions at Guadalajara. The time sequence is identical with the Malraux novel, but the scale of the Regler work is restricted by its narrative form, a limitation which Malraux's "new form" avoided.

Regler's novel borders on factual reporting. Hemingway points out in his Preface to *The Great Crusade:*

> The greatest novels are all made-up. Everything in them is created by the writer. He must create from knowledge, of course, unless his book is to be a tour de force. There have been great tours de force too: *The Red Badge of Courage* and *Wuthering Heights.* But the authors of such books are usually poets who happen to be writing prose. But there are events which are so great that if a writer has participated in them his obligation is to try to write them truly rather than assume the presumption of altering them with invention. It is events of this importance that have produced Regler's book.

Yet the book may justly be called a novel because it does not pretend to be a detailed history of the military events in which the International Brigades took part. Regler's intention is to present various episodes in which his unit participated and to relate the effects of each encounter on the men involved. The intellectual and emotional responses of the men in *The Great Crusade* closely parallel those in *L'espoir*. The episodes involving the foreign volunteers appear the most vital in the book: the Italians of the Garibaldi Battalion, attempting by propaganda to influence Mussolini's conscripts to desert to their side; the Polish Battalion; the French, vanguard of battalions that were supposed to follow but never did. These foreign volunteers represent more than a dozen lands and each is endeavoring to further his conception of a righteous cause. The plight of the men, many of them long-time refugees from fascism, is described by Regler:

> They had to hire themselves to all the road builders of Europe, had passed their winters in the mud, their summers in the blazing heat of the building lot. They were the first to be swept out of the factories, like dirty trash, when a crisis came. Even in their dreams they were pursued by fear of the ticket from the "prefectures" that would ban them from the country. They had opened shoemakers' shops in little holes in the workmen's districts; they have gone through the suburbs with a cart, shouting their melodious cries for rags and worn-out pots up at the house fronts. Their eyes had roamed unsteadily along the windows; weary was the hand that pushed the cart. . . . They had wandered even into the mines of the north of Belgium and when they came back from the coalpits they would sit in tiny dormitories. The riches of earth only passed through their calloused hands, then flowed on, and the riches of their Italy . . . was squandered on senseless wars by the ambitious tyrant. For twenty years they had felt impotent. (384)

The bickerings, jealousies, and hostilities, the political and temperamental differences seem slight compared to the central theme of the novel, the extraordinary but very simple recognition of the concept of human brotherhood in the face of opposing physical and amoral forces that would destroy it. As the war progressed the men developed a reliance on the more authentic caramaderie of their fellows in arms. Thus Regler advances the Loyalist cause and vests it with the aura of a crusade. Undoubtedly, Regler possessed a great gift, for the narrative and the action scenes in his book are vivid; but at times the author indulged in reflections of a pretentious nature which detract from the quality of the novel.

Regler, like Hemingway and, to some extent, Malraux, is concerned in his narrative with the element of betrayal. The men of the International Brigades are betrayed, according to Regler, not only in a material sense but in a spiritual sense, by forces outside Spain. Many lose, or begin to doubt, their faith in previously accepted political principles, particularly communism. But their belief in the necessity for victory and in the justice of the Loyalist cause never falters. While this is not explicit, it is profoundly felt in Regler's novel. Like *L'espoir* and *For Whom the Bell Tolls*, *The Great Crusade* is a sad but not despairing book. Although the Regler and Malraux novels end on a note of victory, both authors are sufficiently realistic not to envision a final, idealized triumph. All three novels have their moments of extreme heroism but not one of them, nor the personal narratives of Orwell, Bernanos, and Koestler, attempts to glorify a war that pits Spaniard against Spaniard, foreign divisions against international brigades, heroic sieges and ghastly slaughtering grounds. The writing, though varied, is always an expression of profound sadness as each writer conveys the emotions that resulted from the pervading sense of historical prescience that inspired the Loyalists.

George Orwell's reasons for going to Spain in December of 1936 were based on a strong faith in common decency and the necessity for defending it. Orwell was not only uninterested in Spain's political situation, but probably unaware of it. He knew nothing about the nature of the war, except that it was against fascism, and he had decided that fascism was an enemy of common decency. To him it seemed that for the first time since World War I democracy was willing to confront fascism in an effort to halt its spread throughout Europe: "When the fighting broke out on 18 July it is probable that every anti-Fascist in Europe felt a thrill of hope. For here at last, apparently, was democracy standing up to Fascism."(48)

Orwell's ostensible purpose for going to Spain was to report on the war for a London socialist weekly. He found Barcelona still under the exciting influence of the anarchists after their successful early counterrevolution against the military rebellion. Barcelona was where, noted Cyril Connolly, "one first became conscious of the extraordinary mixture of patriotic war-fever and revolutionary faith, and that absolutely new and all-pervading sense of moral elevation which since the revolution is the most dominating note in Catalonia."[35] Understanding Orwell's character, it is not difficult to imagine his personal reaction to the young and ragged youths enlisting in the militia, and his desire to join with them.

> I had come to Spain with some notion of writing newspaper articles, but I had joined the militia almost immediately, because at that time and in that atmosphere it seemed the only conceivable thing to do. . . . When one came straight from England the aspect of Barcelona was something startling and overwhelming. It was the first time that I had ever been in a town where the working class was in the saddle. . . . There was much in it that I did not understand, in some ways I did not even like it, but I recognized it immediately as a state of affairs worth fighting for. (4–5)

At that time each of the political parties still had its own militia units, although they were in the process of being absorbed into the Republican army. Because Orwell's letters of introduction were from the British Independent Labour Party, which had close liaison with the Marxist P.O.U.M. in Spain, Orwell joined a militia unit of that party. Being unfamiliar with Spanish politics, the fact that he was assigned to a P.O.U.M. unit seemed to him of no particular significance. Later, during the interparty strife, the P.O.U.M. was represented in Spain and abroad as a Trotskyist party. In fact it was not, although it did join with the small Trotskyist group to oppose certain P.S.U.C. policies which were being promulgated in Barcelona.[36] According to Lionel Trilling, Orwell's personal preference at the time of his enlistment was for the Communist Party line, and because of this he looked forward to a transfer to a communist unit:

> It was natural . . . for Orwell to have been a partisan of the Communist program for the war. It recommended itself to most people on inspection by its apparent simple common sense. It proposed to fight the war without any reference to any particular political idea beyond a defense of democracy from a fascist en-

> emy. When the war was won, the political and social problems would be solved, but until the war should be won, any debate over these problems was to be avoided as leading only to the weakening of the united front against Franco.[37]

After joining the militia, there were a few days of inconceivable chaos in Barcelona while the group received the poorest of equipment. Then the disorganized and confused company was sent to the front. Orwell describes this unit with an affection bordering on pathos:

> You cannot possibly conceive what a rabble we looked. We straggled along with far less cohesion than a flock of sheep. . . . And quite half of the so-called men were children. . . . Yet they were all happy and excited at the prospect of going to the front at last. As we neared the line the boys round the red flag in front began to utter shouts of 'Visca P.O.U.M.' 'Fascistas-maricones!' and so forth—shouts which were meant to be war-like and menacing, but which, from those childish throats, sounded as pathetic as the cries of kittens. It seemed dreadful that the defenders of the Republic should be this mob of ragged children carrying worn-out rifles which they did not know how to use. (19)

Arriving at the Aragon front, Orwell discovered that the Republican offensive had bogged down and no particular military action on this front was contemplated by either the Loyalists or the Nationalists. He settled into the stagnation of life in the trenches where the real enemies were "boredom, cold, dirt and the lice." The only incident resembling a military encounter with the enemy occurred when 15 soldiers volunteered for an assault on the Nationalist trenches, more to relieve the monotony than as a strategic maneuver. Orwell was among the volunteers who made their way into the line of fire between the trenches, only to discover that headquarters had cancelled the attack. In returning to their own trenches through a heavy fog, two of the volunteers lost their lives. Orwell's description of his feelings during this time contrasts sharply with Regler's expression of historical prescience: "When you are taking part in events like these you are, I suppose, in a small way, making history, and you ought by rights to feel like an historical character. But you never do, because at such times, the physical details always outweigh everything else." (138)

After 115 days in the front lines with nothing to break the monotony of trench living, Orwell proceeded to Barcelona, on leave, to visit with his wife and equip himself, at his own expense.[38] The city was a far different place from the one he had left four months before. Earlier he had been aware of the formation of an egalitarian society; an exhilarating atmosphere which persisted, in spite of all discomforts, at the front. Having been cut off from all news either of Barcelona or of the world beyond while at the front, Orwell was totally unprepared for the severe shock on his return to the city, as a result of the transformation which had occurred during his absence. He had departed from a city in which no one dressed better, ate better, slept better, or had more money than his neighbor. He returned to find waiters in boiled shirts, and the bourgeois differences between rich and poor eating places. Even a greater change had occurred in the status of the P.O.U.M. organization and the anarchist militia units, which were being suppressed by government forces as enemies of law and order. Orwell's leave was spent in support of the P.O.U.M., who were actually engaged in street fighting with the government Assault Guards. An armistice was declared, promptly broken by renewed fighting by both sides, and finally the anarchists and the Trotskyists were forced to surrender because of lack of provisions.[39]

Orwell returned to the front at Huesca and soon afterwards was shot in the throat. He tells the story with characteristic detachment because "the whole experience of being hit by a bullet is very interesting and I think it worth describing in detail":

> Roughly speaking it was the sensation of being at the *centre* of an explosion. . . . I had a numb, dazed feeling, a consciousness of being very badly hurt, but no pain in the ordinary sense. . . . This ought to please my wife, I thought; she had always wanted me to be wounded, which would save me from being killed when the great battle came. It was only now that it occurred to me to wonder where I was hit, and how badly; I could feel nothing, but I was conscious that the bullet had struck me somewhere in the front of the body. . . . As soon as I knew that the bullet had gone clean through my neck I took it for granted that I was done

> for. . . . My paralysed right arm came to life and began hurting damnably. . . . The pain reassured me, for I knew that your sensations do not become more acute when you are dying. (185–87)

The wound was not critical, although for a time Orwell's speech organs were paralyzed; even after the wound healed his vocal cords were affected. The trip from the field hospitals at the front—Sietamo, Barbastro, Monzon, Lerida—was an agonizing experience in which medical treatment was primitive and doctors, nurses, and supplies scarce.[40] After his release from the hospital in Barcelona, Orwell discovered that the members of the P.O.U.M. units were being rounded up and jailed, and reports indicated that many, including their leader Andrés Nin, had been executed. Orwell and his wife narrowly escaped arrest by hiding and keeping constantly on the move. They realized that there was little to be accomplished by remaining in Spain and that their lives were in great danger. With the aid of the British Consul, they reached the French border. Fortunately the frontier guards had not yet received the list of persons to be apprehended, on which their names would certainly have figured, and they were able to proceed safely.

Orwell returned to England in the summer of 1937, disappointed by what he considered to be the corruption of a just cause. Although a victim of the internal political strife within the Republican camp, his *Homage to Catalonia,* written only seven months after his original departure for Spain, is neither a rejection of his faith in mankind nor of his faith in the cause of the Spanish people. The conflict in Spain was Orwell's first experience with war, and although the violence and horror of the fighting shocked him, nevertheless he found a comradeship and a sense of dignity and decency in the struggle of the Spanish people.

Orwell's *Homage to Catalonia* is essentially a diary of his adventures in Spain, both in Barcelona and on the Aragon front. It presents the progress of a young writer, at first caught up in the fervor of the popular front, changing from an innocent idealism to the rather resigned yet hopeful "separate peace" of a seasoned veteran. On the next to last page of the book, Orwell writes:

> This war, in which I played so ineffectual a part, has left me with memories that are mostly evil, and yet I do not wish that I had

> missed it. When you have had a glimpse of such a disaster as this —and however it ends the Spanish war will turn out to have been an appalling disaster, quite apart from the slaughter and physical suffering—the result is not necessarily disillusionment and cynicism. Curiously enough the whole experience has left me with not less but more belief in the decency of human beings.

The greater part of Orwell's narrative is straightforward and extremely interesting autobiography. Orwell describes the workers' utopia in Barcelona late in 1936, trench life at the stagnant Aragon front, the return to a changed and bourgeois Barcelona, the serious wounding of the author, and the final flight from Spain as a persecuted veteran of the P.O.U.M. militia. The themes expressed deal with Orwell's political development during the six months he remained in wartime Spain. As a writer he was increasingly dominated by the desire to use literature as a means of forcibly impressing on the outside world some notion of the realities of events in Spain. He writes of the lessons he learned: the experience of war, the comradeship at arms, the dignity and decency of men sacrificing themselves for a just but corrupted cause. Interspersed within the narrative, Orwell attempts his interpretation of the causes of the conflict; he breaks the narrative on one occasion and offers a long analysis of the war in a political context. His perspective is limited to Catalonia, which is a unique section of Spain, but on occasion the universal implications which Orwell draws overcome his rather limited experience. He touches on the inefficiency of the Republican military system, the need to organize and, like Malraux, Regler, and Hemingway, early in the conflict he believes the communists best suited to accomplish the task. The suppression of the P.O.U.M. brings about his complete disillusionment with the communists, not only in their tactics, but also in what Orwell feels is their true motivation. As Orwell viewed the subsequent events in Spain from the safety of his home in England, he was forced to conclude rather pessimistically in his personal narrative: "The fact is that every war suffers a kind of progressive degradation with every month that it continues, because such things as individual liberty and a truthful press are simply not compatible with military efficiency." (180)

*Homage to Catalonia*'s reception in England was remarkably passive; of the 1,500 copies printed in 1938, only 900 had been sold up to Orwell's death, and it was not printed in America until 1952. The personal narrative was probably the only book published in England from 1936 to 1939 which attempted to support the Spanish Republic, but at the same time refused to be classed as wholly adulatory. Orwell, like Hemingway, concedes in his essay, "Looking Back on the Spanish War," that he foresaw the inevitable defeat of the Republicans long before the war ended. *Homage to Catalonia* was written while the war was still in progress, and as a Loyalist supporter he may well have deemed it wrong to prophesy defeat, regardless of his personal opinion at the time. Whether it was right to encourage continued fighting when defeat was inevitable loses its meaning in retrospect. Orwell's basic belief was that though the war might be lost, the fight against fascism was just beginning.

Ernest Hemingway worked hard for the Loyalist cause, although he possessed personal doubts about the foreign communists who were moving into Madrid to join in the struggle against the fascists.[41] Because of his fund-raising activities, from 1936 until the end of the war in 1939, he was either in Spain, or working for the Spanish Republic in the United States, or writing about the course of the conflict. His work took him into the heart of the fighting on four separate occasions. He first sailed for Spain in February 1937 to report the war for the North American Newspaper Alliance. From Toulouse, in mid-March, Hemingway flew south to Barcelona. From there a plane carried him down the east coast of Spain to Alicante, where he found the Loyalists in a joyous mood over their recent defeat of the Italians at Brihuega. When Hemingway reached the actual battlefield, leaving at dawn on a late March morning and driving up through Valencia, the Italian dead still lay where they had fallen. He described the scene in his March 23, 1937 dispatch to the North American Newspaper Alliance:

> Along the roads were piled abandoned machine guns, anti-aircraft guns, light mortars, shells, and boxes of machine-gun ammunition, and stranded trucks, light tanks and tractors were stalled by the side of the tree-lined route. Over the battlefield on the heights above Brihuega were scattered letters and papers, haversacks, entrenching tools and everywhere the dead. The hot weather makes all dead look alike, but these Italian dead lay with waxy grey

faces in the cold rain looking very small and pitiful. They did not look like men, but where a shell burst had caught three of them, the remains took on the shape of curiously broken toys.[42]

Even in his earliest days in Spain, Hemingway, who was extremely contemptuous of Mussolini, contradicted the propaganda disseminated by the Republican press on the fascist rout. In his March 29 communiqué he noted that the defeat of the Italians was not caused by any cowardice on their part:

> Reports that Brihuega was simply an air victory with columns stampeding in panic without fighting, are corrected when the battlefield is studied. It was a bitterly fought seven-day battle, heavy rain and snow making flying impossible much of the time. In the final assault under which the Italians broke and ran, the day was just practicable for flying and one hundred and twenty planes, sixty tanks and about 10,000 Government infantry routed three Italian divisions of 5,000 men each. It is the co-ordination of these planes, tanks and infantry which brings this war into a new phase. You may not like it and wish to believe it is propaganda, but I have seen the battlefield, the booty, the prisoners and the dead.[43]

During April and early May of 1937, Hemingway joined with Joris Ivens on a documentary film, *The Spanish Earth*, working in and near the besieged Madrid. They set up an observation post, witnessed the attacks and counterattacks on the city, and photographed the mangled bodies of the Madrileños in the streets and squares where Insurgent artillery had permanently interrupted their civilian lives. Hemingway was incensed at the fascist terrorist tactics of murdering the nonmilitary population of the city. In his address to the American Writers' Congress that year, he said:

> The Totalitarian fascist states believe in the Totalitarian war. That put simply means that whenever they are beaten by armed forces they take their revenge on unarmed civilians. In this war since the middle of November, they have been beaten at the Parque del Oeste, they have been beaten at the Pardo, they have been beaten at Carabanchel, they have been beaten on the Jarama, they have been beaten at Brihuega and at Cordoba. Every time they are beaten in the field they salvage that strange thing they call their honor, by murdering civilians.[44]

The film, *The Spanish Earth,* was undertaken to aid the Spanish people by an organization called Contemporary Historians, which included John Dos Passos, Lillian Hellman, Archibald MacLeish, and Hemingway. The film was designed to show the efforts of the Spanish peasant to reclaim for agricultural purposes land which had been either misused or neglected for many generations. Its central theme describes how the military rebellion both betrayed these peasants and served to defeat their efforts.[45]

In 1940, looking back on the spring of 1937, Hemingway remarked that "the period of fighting when we thought that the Republic could win was the happiest period of our lives." For the duration of the war, except for his play *The Fifth Column,* he contented himself with his North American Newspaper Alliance dispatches, a few short stories, and the brief script of *The Spanish Earth.* His decision to delay any major writing project of the war was related to his general philosophy on the function of the writer. Delaying further writing until the war was won and the fascist menace reduced in scale, he involved himself in the lives of the young men in the Loyalist ranks, who were fighting for a cause at least as just as that which motivated his own engagement in World War I. Hemingway also believed that if he survived these war experiences, he might then produce a novel superior to any of his earlier works. Speaking through the hero of *For Whom the Bell Tolls,* Hemingway provides some insight into the future of his writing career after having experienced the violence of the war:

> And what you will be like or just exactly what you will be suited for when you leave the service of the Republic is, to me, he thought, extremely doubtful. But my guess is you will get rid of all that by writing about it, he said. Once you write it down it is all gone. It will be a good book if you can write it. (165)

Hemingway's involvement with the Loyalist troops illustrated his belief that comradeship in time of war transcended any political beliefs on the part of the men. His friends in the Eleventh and Twelfth Brigades ranged from militant comintern communists to the liberal, young idealists fighting from a belief in the need to defend a democratic state against fascism. In Hemingway's preface to Regler's *The Great Crusade,* he notes that the

Eleventh Brigade was German, and although they were ardent antifascists, "most of them were communists" and "a little too serious to spend much time with." Hemingway's affection was for the Twelfth Brigade, of which Dr. Werner Heilbrun was a member. He donated his royalties from *The Spanish Earth* to the widow after the doctor was killed during a strafing at Huesca. With the doctor in the Twelfth Brigade were Gustav Regler, whom Hemingway describes as calm, cheerful, tough, and one of the ablest fighting officers in the Brigade, and General Lukacz, Hemingway's closest friend in the group.[46]

After visiting the United States in May to address the Writers' Congress and prepare the sound track for *The Spanish Earth,* he immediately returned to Spain and found conditions deteriorating; Lukacz and Heilbrun were dead and Regler badly wounded. Madrid itself was a tangle of bitter and cynical intrigue. "If the winter and spring of 1937 had been the golden age of the International Brigades, now was the winter of their discontent."[47] During this second trip Hemingway wrote his play, *The Fifth Column,* while living at the Hotel Florida, in Madrid, exposed to German artillery batteries from the surrounding hills. The play was completed and sent out of the country in December 1937, just before the capture of Teruel. In it Hemingway sought to reflect conditions during the siege of Madrid the preceding fall. Civilians had been killed in the daily bombardments, food was scarce, hopes of lifting the siege were dim, and the malignant growth of treason had permeated the city. Whatever its dramatic faults, and there are many, *The Fifth Column* was an attempt to portray conditions in Madrid in the fall of 1937 as they might have appeared in the uncensored dispatches of a very objective war correspondent.

Hemingway's play could hardly be described as Loyalist propaganda, although it was still reservedly sympathetic to the Republic. When it was published in 1938, Hemingway replied to those critics who overlooked its many dramatic flaws and chose to criticize the play for its failure to emphasize the nobility and dignity of the Spanish people:

> Some fanatical defenders of the Spanish Republic, and fanatics do not make good friends for a cause, will criticize the play be-

cause it admits that Fifth Column members were shot. They will also say, and have said, that it does not present the nobility and dignity of the cause of the Spanish people. It does not attempt to. It will take many plays and novels to do that, and the best ones will be written after the war is over.[48]

To complete his experiences in Spain, Hemingway made two more extended visits to the peninsula. The third trip began in March 1938. That summer he told reporters that he thought the Loyalists would win, though they were now clearly on the defensive. Privately, however, he indicated that he knew their defeat was inevitable.[49] Too much of Spain was under control of the Insurgents, and Germany and Italy were pouring men and supplies into the Nationalist zone. By far the most depressing trip of all was the fourth, which began in September 1938. Barcelona fell the following January, and Madrid followed at the end of March. Hemingway remained until the final stages of the struggle and then returned to the United States where, from March 1939 to July 1940, for sixteen intensive months, he embodied his feeling about the Spanish struggle in his novel, *For Whom the Bell Tolls.*

The seventeen-month interim between the close of the war and the completion of *For Whom the Bell Tolls* helped to nurture in Hemingway a feeling that the Republican defeat had been virtually inevitable. In his Preface to Regler's novel, Hemingway recalled that he recognized the inevitability of a Loyalist defeat when the Insurgents captured Irun in the late summer of 1936. But his philosophy would never permit him to admit defeat, even to himself, because "when you admit it is lost you are beaten." With the knowledge of the result influencing his perspective, Hemingway's choice of the early summer of 1937 for the time element in *For Whom the Bell Tolls* assumes particular significance. Carlos Baker offers a meaningful explanation:

> He wanted a period deep enough into the war so that the possibility of republican defeat could be a meaningful psychological force. But the time must also be far enough removed from the end of the war so that some of the people could still believe in a republican victory. The struggle could not seem to be hopeless. Yet, as a study in doom, the novel must early isolate and dramatize those adverse powers and power-failures which would ultimately combine to defeat the Spanish republic.[50]

To present the problems confronting the Spanish people during the later stages of the conflict, Hemingway chose as his focal point a group of Republican partisans, drawn from many parts of Spain, and living under primitive conditions in a cave of the high forested slopes of the Sierra del Guardaramas, sixty miles northwest of besieged Madrid, behind the fascist lines. The central theme of *For Whom the Bell Tolls* is concerned with Hemingway's belief that the Spanish people had been betrayed by forces that they could not understand and were only vaguely aware existed. Although much of the betrayal was perpetrated by outsiders, the Spanish people themselves were partly responsible: the irreparable lack of cohesion, the insubordinate and loose-tongued individualism, and the treachery of comrades-in-arms, must throttle the Republican offensive as surely as the novel's hero must blow up the bridge. In his consideration of the Spanish struggle, Hemingway recognized the need to embody all the foreign elements and then include that quality in the Spanish character which made the betrayal possible.

Hemingway, even more than Malraux, deliberately avoids having his novel assume the function of propaganda. His novel, as well as Malraux's *L'espoir,* and Regler's *The Great Crusade,* attempts to rise above the propaganda of the war with its bloated corpses, fetid latrines, and water-filled trenches. On a political level, Hemingway's account of the fascist atrocities is balanced by the description of the massacre of the leading citizens of a village by a sadistic mob. This in turn is tempered by the implication that the criminal neglect, the inhuman apathy to suffering, has allowed the social situation in villages throughout Spain to deteriorate to this level. Within his narrative Hemingway includes the factors which split the various groups fighting for the Loyalists, the inner religious tensions of the Republican Catholics, the range of political and moral attitudes across the Popular Front. Malraux's belief that communists were best able to organize the Republican forces is echoed by Hemingway's Robert Jordan, a more independent and self-sufficient, though less cerebral, figure than Malraux's Hernandez or Magnin. But Hemingway's main theme involves his conception of the chief weaknesses in the Popular Front during the later stages of the war: the defeatism which affected the Loyalist morale from within, the inefficiency of the government's bureaucracy, the instability of the Spanish temperament, and that quality in the Spanish character which instinctively rebels against discipline.

Possessed with an abundance of courage and determined to meet fascism head-on in Spain, these writers exposed themselves to the physical and emotional stresses of life in a war-torn country for a cause which they supported with their lives, their talents, and their reputations. They accepted the carnage of war as a disagreeable but necessary part of defending the cause which had brought them to Spain. In their best moments, these writers went well beyond trying to embody political lessons in their work or recreating the surface drama of the war. Not only did they assimilate the facts of the war, as well as the powerful human feelings and aspirations behind the sacrifice of human lives, but they managed to portray these human concerns honestly, without expedient political twists. Besides their interest in social reforms and the particular form of government for which the Loyalists were fighting, these novelists were vitally concerned with the immediate effects of the war on the Spanish people.

One critic has written of Spanish Civil War literature that the novelist could never really capture the immediacy of the war available to the poet. Nor could he be expected to recreate completely the feelings that existed during the struggle. The span between observation and creation being of necessity long, allowed the novelist time to formulate a comprehensive view before he entered upon the actual writing. When he started, usually after hostilities had ended, he knew the outcome of the struggle, a factor which unquestionably influenced his presentation.[51]

However, with the exception of Regler and Hemingway, the authors involved in this study composed and published their works while the fighting continued. Yet, even in the case of Regler and Hemingway, the expectation of victory or defeat did little to dampen their enthusiasm for a cause they believed to be noble and just. These six authors shared little of the idealism of the 1930s which found young writers experiencing the thrill of revolutionary ideas and the hope of their realization. Their own experiences and political maturity did not permit them to envisage the dawn of a new world, nor were they inspired to turn political theories into realities. It is undeniable that the generous idealism and compassion and purpose of the younger writers were exhausted on behalf of a worthy cause. But the realistic views of Bernanos, Koestler, Malraux, Hemingway, Regler, and Orwell permitted them to uphold the validity of this same cause, despite the defeat of the Spanish Republic. Their sensibilities were less affected by the violence than many of the young idealists. Often these older writers became suspicious of the political ideologies associated with the Republican cause, but they never lost faith in their belief that the Loyalists stood for tolerance, freedom, and human dignity, and that the fascists must be defeated. Their involvement was not essentially related to any particular illusions, but when encountered, they were quickly dispelled and adjustments made. The only illusions they might have had concerned the morality of politicians and party leaders, and their past experiences minimized that effect. In the widest sense, it made little difference whether they were communists, such as Koestler and Regler, or conservatives, such as Bernanos. Nothing they experienced altered their faith in the cause for which they were fighting.

## ▸ NOTES

[1] *Spanish Civil War,* pp. 235–36.

[2] Malcolm Muggeridge, *The Thirties: 1930–1940 in Great Britain* (London, 1940), p. 247.

[3] See Barea, "The Clash," *The Forging of a Rebel* (New York, 1946) and the polemical pamphlet, *Foreign Journalists under Franco's Terror* (London, 1937).

[4] "Looking Back on the Spanish War," *Such Were the Joys,* p. 139.

[5] Orwell concludes: "Sometimes it is a comfort to me to think that the aero-plane is altering the conditions of war. Perhaps when the next great war comes we may see that sight unprecedented in all history, a jingo with a bullet-hole in him."

[6] *Bernanos,* p. 100.

[7] For an account of the military action in Majorca, see Thomas, *Spanish Civil War,* pp. 253–54, and Frank Jellinek, *The Civil War in Spain* (London, 1938), pp. 432–36. The political importance of the occupation of the island by the Italians is given detailed coverage in Julio Álvarez del Vayo, *Freedom's Battle* (New York, 1940), pp. 103–11.

[8] Eliot Paul's personal narrative, *The Life and Death of a Spanish Town* (New York, 1937), provides significant parallels in his description of the fascist takeover of a small town on Ibiza, a neighboring island.

[9] Bernanos, "Autobiography," *La nef,* 45 (August, 1948), 5.

[10] Louis Fischer, *Men and*

*Politics* (New York, 1941), pp. 351–52. Fischer also became a purchasing agent for the Spanish Republic between 1936 and 1939.

[11] Cot remained France's air minister from June 1936 to January 1938. During this time he was instrumental in sending 100 planes to the Loyalists; 70 of these were sent in 1936 and 30 in 1937. Of these, 20 were old craft and were sold unofficially to Malraux. After 1937, with the French adhering to their policy of "nonintervention," this Republican source disappeared. See Pierre Cot, *The Triumph of Treason* (New York, 1944), Chap. X.

[12] The attempts of the Spanish Republican government to buy desperately needed war materials abroad are described in most of the histories chronicling the effects of "nonintervention" during the conflict. Thomas remarks, "The Spanish Embassy in Paris was a veritable 'caravanserai' where at all hours of the day and during many of the night individuals of every nationality came in and out offering all classes of arms, munitions and aircraft, at all prices." *Spanish Civil War*, p. 225.

[13] *Freedom's Battle*, pp. 63–64. The author computes the numerical inferiority of the Republican air force to that of the Insurgents throughout most of the war as between 1 to 5 and 1 to 6.

[14] Flanner, "The Human Condition," *Men and Monuments*, pp. 38–39.

[15] Frohock, *André Malraux and the Tragic Imagination*, p. 106.

[16] Quoted in Flanner, *Men and Monuments*, p. 42.

[17] *Invisible Writing*, p. 317. This volume is the source of the data on Koestler's visits to Spain. Much of the same material is contained in his section of *The God that Failed*. Both accounts are written in retrospect and differ considerably in perspective and tone from his original version in *Spanish Testament*, although the facts are essentially the same.

[18] *Ibid.*, p. 320.

[19] There are conflicting versions of this story by Koestler and the wife of the reporter. The young man in question was the son of the Swedish playwright, August Strindberg.

[20] The preface to Koestler's *Spanish Testament* was written by the Duchess of Atholl, a conservative MP, whose book, *Searchlight on Spain* (London, 1938), was an outstanding dissertation on behalf of the Loyalists. Members of this "Commission on Inquiry" included Professor Trend of Cambridge and John Langdon-Davies.

[21] *Invisible Writing*, p. 328.

[22] There have been many discussions of the gold transfer, including the polemic between Luis Araquistain and Indalecio Prieto, which occurred as recently as 1958.

[23] The battle of Malaga is given detailed coverage in Thomas, *Spanish Civil War*, 370–73, and Borkenau, *Spanish Cockpit*, pp. 211–27. The details of Koestler's actual arrest are included in the chapter titled "Koestler and I are Arrested," in Sir Peter Chalmers Mitchell's personal recollections of the Spanish Civil War, *My House in Malaga* (London, 1938).

[24] *Invisible Writing*, p. 345. This exchange was negotiated by

Dr. Marcel Junod, Delegate of the International Committee of the Red Cross, and is mentioned in his memoirs, *Warrior Without Weapons* (New York, 1951), pp. 104–107.

[25] *Ibid.*, p. 364. Jean-Paul Sartre's short story, *Le mur* (Paris, 1939), also concerns the subject of arrest and imprisonment during the Spanish Civil War, but provides little insight into the conflict.

[26] *Ibid.*, p. 337.

[27] *Owl of Minerva,* p. 272. Regler's autobiography is the only reliable source of information on his adventures in Spain. Almost all the studies of the International Brigades confirm his role in the events he describes.

[28] *Ibid.*, p. 273.

[29] *Ibid.*, p. 282. The defense of Madrid is probably given more attention by writers and the press than any other event during the Spanish Civil War. Among the Loyalist supporters, Henry Buckley, *Life and Death of the Spanish Republic* (London, 1940), Pacciardi, *Il battaglione Garibaldi,* Álvarez Del Vayo, *Freedom's Battle,* Matthews, *Two Wars and More to Come,* and Vincent Sheean, *Not Peace But a Sword* (New York, 1939), are outstanding. Manuel Aznar's *Historia Militar de la Guerra de España* (*1936–1939*) (Madrid, 1940), provides a detailed account from the Nationalist point of view. The most recent military history of the battle is Robert G. Colodny's extensively documented *The Struggle for Madrid* (New York, 1958).

[30] *Owl of Minerva,* p. 283. "It has often been argued that the International Brigade saved Madrid. . . . This force was too small to have turned the day by numbers alone. . . . The victory was that of the populace of Madrid. The bravery and experience of the Brigades was, however, crucial in several later battles. The example of the International Brigades fired the militiamen to continue to resist, while giving to the Madrileños the feeling that they were not alone," according to Thomas, *Spanish Civil War,* p. 325.

[31] *Owl of Minerva,* pp. 292–93. Fischer also describes the problems experienced when dealing with Marty, in *Men and Politics,* pp. 386–401.

[32] See Pacciardi, *Il battaglione Garibaldi* for confirmation of this incident. For detailed accounts of the battle, see Borkenau, *Spanish Cockpit,* Thomas, *Spanish Civil War,* Aznar, *Historia Militar de la Guerra de España,* Hemingway, *The Spanish War* in *Fact,* and Matthews, *Two Wars and More to Come.* Hemingway's analysis of the fighting at Guadalajara differs from that of Regler, Thomas, Borkenau, and other writers who interpreted the victory as a rout of the Insurgents.

[33] For material on the last days of the International Brigades, see the Rust, Rolfe, and Pacciardi studies, as well as Regler's autobiography.

[34] *Owl of Minerva,* p. 320.

[35] "Barcelona," *The Condemned Playground* (London, 1945), p. 180.

[36] This is Orwell's contention and it is supported by Thomas, *Spanish Civil War,* pp. 424–29, and Borkenau, *Spanish Cockpit,* pp. 173–88.

[37] "George Orwell and the Politics of Truth," *The Opposing Self* (New York, 1950), p. 167.

[38] Conditions on the Aragon front are described by Borkenau, *Spanish Cockpit,* pp. 93–110. Thomas adds, "On every hill-top, in Aragon, for example, there seemed to be a knot of ragged, dirty men, Nationalist or Republican 'shivering round their flag', with occasionally bullets wandering between them—and sometimes voices, encouraging desertion, painting a rosy picture of the comforts to be had on the other side, and shouting insults." *Spanish Civil War,* p. 351.

[39] The suppression of the P.O.U.M. and the anarchists in Barcelona is treated by almost all the later historians of the war, and except for the communist writers, all versions essentially confirm Orwell's account of the events.

[40] *From Spanish Trenches,* ed. Marcel Acier (New York, 1937), contains some accounts of medical units supporting the Loyalists.

[41] Baker, *Hemingway: The Writer as Artist,* p. 229.

[42] In July 1938, *Fact,* a British monthly, compiled a majority of Hemingway's newspaper reports into the single issue. The account, which is in chronological order, provides an excellent guide to Hemingway's whereabouts in Spain during the 14 months he spent there during the conflict.

[43] For detailed accounts of this battle see n.29 above.

[44] "The Writer and War," *Writer in a Changing World,* p. 71.

[45] Guttmann in *Wound in the Heart* provides a detailed analysis of *The Spanish Earth.*

[46] Hemingway's experiences in Spain and his friendships in the International Brigades are recounted in Regler's *Owl of Minerva* and Spender's *World within World.*

[47] Baker, *Hemingway: The Writer as Artist,* p. 234.

[48] Hemingway, *Preface to The Short Stories of Ernest Hemingway: The First Forty-Nine Stories and the Play, the Fifth Column* (New York, 1938), vi. The term, "Fifth Column," is attributed to the Nationalist General Mola. When asked by a group of foreign journalists which of his four columns he expected would take Madrid, he answered in words repeated incessantly during the thirty-five years of treachery and espionage since that time, that it would be the "Fifth Column" of secret Nationalist supporters within the city. Thomas, *The Spanish Civil War,* p. 317.

[49] Baker, *Hemingway: The Writer as Artist,* p. 236.

[50] *Ibid.,* 251.

[51] Ford, *Poets' War,* p. 24.

# IV

# War of Ideas

The Spanish elections of 1936 produced an overwhelming victory for the Popular Front under the direction of Manuel Azaña. Spain's political pendulum which, beginning in 1931, had swung from right to left and, in 1933, from left to right, swung left again in February 1936.[1] As a result, the Azaña government controlled 256 seats in the Cortes, the Spanish assembly, to 165 seats for right-wing factions. Koestler explains that while the Popular Front had won a majority of the total votes cast, it also benefited from those advantages of the Spanish electoral system which tended to increase the margin of victory in the Cortes:

> The proportion of the total votes cast for the Left was less favourable to it than the distribution of Parliamentary seats. The Left had gained a majority of the total votes, but this majority was not as great as the majority gained in the Cortes. The old-fashioned and complicated Spanish electoral system was peculiar in that it increased the victory of the victorious party and intensified the defeat of the vanquished party. (62)

Thus, on February 17, 1936, Spain's second center-left government of the decade began its tragically short and turbulent existence.[2]

Instead of gradually subsiding, the excitement of the Popular Front victory degenerated into savage anti-right demonstrations, rioting and uncontrolled attacks on those institutions which were traditionally symbolic of oppression in the minds of the populace: churches, convents, and large estates. Extremists insisted on immediate release of those prisoners held since the 1934 Asturian revolts. In hope of moderating the agitation, the Republic acquiesced, and thousands of embittered men took to the streets. They lost no time striking back at those elements believed responsible for their years of suffering; and rightist newspapers, churches, and the homes and property of monarchists and conservatives became the targets for incendiaries. The disorders were concentrated in the major cities but soon spread to the provinces where peasants, wearied of waiting for the government's agrarian reform program to improve their conditions, seized the large estates. Claude Bowers, then American ambassador to Spain, indicates that the strikes and disorders during this period were exaggerated, as to their frequency and intensity, in the conservative press in Spain and abroad; that, moreover, they reflected the long-deferred hopes of the peasants and workers and were not revolutionary in a political sense; that often they were the work of fascist agents provocateurs who sought to embarrass and discredit the Republic.[3] Koestler notes that the actual policies of the Republic had little to do with the causes of the rioting:

> A few days after the elections, Azaña, the new Prime Minister and veteran of the Spanish liberals, gave an interview to the correspondent of the "Paris Soir": "Before the elections," he declared, "we drafted a programme of minimum reforms; we intend to adhere to this programme. I wish to govern according to the law. *No dangerous innovations! We want peace and order; we are moderates.*" The propagandists of the Right, however, averred that Azaña was aiming at revolution and the disruption of society. (65)

As lawlessness increased, the new government was forced to impose press censorship and declare a state of emergency. In an attempt to appease the uncontrollable elements, the administration dealt leniently with their offenses and, in the case of expropriation of land by the peasants, frequently acceded to their demands. But under Azaña the government found it more difficult to deny the accusations of the rightists that they lacked the power to control even their own supporters. Within the coalition alliance, the feud between center and left socialists resulted in a series of labor strikes which reduced the nation's economy to a state of complete stagnation, thus further weakening the tottering regime. Unhappy Spain was rapidly moving toward a condition of complete chaos. Naturally, the right-wing parties in the Cortes, numerically strong, lost no opportunity to reproach, and even taunt the government for its impotence.

The Azaña administration, however, was firm in its hostility toward extremists of the right, notably the Falangists. The latter, pessimistic about their position within the rightist minority and heartened by fascist accomplishments in Italy and Germany, split with the minority opposition and succeeded in swelling their numbers with dissatisfied army officers and unhappy conservatives.[4] The prime minister addressed the Cortes in May:

> There is one thing which I wish to make clear with regard to the Government's attitude to Fascism. . . . The purpose of the Fascist groups is to attack the fundamental principles of the democratic Republic. Here the Government cannot maintain an attitude of neutrality. In its relations with Fascism, the Government is a belligerent.[5]

With the arrests of Falangists increasing daily, the revolutionary left harassing the Republic by organized strikes and demonstrations, and the administration apparently powerless to deal with either extreme, the political fight carried on with intense bitterness developed into a series of assassinations. As a reprisal for the assassination of a lieutenant in the Assault Guards, a group of his comrades slew José Calvo Sotelo, the militant leader of the Monarchists in the Cortes. The double murder was the Sarajevo of the Spanish Civil War.[6] Five days later, on July 18th, the military uprising in Morocco began, the opening gambit in a long and bloody civil war.

The risks and problems facing those literary intellectuals involved in trying to assign responsibility for any event as complex as the Spanish Civil War seem almost insurmountable. In retrospect, it appears clear that Generals José Sanjurjo, Francisco Franco, and Emilio Mola set in motion a carefully planned attack against the legally constituted government of Spain.[7] Although the German reporters actually charged that the Spanish government began the war, omitting any reference to the military insurrection, Koestler insists that the Nationalist writers and those Insurgent supporters in France, England, and the United States never openly challenged the military pronunciamiento as the immediate cause of the war. (117-19) But the reasons behind the military pronunciamiento are more difficult to discern. The view that the conflict was indigenous to Spain and grew out of a natural antipathy between the right and left factions within the Republic is expounded by Madariaga:

> It was a civil war. Up to now we have had to refer in no way whatever to the international feud which was to take hold of Spain and open wide the wound of her Civil War making her bleed for causes and interests other than her own. . . . But meanwhile let us not lose sight of this all-important fact. The Spanish Civil War began as a purely Spanish affair, grown out of the Spanish soil in the old Spanish way. It was the outcome of the typical combination of the two predominant political passions of the Spaniard: dictatorship and separatism. It came from the scarcity of water and the excess of fire in the Spanish temperament.[8]

Orwell's comment that "the Spanish bourgeoisie saw their chance of crushing the labour movement, and took it, aided by the Nazis and by the forces of reaction all over the world"[9] seems an oversimplification in this context. The more accurate conclusion would be that the right revolted because their traditional privileges and powers were threatened. Those factions on the right, desperately trying to protect their position and property against a liberal government, which to them appeared revolutionary, did what they could to encourage the dissident generals. The landowners anticipating stringent agrarian reforms, the Church already a victim of extremists and expecting its prerogatives to be drastically curtailed, and the army facing a reduction in its officer corps, all joined in a complex operation to preserve what they felt to be their feudal heritage.[10] But before these factors may be reviewed in the context of the Spanish Civil War literature of Malraux, Regler, Hemingway, Orwell, Bernanos, and Koestler, the element of foreign intervention preceding the outbreak of hostilities should be considered.

Madariaga continues with his thesis that neither Germany, Italy, nor Russia could be held directly responsible for the rebellion: "Neither Communism, Russian or otherwise, nor Nazi-Fascism, German or otherwise, had the slightest possibility of provoking a Spanish Civil War in 1936, even if they had tried, which they did not. . . . This does not mean that Russian Communism had been idle, or that German-Italian Fascism had held aloof. Far from it."[11] The theory that the military pronunciamiento was a plot conceived in Berlin or Rome to destroy democracy in Spain as part of a master plan for the takeover of Europe was advanced by several commentators, including the American ambassador to Spain. *The Nazi Conspiracy in Spain,*[12] containing allegedly incriminating Spanish-German documents, was compiled by the communist propagandist, Willi Muenzenberg, to support this contention; these are the same documents which Koestler collected during his second trip to Spain. In his *Spanish Testament,* however, Koestler states that while Hitler and Mussolini were not the instigators of the military uprising, the liaison between German Nazi agents and the reactionary Spanish generals had long preceded the rebellion:

> Ever since the spring both rumours and authentic information had been disseminated in Spain concerning the conspiratorial activities of the Generals. As early as March, General Sanjurjo had been negotiating with Hitler in Berlin; in May and June, in Alicante and Lisbon, the conspirators made their final arrangements with Italian and German agents. (68)

While Italian and German participation in the revolt of the Spanish generals admits of no doubt, it would be erroneous to conclude that the military insurrection was inspired and directed by Mussolini and Hitler in Rome and Berlin, with the Spanish conspirators merely puppets in a game of European power politics.[13]

Insurgent prospects for success, according to Koestler, were given encouragement since the generals and their followers had received the assurance "of the active political and military support of the three European Dictatorships, the Dictatorships of Germany, Italy and Portugal, the exponents of whose political doctrines they felt themselves to be, and under whose tutelage they acted." (74) Bernanos in *Les grands cimetières sous la lune* derides the assertion that the right-wing conspiracy could have been spontaneous:

> Spaniards on the right were anything but imbeciles so let us give them their due. They had a full three and a half months since the elections in March until the pronunciamiento in July to reflect on their course of action. An infant, however, would understand these few months would be insufficient for an organized revolt of the army and civil guard, unless you can conceive that General Franco confined himself to a quick telegram to his allies: "Rebellion tomorrow. Where do you stand? Reply collect, of course." And Mussolini and Hitler were simply notified by telephone the day Calvo Sotelo was assassinated! (138)

The revolt of the generals thus was the consummation of a plot that required months of preparation, that crossed frontiers and spanned the seas, that sought the destruction of the Republic at almost any price.

Koestler in *Spanish Testament* refutes the antithetical theory offered by Nationalist propagandists in England, France, and the United States: that the Insurgent generals were forced to rid Spain of communist conspirators who were plotting the takeover of the Spanish Republic.[14]

> The main emphasis is laid . . . on the assertion that Franco saved Spain from Communism and on the allegation either that the Communists were already masters of Spain before the revolt, or else that they were planning an insurrection and that Franco stole a march on them at the eleventh hour. (119)

He indicates that the Communist Party had neither portfolio nor any appreciable influence in the Spanish governments that were formed between the elections in February and the outbreak of hostilities in July. At this time, far from contemplating an uprising, they advocated and pursued a policy of collaboration with the middle-class liberals of the Azaña regime. In fact, the Communist Party did not join the government until four months after the fighting began:

> Their inclusion in the Government came about not by virtue of any numerical claim, but because the Republic, engaged as it was in a life and death struggle, was forced to form a war cabinet in which all parties had to share the responsibility. It goes with-

> out saying that in the later phases of the Civil War the Communists considerably increased in strength—periods of crisis always lead to a growth of the more extreme parties. This, however, was not the cause, but a consequence of Franco's insurrection. (121)

The Insurgents' contention that the communists were themselves planning an insurrection is not supported by any available facts. If the Communist International had been planning to establish a soviet in Spain at the end of July 1936, as Franco propagandists claim, no evidence to this effect has been uncovered. Koestler's only comment to this formula was, "I fancy that if there were no Communists the dictators would have had to invent them." (127)

On July 17 and 18 the military hierarchy issued their pronunciamiento, convinced of immediate success. The generals expected the revolt to succeed, the Republic to be overthrown, and a military dictatorship established almost immediately. But these military minds, which had never been distinguished for their political acumen or knowledge of mass psychology, failed to anticipate the violent response of the Spanish people to their plans. Not one had foreseen the resistance of the government and the people. The Republic had been rapidly disintegrating while ruling unchallenged, but the attack on it by an armed force served to unify, at least momentarily, those factions that had been quarreling since the February elections.

The Insurgent troops crossed from Morocco to the mainland in Italian aircraft, occupied Algeciras and Cadiz, and then proceeded north to Seville, which fell after a short but bitter fight. Simultaneously, garrisons were revolting successfully in Saragossa and Pamplona. But in six of the seven largest cities in Spain—Barcelona, Madrid, Toledo, Bilbao, Valencia, Malaga—the rebels met unexpected resistance and were defeated. In these major cities, the workers, peasants, and the "small people," incapable of supporting a peacetime democracy, were supplied arms, united, and fought heroically to subdue the military garrisons. Koestler offers a vivid description of the defense:

> The conspirators had counted on a surprise victory; but they had reckoned without their host. For the first time in their existence the workers' organisations, the trade unions, the anti-Fascist Citizens Defence Units, took the initiative, and within a few hours the People's Front had mobilised its masses. Thousands, tens of

> thousands, hundreds of thousands of people, poured into the streets, armed themselves as best they could, and besieged the mutinous troops in their barracks. . . . The peasants organised defence committees in the villages, built barricades, and took up axes and scythes in defence of the Republic. (73)

Regler in *The Great Crusade* praises the peasant patriots who, unarmed, attacked the military garrisons: "They were almost without arms, but they had not hesitated to advance with bare fists upon the Rebels' barracks. More important than life had been liberty. The working people had shown more dignity and devotion to the nation than all Europe had been able to muster in the last few years." (22)

When confronted by military insurrection on the one hand and a general strike on the other, the moderate Republicans had temporized, endeavoring to steer a middle course between the Scylla of surrender to armed rebels and the Charybdis of submission to armed supporters. But events attendant upon the spreading military insurrection forced Azaña to act decisively. He acceded, albeit reluctantly, to the demands of the union leaders that arms be given to the workers and that the defense of the Republic be swiftly organized. The heroic response of the Spanish masses to the military revolt, the early successes of the workers' militias against the rebels in such important centers as Madrid, Barcelona, Bilbao, and Valencia, carried the government along in its wake and was the decisive element in the determination of the government to defend the Republic.

In half of Spain the real power was now in the hands of the trade unions and the political parties in their respective strongholds, and they exerted this power through the defense committees created in the days of the street fighting. The transformation of the military pronunciamiento into a social revolution as control of the major cities found its way into the hands of a revolutionary proletariat is a central theme in the literature of the Spanish Civil War. Bernanos comments on the immediate effects of this transfer of control within Republican Spain:

> Revolutionary terror in Spain presents no new problem. For instance, in Catalonia, it was clear the military and police uprising provoked the slaughter that followed. Imagine that the military governor of Paris suddenly decided to lead an insurrection. And

> supposing the government, in self-defense, unwisely armed the "man in the street." When the sedition was over, by what means then could the government hope to restrain its dangerous allies? (143)

Bernanos' conservative perspective is in sharp contrast to Orwell's radical view on the causes of the disorders which occurred during the early period of the war:

> Franco was not strictly comparable with Hitler or Mussolini. His rising was a military mutiny backed up by the aristocracy and the Church, and in the main, especially at the beginning, it was an attempt not so much to impose Fascism as to restore feudalism. This meant that Franco had against him not only the working class but also various sections of the liberal bourgeoisie—the very people who are the supporters of Fascism when it appears in a more modern form. More important than this was the fact that the Spanish working class did not . . . resist Franco in the name of 'democracy' and the *status quo;* their resistance was accompanied by—one might almost say it consisted of—a definite revolutionary outbreak. (48–49)

In the provinces excesses often resulted in the execution of the upper classes or the bourgeoisie. Thus, in *For Whom the Bell Tolls,* Hemingway describes how the inhabitants of a small pueblo thrashed male members of the middle class with heavy flails and then flung them over a cliff to their death. (103–29) This seizure of land by the peasants, the expropriation of factories and transport by the trade unions, the persecution of the priests, and the accompanying desecration of churches are parts of the disorders which, from completely different perspectives, the Catholic Bernanos and the socialist Orwell attempt to explain.[15]

In broad terms the Republic could count on the loyalty of the huge unionized labor force, the parties of the Popular Front, farm laborers and peasants, moderates who felt obliged to support the government, and a few professors and intellectuals. The ancient strongholds of the right stood solidly behind the Insurgents: landed aristocrats of the south and central provinces, industrialists such as Juan March, the army, and the Church. For the majority of Spaniards, the intense hatreds provoked by the war left no middle ground. Novelist Pío Baroja, however, speaking for an older generation of Spanish writers, such as José Ortega y Gasset, Ramón Pérez de Ayala, Ramón Menéndez Pidal, and Gregorio Marañón, expresses his distaste for extremism: "We sympathize neither with the Right nor with the Left. At the present time (1937) independent people are not acceptable. . . . The lack of compromise, united to the plebian and rancorous background of Spanish politicians, engenders hatred."[16] But for less privileged Spaniards, their decision was less complex; they either fought with the government or against it, a decision which was frequently determined by their geographic location and the politics of their particular province. Bernanos confirms this circumstance in his discussion of the politics of the young men of Majorca: "In Majorca I lived in a tiny seaside village, actually a suburb of Palma. Even in the midst of the Spanish Civil War, I must admit that Porti-Pi was not a very lively place. The young men were fighting on one side or the other, depending on where they found themselves when the war broke out, for Majorcans are great travelers." (352) Hemingway's conscientious Andrés, whose native village was occupied by the Insurgents in the first days of the fighting, reflects on the circumstances which led him to become a partisan fighter: "If our father had not been a Republican both Eladio and I would be soldiers now with the fascists and if one were a soldier with them then there would be no problem. One would obey orders and one would live or die and in the end it would be however it would be. It was easier to live under a regime than to fight it." (367)

During the first months of the war the Insurgents' strongest opposition was provided by the trade unions. Conceivably the spontaneous actions of the socialist and anarchist organizations were the only effective resistance. In the major cities the fascists were defeated by the efforts of the working class combined with those elements of the armed forces which had remained loyal. Orwell suggests that such resistance was possible only by people who were fighting with revolutionary zeal: "It would be hard to believe that the Anarchists and Socialists who were the backbone of the resistance were doing this kind of thing for the preservation of capitalist democracy, which especially in the Anarchist view was no more than a centralized swindling machine." (50)

Thus, in the opening months of the war, it appeared that the military uprising had, in opposition, triggered a social revolution of enormous proportions. The workers had been armed, and after the initial stages they refused to surrender them. Within a matter of days they would be called upon to use them, not as street fighters and revolutionaries, but as soldiers. Although the Republic had been successful in the large cities, its situation remained desperate. Without an army, its only recourse was to arm as rapidly as possible the militia of the Popular Front parties and unions. With no knowledge of warfare and only the poorest of equipment, political and union officers assumed the leadership of the militia, core of the Republican forces. There was no time for adequate training or instruction. The Insurgents, aware that the outcome of their rebellion depended on moving swiftly against the government, had by the end of July plunged deep into the interior of the country. Unless these advances could be halted immediately, the Republic was in danger of defeat within a month. Each militia unit commandeered its own transport and went forth to engage the rebels.

On the home front the revolutionary movement was not uniform although it probably had progressed further in Catalonia than in the rest of Republican Spain. There were areas where the institutions of local government remained almost unchanged and others where they existed side by side with revolutionary committees. In these early stages, the workers in Catalonia and other sections of the country, had the power to overthrow or replace the traditional governing institutions, but with the fascist threat and the need for support of vast sections of the middle class, radical changes were not advisable. Thus, during the first months of the war, Republican Spain remained in a transitional state.

At the fighting front militia unit losses in the first battles were extremely high. The inexperienced volunteers were no match for the Insurgents' trained regulars. This same militia, which had fought heroically in the old guerrilla manner in its own streets and villages, failed to adapt itself to fighting in close units of modern type in the open field. These men who had been heroes in the streets of Madrid found themselves relatively ineffective in modern warfare. One effect of the hurried formation of organized military units was that the militiamen not only lost the opportunity to employ their guerrilla instinct, but also failed in their training as modern combat soldiers.[17] Moreover, superior Insurgent artillery inflicted heavy damage on the makeshift Loyalist forces. In the first two important encounters of the war, at Alto de León and Somosierra Pass, both main approaches to Madrid, each side fought savagely. Rebel equipment proved decisive, however, and the militia was forced to retreat. With the loss of Toledo by the militia, the need "to organize the apocalypse" grew desperate. Without order, the revolutionary apocalypse would hopelessly succumb to its own irrational romantic passion, its inner contradictions and, above all, to the cruel and mechanized destruction of the fascist forces.

Orwell's contention that the Spanish social revolution was suppressed because "the whole world was determined upon preventing revolution in Spain" (51) requires elucidation. To attribute the halting of the movement to a combination of capitalist and communist pressures from outside the country, appears to overlook an extremely important consideration:

> In particular the Communist Party, with Soviet Russia behind it, had thrown its whole weight against the revolution. It was the Communist thesis that revolution at this stage would be fatal and what was to be aimed at in Spain was not workers' control, but bourgeois democracy. It hardly needs pointing out why 'liberal' capitalist opinion took the same line. Foreign capital was heavily invested in Spain. . . . If the revolution went forward there would be no compensation, or very little; if the capitalist republic prevailed, foreign investments would be safe. And since the revolution had got to be crushed, it greatly simplified things to pretend that no revolution had happened. . . . Outside Spain few people grasped that there was a revolution; inside Spain nobody doubted it. (51)

Orwell does not overlook, but rather refuses to concede, that military necessity demanded a unification of all factions in the Republic to win the war, thus compromising or at least temporarily suspending the revolution. The fact that prior to the Barcelona incident in May 1937 such organization proceeded voluntarily would indicate that the workers recognized such necessity. His negative response that "it appeared that the thing demanded by military necessity was the surrender of something that the workers had won for themselves in 1936," (55) minimizes the fact that the chaotic state in the Loyalist zone was an advantage to the fascists.

Orwell rejects the contentions that pressing forward the revolutionary movement would have weakened the Republican defenses, or that the concept of collectivization would have largely alienated both the peasant and the middle classes. He vigorously disputes the need for a strong central government to replace the local committees in order to produce a properly trained and fully militarized army under a unified command. The contention that fragmentary control by workers and the shouting of revolutionary slogans would do little to halt the advancing Insurgents and would actually hinder Republican efficiency is totally rejected by Orwell. Although Orwell expressed a minority opinion, he was supported by Borkenau, who maintained that "if the Government wanted a broad popular rising, a real people's war, which was the one certain way to beat Franco, it must . . . make every effort to bring about a broad peasant movement and submerge Franco in the waves of revolting villages."[18]

Malraux, however, strongly opposed Orwell's general thesis. In the opening portion of *L'espoir,* Puig views the revolution accompanying the outbreak of fighting with an anarchist's mystique:

> For the first time, Puig had the feeling that he was witnessing not a hopeless struggle like that of 1934—like every other he had ever known—but rather a possible victory. Although he had studied Bakunin (perhaps he was the only member of the group who truly understood the theorist), the revolution had always appeared to him as a *Jacquerie.* Faced with a world without hope, exemplary revolts were the most he could ask from anarchism. And so for him each political crisis had resolved itself into a test of personal character and courage. (30–31)

And later, in response to the statement by the communist García that "henceforth, no social change, much less a revolution, can succeed without war; and no war can succeed without technical organization," Magnin, the liberal idealist, replies, "Men do not sacrifice their lives for such concepts as organization and discipline." García is then able to counter, "In our present circumstances, I am less interested in the reasons men have for sacrificing their lives than in the means they have for disposing of their enemies." (104–105)

García continues to emphasize Malraux's central theme: for a final victory the revolution must be compromised in favor of a unified, organized, and disciplined Republican command:

> Apocalyptic ardor demands everything and will not accept delays; but revolution is a slow and laborious process. The danger is that all men are carried away by their concept of the apocalypse and such fervor spells certain defeat, after a relatively short period, for a very simple reason: by its very nature *an apocalypse has no future,* even when it lays claim to one. . . . Our humble task is to *organize the apocalypse.* (107)

And Hemingway's hero Robert Jordan echoes García's words in response to the question, "Are we to win this war and lose the revolution?": "Nay . . . but if we do not win this war there will be no revolution nor any Republic nor any thou nor any me nor anything but the most grand *carajo.*" (285)

Indications that the war would not remain exclusively Spanish became manifest during the first few days of fighting. The generals of the pronunciamiento had not anticipated the vast and bitter resistance on the part of the populace. They had planned a coup d'etat, but were now faced with a civil war in which the mass of the people, the bulk of Spanish industry, the financial resources of the government, and the legitimate authority of the Spanish state were aligned against them. Left to their own resources, they faced inevitable defeat. "But beyond Spain were men of great power who stood ready to succor them and to these the generals turned."[19]

By the end of July, German aircraft, arms, munitions, and other supplies began to reach the Insurgent forces. The rebels were being ferried from Morocco to Andalusia in German Junkers transport planes, complete with Luftwaffe crews, and by this means thousands of fully-armed Legionnaires and Moors arrived at the Seville airport. In this manner the Insurgents were able to bypass the obstacle of the Republican fleet in the Straits of Gibraltar. Koestler summarizes the period immediately following the rebellion:

> Two weeks later the rebels were in possession of a brand-new airfleet of German and Italian planes, manned by German and Italian pilots, mechanics and instructors; Italian tanks were already

> in action at Badajoz; Irun was being bombarded by German heavy artillery. Together with war material, technicians also were pouring into the country, from tank mechanics to General Staff Officers. Italian regular troops landed in Majorca; and by the end of October this largest of the Balearic Islands had become virtually an Italian possession. Week by week the number of foreigners in the rebel army grew. (96)

Fearful that contravention of international law, which forbade furnishing aid to the Insurgents, might create strained international tensions, both Hitler and Mussolini intervened covertly, perhaps hoping that the Insurgents would seize control before their participation could be exposed. Thus, in retrospect, the duplicity of the Axis powers is disclosed; while clandestinely dispatching enormous quantities of aid to the Spanish rebels, both dictators continued to proclaim their strict neutrality in the Spanish conflict. Koestler points out, "It was only bit by bit that the world learned these facts. But Franco and his friends knew, long before they precipitated the insurrection, that they could count on events taking the course they did." (98)

The intervention of fascist Italy and Germany in the Spanish conflict occurred simultaneously, but there were important differences between the Italian and German contributions to the rebel victory. Quantitatively, the Italian military effort in Spain was greater than that of Germany; however, qualitatively, the German military effort was superior to the Italian. The swift efficiency with which the Germans, once they had decided to intervene in the conflict, organized and dispatched assistance to the rebel generals, contrasts sharply with Italian aid which, while not negligible, was committed to the struggle in a hesitant and piecemeal fashion.

The part played by Portugal in these events was not of the magnitude of either Italy or Germany and was collateral to the efforts of the fascist powers in some respects. During the first weeks of the war, Portugal exerted an influence on the course of events in disproportion to the very limited resources and power at its disposal. The response of Portugal throughout the war reflected the pressures and counterpressures of the various European powers to whom the Iberian Peninsula represented an area of strategic importance.

With German, Italian, and Portuguese support for the rebels assuming alarming proportions, it now became apparent that unless equally prompt and commensurate military assistance reached the Loyalists from abroad, their situation would be desperate. The Spanish Republic expected support from peaceful and friendly states in general and from France and Great Britain in particular. Such an expectation was warranted by both the course of Spanish diplomacy with these countries under the Republic, as well as by the requirements and practices of international law relative to rebellion. An armed assault on the duly established government of a state is, by the laws of all nations, an act of treason.[20] When it became evident that the Republic had to contend with a widespread and formidable military rebellion, the Spanish government sought to purchase arms and munitions from friendly foreign powers. Except for detachments of Civil Guards and Assault Guards, most of the poorly-equipped air force, and the virtually autonomous and inadequately armed workers' militia, it had been stripped of military power when the army, almost en masse, deserted to the rebels. This move to acquire war materiel was not only the legitimate exercise of its sovereignty under international law but a desperate effort to counterbalance the military advantage possessed by the Insurgents.

In the first days of the war the Republicans succeeded in obtaining an odd collection of civilian and obsolete military aircraft and various types of arms and supplies from England and France. This was before the Anglo-French announced policy of nonintervention; such procurement of arms and supplies had no relation to their national policies. In addition to negligible arms and supplies, Spain received many expressions of sympathy and moral support and some financial assistance from liberal and radical groups in the Western democracies, some from places as distant as Soviet Russia and Latin America.[21]

But it was France upon whom the Spanish Republic ultimately placed its hopes. Geographical proximity and the fact that France was governed by a Popular Front ideologically analogous to that of Spain raised Loyalist expectations of support. It was appreciated in Madrid that France would be most directly menaced by a fascist victory south of the Pyrenees. Thus Madrid approached the French government within a few days after the uprising in Morocco. The Spanish request produced a sharp division of opinion within the French government. Its decision not to supply arms to the Loyalists was a tragic one; in retrospect, it is now clear that this act forecast the eventual defeat and destruction of the Spanish Republic. Regler's commissar, Albert, bluntly concludes: "I told you, Blum is on vacation and the whole People's Front has swallowed Non-Intervention." (53) As this failure of the democracies to come to the aid of the Republic manifests itself in lost battles for the Loyalists, Albert bitterly remarks:

> Should he really inform this man . . . that the international outlook was even worse than the Spanish? That the Fascist Grand Council had openly and loudly declared its solidarity with Franco? That there was talk of tens of thousands of Italians being sent to Spain? That England had already dispatched a trade delegation to Burgos? That the French Right was demanding a peace proposal that would hand over most of the country and all the mines to Franco? What could be the use of this report of bourgeois cynicism? For matters were no better with the labor organizations. . . . The Revolution is forsaken, the Right is playing blindman's buff, cowardice walks the world. (371–72)

One result of the decision by France, followed by England, to remain neutral and not intervene in the Spanish struggle, was the creation of a situation within Spain extremely favorable to a rapid growth of communist influence. Thus, the rapid proliferation of communist power following the rebellion may be attributed to the refusal of the Western democracies, particularly France, to sell arms and supplies to the Spanish Republic, without which it could could not cope with the fascist threat. This default by the Western democracies created a vacuum which Soviet Russia swiftly and at least partially attempted to fill. The growth of communist power within Loyalist Spain was an inevitable concomitant of the emergence of Soviet Russia as the principal source of war materiel of the Spanish Republic.[22]

What were the decisive factors in determining foreign policy of both the democracies and the fascist states during the Spanish Civil War? In Britain and France the threat of a general European war aroused considerable anxiety and, as an aftermath of the bloodshed and destruction of the First World War, an abiding pacifism prevailed. Moreover, important conservative and Catholic groups in the democracies viewed the Popular Front government in Spain with open hostility, an attitude that was considerably strengthened by reports of revolutionary seizures of property, massacres, looting and burning of churches, and other outrages perpetrated in Republican Spain during the first days of the war.

After the formation of the Nonintervention Agreement in August 1936, to which 27 European nations including Italy, Germany, and Russia pledged support, foreign interference in the Spanish conflict neither ceased nor appreciably diminished. As the flow of war supplies from England and France to Republican Spain was reduced substantially, that from Germany, Italy, and Portugal to the Spanish rebels increased enormously. Meanwhile, from places as far distant as Soviet Russia and Mexico came arms, munitions, and supplies for the embattled Republic. The help that Soviet Russia sent was to expand in volume and importance. Koestler reflects on the nature of the foreign intervention on behalf of the Loyalists and the Insurgents:

> The world learned also, of course, about the French airplanes, Russian tanks and Mexican munitions supplied to the Spanish Government. Some of the reports in this connection were exaggerated, most of them were true. The simple truth is that the Non-Intervention agreement, which was based on the absurd assumption that the legal Government and the leaders of an open rebellion should be treated on equal terms, never really worked on either side. But the help from abroad which the Spanish Government received was only a fraction of what was due it as the legal Government of a sovereign state with the full right to purchase war material—the help from abroad which the rebels received in the preparation and the carrying out of the insurrection, constituted, on the other hand, an open breach of international law, and arbitrary interference in the internal affairs of a sovereign state. (98)

And Regler's volunteer in the International Brigades bitterly laments the failure of the democracies to aid a sister Republic:

> For the Republicans there were no re-enforcements. But across the Strait of Gibraltar more ship loads of Moors were heading for Franco. In Ibiza bigger and better squadrons of Italians were ar-

> riving—for Franco: and the enemy's overheated cannon were replaced by Krupp for Franco. Would it be that way always? (320)

The motives behind the fascist dictators' support of the Burgos regime are not difficult to discern. But their generosity threatened to abrogate much of what it allowed the Nationalists to gain. Besides raiding Spanish mineral deposits to feed burgeoning war industries at home, both Hitler and Mussolini desired strategic Spain to advance their future European ambitions. Nazi Germany saw the opportunity to isolate France by gaining an ally in Spain, and even should Franco demur at becoming embroiled in a European struggle, he would at least make an inhospitable neighbor to the south of France. Mussolini's aspiration centered on achieving hegemony in the Mediterranean. With this objective, Italy occupied Majorca and the strategically valuable seaports of Cadiz and Malaga. In return for military assistance, the Burgos government had to go beyond permitting Hitler and Mussolini to use Spain as a proving ground for war and to exploit her raw materials: it meant offering them a chance to control the western portion of the Mediterranean, from which they might neutralize the British bastion at Gibraltar and harass the French.[23] The communist García in Malraux's *L'espoir* provides a fair analysis of Italy's intentions:

> Mussolini doesn't give a damn about establishing a fascist state in Spain. Moral questions are not related to foreign policy. Mussolini desires a government he can control. . . . I suspect his idea is to gain a foothold on Gibraltar; to be able to convert, automatically, an Anglo-Italian war into a European war by forcing England to operate across the territory of a European ally. British disarmament would have encouraged Mussolini to attack them single-handedly; now that they are rearming, Italian policy must change drastically. (106)

The motives behind Russian intervention in Spain were extremely complex. The fascists and many conservative groups charged that the communists intended to set up a Soviet satellite; the communists in contradiction asserted that they were merely aiding bourgeois democracy in Spain. Neither explanation approached the truth.[24] When it was acknowledged that France and England had decided to subscribe to the Nonintervention Agreement despite the fact that Germany and Italy were brazenly supporting the Insurgents, Stalin agreed to send technicians and materiel to the Loyalists. According to Borkenau, Stalin's decision not to send troops was prompted by fear that Russian force in Spain might effect a "rapprochement between Britain and Germany, and between France and Italy against Russia."[25] If Russia were permitted to furnish the Republic with arms without becoming involved in the struggle herself, it might be possible to allay suspicion by the democracies of her intentions and at the same time reduce the threat of a German attack on Russia by keeping Hitler occupied in Spain. Nazi Germany's ominous rise to power and the accompanying recrudescence of Prussian militarism had led to the signing of the Franco-Soviet Security Pact of 1935. In Spain Stalin might have seen an opportunity to frustrate any plans the dictator had for aggression in the East by involving him in a war of attrition on the Iberian Peninsula. There was even the possibility that England and France might eventually join with Russia in support of the Loyalists. For Stalin, the Spanish Civil War might have been merely a delaying action which provided time to prepare for the eventuality of German aggression.[26]

Robert Jordan, Hemingway's hero, translates this holding action in Spain into a defense of all the democracies:

> But remember this that as long as we can hold them here we keep the fascists tied up. They can't attack any other country until they finish with us and they can never finish with us. If the French help at all, if only they leave the frontier open and if we get planes from America they can never finish with us. Never, if we get anything at all. These people will fight forever if they're well armed. No you must not expect a victory here, not for several years maybe. This is just a holding attack. (432)

And Regler's commissar Albert during the defense of Madrid reiterates this theme:

> There, that very night, the little battle had blazed. There the dam had held, the dam of the International Brigades. And yonder, in that red heart, a hundred thousand children heard in their sleep the rattle of the deadly toys. There, when the uproar died down, a hundred thousand mothers closed their windows, reassured. And far to the rear of the great city, in all the villages and cities

> of Republican Spain, another day has been gained. And still farther away, in all the countries of Europe, people would be saying: "It's holding! The city is holding out! The dam of the International Brigades has been thrown up, and the dam is standing firm." (38)

Such idealism is transformed later in *The Great Crusade* into a cynicism which also finds expression in Malraux's *L'espoir.* The bitter resentment of the democracies' policy of nonintervention in *L'espoir* is expressed by the American journalist Slade in his dispatch to his newspaper:

> Fate is raising her curtain on a dress rehearsal for the coming war. Fellow Americans, I say to you: Down with Europe! Let us discover what it is we want. When a communist addresses an international conference, he bangs his fist on the table. When a fascist addresses an international conference, he puts his feet on the table. When a democrat—American, English, French—addresses an international conference, he scratches his head and asks questions. The fascists come to the aid of the fascists; communists come to the aid of communists and have even assisted the Spanish Republic; but democracies do not come to the aid of democracies. We, the democratic people of the world, believe in everything except ourselves. (329)

The focal point in Regler's novel depicts those French and German refugees fighting for the Loyalists as representative of the thousands of volunteers from all parts of the world who had flocked to Madrid to form the International Brigades. At the same time that Soviet materiel and personnel began arriving in Spain, communist groups in Europe and the United States began recruiting volunteers for the Loyalist cause. A military command was established at Albacete and commenced building an army with, as its nucleus, the volunteers who began arriving in October 1936. The International Brigades were led by experienced revolutionaries, and political commissars filtered through the troops, seeking to "coordinate political and military decisions."[27] The formation of the International Brigades, in addition to raising morale, materially strengthened the Loyalist forces and symbolized the international solidarity, perhaps only on a moral plane, behind the Spanish Republic.

Koestler examines the differences in composition between the international forces on both sides of the Spanish struggle:

> On the one side is the International Brigade, the strength of which, after a year of civil war, is estimated at 15,000. It consists of volunteers from all parts of the world, private individuals actuated by purely personal convictions. There have been men of this kind in Europe ever since the time of Lafayette and of Byron. More than half of the International Brigade consists of political refugees from the Dictator States of Germany, Italy and Austria. The remaining large contingents are made up of Englishmen and Frenchmen who have managed to make their way to Spain despite the veto of their own governments. (98–99)

In sharp contrast are those foreign troops on the side of the Insurgents:

> On the other side are the 8,000 to 10,000 military experts and technicians officially despatched by the Reichswehr and about 100,000 Italian infantry. . . . They form an army of intervention, which is waging war against the Spanish Government—a regular war with the only difference that, in accordance with the new practice in diplomacy, there has been no declaration of war. (99)

Regler notes that the foreign troops on both sides are in Spain illegally, but where casualty lists of the fascists can be published by the Italian government and their deeds officially glorified by Mussolini, those of the volunteers of the International Brigades remain unreported:

> By the way, how do they find out whether we have relatives? Can they even report such deaths outside? Are not all the volunteers here illegally anyway. A weird thought. They could no longer say openly that they were willing to die for their ideas. They were thrown in here, cut off, soldiers for good or ill, that and nothing more. (41)

Regler concludes: "No pride. No romanticism. And ask yourself quite simply: Is it worth it? Isn't Europe bleeding her best men to death here?" (85)

The warm response given the International Brigades after their defense of Madrid was not a unanimous expression of the Spanish reaction to the internationalization of their struggle. Certain qualities in the Spanish character caused many of them to regard all outside intervention as unwelcome, to resent foreign troops of any nationality on Spanish soil, and to look forward to the time when Spain might once again be permitted to settle her own problems. Koestler, while a prisoner in Nationalist Spain, records one aspect of this sentiment: "The grandmother said that it was foreigners who were to blame for the whole tragedy; on the other side Russians, and on this side the Germans and Italians." (259–60) And Hemingway's Pablo, the shrewd Spanish peasant, reflects on the motives behind foreign intervention: "This foreigner comes here to do a thing for the good of the foreigners. For his good we must be sacrificed." (54) Orwell, in contrast, encountered no hostility during the time spent in Catalonia:

> A Spaniard's generosity, in the ordinary sense of the word, is at times almost embarrassing. . . . And beyond this there is generosity in a deeper sense, a real largeness of spirit, which I have met with again and again in the most unpromising circumstances. Some of the journalists and other foreigners who traveled in Spain during the war have declared that in secret the Spaniards were bitterly jealous of foreign aid. All I can say is that I never observed anything of the kind. (12)

And, at the end of *Homage to Catalonia,* Orwell himself has developed a resentment of foreign intervention in the Spanish struggle. He speaks affectionately of friends among the Spanish militia units and bids them farewell with the wish: "Most of them, I hope [are] still safe and sound. Good luck to them all; I hope they win their war and drive all the foreigners out of Spain, Germans, Russians and Italians alike." (230)

The view of the Spanish Civil War in a European and world context as a prelude to World War II is a prevalent theme in the literature of most novelists treating the conflict. Even those works published early in the Spanish struggle, perhaps because of the international perspective of their authors, contain references to the approaching holocaust and the position of the Spanish war leading up to it. Koestler focuses on the aerial bombardment of Madrid and notes: "The capital of Spain served, so to speak, as an experiment in vivisection for the next war." (164) Malraux's Magnin, the leader of the foreign pilots flying for the Republic, after observing that the German aircraft had not measured up to expectations, remarks:

> They could not have held their own against modern French aircraft, nor against Russian aviation. But now all that would be changed; the bloody military maneuvers had tragically begun here. For two years Europe had been frightened by the constant menace of a war which Hitler had not been equipped to wage. (99–100)

Koestler points out that the dictatorships were using Spain, not only as a military rehearsal, but also in an attempt to perfect their propaganda techniques for the next war:

> The Spanish War is for the dictatorships in many respects a dress rehearsal for the world war for which it is preparing the way; it is so, alas, in the matter of propaganda. The laying of the responsibility for the Civil War at the door of their opponents, the designation of the war of aggression as a retaliatory measure, the representing of acts of arson as the extinguishing of fires, of declarations of war as offers of peace—this is how the coming world war is being prepared. (146)

And a foreign volunteer in *The Great Crusade* reflects: "It's begun already . . . and it won't stop until they are all at war, all Europe." (248)

Bernanos' comments on the Spanish Civil War in a European context deserve special attention because not only is his analysis extremely incisive, but his final statement on the role Spain will play in the global war is prophetic. In relation to modern European history, Bernanos views the Spanish struggle as one phase in a movement toward a monstrous holocaust:

> Europe is saturated with wars, but even the biggest fool is beginning to realize that all these conflicts are merely a pretext and alibi for the one great war which is not far off. And this coming absolute war will be neither political nor social nor religious in the strict sense of the word; rather it will be the result of the natural condition of human society whose extraordinary complexity bears no relation to the primitive emotions—vanity, greed, envy—which presently govern it. (215)

The adventure of the generals of the pronunciamiento will eventually prove costly for Spain, but at the same time Bernanos believes it will render her incapable of taking part in an even more horrifying struggle:

> This adventure by the generals will have cost a million lives; certainly an enormous sacrifice. But it may be worth it in order to disqualify Spain from taking part in any sort of "crusade" for a long time to come. Spain will continue to dwell behind her mountains, as in the past, on the fringe of Europe, and for her the purge is over. (230–31)

Hemingway, Malraux, Regler, Koestler, Orwell, and Bernanos, in their novels and personal narratives, display a keen understanding of the international complications of the Spanish Civil War. Their knowledge of the European rivalries and the political machinations of the great powers in exploiting one side or the other is apparent in their writing. And each writer properly deplores the fact that it was necessary to further German, Italian, and Russian political ambitions on Spanish soil and, in the main, with Spanish blood. The strategic position and mineral wealth of Spain had become an important factor in the European power-struggle and was rendered even more significant beyond the Pyrenees by the thrust and direction of Spanish politics. Yet, while evidence exists of the intrigues and machinations of foreign powers in Spain even prior to the outbreak of hostilities, nevertheless historians agree that the immediate cause of the war was the result of tensions within the country, specifically the conflict between a feudal ruling class and a section of reformers who drew their principal support from middle-class liberalism, organized labor, and the distress of an impoverished, landless peasantry. The limited extent to which these novelists understood the history of the social and economic conditions in Spain during the period preceding the Spanish Civil War contrasts sharply with their extensive knowledge of international politics.

The origin of the Spanish conflict cannot be attributed to either foreign intervention or influence. The roots are firmly planted in Spanish history, and during the 1930s were manifest in the social problems within the country. In examining social conditions in Spain, it is important to stress the distinction between the upper and middle classes and the peasants and workers. The former, which constituted approximately one-fifth of the population, voted, were knowledgeable concerning politics, held government positions, and generally operated the national agencies; the latter were peasants and workers who ordinarily were unconcerned with politics, often were illiterate, and primarily interested in the matter of survival. Between these two completely different levels, but failing to serve as a buffer, were the small trades people and artisans.[28] While the two classes lived side by side in towns and villages, they lacked any mutual interests. The need of education and the deficiencies of the economic structure prevented any upward movement by the peasants and workers. It is not difficult to understand why Spanish politics appeared futile and of little consequence to the lower classes. So convinced were the workers and the peasant class that the government and its laws were not their concern, and that politicians existed for their own self-interest, that they consistently refused to consider suggestions by Republican candidates for the improvement of their own conditions. Madariaga attributes this failure to participate in social projects as an indication of Spanish individuality:

> The instinct for preserving his own liberty makes him eschew all forms of social cooperation, since all collective work tends to enslave the individual and to reduce him to the status of a piece of machinery. His anti-cooperative instinct comes to reinforce his tendency to dwell on the two poles of his psychology—man and the universe—leaving uncultivated the middle stretches in which social and political communities lie.[29]

Thus the Spanish pueblo had a totally different character from any other body of peasants or laborers in Europe. At regular intervals in the course of its history, whenever its deepest interests were threatened, it successfully repulsed the threat. However, it is to be noted that all the popular movements had the object not of redressing their grievances but simply the expulsion of a foreign body which had provoked and irritated them. The lower classes exhibited a fanaticism, a capacity for self-sacrifice, and a spontaneity of action, but always in a narrow, local, and prejudiced sense, without constructive efforts on a wide scale.

The enthusiasm of the Spanish people contrasts sharply with the inertia of the Spanish upper classes to take affirmative action regarding both national and international matters. Even the Spanish aristocracy recognized the pueblo as the great repository of the virtues of the race and the source of all that was sane and healthy in the country. Among the Spanish upper classes were to be found such qualities as decay, corruption, political incapacity, as well as a complete lack of creative talent. The Spanish middle class suffered from a spiritless sense of inferiority, of superficiality, and inadequacy. They had lost faith in themselves and in their religion. Under an air of assumed self-confidence, they nevertheless felt themselves excluded from the true sources of life in their country.

On the part of the pueblo in the twentieth century there had been a gradual transfer of allegiance from the Church to revolutionary ideologies hostile to it. The effect of these new social theories, particularly socialism and anarchism, was to make the workers and peasants regard the factory owners and landlords as aliens who interfered with their ambitions and prevented their free development. To reach such a conclusion required little convincing argument if one understood the gross and unmitigated parasitism of the Spanish upper classes. The incurable selfishness of the Spanish ruling classes and their governments, and the ignorance of the traditionalist parties who seemed to have no idea of the conditions under which the Spanish peasants and workers actually existed, prevented the introduction of social reform long before the formation of the Republic.[30]

It is necessary to emphasize that the most important single cause of the Spanish Civil War was the refusal of the Spanish ruling classes to institute social reform programs, particularly of an agrarian nature. The ruling classes and the Church should have realized that their obstinacy was at complete variance with the times and conditions in the other European countries. "But," according to Brenan, "Spain is a peninsula, cut off from the rest of Europe, psychologically and climatically at variance with its neighbors, and this isolation has produced among certain classes an obstinacy and resistance to change which neither facts nor arguments have any effect upon."[31] In this situation the ruling classes, either incapable of, or refusing to permit social reform, undertook a policy of economic and military repression to maintain order and protect and preserve their prerogatives.

The closed economic system in Spain created a feeling of hopelessness on the part of the peasant and the industrial worker, who usually was a former peasant or the son of a peasant who had migrated to the city. Such conditions were conducive to revolutionary experiments.[32] These in turn led to further repression in the form of counterrevolutionary measures. Bernanos addresses a protest to the injustice of the ruling classes:

> Human society is full of contradictions that will never be resolved. Revolution is always initiated by the poor, though the poor seldom gain much advantage from it. The counterrevolution inevitably follows, waged by a class of people often with real grievances but more so because they see their own position threatened and are desperate. The result is a condition in which despair is infectious. Society assimilates the poor contentedly enough, so long as it can eliminate potential threats by accommodating them either in hospitals or prisons. When the proportion of malcontents becomes dangerously increased, the upper classes then summon their police officials who in turn throw open the cemeteries. (249–50)

The instrument of repression is the army, an organization in Spain whose essential function was not national defense but, rather, the maintenance of a social order. It should not be assumed that the army was the tool of the aristocracy, as Malraux implies in *L'espoir:*

> What is referred to as a comic-opera army is actually an army intending to fight a civil war. In the Spanish Army there is an officer for every half dozen men. Do you truly believe that the army budget is meant to pay for war? Actually it is to pay the officers —who belong to the propertied class and serve its interests—and to buy automatic weapons quite inadequate for real warfare (too much goes into graft) but quite adequate to police the country. (81)

Its frequent intervention into the political life of Spain had made of the Spanish army, essentially the officer cadres, a quasipolitical party. Because of the inability of any single political group to obtain sufficient support to perpetuate itself in office, the military, by no means a caste, assumed a dominant role in the political life of the nation. Emulating the individual political factions, they gave little thought to foreign affairs and were intent on preserving the status quo, the administration and enjoyment of a disproportionate amount of the budget.[33]

With the institution of the Republic in 1931, the landed aristocrats, the factory owners, the military, and the Church (which will be discussed separately), all recognized the possibility of nonviolent revolution in which they would be stripped of their traditional privileges. Whether these threats were more imaginary than real, in retrospect it appears no longer important. From 1931 to 1936, each special interest group in its own way did what it could to sabotage the efforts of the Republic at social reform.

The land question was most acute in Andalusia and Estremadura where there were numerically few landlords. These aristocrats owned huge estates which were surrounded by a landless proletariat whose very subsistence depended on the day-to-day caprices of the landlord stewards. Koestler describes the plight of the landless laborers in areas where approximately 1 per cent of the total rural population controlled over half the cultivable land:

> The millions of small peasants and agricultural workers live in abject poverty and misery. . . . Agricultural labourers possessed neither rights nor means of protecting their interests. In the village the only law, the only authority, was the despotic rule of the "cacique," the local boss, backed up by the rifles of the Civil Guard. Moreover, work was available only on a hundred to two hundred days in the year. Spanish agricultural labourers have always lived under the threat of starvation. For centuries their unspeakably wretched condition has been the most urgent social problem of the Iberian Peninsula. (42–43)

This was the foremost evil which the Republic set out to remedy with its agrarian reform program. After spending almost two years studying the land and taking a census of the workers, a law was passed which provided for the expropriation of large estates. Feudal estates would be taken without compensation; other lands would be paid for by capitalizing the farm income shown on the tax registers. The lands secured would remain the property of the state, which would distribute it either to individual farmers or to collective farming associations. This reform program was on the whole well-intentioned and statesmanlike, but progressed slowly, owing to the inefficiency of the civil service which was to administer it.[34]

The Republic approached the labor problem, which was not nearly as acute as the agricultural situation, with much idealism. Into the constitution they drafted Article 46, which read:

> Work, in its several forms, is a social duty and will enjoy the protection of the law. The Republic will guarantee to every worker the necessary conditions for a dignified existence. Its social legislation will regulate: cases of sickness, accident, unemployment, old age, infirmity and life insurance; the labor of women and children, and in particular, the protection of motherhood; the working day and minimum and family wages; yearly paid vacations; the conditions of Spanish workers abroad; cooperative institutions; the economic-juridical relations among the several factors which make up production; the participation of the workers in the management, administration and profits of businesses, and all that concerns the welfare of the workers.

No attempt was made to confront the problem of Spain's economy as an organic whole, and without such a confrontation the criteria contained in Article 46 were doomed to failure. Madariaga attributes much of the failure to an overambitious program instituted by the socialists, who were now in office, to impress the syndicalists that the political-democratic way was the superior way for labor to triumph.[35]

The Republican threat to the army consisted in rescinding the law which permitted the military courts to invade the sphere of strictly civil life. It also abolished all ranks above that of division general, and gave all officers the choice of swearing allegiance to the Republic or resigning, generously, with full pay. Finally, the Republic attempted to convert the army, through proper training and equipment, into an efficient weapon of defense rather than as an active political force. Unfortunately, the majority of officers who chose to retire on full pay made use of their leisure time to conspire against the Republic.

The new Republic, facing so many difficult problems, was also forced to contend with opposition in open parliamentary civil war and with an uninterrupted series of labor strikes, all of a political and revolutionary nature, which paralyzed business life and threw many of the major cities into bloody turmoil. In opposition to the agrarian reform, the landed aristocracy successfully sabotaged the already lagging efforts of the administration. Koestler describes the methods employed:

> The offensive on the part of the reactionaries began with a highly organized plan of sabotage on the part of the big landowners in

> the spring of 1933. All of a sudden there was no more work to be had on the land. True, the agricultural labourer had the right to demand an eight-hour day and a wage of eight pesetas, but work he could not find. The landowners persisted in this tacit lock-out: they let their land lie fallow, and turned it over to pasturage; where formerly two hundred labourers had been employed, two or three shepherds now sufficed. The position rapidly worsened; this policy of blackmail on the part of the governing caste succeeded in defeating almost every one of the Government's paper reforms. Expectation turned to disappointment; and in the elections of the autumn of 1933 the Right scored a victory. (52)

In the interim the forces of the right had united behind Gil Robles' C.E.D.A., while factionalism completely devastated the left. In the elections held during the winter of 1933, the left was routed.

With the right-wing parties now in power, the labor strikes continued, but concessions were made to the army and Church which secured their support. The agrarian reform program was suspended and, in terms of the land worker's family, the political change proved disastrous.[36] The Spanish landlords had forgotten nothing and learned nothing, and their callous and shortsighted policy now assumed a vindictiveness for the insults and injuries received when the left had been in power. Koestler describes the plight of the peasant under the new regime:

> The unrestrained tyranny of the feudal aristocracy was driving the Spanish economic system once more towards ruin. Whilst in most European countries a gradual recovery after the slump was discernible between 1933 and 1935, the curve of unemployment in Spain mounted steadily, reaching its peak in 1935. Meanwhile Spain became the country with the highest duties on consumers' goods in Europe. The masses had returned to their old state of unspeakable misery and suffering. (64)

The agricultural worker saw his wages drop to famine level, the security of his employment disappear, and his hope for land vanish. These frustrations, confined to the south and southeast of Spain, were one of the most potent causes of the civil war which two years later was to tear the nation asunder.

The inability and possible lack of desire on the part of the ruling classes to alleviate these social problems are soundly denounced by Bernanos, and in so doing, he denounces the Church for condoning these practices:

> The misery in Spain is growing and, as if related, the military budget is also increasing; such a coincidence is extremely disturbing. After all, whether we wipe out the superfluous poor with guns, or destroy entire harvests by fire, or throw tons of milk into the river, these are all, in essence, identical ways of meeting the situation. If our materialistic society demanded that we sanction the extermination of the unemployed, we should certainly refuse. But such a measure would be less barbarous than our constant refusal to alleviate the growth of the indigent population—that is, the anti-social elements which cannot be absorbed. For then we are forced into the inevitable bloody repressions, which in turn fill the cemeteries, empty the treasury, and are invariably the cause of economic crises, thus begetting new poor. And so the vicious cycle continues. (251–52)

Meanwhile the revolutionary ferment spread from the countryside into the cities. The state of the peasants in the mid-1930s had reached limits which a less volatile people could not endure. As a consequence the highly volatile temperament of the Spanish masses responded in violent fashion to these wretched conditions. The labor unions, particularly those affiliated with the Socialist Party, felt a sense of betrayal by the Republic and did not conceal their discontent. Threats and counterthreats and the discovery of caches of arms in the possession of right-wing and left-wing groups further aggravated the situation. In October 1934, a general strike was called which paralyzed the major cities of Spain. The strike was quickly suppressed in most of the cities, but in Madrid and Barcelona there was some bloodshed, and in Oviedo the repression of the Asturian miners, with the aid of Moors and Legionnaires, became a black page in Spain's history.

In order to protect themselves from the social revolution instigated by the lower classes, the Spanish bourgeoisie and aristocracy invoked their right of lawful defense. The moral question of such a defense is raised by Bernanos and is addressed to the Church:

> This right seems to be reserved more and more for a particular class of citizens and held to be inseparable from their property rights. Thus a man may fairly defend his house by shooting, but

> another man may not defend his wage by the same methods, even if he possess nothing else. Greater harmony would be achieved—considering the many discourses in the past by the Church on the wretched condition of the Spanish peasants and workers, the selfishness of the wealthy, and the anti-social nature of the monarchy—if this same Church restrained itself from proclaiming to the world that the peasants and workers were responsible for the diverse misfortunes now befalling Spain. These are the same men who suffered most from those deprivations which the Church had previously spent its time lamenting. (261)

At the same time Bernanos indicates that the social changes desired by the suffering peasant classes cannot be effected through the intervention of the Spanish courts. The law courts concern themselves with the injustices to the upper classes, but should the peasant seek redress for social wrongs inflicted on him, he is unable to obtain the guidance and protection of these same courts, and hence is compelled to resort to violence. Bernanos comments on the difficulty of the peasant in obtaining social justice in Spain:

> An obligation to be just is imposed on the masters and a duty of resignation is imposed on the slaves. But when a slave takes to shooting, how can he be considered as resigned? The injustice of the master is a matter for assessment and it cannot be denied that the injustice of a master is often more costly to society than the violent rebellion of the slave. But even were the damages equal, the penalties would be very different. The injustice of the master is referred to the law courts, but the rebellion of the slave is the province of the civil guard. And unfortunately there is no appeal from the verdict of a machine-gun. (255)

The period from October 1934, when the left tried to seize power by violent methods and failed, until February 1936, when they sought to seize power by democratic means and succeeded, was one in which the right governed unopposed. The atmosphere was one of petty vindictiveness in politics, harsh repression, particularly in the Asturias, and exploitation of the rebellion to gain the maximum political advantages for the right. Some of these political advantages consisted in the repeal of many of the social reforms enacted by the Republic during the 1931–1933 period.

The events which followed the 1936 elections have been

recounted, and the military revolt which occurred that summer found the Popular Front at least temporarily united against the forces of reaction. The difference in attitudes within the Popular Front can perhaps best be expressed by the thoughts of two characters in the novels of the war. The anarchists were one extreme, exemplified in *L'espoir* by Malraux's Negus, whose philosophy demanded that the country be freed from all political authority. The natural explanation of the Spanish peasants' receptivity to such a philosophy is simply that the peasant has always been the victim of the worst forms of authority. As Negus faces the military officers who had just revolted in July 1936, he expresses all the frustrations experienced by the peasant in his lifetime:

> This was not the first time he had seen these officers. They were the men who had interned thirty thousand captives in the Asturias, the men who had been so ruthless in 1933 at Saragossa, who had schemed the repression of the agrarian revolt; thanks to whom the confiscation of the Jesuits' wealth, ordered for the sixth time in a century, had remained a dead issue. And these were the men who had dispossessed Negus' parents from the vineyards which they had planted and cultivated for decades. (21–22)

In contrast to Negus, about to kill these same officers who symbolized for him the decades of oppression, Hemingway's noble peasant, the Republican Anselmo, offers a more civilized approach to the social revolution sweeping Spain:

> I would not kill even a Bishop. I would not kill a proprietor of any kind. I would make them work each day as we have worked in the fields and as we work in the mountains with the timber, all of the rest of their lives. So they would see what man is born to. That they should sleep where we sleep. That they should eat as we eat. But above all that they should work. Thus they would learn. (41)

To Hemingway, Malraux, Regler, Orwell, Koestler, and Bernanos, the Spanish Civil War exerted a strong attraction, both for humanistic and ideolgical reasons. Although the Spanish struggle possessed contemporary interest and importance, in the rest of Europe and the United States little of this fundamental attraction was grounded on a knowledge of the country's social structure and the events leading to the war. Even Bernanos, who had lived in Majorca for two years preceding the military pronunciamiento, and Hemingway, who had been a frequent visitor to Spain, displayed only a minimal knowledge of the indigenous social causes of the war. Their failure to even mention the separatism and desire for regional autonomy which divided Spain and contributed to the failure of the Spanish Republic to gain the united support of the people is evidence of this lack of knowledge on the part of the writers. To be sure, the Spanish struggle inspired them and they were concerned with the topical aspects of the conflict: the perils of nonintervention, the military offensives, the capture of a particular town or sector and, above all, the dangers of a fascist victory. But, being essentially novelists and not contemporary historians, an insight into Spain's history and social problems was often lacking in their work. Of the six novelists, only Koestler displays significant understanding of Spain's social structure and the problems inherent in it.

Perhaps this disregard for details of a historical and sociological nature, except in the case of Koestler's *Spanish Testament,* is to the novelist's advantage. Those writers who expounded too lengthily and enthusiastically on the social and economic causes of the Spanish struggle produced historical tracts which often left untouched, or developed only superficially, the deeper meanings involved in the conflict. In contrast, in other cases the violence and excitement of the immediacy of the war served to obscure the more universal issues. The major novelists, however, strove to achieve a balance between descriptions of the immediate effects of the conflict, at the same time providing some insight into the basic issues and the universal significance emerging from the Spanish struggle.

From the earlier quotations of these writers, it is clear that they did not choose to completely ignore the social and economic aspects of the Spanish struggle, nor did they fail to recreate the presence of the war in Spain. But these purposes were often secondary to the author's involvement with the universal themes suggested by the struggle of the Spanish people: the examination of the human predicament, the hopeless confusion of elemental man caught up in the chaos of war, the fraternity of men involved in a meaningful cause, the potential for good and evil within man, the emergence of man as a transcendental figure during the conflict.

One subject, however, that the novelists did not choose to relegate to a secondary position in their writing about this most political of wars was the factionalism which divided the Loyalists. Orwell states the case for the novelists:

> At the beginning I had ignored the political side of the war, and it was only about this time that it began to force itself upon my attention. . . . But at the same time it would be quite impossible to write about the Spanish war from a purely military angle. It was above all things a political war. No event in it, at any rate during the first year, is intelligible unless one has some grasp of the inter-party struggle that was going on behind the Government lines. (46)

To a world unaware of the internecine conflict between the Spanish right and left which had precipitated the war, the Spanish struggle seemed less concerned with the political issues indigenous to Spain than with international problems. If the war appeared to many less knowledgeable foreigners to be involved with issues outside the country, to many Spaniards it seemed a continuation of a long and tragic domestic struggle among Spain's political parties. This fact was evident in the political composition of the belligerents. The rebel side was first and foremost a military dictatorship. Although they accepted support from the Falange and right-wing parties that had been active during the Republic, the generals never relinquished their power nor chose to share it with politicians. But the division between the right and left merely obscured the fact that within the opposing factions were even further divisions, particularly on the side of the left. According to Madariaga, in a rather cynical cataloguing of factions:

> From that moment on the Civil War became a duel between a fairly well-held army and state under military discipline and an ill-assorted, loose group of tribes known as the UGT, the FAI, the POUM, the PSUC, the Communist Party, the Generalitat, Euzkadi, and several others, each pulling its way. This ill-assorted crowd could by no means be described as an alliance. They lived in a constant state of civil war, by which no mere metaphor is intended, for it is a matter-of-fact description of reality, with its battles and casualties and plans of campaign. The very aim of

> these tribes was not—as one might have thought—to win the war against the Rebels. For most of them it was to achieve a proletarian revolution, though not the same, for each tribe had a revolution of its own to achieve and one wholly incompatible with that of its adversaries; while others of these tribes, like the Catalans or the Basques, dreamed of achieving their own political statehood under cover of war.[37]

In the opening months of the war, President Azaña, in an effort to control various political factions which threatened to destroy the unity of the Popular Front—largely revolutionary socialists and anarchists—was forced to take extreme measures. Azaña deliberately appointed Largo Caballero, leader of the Socialist Party and one of the chief instigators of the unrest, to the post of prime minister. A cabinet was formed in September 1936, with moderate as well as revolutionary elements, as Azaña had planned; the Caballero Cabinet contained a majority of six socialists and two communists. It was still some time before the anarchists would consent to cooperate with the center-left regime. The exaggerated optimism of Malraux's Puig regarding a united antifascist front in the opening days of the fighting appears a premature miscalculation:

> Around Puig were grouped the standards of all the left-wing parties with thousands of men behind them. For the first time, liberals, members of the U.G.T. and C.N.T., anarchists, republicans, syndicalists and socialists joined forces in an attack on their common enemy with his machine guns. For the first time the anarchists had voted, so as to ensure liberation of the Asturian prisoners. It was the blood of the Asturians which brought about this unity of political forces in Barcelona, quickening Puig's hope that at last the black-and-red banner, so long kept undercover, would now unfurl triumphantly. (27)

Orwell provides an explanation of the basic weakness in Puig's conception of the Popular Front. But it must be remembered that this is a politically disillusioned and cynical Orwell who is reflecting in retrospect:

> The whole process is easy to understand if one remembers that it proceeds from the temporary alliance that Fascism, in certain forms, forces upon the bourgeois and the worker. This alliance, known as the Popular Front, is in essential an alliance of enemies,

and it seems probable that it must always end by one partner swallowing the other. (56)

The Nationalists had no such problems because, although there was sharp disagreement in basic tenets among various factions, particularly the Falangists and the Carlists within the Burgos government, the might of the army served as a cohesive force which neither tolerated ideological disagreements nor permitted any form of dissension to interfere with its military functions. Bernanos comments rather sarcastically on the unity of the dissimilar interests within the Nationalist camp:

> Anarchists, communists, socialists, radicals and parliamentarians, from Prieto to Robles—a strange melange, these reds of Spain. But the whites are no less incomprehensible. Is it possible that the millionaire Juan March—enriched, as every Spaniard knows, by fraud and embezzlement, imprisoned under the Monarchy and now a leading supporter of the rebels—shares the same political and social aims as the Falange leaders, who publicly promised to have him executed in 1936? And what in the world can the peasants of Fal Conde have in common with the semi-Jewish aristocrats in the Nationalist camp? (287–88)

In the rapidly reorganizing Popular Front, the Spanish communists, although they represented an expanded but certainly far from large electorate, skillfully sought to exploit the power they derived by virtue of Russian aid. With Russia the only major nation supporting the Republic, the Spanish Communist Party grew from an unimpressive total of 1,000 members in 1931 to a total of 249,000 in March 1937, and from a minority faction with almost no voice in the government, to the role of a major decision-making force, although not distinguishing itself in that role. The communists, who by now included in their number the Soviet military cadre and members of the Comintern working in close collaboration, utilized the fact of Soviet aid as a lever to exert pressure on the Republic to grant their demands, and even ventured to decrease or completely discontinue supplies when the government proved intractable.[38]

The communists were able to pressure Azaña into disbanding the workers' militias in favor of a People's Army, which they intended to control and for which the communist-organized International Brigades would serve as a model. But the prospect of integrating all divergent groups into a People's Army was especially distasteful to the anarchists, who since the beginning of the war had opposed the communists' "reactionary" view that the defeat of fascism must precede the social revolution. Orwell indicates the factionalism thus dividing the Popular Front:

> So, roughly speaking, the alignment of forces was this. On the one side the C.N.T.-F.A.I., the P.O.U.M., and a section of the Socialists, standing for workers' control: on the other side the Right-wing Socialists, Liberals, and Communists, standing for centralized government and a militarized army. (62)

This issue, the need for military discipline and organization demanded by the communists, in opposition to the desire for an admittedly chaotic version of libertarianism advocated by the anarchists, often overshadowed the basic conflict between democracy and fascism in the literature of such writers as Orwell and Malraux. Malraux expresses the problem involved by the failure of the various factions within the Popular Front to cooperate and also provides an insight into the Spanish character:

> Rather than enter into political debates, the time would have been much better utilized in establishing some basis for cooperation among the various factions, thus enabling them to implement the orders of the Government by joint action—the communists, C.N.T., F.A.I. and the U.G.T.! Strange, the weakness people have for debating about everything and anything rather than providing a practical line of action to be followed, even at the moment when their lives depend on the line of action chosen. (183–84)

Orwell is probably the leading spokesman in defense of the anarchist cause, but Malraux, never one to conform to a communist line, presents fairly the anarchists' contentions. Anarchists, notably in Catalonia, long the center of political extremism, had begun an intensive program of collectivism, which they feared would collapse if it did not function concurrently with the war against Franco.[39] Orwell indicates the basis for their fear:

> The country was in a transitional state that was capable either of developing in the direction of Socialism or of reverting to an ordinary capitalist republic. The peasants had won most of the land,

and they were likely to keep it, unless Franco won; all large industries had been collectivized, but whether they remained collectivized, or whether capitalism was reintroduced, would depend finally upon which group gained control. (52)

Both the P.O.U.M. and the anarchists agreed that the war and the revolution were inseparable.[40] Orwell advances this reasoning although it is doubtful that under either group was it ever as clearly enunciated:

> It is nonsense to talk of opposing fascism by any bourgeois "democracy." Bourgeois "democracy" is only another name for capitalism, and so is Fascism; to fight against Fascism on behalf of "democracy" is to fight against one form of capitalism on behalf of a second which is liable to turn into the first at any moment. The only real alternative to Fascism is workers' control. If you set up any less goal than this, you will either hand the victory to Franco, or, at best, let in Fascism by the back door. Meanwhile the workers must cling to every scrap of what they have won; if they yield anything to the semi-bourgeois Government they can depend upon being cheated. The workers' militias and police-forces must be preserved in their present form and every effort to "bourgeoisify" them must be resisted. If the workers do not control the armed forces, the armed forces will control the workers. The war and the revolution are inseparable. (60–61)

Similarly, from the anarchists' viewpoint, the communists appeared to have abandoned the principles of revolution and to have adopted those of right-wing reactionaries, establishing them as dangerous as the fascists. Malraux's Negus offers an emotional appeal in a debate with the communist García over revolutionary tactics:

> It isn't very easy for men to join together. There is not much courage left in the world, and it is courage that gets things done. Let's not fool ourselves! When men are ready to sacrifice themselves for something, they stand out from the rest. But such men have no use for "dialectics" or bureaucratic red tape; delegates are all right, but bureaucrats never! Nor an army to defeat an army, inequality to eradicate inequality, or playing the bourgeois game. What we desire is to live the way men ought to live, here and now; or else we are ready to die. If we fail, that's the end of it. No return ticket for me! (176)

Negus concludes his case against Marxist dialectics and enforced discipline in the same vein: "And I suppose tomorrow there will be free shaves for everyone. . . . Nonsense! Political parties are made for men, not men for parties. We are not attempting to establish a state or a church or an army. Just free men." (178)

Suspicion of the communists' motives in aiding the Spanish Republic is raised by Orwell. The communists' desire to unite with the bourgeois elements in fighting the war, according to Orwell, may be attributed to Russian foreign policy at that moment. In order for Russia to remain allied with France in the face of the German threat, the Spanish Loyalists were forced to abandon any hope of a radical social revolution and were to channel their energies on a nonrevolutionary course. "The clue to the behaviour of the Communist Party in any country," theorizes Orwell, "is the military relation of that country, actual or potential, toward the U.S.S.R." (57) In Spain the communist policy was undoubtedly influenced by the fact that France, Russia's ally, would strongly object to a radically-oriented neighbor and would never condone the possible liberation of Spanish Morocco, thus threatening France's African colonial holdings.

The idea that communists no longer desired to propagate a revolutionary line and, in fact, had lost faith in their cause is expressed by Negus:

> We are anything but Christians! But your group is evolving into a bunch of priests. I do not say that communism has become a religion, but for you being a revolutionary now means merely being more clever than anyone else. Not so for Bakunin or Kropotkin—not at all! You have become immersed in the party, in its discipline, its plotting, its scheming. If one is not a member of your order, he cannot expect a fair deal, a scrap of decency, or even loyalty while sharing in the same fight. (177)

Beneath the communist campaign for "order and discipline," the anarchists thought they detected the first step toward totalitarian regimentation.

The case for the communists is only partially hinted at by Hemingway's young idealist, Robert Jordan:

> He was under Communist discipline for the duration of the war. Here in Spain the Communists offered the best discipline and the

> soundest and sanest for the prosecution of the war. He accepted their discipline for the duration of the war because, in the conduct of the war, they were the only party whose program and whose discipline he could respect. (163)

The general increase in the influence of the communists dated from about October-November 1936, when Russian supplies first began arriving in Spain. Orwell attributes the improved communist position to three specific factors:

> Once the U.S.S.R. had intervened the triumph of the Communist Party was assured. To begin with, gratitude to Russia for the arms and the fact that the Communist Party, especially since the arrival of the International Brigades, looked capable of winning the war, immensely raised the Communist prestige. Secondly, the Russian arms were supplied via the Communist Party and the parties allied to them, who saw to it that as few as possible got to their political opponents. Thirdly, by proclaiming a non-revolutionary policy the Communists were able to gather in all those whom the extremists had scared. (54)

The communist position, criticizing the revolutionary mystique of the anarchists, at least in theory, is stated by Malraux's García in his conversation with the liberal Republican Hernandez:

> The communists wish *to do* something. You and the anarchists, on the other hand and for different reasons, want *to be* something. That is the tragedy of this revolution and all revolutions such as this one. We must live with a multitude of contradictions: pacificism and the necessity to defend oneself; political organization and Christian sentiment; military efficiency and justice—a combination of incompatible myths. It is necessary for us to make some sense out of these contradictions, transform the apocalyptic vision into a potent military force or submit to extermination. That's all! (186)

The means by which the communists set about to accomplish this task are also described in *L'espoir*. In a conversation between Magnin, leader of the air squadron, and the visiting communist commissar, the latter expounds upon the method of reorganization within the old militia units:

> The communists are disciplined already. They obey their political and military leaders, often the same men. Many now consider

> joining the party because this sense of organization appeals to them. Formerly, our people were disciplined because they were communists; now people wish to become communists because the party stands for discipline. In each army unit are communists who set an example and help enforce military discipline. Each of these groups is a solid nucleus around which new men gravitate, who in time help to discipline other recruits. More and more realize that by aligning with us, they are effectively combating fascism. (137)

Orwell maintains that the communists were playing a double role at this time. On the one hand they offered the best defense against the fascist threat; at the same time they were attempting to suppress all political parties which would not accept their policies. Chief target on their list was the destruction of anarchist influence, which was usually accomplished through their trade unions:

> The fight against Franco had to continue, but the simultaneous aim of the Government was to recover such power as remained in the hands of the trade unions. It was done by a series of small moves—a policy of pinpricks, as somebody called it—and on the whole very cleverly. There was no general and obvious counter-revolutionary move, and until May 1937 it was scarcely necessary to use force. (54)

The transformation of the militia into a disciplined People's Army is manifested in the change of attitude on the part of Malraux's Negus from a desire for anarchical libertarianism to a compromise with military necessity. This change occurred during December 1936, while the International Brigades were defending Madrid:

> For a whole month he had ceased believing in the revolution. The apocalypse was over, but there remained the struggle against fascism. . . . The fight against the bourgeoisie had been his cause for so long that Negus found it easy to go on living for the battle against fascism. He listened to his own men making their radio appeals for discipline and he envied the young communists who spoke after them. . . . The fascists must be eliminated first, he guessed; plenty of time afterwards to argue. "You know," he once remarked, "the communists are good workers. I can work

with them, but no matter how hard I try, I cannot get to like them." (354)

Both Hemingway and Regler express their distaste for the communist and the anarchist tactics, but in their novels concede that the communists possessed the only solution to a Loyalist military victory. Regler's Republican surgeon for the International Brigades notes: "The thing I hate about the Anarchists is what we just saw there. Corpses by the roadside. Dramatics and death. They're a little too spontaneous and a little too public for me." In contrast, the doctor says of the communists: "And what I dislike about the Communists is just the opposite. Not spontaneous enough and too secretive. With them everything has to be just exactly so. Everything strictly according to rule. . . . Everybody always spying on himself, every man his own little Commissar. They never can let their foot slip for a minute, just for the hell of it." (34)

On a dangerous mission, Hemingway's Andrés, in *For Whom the Bell Tolls,* must cross from fascist lines into Loyalist territory to deliver a message. As he crosses the trenches, Andrés reflects on the anarchist troops who are holding the Republican line in this area:

> They started down the shallow trench behind the crest of the hill and in the dark Andrés smelt the foulness the defenders of the hill crest had made all through the bracken on that slope. He did not like these people who were like dangerous children; dirty, foul, undisciplined, kind, loving, silly and ignorant but always dangerous because they were armed. He, Andrés, was without politics except that he was for the Republic. He had heard these people talk many times and he thought what they said was often beautiful and fine to hear but he did not like them. It is not liberty not to bury the mess one makes, he thought. No animal has more liberty than the cat; but it buries the mess it makes. The cat is the best anarchist. Until they learn from the cat I cannot respect them. (376–77)

At the same time the cold terrorism of the communists is also repellent to Hemingway. In a discussion of political assassination with a Marxist theorist, Robert Jordan discovers the doublethink attitude of the communists. Although the communists claim not to believe in political assassination as a revolutionary method, they are able to practice it by a change in semantics:

> We do not believe in acts of terrorism by individuals. . . . Not of course by criminal terrorist and counter-revolutionary organizations. We detest with horror the duplicity and villainy of the murderous hyenas of Bukharinite wreckers and such dregs of humanity as Zinoviev, Kamenev, Rykov and their henchmen. We hate and loathe these veritable fiends. . . . But certainly we execute and destroy such veritable fiends and dregs of humanity and the treacherous dogs of generals and the revolting spectacle of admirals unfaithful to their trust. These are destroyed. They are not assassinated. You see the difference? (245)

Despite the deliveries of Soviet supplies and the assistance of the International Brigades and the Russian military command, the Loyalists lost ground during the first year of the war. Madrid, however, which the Republicans realized had symbolic significance for Spaniards, as well as international observers, was kept well fortified and continued under Republican control. During this period an attempt was made to forge a formidable military force out of a conscript army. Hemingway's communist theoretician discusses the problems encountered:

> We are building a huge army now and some of the elements, those of Modesto, of El Campesino, of Lister and of Duran, are reliable. They are more than reliable. They are magnificent. . . . Also we still have the Brigades although their role is changing. But an army that is made up of good and bad elements cannot win a war. All must be brought to a certain level of political development; all must know why they are fighting, and its importance. All must believe in the fight they are to make and all must accept discipline. We are making a huge conscript army without the time to implant the discipline that a conscript army must have, to behave properly under fire. We call it a people's army but it will not have the assets of a true people's army and it will not have the iron discipline that a conscript army needs. (246)

But in February 1937 Malaga fell to the Italians, who were experimenting with the coordinated use of tanks, planes, and infantry in battle. This experiment in blitzkrieg methods of war went unchallenged at Malaga because the city surrendered without a battle. Regler bitterly blames the Valencia government for abandoning Malaga and expresses his suspicion of betrayal within the Loyalist ranks:

> The city was given up in a cowardly fashion. The civil governor fled. The military authorities were asleep. No barricades had been erected. Nobody called out the workers to help in the defense. They deceived them, and kept them in uncertainty. There was a good working class down there. Now it will be killed off. Of course, that was not only the fault of the underofficers. Valencia behaved just as criminally. They sent hardly any ammunition to Malaga, not to speak of re-enforcements. In general the Government never investigated the city. Nobody knew anything about the strength of the enemy. The navy was asleep in some harbor near Valencia. I personally have always been of the opinion that there are traitors in the High Command. Today the newspapers are saying so openly. (296)

Koestler's description in *Spanish Testament* of the fall of Malaga appears to confirm Regler's version of a defenseless city betrayed by Valencia.

The Italian attempt to utilize the blitzkrieg method[41] failed them a month later at Guadalajara, however, where the Loyalists won their first major battle of the war. With Madrid a stalemate, Insurgent General Mola began a campaign to subdue northern Spain. Beginning in June, his troops swept along the frontier, capturing, at two-month intervals, Bilbao, Santander, and Gijon. It was during Mola's campaign that German bombers demolished the Basque town of Guernica, killing 1,654 and wounding 889. Nationalists blamed fanatical Basques for deliberately destroying the town before retreating, but more reliable evidence pointed to a planned aerial bombardment which became the first blitz of the Second World War.[42]

Meanwhile, during the month of April, the communists had precipitated a cabinet crisis designed to force Caballero to resign. Often at variance with the Soviets on matters of military strategy and clearly opposed to their efforts to eliminate intransigents, Caballero had increasingly obstructed the communists and eventually developed into an outright antagonist. Regler, from the communist point of view, notes the dissension among the Republican factions:

> The period of militia anarchy was over. The masses saw that an old man was leading them. They could not triumph unless a real army was organized. Industry must be mobilized. They had discovered an espionage center of two hundred Fascists in Madrid; foreign consulates had hidden them. . . . A member of the General Staff in Valencia had declared that Madrid must be given up —it had no strategic value. There was also the old strife between Anarchists and Communists. Caballero protected himself from all criticism behind the Anarchist clan. Besides there was the POUM, which maintained that the revolution was being betrayed if the workers were compelled to do more work because it was wartime. The bourgeois Left Parties were in agreement with the Communists, demanding that the General Staff be moved back to Madrid. . . . There was talk of a purely trade-union government, of jettisoning the Communists; Catalonia was threatening with separatism. (368–69)

Even in Madrid, personal as well as political jealousies threatened an effective defense of the city. Hemingway's Robert Jordan comments on this phase:

> He had certainly not seen any military geniuses in this war. Not a one. Nor anything resembling one. Kleber, Lucasz, and Hans had done a fine job of their share in the defense of Madrid with the International Brigades and then the old bald, spectacled, conceited, stupid-as-an-owl, unintelligent-in-conversation, brave-and-as-dumb-as-a-bull, propaganda-built-up defender of Madrid, Miaja, had been so jealous of the publicity Kleber received that he had forced the Russians to relieve Kleber of his command and send him to Valencia. (233)

Fearful lest Caballero become openly hostile, the Soviets persuaded Republicans and the rightist socialists to join them in walking out of a cabinet meeting. This caused the immediate collapse of the government and forced Caballero, despite strong anarchist support, to resign.

Meanwhile, on May 3, a handful of anarchist C.N.T. workers in the Barcelona Telephonica thought that the presence of the chief of police at their headquarters signaled the long-expected government takeover of the telephone exchange. They opened fire, and before the end of the day all the political organizations in Barcelona had taken up arms and prepared for battle. Orwell presents a fair commentary of the forces at work in Barcelona in May 1937:

> On the surface the quarrel between the Communists and the P.O.U.M. was one of tactics. The P.O.U.M. was for immediate revolution, the Communists not. . . . Further, the Communists contended that the P.O.U.M. propaganda divided and weakened the Government forces and thus endangered the war. . . . But here the peculiarity of Communist tactics came in. Tentatively at first, then more loudly, they began to assert that the P.O.U.M. was splitting the Government forces not by bad judgment but by deliberate design. The P.O.U.M. was declared to be no more than a gang of disguised Fascists, in the pay of Franco and Hitler, who were pressing a pseudo-revolutionary policy as a way of aiding the Fascist cause. . . . This implied that scores of thousands of working-class people, including eight or ten thousand soldiers who were freezing in the front-line trenches and hundreds of foreigners who had come to Spain to fight against Fascism, often sacrificing their livelihood and their nationality by doing so, were simply traitors in the pay of the enemy. (64)

The communist-socialist coalition along with Catalan government forces controlled half the city, the anarchists controlled the other half and, with the aid of the C.N.T., controlled the suburbs. Sporadic gunfire kept the combatants alert and the civilians tense. While the Catalan government and the anarchists began negotiations, the P.O.U.M. and anarchist extremists continued the rebellion behind barricades. The street fighting persisted and, on May 6, four thousand Assault Guards arrived in Barcelona from Valencia. The Barcelona struggle was terminated on May 9, and according to the Soviets, clearly showed the perils of tolerating opposition elements.[43] The communist attitude toward the Barcelona incident is expressed by Regler's commissar Albert:

> There are still innocents . . . who think those are honest revolutionists. And yet it is the most brazen example of treason. You know all winter long their press has been complaining that the 'Marxist Parties' were being unfairly preferred in the matter of arms. I don't have to tell you that these very 'Marxist Parties' were constantly in the midst of the heaviest fighting, while here they were playing football between the lines. (432)

Such an attack is deemed completely unwarranted by Orwell and he stresses that all the accusations "of espionage against the P.O.U.M. rested solely upon articles in the Communist Press and the activities of the Communist-controlled secret police." (175) And in his discussion of the propaganda treatment of the events, Orwell notes, "Compared with the huge miseries of a civil war, this kind of internecine squabble between parties, with its inevitable injustices and false accusations may appear trivial. It is not really so. I believe that libels and press-campaigns of this kind, and the habits of mind they indicate, are capable of doing the most deadly damage to the anti-Fascist cause." (177–78) Within a few months O.G.P.U. agents rounded up members of the P.O.U.M. and its leader, Andrés Nin. In most cases they were either imprisoned or executed. It is significant, in support of Orwell's contention, that several months later, when the anarchist and P.O.U.M. leaders were brought to trial, they were completely exonerated of the communists' charges of fascist complicity.[44] The aftereffects of the Barcelona fighting are analyzed by Orwell:

> There is no evidence that the outbreak had any direct effect upon the course of the war, though obviously it must have had if it had continued even a few days longer. It was made the excuse for bringing Catalonia under the direct control of Valencia, for hastening the break-up of the militias, and for the suppression of the P.O.U.M., and no doubt it also had its share in bringing down the Caballero Government. (152)

The new government, headed by the moderate socialist, Juan Negrín, took office on May 17 and lasted, with relatively few changes, until the end of the war. Cooperative but by no means a communist puppet, Negrín opposed a Soviet campaign to unify the Socialist and Communist Parties, and permitted Defense Minister Prieto to draw up and put into effect a plan to reduce the large force of Soviet military commissars. Prieto's plan, almost a duplicate of a scheme once devised by Caballero, threatened seriously to weaken the communist grip on the People's Army. Again, as in the case of obtaining the resignation of the former prime minister, a military crisis came to the aid of the communists. Using the defeats at the front as "evidence" of Prieto's incompetence, the Soviets were able to agitate for his immediate dismissal. As usual, Soviet supplies began to dwindle. Worried lest Russia completely cease to support the Loyalists, Negrín complied with the communist demands and accepted Prieto's resignation.

Throughout the second year of the war and the remainder of 1938 Republican politics maintained a degree of stability. Negrín remained at the controls and the communists exerted constant pressure on him to institute their policies. This internal political stalemate within the Republic was virtually unchanged until the closing days of the war. Several bitter arguments ensued and a revolt occurred before the war was officially ended. Since, in 1939, the Republic still controlled a large part of central Spain, including Madrid, and several hundred thousand troops, some members of the government—including the communists, Premier Negrín, and Madrid-defender Miaja—favored continuing the fight. Opposed were the other members of the Popular Front who considered further opposition futile and urged immediate surrender. Negrín's motives for continued resistance were twofold: he believed, not without foundation, that a general European war —surely not far off in February 1939—might save the Republic and even bring French and English aid; realistically, he wanted time to negotiate with Franco on such matters as reprisals, prisoner exchanges, and amnesties. On February 1, 1939, in a cellar of the ancient fortress of Figueras, he outlined his peace terms before a much depleted Cortes. Franco chose to ignore them. On February 28, both England and France officially recognized the Burgos regime. President Azaña resigned and left for France to join other Republican officials who had already fled. But Negrín, determined to carry on the war, attempted to replace unenthusiastic commanders with communists who supported his policies. This action, however, precipitated a revolt led by Colonel Segismundo Casado in Madrid that removed the fate of Spain from the government's hands and forced Negrín and his cabinet into exile in Algiers.[45] Casado set up a defense council, which opened peace negotiations with Franco and ended the war on March 26, 1939.

Most historians agree with Hemingway, Malraux, Regler, Koestler, and Orwell that one of the primary causes of the downfall of the Spanish Republic was the internal strife and anarchy which characterized Loyalist politics during the war. Their novels and personal narratives reflect the sense of betrayal through internal factionalism, caused by the government's inability to coordinate and restrain the dispersive tendencies of the Spanish character and to channel them into a spirit of national unity. Moreover, these authors considered the betrayal of France, England, and the United States, who failed to come to the aid of a sister democracy and even permitted the fascist dictatorships of Italy, Germany, and Portugal to assist in its overthrow. The issue of Russian intervention and its selfish motives, devious tactics, and eventual subversive plans are considered a contributing factor by Hemingway and Orwell. Malraux's explanation of the political dissension within the Republican camp is as valid as Orwell's contention that the failure to implement the social revolution contributed to the Republic's eventual defeat. The latter's statement that the failure to establish any sort of espionage system behind fascist lines, in territory occupied by a hostile army, also is a valid contention. The analyses by these novelists of Spanish politics are incisive and for the most part irrefutable. Often they were better informed than the Spaniards themselves, particularly about conditions outside Valencia once the government had moved.

Now that the Spanish Civil War may be viewed in retrospect and its politics examined with the aid of the personal narratives and novels of the six authors involved in this study, certain conclusions may reasonably be drawn. Undoubtedly, the Spanish Republic was betrayed both by its supposed friends, as well as enemies. According to such historians as Hugh Thomas, Stalin in particular betrayed the Loyalists and used the Spanish struggle in an attempt to eliminate his political foes; he disposed of many Russians and Spaniards after hostilities ended, fearing their knowledge of events in Spain would expose his involvement in the Spanish struggle.[46]

The conclusion that at times the writings of Orwell and Bernanos on the war were politically naïve fails to note two important considerations: the knowledge that was not available to most people, including these writers at the time, and the possibility that they retained a belief in the justice and moral integrity of the Spanish cause, despite the selfish designs of the various political groups involved. Few were perspicacious enough, as was

Malraux, to suspect or be able to distinguish, amidst all the bloodshed, courage, propaganda, and sincere enthusiasm, the extent of the falsehoods and distortions which existed beneath the surface. Both Hemingway and Orwell had registered their belief that politics was a relatively unimportant factor to the soldier in the trenches, that good training and equipment were what mattered, and political matters were reserved for the home front.

Even if these novelists, particularly Hemingway, Orwell, and Malraux, did uncover instances of dishonesty and ruthlessness on the part of the Loyalists, such exposures were tempered by the knowledge that war by its very nature necessitated both chicanery and cruelty. In the writings of Koestler and Regler, both of whom were experienced in communist tactics, and neither of whom was easily shocked by the cruelty of war or the ruthlessness of political machinations, such criticism is lacking, perhaps taken for granted because of the authors' previous experiences with party politics. The human failures and petty jealousies among the political factions did not impair their belief in a just cause. Nor, in the case of these authors, was a willingness to condone what seemed wrong a matter of simple self-deception. Not one of these six novelists was insincere in his attitude toward the Spanish people. If the war contained the sordid, it also contained much that was noble, and if the latter had to exist alongside the former, then they concluded this was a paradox of war.

## ▸ NOTES

[1] Essentially to a center-left coalition.

[2] For explanations in depth of this pendulum movement in Spanish politics, see Borkenau, *Spanish Cockpit*, pp. 47–63, Madariaga, *Spain*, pp. 377–477, Brenan, *Spanish Labyrinth*, pp. 229–315, Jellinek, *Civil War in Spain*, pp. 119–228, and Thomas, *Spanish Civil War*, pp. 21–109. These books and Álvarez del Vayo's *Freedom's Battle*, Jackson's *Spanish Republic and the Civil War*, Peers' *Spanish Tragedy* and Puzzo's *Spain and the Great Powers* are the sources for the background material on the political situation in Republican Spain from 1931 to 1939.

[3] *My Mission to Spain* (New York, 1954), pp. 197–238. For a complete account of the lawlessness, see Arnold Toynbee, *Survey of International Affairs, 1937*, Vol. II (London, 1938), p. 21 ff.

[4] Payne, *Falange*, pp. 98–115, recounts their growth during this period, their participation in terror-

ist activities, and their suppression by the Republic.

[5] Quoted in Peers, *Spanish Tragedy,* p. 208.

[6] Most historians agree on this as the immediate cause of the Spanish Civil War. For highly dramatic accounts of the double assassination, see Madariaga, *Spain,* p. 460, and John Langdon-Davies, *Behind the Spanish Barricades* (London, 1936), p. 86.

[7] This view is supported by such historians as Madariaga, Peers, Álvarez del Vayo, Matthews, Langdon-Davies, and Antonio Ruiz Vilaplana in his *Burgos Justice* (New York, 1938).

[8] *Spain,* pp. 460–61.

[9] "Looking Back on the Spanish War," *Such Were the Joys,* pp. 138–39.

[10] Borkenau discusses the general inability of the Republic to institute reforms, particularly of an agrarian nature, and concludes that, for the most part, the right had little to justify its fears. *Spanish Cockpit,* pp. 47–62. Puzzo notes that the program of the Republic was closer to Roosevelt's New Deal than to a revolutionary doctrine. *Spain and the Great Powers,* p. 35.

[11] *Spain,* p. 482.

[12] London, 1937.

[13] See Puzzo, *Spain and the Great Powers,* p. 47. Puzzo agrees with Koestler's observation and elaborates on the strategic and economic interests of both Germany and Italy at this time. Following the establishment of the Third Reich, German activity in Spain increased enormously; it became a bold, vast and coordinated effort to win a position of influence in Spanish affairs. See also Buckley, *Life and Death of the Spanish Republic,* pp. 207–208.

[14] *A Preliminary Report on Communist Atrocities in Southern Spain* (London, 1936–37) is the Burgos work which first propounded these charges. Such right-wing commentators as Yeats-Brown in *European Jungle,* pp. 298–99, and Robert Sencourt, *Spain's Ordeal,* p. 77 ff, enlarged on them.

[15] For gruesome descriptions of the assassinations, destruction, and spoilage, see Thomas, *Spanish Civil War,* pp. 171–79.

[16] *Spanish Liberals Speak on the Counter-Revolution in Spain* (San Francisco, 1937), p. 28. Madariaga agrees that Baroja's attitude was true of many of the Spanish intellectuals, appalled by the irrationality accompanying the war: "In this atmosphere of violence the life of the mind could not thrive." *Spain,* p. 497.

[17] See Borkenau, *Spanish Cockpit,* pp. 283–84, for this explanation of the militia's failure to make a stand against air raids and artillery bombardments.

[18] *Ibid.,* p. 284.

[19] Puzzo, *Spain and the Great Powers,* p. 58. See also Álvarez del Vayo, *Freedom's Battle,* p. 73, and Madariaga, *Spain,* pp. 502–503.

[20] Norman J. Padelford, *International Law and Diplomacy in the Spanish Strife* (New York, 1939), p. 1.

[21] See Buckley, *Life and Death of the Spanish Republic,* p. 234, and Puzzo, *Spain and the Great Powers,* p. 80. Most of this

material consisted of the machines Malraux had purchased in France with Republican funds.

[22] See Puzzo, *Spain and the Great Powers,* p. 73, and Bowers, *My Mission to Spain,* pp. 288–303.

[23] See Álvarez del Vayo, *Freedom's Battle,* pp. 79–95, for a complete account of the Axis' ambitions; also Thomas, *Spanish Civil War,* pp. 226–29, and Ford, *Poets' War,* p. 37.

[24] See Cattell's *Communism and the Spanish Civil War,* p. 73, and *Soviet Diplomacy and the Spanish War,* p. 33.

[25] *European Communism* (London, 1953), p. 169.

[26] See Cattell, *Soviet Diplomacy and the Spanish Civil War,* pp. 32–37. For an analysis of Soviet activities in Spain sympathetic to the Soviet position, see Louis Fischer's *Men and Politics.* Burnett Bolloten, *The Grand Camouflage* (London, 1961), depicts the communists as cynical conspirators, trading on the idealism of others. While containing some element of truth, the psychology of his study has been anachronistically distorted to fit the logic of the current cold war.

[27] Hugh Thomas, "The International Brigades in Spain," *History Today,* II (May 1961), p. 318.

[28] See Brenan, *Spanish Labyrinth,* pp. 87–88, and Borkenau, *Spanish Cockpit,* pp. 4–6. These books, along with Madariaga's *Spain,* are the basis for the discussion of Spanish social conditions.

[29] *Spain,* p. 22; see also Brenan, *Spanish Labyrinth,* pp. 88–89.

[30] Brenan, *Spanish Labyrinth,* pp. 123–24. See Madariaga on the feudal despotism of the landlord and the plight of the small farmers and agricultural workers. *Spain,* pp. 137–39.

[31] *Spanish Labyrinth,* p. 124.

[32] Vicente Blasco Ibáñez's novel, *La Bodega* (Madrid, 1904), is concerned with the revolt of the peasants and their march on Jerez in 1892. It presents an excellent picture of the rural conditions which could incite such an uprising.

[33] Madariaga, *Spain,* p. 170. See also Borkenau, *Spanish Cockpit,* pp. 11–13, Jellinek, *Civil War in Spain,* pp. 54–65, and for an ironic description of the Spanish military mind, José Ortega y Gasset's essays in *España Invertebrada* (Madrid, 1921).

[34] Madariaga, *Spain,* pp. 409–10; Jackson, *Spanish Republic and the Civil War,* pp. 78–85; Peers, *The Spanish Tragedy,* pp. 99–101; and Brenan, *Spanish Labyrinth,* pp. 242–46. Brenan maintains that the solution to the agrarian problem was not to be found, as in other European countries, by distributing plots of land to individual peasants and advancing them credits. He advocates, rather, a collectivism which presupposes a large staff of technical advisers, a fair amount of time and patience, and an organizing capacity—precisely virtues which no Spanish administration had ever possessed.

[35] *Spain,* pp. 410–12. For an analysis of the complex problems facing the Republic with reference to such commodities as wheat, coal, and citrus fruits, and the effects of

the international depression on the Spanish steel industry, see Jackson, *Spanish Republic and the Civil War,* pp. 85–91.

[36] The most objective sources on the government administration from 1933 to 1935 under the right are Jackson, Brenan's *Spanish Labyrinth,* Madariaga, Peers' *Spanish Tragedy,* and Jellinek.

[37] *Spain,* p. 548.

[38] See Cattell, *Communism and the Spanish Civil War,* Chap. IX.

[39] See Borkenau's *Spanish Cockpit,* for an excellent study of this aspect of the Spanish Civil War.

[40] Besides Orwell and Malraux, John Dos Passos served as a competent spokesman for the anarchist position in his two books, *The Villages Are the Heart of Spain* (Chicago, 1937), and *Journeys Between Wars* (New York, 1938).

[41] For detailed accounts of the military strategy employed by both sides during the Spanish Civil War, see Ludwig Renn's technical appraisal of tactics in *Warfare* (London, 1939).

[42] A detailed documentation of this incident is found in G. L. Steer's *Tree of Gernika* (London, 1938).

[43] Orwell's *Homage to Catalonia,* pp. 150–51, contains an accurate detailed account of the actual fighting. Bernanos, Hemingway, Koestler, and Regler mention the events also, but Orwell treats the Barcelona fighting as the central action in his narrative. Hemingway views this internal conflict as not particularly serious. (247)

[44] See Jackson, *Spanish Republic and the Civil War,* p. 462.

[45] See Segismundo Casado, *The Last Days of Madrid* (London, 1939).

[46] See Thomas, *Spanish Civil War,* pp. 618–24.

# V

# The Holy War

The Spanish Civil War was the consequence of the intense passions seething through centuries of Spanish history. If the conflagration was the predictable result of the polarization of political, economic, and social life, the war also served to bring the religious tensions endemic to Spain to a climax. Although a survey of the role of the Roman Catholic Church in the history of Spain is too complex to be attempted here, nevertheless some generalizations concerning the nature of the Spanish Church can profitably be made. All six novelists included in this study chose to treat the subject, but in each case, with the possible exception of Bernanos, a serious scholar of Catholic history and theology, their treatment was essentially subjective. For this reason the introduction of some substantive material should help to clarify the position of each writer in the context of the actual role of the Church in the life of the Spanish people.[1]

In Spain, as in most Western countries, the relations between the Church and the State have not been conditioned primarily by the legal status of the Church within the State as they have been by the amount of power and influence the Church has wielded on the body politic and the social fabric of the nation. The Roman Catholic Church in Spain has, while maintaining the universality of dogma necessary for a catholic institution, developed certain distinct national qualities. In modern Spain's history the Church has traditionally been a politically conservative institution. Its support of conservative governments has been predicated on its need to survive. Therefore the Church has preferred those governments which have promised it a privileged position and which have guaranteed it order and domestic stability so that it might best fulfill what it considered to be its function. In its conflicts with radical and progressive administrations, the Church has sought the support of conservative factions, and the latter, in return, have used the Church to further their political ambitions. Hemingway distinguishes between that special brand of Spanish Catholicism, which is the product of that country, and the French and Italian embodiments, which are so different:

> There is no finer and no worse people in the world. No kinder people and no crueler. And who understands them? Not me, because if I did I would forgive it all. To understand is to forgive. That's not true. Forgiveness has been exaggerated. Forgiveness is a Christian idea and Spain has never been a Christian country. It has always had its own special idol worship within the Church, *Otra Virgen más.* I suppose that is why they had to destroy the virgins of their enemies. Surely it was deeper with them, with the Spanish religious fanatics, than it was with the people. The people had grown away from the Church because the Church was in the government and the government had always been rotten. (355)

Despite Hemingway's allegation that "the people had grown away from the Church," the spiritual strength of the Roman Catholic Church should not be underestimated in Spain. The conflict between the Church and the people had never been of a religious nature. Koestler observes that the struggle had always been on a secular and political plane:

> It is essential to appreciate the peculiar position of the Spanish Church in order to realize that the struggle of the Spanish democracy against the clergy is not an anti-religious struggle, but a purely secular, political struggle waged against an extremely secular, extremely political opponent—a struggle which all the Western democracies waged successfully centuries ago when they set to work to lay the foundations of a liberal era. It was the

> struggle of Henry VIII against Rome, the struggle of France in the eighteenth century for the Rights of Man. (44)

The apostasy of a great number of the working class and the intellectuals had not lessened the support for the Church of a large section of the middle and upper classes, as well as the women of all classes, in Spain. It was Orwell's contention that everywhere only a small number of those who professed the Christian faith really believed in it. His statement that the people of Catalonia and Aragon had through the years forsaken Catholicism, however, should not be accepted as completely accurate:

> It struck me that the people in this part of Spain must be genuinely without religious feeling—religious feeling, I mean, in the orthodox sense. It is curious that all the time I was in Spain I never once saw a person cross himself; yet you would think such a movement would become instinctive, revolution or no revolution. Obviously the Spanish Church will come back . . . but there is no doubt that at the outbreak of the revolution it collapsed and was smashed up to an extent that would be unthinkable even for the moribund C. of E. in like circumstances. To the Spanish people, at any rate in Catalonia and Aragon, the Church was a racket pure and simple. And possibly Christian belief was replaced to some extent by Anarchism, whose influence is widely spread and which undoubtedly has a religious tinge. (81)

Orwell's conclusion that the religious feelings of the Spanish people had been transferred from a corrupt Church to a revolutionary social movement is only partially valid in light of the history of the relationship between the Church and the masses in Spain. Of the literary and devotional record of Spanish Catholicism he knew little, but he claimed that the ordinary Spanish worker and peasant in 1936 also knew little of it.

During the nineteenth century the State, in an attempt to restrain a powerful Church, had confiscated its landed property. Never since has the Church regained this wealth. The claim by Koestler that the Church in the twentieth century is the largest landlord in Spain requires some clarification:

> The Catholic Church is the largest landowner in Spain. This explains why the Spanish peasants' struggle for existence was bound at the same time to be a struggle against the secular power of the

> Church. The anti-clerical character of all Spanish mass movements since the seventeenth century is a direct and inevitable consequence of the temporal power exercised by the Spanish clergy ever since the expulsion of the Moors. (44)

Objective historians of the Spanish Church, among them Brenan, Madariaga, and Peers, are in accord that since the middle of the nineteenth century the Church has been able to regain only a small fraction of its real estate, although they concede that under favorable regimes it has managed to accumulate considerable capital. The effects of the disfranchisement of the Church to own real property were twofold, but neither one confirms Koestler's implication that the lower classes were alienated from the Church because they considered it one more tyrannical landlord attempting to exploit their poverty.

The first result of the confiscation of Church lands served to alienate the Church from the masses by forcing the Church to seek support from the wealthier classes throughout the greater part of Spain. This dependence on the wealthier classes has continued ever since. The general detachment of the Church from the people was succeeded by an avariciousness and an accompanying violently aggressive attitude on its part. Thus, in the twentieth century, the Spanish Church, particularly the Jesuits, became the single most wealthy power in the country. The second effect of this shift in the wealth of the Church from land to other capital also resulted in a gradual severance of the Church from the masses. Never would the masses have so readily abandoned a Church firmly established on the land; but they were easily alienated from a Church which was the wealthiest shareholder in the country. It followed that the Spanish pueblos gradually and reluctantly considered the Church to be a self-seeking institution with no real concern for their interests.

Throughout the history of modern Spain the State, which includes monarchies and dictatorships as well as republics, has attempted to limit the power of the Church. In this struggle for power the Catholic Church has relegated its pastoral duties, its interest in the people, to a secondary position. Instead, it has become more acquisitive, seeking to gain special privileges in economic matters. Koestler examines the nature of this shift in Church policy during the twentieth century:

> The temporal, material interests of the Spanish Church were as great as those of the French Church about the time of Richelieu, and those of the English Church up to the Reformation. We have further seen that the Spanish Church had such considerable sums invested in banking, industry, and even in large-scale commercial undertakings and shipping, that in order to safeguard these material interests it was obliged to meddle even in the petty inrigues of day-to-day political life. The political attitude of the Spanish Church has been determined in no uncertain fashion by these secular interests. (100–101)

The historical allusions of Koestler concerning the Church in modern Spain are confirmed by Borkenau when he notes that to understand its position in society, one must not think of Catholicism as it now exists in Germany, France, Britain, and other European countries. Rather, the late medieval Church in the periods of its deepest decay, before the Counter-Reformation, should be the point of reference. Most of the work of the Council of Trent had been undone, in deed if not in words, in Spain during the nineteenth century.[2]

From the middle of the nineteenth century until 1931, the Church, though steadily losing its influence with the poorer classes, was gaining constantly in wealth and political power. The leaders of this movement were the Jesuits; their policy—originated years before by their founder—was dedicated to winning the support of the rich and the powerful. Thus the rift grew wider between the peasants and this socially distant institution; the peasants' only contact with the Church was now a poorly educated, morally lax lower clergy, acting in a commensal relationship with the local guardia, and a distant, worldly episcopacy which seldom indicated awareness of their existence. Koestler reflects that this alienation was not due to outside forces working against the Church, but rather was caused by the attitude of the Church itself:

> It is quite understandable that the provocative attitude of the clergy should have aroused violent anti-clerical feeling amongst the people. Their attitude, as has already been said, was not anti-religious, but anti-clerical. There are large sections of the people who, while to this very day imbued with strong traditional religious feelings, are yet opposed to the attitude of the Spanish

> Church. The Church has increasingly cut itself off from the masses. The Church dignitaries' identification of themselves with the ruling caste, their open resentment of even the most elementary demands of the poor peasants, their cold and calculated policy of encouraging the wealthier peasants, has increasingly intensified this process of isolation. Not only those workers who have come under Socialist or Syndicalist influence, but the illiterate rural population too, have turned away from the Church. (102)

Malraux's anarchist, the brave Puig, attempts an explanation of his personal alienation from the priests, which provides some insight into the psychology of the peasant when confronted by a clergy that offers him little in the way of understanding and much in the way of condescension. In his dialogue with the Catholic Ximenes, Puig must reply to the question: "Suppose the Church in Spain has fallen short in its moral obligations to your countrymen. But why should those assassins who pretend to share your views—and heaven knows there are enough of them—why should they prevent you from carrying out your own duty? It is a mistake appraising men by what is lowest in them." Puig articulates the silent suffering of the peasant in Spain:

> When you condemn a people to low living, you should not expect high thoughts to emanate from them. During the last four centuries, who has taken charge of the "curing of souls," as you would call it? If the people had not been taught so well to hate, perhaps they could learn better how to love. . . . Your catechism and mine are not the same; our lives are too different. I reread the catechism when I was twenty-five; I picked it up near here in a gutter—sounds like a morality tale. There is just no use in telling people who have been having their cheeks slapped for the last two thousand years to "turn the other cheek." . . . As for the clergy, I do not care for people who talk a lot and do nothing. . . . I'll tell you something but you won't understand because you have never been poor: I hate a man who says that he forgives me for doing the best thing I have ever done. *I don't want to be forgiven!* (35–36)

To the various liberals in Spanish government, as they viewed a militant Church each year controlling a larger share of the industrial life of the country, the national interests appeared in danger. These liberals recognized that much of the Church's wealth was the result of gifts and bequests from the rich who in turn expected some form of recompense for their contributions. As one form of repayment, the Church was obligated to defend their benefactors' interests against the revolutionary tendencies of the lower classes. The politics of the Church in modern Spain, as Koestler explains, were formulated to champion unpopular causes: "As a result the clergy in Spain has always pursued a strictly anti-liberal and anti-Republican policy." (101) In return for this hostility, liberalism in Spain evolved in part to include a general anticlerical attitude.

In contrast to a wealthy and distant hierarchy, the country priests were poor; some received scarcely more than a manual laborer. But their poverty was not an essential factor in their efforts to command the respect of the peasant. On the contrary, this poverty lessened the general hostility toward these badly educated and somewhat lax rural clergy who, as plain, honest men, in an age when faith in the Church was waning, did their best to perform their duties. Malraux indirectly offers them praise while at the same time castigating the hierarchy. When Lopez, in *L'espoir,* attempts to secure a priest for a mission of mercy, he encounters a reluctant canon:

> Backing out, was he? Those lousy swine won't even do their job! Then they explained to me that he was a canon at the cathedral, one of the higher-ups in the ecclesiastical hierarchy. If he had been a country priest, he wouldn't have made such a commotion. (162)

Koestler's accusations against the episcopacy are even more explicit: "The indictment . . . is directed against only a section of the Spanish clergy, primarily against the hierarchy at the top, the Princes of the Church and the Bishops. A considerable section of the clergy with a social conscience was staunchly Republican." (108)

Although social advances in Spain did not keep pace with the rest of Europe, nevertheless the impact of the twentieth century on the Spanish people grew stronger, literacy more general, and new social problems arose. The increase in industrial employment created economic and labor questions for which the Church was not prepared to offer any solutions, nor sufficiently informed to provide some form of guidance. The Spanish Church had no understanding of modern social problems, welfare organizations, cooperatives and trade unions, and made little effort to educate itself in these areas. Borkenau, as a sociologist, in contrasting the Spanish Church with the role of other European Catholic institutions, notes that the success of the Catholic Church in countries where it had little or no political power when it started to take an active interest in the problems of modern life, and its wholesale failure in Spain, where it wielded enormous political power, indicates that the responsibility for its failure must be attributed to the Spanish Catholic hierarchy itself.[3]

During the one hundred years preceding 1930, the Spanish Church gradually lost any real influence it had exerted on the great mass of Spanish people. In most sections the Spanish devotion, theretofore expressed in religious fervor, was transferred with the same intense faith to social ideologies, often revolutionary in nature—anarchism being the most radical. The need to expend themselves, so characteristic of the Spanish temperament, was channeled into political action whose very instability was an indication of the passions aroused. The exception was in those districts—Navarre and the Basque country—where provincial clergy had maintained a close relationship with their parishioners. The fervent Catholicism of both districts is evident, but in the Spanish Civil War the Basques were aligned with the Republic, while Navarre provided some of the strongest units in the Insurgent army. The causes of such antithetical responses to the Spanish struggle merit further comment.

In Navarre, the clergy, continuing to live among the people in a primitive community which had varied little since the Middle Ages, had no need to adapt themselves to modern conditions. In the Basque country, which with Catalonia constitutes the total industrial complex of Spain, the Catholic clergy were in close contact with the masses from the start in the traditional defense of the Basque language against the influence of a centralizing Castile. Utilizing this foundation, the Basque Church interested itself in the cooperative and trade union movements, and took a generally active role in social welfare work. Thus, the Basque clergy, by conscientiously demonstrating its allegiance to the people through years of political and social unheaval, was the major influence that kept that section of the country from following a trend away from the Church, when such a trend was prevalent throughout much of Spain. Such success serves as a further indictment of the Spanish episcopacy, which might have accomplished the same result throughout Spain had they attempted to exercise some initiative.

Prior to World War I, the Spanish Church had experienced a steady increase in financial resources and political influence. The Church had never been resigned to its displacement as the dominating force in the social, political, and educational life of the country. In an effort to reestablish its position in the political structure of Spain, the Church had endorsed a clerical party which seemed to offer one more opportunity in its quest for power. In opposition, the forces of anticlericalism had initiated a proselytizing campaign of their own and gained intellectual support from the movement in contemporary European thought which had manifested itself in the disestablishment of the French Church. During the early years of the twentieth century, the chief issues centered around the liberals' attempt to limit the number of religious orders, to enforce the toleration of other religious groups, and to gain control of education in Spain. In this struggle neither side made appreciable gains, but as the conflict progressed the Church alienated itself even further from the masses. Only the support given by the richer classes enabled it to withstand the pressures of public opinion. By the time of the proclamation of the Republic in 1931, Spanish liberalism had been identified with anticlericalism, and although the Spanish masses, particularly the women, had retained some instinctive elements of traditional Catholicism, the Church throughout much of Spain commanded little respect.

The most prominent issue in the conflict between the Church and the liberals was that of education. Brenan points out the backwardness of the system in the hands of the Church during the nineteenth century:

> The Church at this time had not yet recovered from the shock which the French Revolution had given it and had a mortal dread of learning. Science, mathematics, agriculture and political economy were therefore not taught, as they were considered dan-

> gerous subjects for any but trained theologians. The Jesuits frowned on history, which offered so many bad examples to the young and innocent. Almost the only subject which could usefully be studied at the universities was law. For though medicine was taught, it suffered from the suppression of that erroneous Lutheran notion upon the circulation of the blood, whilst if one touched on physics one had to remember that the Copernican system was still a "cosa de Inquisición." In the elementary schools the children of the poor were deliberately not taught to read, but only to sew and to recite the Catechism.[4]

As successive liberal governments exerted their influence, the institutions of higher learning were gradually freed from control of the clerics, and the foundation for universal elementary education was established. Considering how reasonable and conservative the requests by the liberals were, and how the maximum demanded was that freedom prevalent in all other countries of the Western world be accorded them, the increasing hostility of these men toward the Church is understandable. In revulsion they finally assumed an attitude of violent resistance to a religious institution which appeared to them to have learned nothing in the last three centuries. The frustrations caused by the Church's political intransigence finally determined the majority of the population to abandon it in disgust.

The errors of the Spanish Church are not attributable to a lack of religious conviction, but instead to an absence of Christian sympathy for, and understanding of, the people. Rather than attempt to influence the masses by precept or persuasion, the Church preferred to resort to force exerted through its political power. Instead of adjusting to social conditions and combating antithetical revolutionary movements through a constructive program of labor organizations, friendly societies, and the institution of social reforms, the Church concentrated its efforts in search of a governmental administration which would help to suppress its enemies by force and restore to the Catholic Church the privileged position it had formerly enjoyed. Thus the Church centered its activities in the area of politics and chose for its allies the wealthiest and most reactionary groups. In following this course, it incurred the hostility of many of the decent and progressive elements in Spain. The educated classes had come to consider the Church the enemy of representative government and the leading factor inhibiting the spread of modern European culture in Spain; the working classes were forced to regard it as a barrier to their hopes for a better standard of living. Behind every governmental repression, every curtailment of individual liberty, every judicial murder, there stood the episcopacy with a leading article in the Catholic press or a pastoral demonstrating its approval. Considering that this uncompromising attitude often concealed the greatest laxity in conduct and a dearth of Christian virtues, it is not surprising later to hear Malraux's Manuel denounce the Church as vile, stupid, and hypocritical:

> The peasants reproached the Church for having consistently supported the upper class, approved the punitive measures which followed the Asturian revolt, condoned the spoliation of the Catalonians, taught the poor a meek submission to injustice, and now the Church was backing a Holy War against these same peasants. Some resented the self-righteous tone of the priests; many resented the harshness and hypocrisy of the clergy. All were indignant that, in conquered villages, priests had denounced to the fascists all whom they considered guilty of "irreligious thought," knowing full well that this action consigned those men to a firing squad. And all reproached the clergy for their wealth. (155–56)

The devotion of individual priests and monks, the sincerity and humanity of a large number of the lay Catholics, were all overshadowed in the minds of the people by the militant and reactionary attitude of the hierarchy.

In the final days preceding the "self-imposed" exile of Alphonso XIII, municipal elections were held throughout Spain. The episcopacy supported the monarchy and forbade Catholics to vote for the socialist-republican coalition opposing it. In April 1931, the electorate went to the polls. Viewing the surprising election results, it seemed the religious issue was momentarily overlooked. In what seemed a true mandate from the people, the Second Spanish Republic was proclaimed amid orderly rejoicing throughout the country. Contrary to Spanish tradition, no blood was spilled and no churches burned. Koestler comments that the Church absented itself from this acclamation and continued its campaign against the new administration:

> The Spanish clergy's immediate reaction to the proclamation of the Spanish Republic in the year 1931 was of a most violent and aggressive character. The arch-bishops and priests turned themselves into electioneering agents, issuing pastoral letters against the Republican parties, the workers' organizations and their leaders, and not scrupling to employ the most unsavoury methods in their campaign against the Republic. (102)

The Second Spanish Republic from its inception was plagued with problems for which practical solutions were virtually impossible. The reasons for these problems, so common in Spanish history, were the threats posed by extremist elements of both the right and the left. At the extremes, a large section of belligerent monarchists was demanding the return of the king and the predominance of the Church, army, and oligarchy, while in opposition the radical elements were demanding immediate reforms as a prelude to their vision of a social revolution. The regionalists demanded autonomy, and the Catalans had taken advantage of the collapse of the regime under Alphonso to proclaim themselves an independent state.

Despite all these problems, the government chose immediately to concern itself with the chief religious issue, the removal of the Church from its privileged position. Moderate elements counseled the advantages to be gained for Republican stability by proceeding cautiously with these anticlerical measures. In the early days of the Republic, these moderates in the administration were in control of policy. But early in May 1931, because of rumors that the Church was planning to liquidate some of its investments and remove its wealth from reach of the Republic, the government initiated its first legislation to frustrate this effort. On May 2, a decree was issued which forbade the sale or transfer of Church property. In opposition, a pastoral letter by the militant Cardinal Pedro Segura, Archbishop of Toledo and head of the Catholic hierarchy in Spain, was issued, making frequent mention therein to the serious disturbances and threats of anarchy; he expressed gratitude to the expelled monarchy and urged the women of the country to embark on a crusade offering prayers and sacrifices in behalf of the Church against the many inroads on its traditional rights.[5]

Immediately thereafter, in a test of strength between the

new government and the Roman Catholic Church, the Republicans announced their determination to institute a laic school system, permit divorce, secularize cemeteries and hospitals, and greatly reduce, if not eliminate, the number of religious orders in Spain. Koestler points out that the young Republic in its policy was not particularly militant and was merely executing long overdue reforms consonant with twentieth-century Western civilization:

> It never attempted to introduce, let alone enforce, a single reform that had not long since been embodied in the constitutions of many of the democracies of Europe; such as, for example, the separation of Church and State, the confiscation of Church property, the right of divorce, secular education in the State schools, the dissolution of the Jesuit order. The Republic respected the Concordat concluded in 1851 with the Holy See; it allowed all the religious orders, with the exception of the Jesuits, to continue to exist on Spanish soil; it allowed the Church schools for adults and children to continue to exist as private institutions, it permitted all the churches to remain open, and made no attempt to interfere with practising Catholics in the observance of their religion. (103)

Although what Koestler states may be the truth from the viewpoint of a French or English national, in Spain such reforms imposed upon an inflexible and openly belligerent Church almost resulted in the overthrow of the government.

In a series of measures and countermeasures the Republic and the Church engaged in a bitter dispute. As tensions increased, the Spanish temperament exploded, and from May 6 to May 14 convents were burned and churches sacked in Madrid, Malaga, Seville, Cadiz, and Alicante. While no priests or nuns were killed, the laboratories of the Jesuit industrial and technical school in Madrid and many works of art were destroyed.[6] The less visible but more important result of the burnings and pillaging was the shock effect upon the Spanish middle class. Less than a month after the founding of the Republic, the country was forcefully awakened to the possible violent repercussions which could be caused by extremists of the left and right should the government persist in its policy of religious reforms. Many members of the government, particularly Catholics, were not willing to accept responsibility for the consequences should the conflict increase in intensity. Thus, the May church burnings, apparently unopposed by the new government since no arrests had been made, delineated the positions of the two factions. By its inaction the government had exposed its anticlerical position, in accord with traditional Spanish liberal politics. No longer did the moderates caution the Republic in an effort to ease the situation.

In swift succession the Republic proclaimed complete religious liberty; all faiths were authorized to perform their functions unrestricted. By its very nature such action defined the Republican position in the area of religious reform. It vested in itself inflexible opposition to the Church. While the Church might have suffered a separation between the Church and State, the prohibition against its teaching orders, and the dissolution of the Jesuits, it could not accept the loss of its economic privileges—its subjection to taxes and prohibition from commercial transactions, the elimination of government subsidies, the need to register its properties and account for its income and investments—which struck a mortal blow. Other governmental decrees pertaining to religion established freedom of conscience, State control of marriage and divorce, implied State control of Church property and laic education. The results of these policies were not what the state had anticipated. The Catholic deputies, including those from the Basque country and Navarre, walked out of the Cortes, and the Spanish Republic was seriously divided. Such historians of modern Spain as Madariaga, Brenan, and Sánchez agree that its anticlericalism proved disastrous to the new government. At this time the moderates could only hope for a nonviolent resolution to the religious issues through faith in the bureaucratic ministry's traditional failure to implement its own laws.

On January 23, 1932, the government enacted its decree for dissolution of the Jesuits. The realization that religious laws were to be promulgated united the opposition. The failure of the Republic to synchronize its reform program with constructive measures was soon evident in the field of education when almost 7,000 students were turned out of the Jesuit schools, many to burden the already overcrowded state schools. The government's plan to eliminate general education by the Church posed a serious threat to its own existence. In 1931 there were some 400,000 students in church schools, while at least 500,000 children were receiving no education whatever. Therefore, to comply with the law, the State would have had to provide schooling for nearly one million children, something they were not prepared to do.

These religious laws not only did little toward extirpating the Church's political influence but also proved politically disastrous for the State. In addition, the petty quality of much of the anticlericalism served no constructive purpose in solving the politico-religious problem; it rather tended to strengthen the position of the Church. Responsible leaders in the administration found it difficult to gain support in other desperately needed areas of attention because of this division afflicting Spanish life. The stage was now prepared for the swing of the Spanish political pendulum. The struggle with the Church had assumed a petty vindictiveness which cost the Republic much of its original popularity with the middle classes. Many Catholic Republicans were unable to support the anticlerical aspects of the administration's policy. The politico-religious conflict had weakened Republican support while at the same time bestowing on the conservative and right-wing elements a common unifying bond—the defense of Catholicism.

The subsequent victory and rule by the right, from December 1933 to December 1935, have been recorded in Spanish history as the "bienio negro." This sobriquet, conferred by the left, is descriptive of the paralysis of official action and the repeal or nonenactment of the earlier Republican legislation, particularly that legislation dealing with the religious question. This inaction brought about charges of anti-Republicanism from the left, for the reformers saw their constitution violated. Once having accomplished its aims with respect to the Church, the new administration, having no obligation to enact a social program which would conflict with its commitment to the upper classes, nullified any ambitions in the areas of social or agrarian reforms, and merely stagnated. The single instance during the two-year period in which the government took vigorous action was in the repression of the Asturian miners after breaking the general strike. Again the actions of the Catholic Church further alienated it from the masses. Instead of counseling moderation, it chose to voice its approval of the government's position in the affair. Koestler's accusation that "during the rising in Asturias in October, 1934, certain fanatical priests went so far as to denounce Socialist workers to Lopez Ochoa's hangmen," (103) is not without foundation. Koestler later notes that during November 1935, in the waning days of the "bienio negro," one of the leaders of Gil Robles' Catholic Party declared "that the only means of putting an end to the prevalence of Godless Socialism in Spain was to set up a new Inquisition." (103) By the end of 1935, the moderate Catholic elements in the government were pushing for constitutional revision. But the coalition of parties on the right was rapidly disintegrating and time was running out before there was an opportunity to execute this plan.

In the subsequent elections, despite the Church's vigorous campaign against it, the Popular Front triumphed because of the strength of its union and the general frustration and dissatisfaction felt by the masses during the bienio negro. Almost immediately after the Popular Front took office, there was a new and violent wave of church burnings. Throughout Spain, churches were burned by an aroused lower class, and Azaña, rather than further provoke the masses, including many who had recently been released from prison where they had been incarcerated as a result of the 1934 uprising, did little to prevent the destruction. In the Cortes a socialist minister replied to charges that the government was responsible for the disorder:

> The Church had always taken sides against the workers . . . and the Church had lost its neutral position because "each pulpit and confessional had been a campaign headquarters against the Popular Front. . . . We would like the religious problem to be one of conscience, but if the Church is going to play politics, it is going to get hurt."[7]

In addition to the violence, the Church faced the renewed threat of implementation of the religious laws. After two years of the bienio negro, in which such execution was deliberately deferred, the Popular Front was determined not to permit any further delay. The Church, denied the protection of the C.E.D.A.-controlled government, sought its allies among the forces of reaction, particularly the army and the oligarchy. Koestler again expounds that the legislation to be enacted by the new Popular

Front government was not only radical in content, but had been accomplished in the rest of Europe several centuries before:

> The anti-clerical demands of the Spanish Popular Front in the year 1936 were not a whit more radical or "red" than those of the writers of the age of enlightenment: separation of Church and State, distribution of Church lands amongst the landless peasants, secular education, freedom of religious worship, freedom of speech and freedom of the pen. If this is anarchism, then John Stuart Mill was an anarchist; if it needed the inspiration of Moscow to raise these demands, then Cromwell was a hireling of Stalin. The truth is that the Spanish Popular Front was not striving towards a Soviet State or a Bakunian Utopia, but towards one goal alone: the raising of the Spanish State, which had not yet succeeded in emerging from the clerical, feudal stage, to the constitutional, material and spiritual level of the great European democracies. (45)

This last charge of Russian influence within the Popular Front was sounded by the Church and reactionary factions immediately after the election results and the proposed policies of the Popular Front were made clear. Bernanos counters these accusations by reminding the Church that this same electorate gave the C.E.D.A. a majority in 1934:

> Spain must have been even more corrupt than was imagined. But is it not this same Spain which, in 1934, gave the Catholic C.E.D.A. a majority in the Cortes? Then your purification crusade must be working in reverse, and your methods cannot be worth much. (141–42)

And earlier he noted concerning the legality of this government: "Try to remember that Spain had just established her republic—*Viva la republica!*—and that on the evening of July 18th—the time of the military insurrection—it was still the legal regime, recognized by all, acclaimed by the army, approved by the pharmacists, doctors, professors, and even by the intellectuals." (97–98)

In the days preceding the pronunciamiento, the Church aligned itself with the one group which could most effectively protect its interests—the army. No longer able to rely on the moderate Catholic C.E.D.A., the Church joined forces with the militant monarchists and the fanatical Falangists. The polarization of the nation into extremist groups was inevitable, and a mass desertion from the moderate parties followed. The recognition of the Church's contribution to the approaching cataclysm is succinctly expressed by Bernanos: "Spanish air is not favorable for the lungs of Christians. And the anguish of suffocation seems even more intolerable because there appears no justification for it, since the entire country is in the firm control of Catholic elements." (274) In the alliance with the military, the Church had rallied to the obviously stronger side, disregarding the moral aspects of its decision. Bernanos expounds the rationale later, in *Les grands cimetières sous la lune,* only to destroy it:

> "Let us reason practically," my eminent detractor will no doubt reply. "The dignitaries of the Church would have willingly served as a mediator and moderating influence in the Spanish conflict. Unfortunately such a task was made impossible by the circumstances created in the rapid transition from Monarchy to Republic, from Democracy to Dictatorship. In short, we lacked the means necessary for assuming the role of successful peacemaker. Discretion constrains us to rally to the side of the stronger, and since the strength of our chosen side is still in question, we must not be reticent in our support." (199–200)

Bernanos contends that when the Civil War erupted, the Spanish Church should have assumed a moderating position and offered its services, in a gesture of peace and union, at the disposal of both the left and right. But from the outset the Church chose to align itself with the Insurgent generals, and on July 10, 1937, the Spanish Episcopate published a collective pastoral letter officially siding with the rebels.

The Spanish hierarchy espoused the position that the uprising had been a "civil-military" affair, with the healthiest and best qualified civilians and the army united within the Insurgent faction. The first statements justifying the pronunciamiento omitted the subject of religion, but as the war progressed the influence of the Church increased steadily in the Nationalist zone. The Spanish Church maintained that it had not wanted a war but was grateful for the protection which the Nationalists afforded. However, even the more amenable section of the Church could not wholeheartedly endorse the fascist tenets in the Insurgents' social and political program. This faction assumed a more philosophical view of the war which, according to Bernanos, envisioned Franco as a "temporary" alternative who would not remain in power very long after the successful military rebellion, while the Church in its infinite patience would gradually be able to assume the functions it had neglected for so many years before the conflict:

> Compromise for compromise, General Franco is the least embarrassing to us because he will not remain in power very long. Our doctrines on respect for established power, our strictures against the use of force, the deference we showed toward universal suffrage—all these things will develop significance again, sooner or later. We need only be patient. (201)

Bernanos would willingly have accepted such contentions had the support of the Church on behalf of Franco's forces consisted of a passive resignation to an unfortunate situation, or a moderating influence within the Nationalist camp. Instead, the Church chose to campaign actively for the Insurgents and, using the rationale of expediency, condoned and often encouraged the most unchristian acts during the course of the war. The Catholic hierarchy completely disregarded the moral considerations involved in such a position and, Bernanos contends, would more than likely have changed sides, forsaking its previous commitments, also on the grounds of expediency, should a Republican victory have appeared probable:

> No doubt in the case of a Loyalist victory, however improbable, the Church would enter into negotiations with the Republican regime, but this would surprise nobody. Such a privilege, such duplicity, I am pleased rests on shoulders other than mine. To transcend human honor! To remain faithful to your allies only in success and to abandon them in defeat—is there a more rigorous, more abnormal sense of loyalty? (206)

With the declaration of the pronunciamiento, the anticlerical fury of the people reached its climax. Although the response varied throughout the cities and villages of Spain, across the Republic churches were attacked and desecrated, and in the anarchist stronghold of Barcelona, virtually every church in the city with the exception of the cathedral was set afire. There were macabre scenes of executions and spoilage; vandalism rather than loot was the objective. Certain churches and convents in central positions, mostly around Madrid, were protected by the government, but in the provinces the destruction was most thorough. Although the great works of art were preserved, the breaking of images and sacred objects, and the wearing of ecclesiastical robes by militiamen were widespread. These attacks were accompanied by an uncontrollable onslaught on the lives of members of the clergy. During the first year of the war conservative estimates of clerical deaths reached 8,000, an overwhelming figure.

When the civil war erupted, there were rumors that arms and ammunition had been secreted in churches, convents, and monasteries. According to the historian Thomas, practically nowhere had the Church taken an active part in the rebellion.[8] His claim that the stories of rebels firing from church towers were without foundation is countered by Regler's description of just such an incident, during the first days of the fighting, in a small town where the rebel leaders were young Falangists:

> The rebellion had begun at the town hall, and the strange boys had killed the Alcalde. Then they retreated to the church and fired through the half-opened portal at the advancing crowd. And the priest had actually played the organ in the loft while the shots were crackling in the street, where the Alcalde's wife had come with the citizens. A nice kind of church where you got bullets for communion. A devil's church, and so they piled straw around it and set it on fire. The devils had got a singeing they said, but the head devil, the priest, had got away through a back door and taken to the mountains. (167)

Koestler's personal narrative confirms the basis for Regler's description. In *Spanish Testament,* Koestler cites specific churches in Madrid which were used by the Falangists during the first days of the insurrection:

> During the first few days of the insurrection churches were again used as strategic points. On July 19th, in Madrid, machine-guns were fired from the Salesian monastery in the Calle de Francisco Rodriguez, . . . from the Cathedral of Saint Isidor and from several priests' seminaries. After the fighting barricades of mattresses were found behind the windows of a convent in 7, Calle del Sacramento. Twenty-four hours before the insurrection the nuns had been evacuated, and a troop of Phalangists had taken up their quarters there. The same thing happened in other towns of Spain.

> In the smaller towns in Catalonia the inadequately armed or entirely unarmed Militiamen were frequently obliged to smoke out the machine-gun nests set up in the monasteries or to blast the walls with dynamite. (104)

At no time in the history of Europe, or perhaps the world, had so passionate a hatred of the Church and all its corruption been demonstrated. The foreign press carried detailed accounts of the demolished churches, with appropriate pictures, thus inflaming the feelings of Catholics and non-Catholics, and further internationalizing the issues inherent in the conflict. Koestler recognized the propaganda value of such material in the democracies where it could be used by Nationalist sympathizers to discourage support for the Republic:

> I have seen the ruins of churches and monasteries in Catalonia; the sight of them is staggering. I have also seen the Churches in Madrid which were blown to bits by Franco's artillery and aircraft and the hospitals that suffered a like fate; the sight was equally staggering. It is to be expected that the propagandists of both sides should make all the capital they can out of their demolished churches; in the Great War the Allies and the Central Powers also denounced each other for the destruction of church buildings. But that there should be journalists who never weary of returning again and again to the subject of the burned churches of Catalonia, expressing their horror at the effect, without mentioning the cause, is a thing I have never been able to understand. (104–105)

Koestler calls attention to the many causes for the ferocious persecution of the Church. While the mind recoils at the horrors of such events and while the persecution of the Church and its priests can never be condoned on moral grounds, nevertheless it is necessary to consider the feelings of the people toward the Church at that time and to seek to explain why they harbored such animosity toward a "Christian" institution. The Church had sadly neglected its chief duty in Spain. No institution in any country had at its disposal such vast assets which might have been used to assist the people in the direction of social progress and a Christian life to the extent possessed by the Roman Catholic Church in Spain. The failure to thus utilize its resources and to function according to its tenets were major crimes.

In addition, coursing through many Spanish veins was a mortal hatred of the condescending Church which had, throughout modern history, almost invariably espoused the worst causes in national life. Malraux's anarchist Puig responds violently to this feeling:

> "My comrades say we are foolish to be attending to the churches when we should be burning the banks. I tell them to leave the burning of banks to the bourgeoisie; that is their line. The priests are another matter. Those churches, where they have retreated after having thirty thousand good men arrested and tortured, and the rest of it—let them burn, and a good thing too!" (36)

Always on the side of the powerful, the rich, the oppressive authority, the Church had become an object of general aversion. The Spanish working classes attacked priests because they thought of them as hypocrites and because the clergy seemed to provide a spiritual front for a tyrannical ruling caste. Whether the military had taken the Church into its confidence regarding its plot is less important than the fact that public esteem of the Church had fallen so low that people easily believed the priests were capable of firing on the workers. And one priest who had escaped to France from Barcelona was frank to admit that "the Reds have destroyed our churches . . . but we priests had first destroyed the Church."[9] Malraux's Catholic Ximenes sadly confirms that in Barcelona, "on certain churches, instead of the usual scrawled notice, *Under the People's Management,* I saw written, *Appropriated by the People's Vengeance.*" (160)

Under such tense circumstances it was inevitable that a combination of three forces—the violently anticlerical passions of the extremists, the general antagonism of the masses toward the Church, and the spirited rather than spiritual attitude of the priests themselves—should result in excesses. And if the extremist elements committed the actual violence, the Spanish people's conscience was quiescent, if not actually approving. Attacks on the Church were not new to Spain, and the particular ferocity of this one was based on a deep-seated necessity for revenge and punishment for a betrayed trust. The people in the street could not yet destroy the economic basis for the tyranny to which they had been subjected, but they could at least strike back at the one institution which personified this tyranny.

With the outbreak of hostilities, Catholic and monarchist Navarre had aligned itself with the rebels, and had supplied them with some of the outstanding troops, the Requetés, recruited from the far right of the traditionalist movement in Spanish politics. Koestler relates the cause of this alignment to the social and political nature of Navarre:

> The great majority of the Catholics of Navarra have been without doubt behind Franco from the beginning. . . . The Pyrenean valleys of Navarra had remained a stronghold of medieval tradition; it was Spain's Vendee and the birthplace of the Carlist movement. In Navarra Catholicism was synonymous with the political programme of absolute monarchy, with the retention of patriarchal, feudal conditions in agriculture. . . . The Catholicism of Navarra professed the faith of the Church of Torquemada, of the quarrelsome and worldly Popes of the Middle Ages, of the Church Militant. (111–12)

And Regler's internationals, sounding a great deal like Hemingway, begrudgingly express their admiration for the fighting ability of these men from Navarre.

> "You mustn't underestimate the enemy; those Requétes fight like wild beasts." . . . "A king may be replaced by a duce, and neither is enough against shells and machine-guns. But when a man fights for the Virgin, for the sacrament, for the glory in the skies, you get savage soldiers, crusaders." (146)

A rift separated the Catholic Church in northern Spain as the great majority of the Basque Catholics sided with the Republic. The Basque country is generally conceded to be the one province of Spain which has most strictly adhered to the fundamental principles of Christian faith. It is also the only province of Spain in which a Christian social movement, with its roots in an alliance between the people and the Church, can be compared in strength with the socialist movements among the workers. Part of the Basque support was due to the desire for regional autonomy. Koestler notes that the Basques' recognition of the Nationalists' attitude toward separation was a major factor in their decision to commit themselves to the Loyalist cause:

> The Basques have striven for centuries to attain linguistic, cultural and economic autonomy. History has taught them that the liberal democratic movement in Spain favours the cause of racial minorities and that movements aiming at absolute monarchy and dictatorship, on the other hand, are bitterly opposed to all demands for autonomy. The Catholics of the Basque country had everything to hope for from the Republic and nothing from the Generals. Franco's first act after the taking of Bilbao was to abolish Basque fiscal autonomy. (110–11)

The liberal Catholic Guernico in Malraux's *L'espoir* compares the Basque and Navarre priests and proposes a condemnation of the Spanish Church:

> "What do those priests of Navarre, who permit men to be executed for the 'glory of the Holy Virgin,' know of charity? Rather it is the Basque priests who truly understand the meaning of Christian charity; those priests who till the fascists killed them went on administering the benediction, in the cellars of Irun, to the anarchists who had burned their churches. I recognize the Church of Spain, but—all the faith I have bears me out—I'm against it in the name of the three major virtues of our creed: Faith, Hope and Charity." (269–70)

The situation of the Church in the Insurgent zone differed greatly from that in the Republican zone. There was nothing specifically religious in the first public pronouncements of the rebel military authorities. As the Church publicly supported the Insurgents at every opportunity, however, it gradually assumed a prominent position in the Nationalist regime; in return for this support the generals expected and generously received the Church's active cooperation. On the whole the Church cooperated willingly: the bishops and archbishops appeared in the company of the military officials at all public ceremonies; they blessed the troops and provided confessors for the prisons. As the war progressed, religious persecution subsided in Republican Spain, but with the tide of the war turning in favor of the Nationalists, the Franco regime began a massive purge. Occasionally, parish priests pleaded for the lives of particular individuals sentenced to death, but no section of the Roman Catholic Church questioned the principle of execution or the general extent of the purge itself. Village priests were expected to serve on local purge committees, and they were neither less cruel nor more generous than their fellow members in handing down death sentences.

Koestler asserts that since World War I the Spanish clergy had been exceptionally vocal in the praise of the fascist regimes in Germany and Italy. The clerical press in Spain enthusiastically acclaimed the Italian campaign in Abyssinia and systematically avoided all references to the persecution of German priests and pastors by the Nazis. They were also forced to overlook the treatment of their own priests when these clergy fell out of favor with the military:

> The crusading spirit of the rebel Generals only persists so long as believers and priests identify themselves with the purely political aims of the insurrection. The moment that priests, and even bishops, cease to see eye to eye with these political aims they are treated as enemies, and either imprisoned or shot. A well-known case in point is that of the Bishop of Vitoria. . . . (112)

And Koestler continues his analysis of the attitude of the Nationalist regime toward the Church, which he claims is a symbiotic relationship:

> Franco does not represent the interests of believers as against the forces that threaten religion. He represents the interests of that section of the Catholic population which is Catholic *and* reactionary. Catholics with Republican sympathies are persecuted by him with the same ruthlessness as are Republicans who profess no religion. The Protestants who, owing to their social status, are almost entirely Republican, are treated as out-and-out enemies, as are the Jews. (115–16)

Regler's Albert and Malraux's Guernico are both Catholics who have totally abandoned their faith in the present Church. Each regards the Spanish Church with contempt, yet neither has truly freed himself from his own Catholicism, his vision of what the Church should be. Regler writes of his commissar:

> Albert had been a Catholic: he abandoned the Church when he could no longer reconcile its decay and its veniality with his ideas of universal moral law. What remained to him, something of an

> awkward encumbrance, was a passion for the logic of justice and of chivalry, even toward an opponent. And of this he had preserved more than the descendants of the Crusaders, in their mixture of spineless complacence and rigid intolerance, could show in our time. (20)

And Malraux's Guernico tries to communicate this same feeling to the communist García:

> I am neither a protestant nor a heretic; I am a Spanish Catholic. If you were a theologian, I would explain that I am appealing to the soul of the Church against its body. Faith doesn't imply a lack of love nor does hope imply a vision of a world seeking self-justification by forcing people to worship, like a fetish, that crucifix in Seville which they call the *Christ of the Rich.* (Our Church's problem is simony, not heresy.) Nor is it seeking a Spanish empire, a state in which no sound is heard because those who suffer must hide themselves to weep. Even the best of fascists hasn't a single hope that isn't founded on pride. What has Christ to do with such a vision? (269)

For sensitive Catholics, the fate of the Church was possibly worse in the Insurgent zone than in the Loyalist zone. In Madrid and Barcelona, Catholics lived through an experience mildly comparable to the catacombs. But sacrifice, and even martyrdom, had spiritual compensations. In the Insurgent zone power and prestige were on the side of the Church. Bernanos, in Nationalist occupied Majorca, could do little more than condemn the Church for its role in the purge of the island:

> Terrorism at the time perhaps appeared inseparable from all revolutionary disorder; but of all the destructive forces, terrorism is the most far-reaching, pierces the deepest, extending to the roots of the soul. When I see an acid poured over a limb of Christianity —even though it be gangrened—I realize the burning will destroy it completely, down to the last fiber, the final seed. . . . It is clear that the reign of terror would long ago have burned itself out were it not for the open and conscious endorsement of priests and church-goers, who have finally succeeded in endowing it with a religious aspect. (145–46)

Condonation by the clergy of the violence and atrocities outraged his humanist conscience. All that the Church officially insisted upon was that those killed should have the opportunity for confession. Bernanos relates that the Majorcan clergy actually boasted of a 90 per cent conversion of Loyalists immediately prior to execution: " 'No doubt they were quite decent fellows,' the Spanish bishops will probably answer, 'for the majority were converted *in extremis*. According to the report of our Venerable Brother in Majorca, only 10 per cent of those dear children refused the last sacraments before being dispatched by our good officers.' " (98)

As archbishops, bishops, canons, and priests daily implored the protection of the Virgin for the Insurgent troops, others of the clergy actually fought with the Nationalist forces. For the majority of the clergy in Nationalist territory, their alliance consisted of giving the full support of their position and prestige to the "Movement." Among their duties they were active in Nationalist prisons, particularly when death sentences were to be carried out. One of the peasants held prisoner by the Nationalists describes in Malraux's *L'espoir* how the coming of the priests during the night alerted the condemned men:

> The fascists opened a door and pushed a poor devil out. Then it started all over again. We never heard the firing squad, only the priest's bell. When that swine started ringing, we knew what it meant: one of us was in for it. Try to confess, to give us absolution, according to him. Surely not for defending ourselves against the generals. After fifteen days of listening to that bell ring, I realized that those "pardons" are a racket; it isn't only a matter of money. What does a priest tell you when he is confessing you? He tells you to repent. If there is a single priest who convinced a single one of us to repent for having defended himself—well, there is no fate too bad for him. Because repentence is about the best thing a man has in him. (157)

And as the civilians were executed in Majorca, Bernanos caustically comments: "The personage whom good manners require that I should refer to as Archbishop, had delegated a priest who was forced to stand with his boots paddling in the blood, distributing absolutions between the executions." (140)

The association of religion and acts of violence in the Nationalist camp is echoed by both Regler and Hemingway. As the Insurgents with the aid of the Church attempted to create an image of themselves as defenders of Christianity, Regler called attention to their use of the historical enemies of the Spanish Church—the Moors—in their fight against the people of Spain:

> Albert wrenched his briefcase open, and took out the banner of the Tercios. . . . It was red and yellow, embroidered with a blue Virgin. . . . This fascist Mary floated over Badajoz, over the twitching bodies, over the groaning women and the bloody grunting Moors. (175)

And in *For Whom the Bell Tolls,* Hemingway has the fascist Lieutenant Berrendo give the order for the decapitation of the dead after the battle with El Sordo, and "then he made the sign of the cross again and as he walked down the hill he said five Our Fathers and five Hail Marys for the repose of the soul of his dead comrade." (322)

As the war progressed the already heated controversy over the religious implications of the Spanish Civil War was intensified. Although the Vatican bestowed official recognition on the Burgos regime, the controversy nevertheless continued throughout the war. The hierarchy of the Spanish Church, led by Cardinal Goma, the Archbishop of Toledo, took the extraordinary step of dispatching a joint letter to the "Bishops of the Whole World" in which they explained that they had not wished an "armed plebiscite" in Spain, though thousands of Christians "had taken up arms on their personal responsibility to save the principles of religion."[10] In their effort to justify the Nationalists' position theologically, these members of the Spanish episcopacy attached to it the aura of a modern "crusade." Koestler attempts to expose the fundamental lie behind such propaganda:

> It is one of the fundamental untruths of the rebal propaganda to designate this war as a religious war. One need not be an orthodox Christian to consider it blasphemy for ambitious Generals to use God as an excuse for their insurrection. The struggle between feudalism and democracy in Spain has as little to do with religion as had those picture postcards in 1914 which portrayed God as blessing a French mine-layer or a German submarine. (112)

Such criticism does not carry with it nearly the force of Bernanos' denunciation of the concept of a "holy war" which he expressed in *Les grands cimetières sous la lune.* That the Spanish Civil War—social war, political war, class war, war of international intervention—should take on an additional dimension, that of a war of religion, is completely rejected by Bernanos:

> I consider the concept of a Spanish "crusade" a farce, for set against each other are the two same heterogeneous, partisan groups which had opposed each other during the election and which will always be opposed to no purpose since neither truly knows what it wants and because each exploits the use of force lacking the insight to use it advantageously. . . . Naturally you may say that the Reds are not worth much and that all slogans in time of war are good: You can also say that the Mikado is a good Catholic, that Italy has always been the defender of the faith, or even that General Queipo de Llano is cast in the mold of Bayard or Godefroy de Bouillon—do as you wish! But don't speak to me of "crusades." (197–98)

Bernanos maintains that such terminology has no basis in the facts of the conflict. In the modern history of Western civilization, war between foreign powers, or war against fellow-citizens, is, of necessity, profane and secular. And if religious values are in question, defended by one side and attacked by the other, the religious values are themselves secularized. In civil wars there are sufficient human values and partial truths, on either side, for one to characterize the war as "holy" and to assert that he is fighting and dying for justice. Bernanos anticipates that a time may come when the last free men will be compelled to defend their Christian principles in a degenerate Europe, or Christianity shall become extinct:

> I truly do believe in a Holy War, and I also believe that it is inevitable. In a world steeped in lies and hypocrisy, the revolt of the few remaining free and honest men is inevitable. The phrase Holy War half pleases me: saints rarely make war, and as for the others—those who flatter themselves into thinking they are saints —God protect me from such men! I believe in the war of free men, men of good will. . . . I should be glad to call men free when they ask nothing better than to live and die in peace, but who now blame your civilization for making a muddle of such values. (211)

Expecting to be accused of attacking ecclesiastics and possibly being regarded as a seditious influence, Bernanos remarks that this same Church may, not without historical precedent, some day in the future use *Les grands cimetières sous la lune* in its own defense: "Perhaps the future Church historians may use these few modest pages to prove the argument that Catholic opinion was not unanimous in its support of Franco and his followers." (145)

The most notable aspect of the reaction of these novelists to the Church's responsibility for the Spanish tragedy and the role it chose to play throughout the conflict is that not one of them truly condemned the Roman Catholic Church. Even communists, such as Koestler and Regler, tempered their criticism of the Church with references to the corruption of the Spanish episcopacy while recognizing the victimization of the lower clergy. Undeniably an undercurrent of latent anti-Catholicism existed in modern Europe and the United States, but these writers were not anti-Catholic, nor were they seeking to perpetuate an ugly tradition of "Catholic-baiting." Their response was prompted by a firm belief in a democracy's ability, despite its past mistakes, to come to terms with its religious problems. The criticism of the Spanish Church was not provoked by feelings of animosity toward Catholicism, nor did these writers rejoice in the suffering inflicted upon the Church itself. In their writings they never attempted to fix all the responsibility for the Spanish tragedy on the Church, or deny the anticlerical charges against the Spanish Republic, or seek comfort in the disasters that befell the Church.

Bernanos, the only devout Catholic of the six novelists involved in this study,[11] sets the tone for these critics when he writes movingly of the human failings of the Spanish Church:

> If I happen to hold the Church responsible, it is not with the absurd notion of reforming it. I do not consider the Church capable of human reformation, at all events in the manner of Luther. I do not expect the Church to be perfect, for the Church is a living thing. Like the most lowly, the most destitute of her sons, the Church stumbles haltingly from this world to the next; she sins, she expiates, and those who can see through her pomp and ritual hear her praying and crying in the darkness. But she must be held responsible because she is always responsible. I am dependent upon her and her offense has touched me, has pierced my soul, and has struck at the very roots of my hope. . . . It is not that

> we wish to charge her with her faults; it is not the faults that shatter our soul, but rather the false pride. (147–48)

For religious Catholics such as Bernanos, the failure of the Church to fulfill his hopes was tragic, but never unforgivable.

Nor can Hemingway's peasants forsake their religious beliefs. While at first the Christian Anselmo, "something very rare in Catholic countries," has renounced the Church, he can never free himself from its precepts. In his disgust with the killing, which cuts cruelly across the Christian grain of this admirable old man and which has become a necessary part of his existence as a partisan fighter, he reflects on the penitence that some day he must make with a secular substitute for religion—a substitute which fulfills his old Catholic conception and the new revolutionary vision of which he feels he is a part:

> It must really be a great sin, he thought. But certainly it is the one thing we have no right to do even though, as I know, it is necessary. . . . I wish I did not think about it so much, he thought. I wish there were a penance for it that one could commence now because it is the only thing that I have done in all my life that makes me feel badly when I am alone. . . . Later on there may be certain days that one can work for the state or something that one can do that will remove it. It will probably be something that one pays as in the days of the Church, he thought, and smiled. The Church was well organized for sin. (197–98)

And, later, when Hemingway's young and innocent neo-communist Joaquin lies trapped on a hilltop with El Sordo's band, he first appeals for help to La Pasionaria, the communist "Virgin" in a Marxist Spain, and then, as death approaches, he reverts to his ingrained Catholicism. The conflict between his Catholic faith and the pseudo religion of the communists is debated by him as the fascist bombers drone overhead. As Joaquin starts to intone the words of La Pasionaria for help, the closeness of death forces him to return to the religion of his first eighteen years:

> "Pasionaria says 'Better to die on thy—'" Joaquin was saying to himself as the drone came nearer them. Then he shifted suddenly into "Hail Mary, full of grace, the Lord is with thee; Blessed art thou among women and Blessed is the fruit of thy womb, Jesus. Holy Mary, Mother of God, pray for us sinners now and at the

hour of our death. Amen. Holy Mary, Mother of God," he started, then he remembered quickly as the roar came now unbearably and started an act of contrition racing in it, "Oh my God, I am heartily sorry for having offended thee who art worthy of all my love—" (321)

To the serious Guernico in Malraux's *L'espoir*, the Spanish Civil War is a chance for the Spanish Church to redeem itself and proceed to a spiritual renaissance. Prior to the war, Guernico recalls, the Church had neglected its duties and Spain had become a spiritual wasteland:

> I believe that what is now happening—even the burning of the churches in Catalonia—may do more for my Church than the last hundred years of Spanish Catholicism have done for it. For my twenty years I have seen the priests exercising their ministry here and in Andalusia, and I have never truly glimpsed a Catholic Spain. Only ritual and ceremony, and in the people's hearts as on the face of nature—a wasteland! (268–69)

The spiritual trials of the clergy during the fighting, especially those priests in Republican Spain, may do much to revitalize a Church which has fallen into decay:

> At this moment in those squalid buildings as well as in hospitals, there are priests, collarless, in waistcoats like Parisian waiters, and they are hearing confessions, giving extreme unction, even baptising children. I have said that for twenty years Christ's word was not heard in Spain, but I am hearing it now. And those priests are being listened to but nobody will listen to those clergy who tomorrow again don their cassocks to bless Franco. How many priests are now carrying out their ministry: fifty, perhaps one hundred. Napoleon once walked through these arcades; in those days the Church of Spain protected its flock; and since then I doubt that there has been a single night, until now, when Christ's words were truly living in our midst. But tonight they are a living presence. (270)

Malraux concludes that much of the fault of the Spanish Church may be attributed to its wealth, which had enabled the clergy to live a life of ease. Such a life, according to Guernico, is not what God intended for his ministers: "God alone knows the trials He is about to impose on the priesthood; but I believe that a priest's work *should* become a difficult task once again. . . . As indeed the life of each Christian is a struggle." (217)

## NOTES

[1] The sources consulted for background material on the position of the Church in Spanish social and political life include Borkenau, *Spanish Cockpit,* Brenan, *Spanish Labyrinth,* José Castillejo, *War on Ideas in Spain* (London, 1937), Madariaga, Mendizábal, E. Allison Peers, *Spain, the Church and the Orders* (London, 1939), Sánchez, and John B. Trend, *The Origins of Modern Spain* (Cambridge, 1934).

[2] *Spanish Cockpit,* p. 9.

[3] *Ibid.,* p. 10.

[4] *Spanish Labyrinth,* pp. 49–50.

[5] In *El Siglo Futuro,* May 6, 1931.

[6] Regarding the number of churches burned, the figures vary from 119 attacks listed in Catholic author Moreno's *Historia de la Persecución Religiosa en España,* to the *New York Times* reports of 21 actual serious incidents. Fixing the blame also offers a wide range of diverse interpretations extending from premeditated acts of fanatical anarchists, spontaneous rioting of the populace, to a plot by monarchist extremists to discredit the Republic.

[7] Quoted in Sánchez, *Reform and Reaction,* p. 206.

[8] *Spanish Civil War,* p. 172.

[9] Madariaga, *Spain,* p. 495.

[10] Quoted in Thomas, *Spanish Civil War,* p. 450.

[11] Hemingway and Regler were reared as nominal Catholics.

# ▸ VI

## ▸ The Pornography of Violence

Irrational impulses are not surprising in the stress and tension of a civil war. In an atmosphere of violence, reason is sometimes abandoned and humanitarian principles forgotten. The inflamed passions of the time lead men to commit atrocities. But the concern in this study is not with the psychological pathology of those who commit atrocities but rather with the literary treatment of such acts of violence. Throughout modern history atrocity propaganda has often mesmerized readers thousands of miles from the scene of the conflict. Often the improbability of the actions described suggests that the stories were little more than fantasies concocted for diverse reasons from even more diverse sources. But the reading public has invariably evinced a morbid absorption with the most nightmarish aspects of this form of sensationalism. William James cynically observed that material which should create a moral aversion to the cruelty of war often produces a perverse fascination instead.

The precedent for atrocity propaganda was established well before the twentieth century, but the techniques perfected attained new heights during World War I. Koestler speaks for most journalists who covered that conflict when he notes, "We know how much harm the preposterous atrocity propaganda engaged in by both sides caused during the Great War, and the author shares the repugnance felt by every newspaper man with a conscience at the thought of allowing himself to be drawn into such slimy depths." (84) Various studies have been made of the atrocity propaganda of the First World War—the ghastly stories of handless babies, crucified soldiers, corpse factories, and other deliberately contrived falsehoods which were fed to an avid public. This form of propaganda was highly successful in arousing resentment, and its advantages were well known to supporters of the Republic and the Insurgents at the beginning of the Spanish Civil War.

The Spanish conflict aroused such emotionalism that partisans of both sides exceeded the professional journalists in inventing tales of horror. Fortunately, the sophisticated and more intellectual writers recognized that the emotions stirred by such stories held greater appeal for savages than for civilized human beings. These writers did not deny the truth of the atrocities, nor did they refuse to treat the subject. But each author realized that to present such material without first including extenuating circumstances surrounding each incident would be to sacrifice literary integrity for journalistic expediency and sensationalism. While Hemingway, Orwell, Malraux, Bernanos, Regler, and Koestler refrained from such writing, extremist publications throughout the democracies printed gruesome stories of rapes, mutilations, perversities, and child murders. An extremely partisan and sympathetic public was willing to read and believe almost anything, if it were tinged with sadism. Gamel Woolsey, American wife of the British historian Gerald Brenan, termed this obsession with atrocity stories "the pornography of violence": "The dreamy lustful look that accompanies them, the full enjoyment of horror (especially noticeable in respectable elderly Englishmen speaking of the rape or tortue of naked nuns: it is significant that they are always 'naked' in such stories), show only too plainly their erotic source."[1] Orwell comments on this propaganda in England during the 1936–1939 period:

> We all remember the *Daily Mail's* poster: 'REDS CRUCIFY NUNS,' while to the *Daily Worker* Franco's Foreign Legion was 'composed of murderers, white-slavers, dope-fiends and the offal of every European country.' As late as October 1937 the *New Statesman* was treating us to tales of Fascist barricades made of

> the bodies of living children (a most unhandy thing to make barricades with), and Mr. Arthur Bryant was declaring that 'the sawing-off of a Conservative tradesman's legs' was 'a commonplace' in Loyalist Spain. The people who write that kind of stuff never fight; possibly they believe that to write it is a substitute for fighting. (65–66)

The novelists in this study recognized that much of the savagery connected with the war in Spain could be explained in the violence inherent in the character of the Spanish people. Not only are the Spaniards more passionate than northern Europeans and North Americans, but they hate more bitterly as well. Orwell, Koestler, Malraux, Hemingway, Bernanos, and Regler never lost sight of this bitterness within the civil war, in which the opposing ideologies struggled, inextricably locked in combat throughout every town and village. And added to this flame were the intense religious feelings, class hatreds, political feuds, sectional differences—all serving to intensify the bitterness. Madariaga believes that too much stress has been placed on the anarchical, irregular, and irresponsible nature of the terror which shook Spain at the beginning of the war. He maintains that impartial information after the conflict had ended has proven that both sides sinned equally, that terrorism was rife, systematic, and prolonged. In a sense it was inevitable and irrelevant, and it can at least partially be attributed to the Spanish temperament.[2] Koestler acknowledges that the Spanish character may, at least partly, explain the exceptional violence of their civil war:

> It would, of course, be absurd to deny that atrocities have been committed on the Government side. The Spaniards show an undeniable tendency towards cruelty; the celebrating of bull fights as national festivals is hardly an engaging trait in the character of a people. I am convinced that enough acts of brutality have been committed on both sides to satisfy Europe's demand for horrors for the next hundred years.

But at the same time Koestler reacts strongly to those tales of atrocities which tend to depict one side or the other as monsters:

> The "black-is-black" and "white-is-white" technique of many propagandists of the Left—Fascist devils on the one hand, democratic angels on the other—is just as absurd as the "red-and-white"

> technique of the rebel propagandists. The stories of the burning of churches in Barcelona and the villages of Andalusia are no fable; I have seen such churches with my own eyes. A good many of them served as hiding-places for rebels and priests armed with rifles. Others, however, did not, and were burned nevertheless. Let me repeat: only demagogues and abstract doctrinaires with no first-hand experience of the Civil War can deny that a great number of abominable acts have been committed on both sides. (130)

Though these novelists willingly admitted the perpetration of atrocities by the Loyalists as well as the Insurgents, they made a definite distinction betwen the two. Those acts of violence involving civilians, which occurred in Republican territory, took place early in the war, amidst considerable chaos and confusion. The government had no organized army or police force during this period and had been forced to arm the masses indiscriminately. The inevitable consequence was that some of these arms found their way into the hands of irresponsible elements. During the first few days after the outbreak of the insurrection, the government had no real control over the masses. In this interim period, while the Republican army was assuming shape, the administration attempted to master the situation, declared martial law, and demanded the death penalty for looting and molesting private citizens; the militia officers were made personally responsible for the fate of the civilian population in the cities and villages throughout Loyalist Spain. Koestler describes the conditions at this time:

> The most difficult task of all was to restrain the peasants in the outlying districts of Andalusia and Estramadura, who were in a state of raging fury. . . . Ninety per cent of all the excesses committed by the armed forces of the Government were committed during this period of chaos and confusion, which lasted no longer than from two to three days in the large towns, and from eight to ten in the villages. With astounding speed the Government made itself master of the situation in those districts where the revolt was stemmed. (131–32)

Hemingway's Pilar in *For Whom the Bell Tolls* (99–129) describes the massacre in a small town near Avila in Old Castile. An enraged peasant group led by Pablo put down the insurrection. Gradually these peasant defenders were transformed into a bloodthirsty mob which began a purge of the leading citizens of the town. Pilar recounts with clinical interest the death of each fascist as Pablo personally executes the four prisoners, members of the "guardia civil" who had surrendered. Although she watches the slaughter that follows with cold fascination and no thought of protest, Pilar experiences a sympathy for the victims and disgust at the combination of bestiality and drunkenness exhibited by the mob. This sense of humanity manifests itself in her revulsion as she recalls the atrocities: "It was as after a storm or a flood or a battle and every one was tired and no one spoke much. I, myself, felt hollow and not well and I was full of shame and a sense of wrong doing and I had a great feeling of oppression and of bad to come." (127) Pilar's loathing is shared by other individuals within the mob, as is a feeling of regret that their revolution should start on such an inhuman note: "If it is necessary to kill them all, and I am not convinced of that necessity, let them be killed decently and without mockery." (119) The failure of social conditions to provide these peasants with a more civilized alternative than mob action was an implicit indictment of the ruling classes. In the inhuman apathy of the landlords to the suffering of these people may be traced the sources of this violence. But even then Hemingway is not attempting to condone such atrocities. After the massacre Pilar remembers, "Then I went back inside the room and I sat there and I did not wish to think for that was the worst day of my life until one other day . . . three days later when the fascists took the town." (129)

Conditions in those sections of Spain immediately occupied by the Insurgent forces were not dissimilar. Bernanos describes an incident involving a Republican mayor in a village on the island of Majorca. Since the war began the island had never been in Republican hands, so that the murder and cruelty accompanying it cannot be ascribed to retaliation for earlier crimes committed against that portion of the population sympathetic to the rebels:

> The mayor of a small village was hidden by his wife in a cistern. At each sign of danger the poor fellow hid himself in a small niche, a few inches above the still water. They dragged him out one December night, shivering with fever. They took him to the

> cemetery and shot him in the stomach. Then, since he was in no hurry to die, his executioners who were drinking close by returned with a bottle of brandy, forced it into the mouth of the dying man, and then smashed his head in with the empty bottle. I repeat that these facts are public knowledge. (169–70)

Hemingway's Joaquin indicates the reasoning, often the result of long-standing political, religious, and social hatreds, used by the Insurgents after gaining control of Valladolid, to determine whom to execute:

> They were of the left as many others in Valladolid. When the fascists purified the town they shot first the father. He had voted Socialist. Then they shot mother. She had voted the same. It was the first time she had ever voted. After that they shot the husband of one of the sisters. He was a member of the syndicate of tramway drivers. Clearly he could not drive a tram without belonging to the syndicate. But he was without politics. I knew him well. He was even a little bit shameless. I do not think he was even a good comrade. Then the husband of the other girl, the other sister, who was also in the trams, had gone to the hills as I had. They thought she knew where he was. But she did not. So they shot her because she would not tell them where he was. (138)

As the Republic gradually reorganized the armed masses from independent militia units into a disciplined army, isolated acts of uncontrolled violence ceased. The Republican army in this early stage consisted almost entirely of armed civilians. Koestler analyzes the composition of such a military force and concludes that psychologically this heterogeneous group was incapable of the cruelty normally associated with hardened soldiers involved in a civil struggle:

> They came fresh from civilized life. They lacked the ruthlessness towards civilians of the professional soldier. They lacked the African ferocity of the Moors. They lacked the notorious unscrupulousness of the Foreign Legionaries. Soldierly cruelty was as little a part of their character as were other soldierly qualities. They were humane and not soldierly, and they lost one battle after another. They had neither the inclination nor the need to terrorise the population, to make warning examples, to safeguard the territory behind the lines by the application of methods of Terror. For they were literally of the people; they enjoyed the confidence

> and sympathy of the civilian population, whose life they had shared but the day before and whose sympathies they could but alienate by terrorist acts. (132)

In this analysis Koestler reveals the fundamental distinction which these literary intellectuals discerned between those acts of violence committed by the Loyalists and the Insurgents. This essential difference lies in the knowledge that the crimes perpetrated in the Republican zone were the result of spontaneous and sporadic outbursts on the part of widely diverse, undisciplined, and often uncontrollable elements. In contrast, the crimes committed in the Nationalist zone were recognized as part of a systematic campaign of terror, perpetrated with the full knowledge and consent of the responsible authorities. Koestler compares the behavior within the two camps in his *Spanish Testament:*

> Therein lies the fundamental difference between the behaviour of the two armies. Just as fundamentally different was the attitude of the two Commands. The very principles which the Madrid Government was upholding—democracy, humanitarianism, liberalism—are terms of derision in the mouths of Generals in backward, feudal countries. One could accuse these newly-fledged ministers of almost every failing—of being amateur, dilettante, irresolute, timid, incompetent; of being blind and of having allowed themselves to be taken unawares; of believing in compromise at the very moment when the guns of Generals were trained on them. But the very idea that a Caballero, an Azaña, a del Vayo or a Prieto could have displayed tendencies towards terrorism and cruelty, will seem to anyone with even a slight knowledge of Spain a very poor joke. (132–33)

Orwell calls attention to the fact that as the war progressed, the Insurgents, of necessity, eventually held a larger land area and civilian population under control than did the Republic. (69) With a generally hostile population to contend with in their occupied territory, the Insurgents were forced to resort to the cruelest forms of repression in order to protect themselves and the supply lines to their troops at the front. Koestler is able to assume a fascist point of view in analyzing the situation: "The Spanish rebels found themselves objectively in the position of an alien invading army. The masses sympathized either actively or passively with their opponents. There was only one method of forcing the masses in the district which they took to become neutral: the method of terror." (80) That the motives behind the Insurgents' actions were not based on revenge for crimes committed in territory once under Loyalist domination is confirmed by Bernanos:

> "But there was killing in Spain, one hundred and thirty-five political assassinations between March and July 1936." True, and so fascist terrorism could conceivably be regarded as a form of revenge, despite its blind viciousness which caused the death of so many innocents. But in Majorca there were no crimes to avenge, and so the terror could at best be termed a preventative action, the systematic extermination of suspects. Thus the majority of "legal" executions on the island—later for those without benefit of trial—were merely for *desafección al movimiento salvador*. (131)

Koestler and Malraux attest the "preventative action" in this systematic extermination of elements within Nationalist occupied territory. Koestler pictures the rebel General Franco as "the helpless tool of that logic of history which leaves a minority determined to assert itself against the majority no choice of methods. Terror was not merely an attendant phenomenon, but a vital function of his insurrection." (80) Both writers refer to a specific document, a circular addressed to the higher ranks of the officers in the rebel army, as proof of the deliberate character of the terror. This conclusive evidence was taken from a captured rebel officer after the battle of Guadalajara. Malraux's García paraphrases the Koestler version (81–82) of this document:

> One of the conditions essential to victory is that the morale of the enemy troops shall be shaken. Our enemies have at their disposal neither sufficient troops nor sufficient arms to resist us; nevertheless, it is indispensable that you strictly follow these instructions:
>
> To secure our occupation of the countryside, it is essential to inspire a certain salutary dread in the population. Therefore all measures adopted should be both impressive and spectacular.
>
> All points situated in line with the enemy's retreat and, in general, all points to the rear of the enemy front, should be considered attack zones. Even if these localities do not harbor enemy troops, panic prevailing along the line of the enemy's retreat tends to lower the morale of their troops.
>
> Experiences during World War I show that damage unin-

> tentionally inflicted on enemy ambulances and hospital trains greatly contributes to the demoralization of the troops. . . .
>
> The more uncompromising our attitude and the more ruthless our elimination of all resistance on the part of the population, the sooner will our triumph bring about the renovation of Spain. (322)

Atrocity propaganda from Republican and Nationalist sources was an attempt to win sympathy within the democracies for their respective factions. Because a Nationalist victory implied a military dictatorship, a corporate state, and clericalism—causes which have never been popular in England, France, and the United States—and because the pronunciamiento of the generals was against a liberal, democratic Republic whose constitution and political program were modeled after these Western democracies, normal political propaganda on behalf of the Insurgents would have proved entirely ineffective. Except for the fears concerning Russian influence in Spain, there could be little political sympathy in the democracies for the rebellious Spanish military. Koestler concludes that the Nationalist propaganda agents had no real alternative but to resort to atrocity reports:

> So he deliberately chose a form of propaganda that from the time of the ritual murder myths of the Middle Ages until the time of the Reichstag fire and the Abyssinian campaign has always proved an unfailing standby whenever it had been essential to avoid awkward political discussions and to justify one's own terroristic acts by pointing to those of the other side: what has come to be known as atrocity propaganda. . . . He preferred to tell them [the democracies] stories of mangled corpses, of the putting-out of eyes, and of Red cannibalism. This kind of propaganda is always more effective and sensational and saves one the necessity of logical argument. (129–30)

The extent of atrocity propaganda varied from documented accounts to completely invented fiction. The official reports and accounts by fugitives were not easily authenticated. For this reason Orwell and Bernanos, in their personal narratives, and Koestler in his revised text, relied solely on firsthand accounts, taking into consideration only those facts personally witnessed or reported to them by people whose trustworthiness was unquestionable. The novels of Malraux, Hemingway, and Regler naturally do not require such documentation, but nevertheless they do not exceed the bounds of probability.

The Nationalists' concept of total war shocked the literary intellectuals and represented for them a new barbarism and a repudiation of the humaneness of man. The one act of horror which aroused the abhorrence of most of these authors was the aerial bombardment of civilian populations. Malraux and Regler in their novels describe the horrible effects of the bombing of Madrid in terms of death visited upon helpless women and children. Regler's International Brigade member relates his impressions during the bombardment of the city:

> "You can't imagine! They rushed out of all the houses into the street and over to the demolished building, and began lifting up beams and digging in the plaster, exactly as if the booming had stopped and these bastards weren't flying around up there. They just wanted to help, and pretty soon the first pair of legs came out of the rubbish. Bloody and covered with plaster. It was a woman, her breast was still soft as it slipped out of her dress. Well, sir, I thought of my own girl. And later they got a child out too, it dangled its arms when the soldier took it up—just like my Veronica when she falls asleep at the circus." (108–109)

In *L'espoir,* Malraux's Lopez offers two similar incidents in which the victims of the bombing bear no resemblance to the Loyalist troops. He describes the slaughter of innocent women and children by explosives dropped mercilessly from military planes on the helpless victims below:

> One morning in the nursery school of the Plaza del Progreso, three children were playing at war, looking at the sky. "A bomb!," cried one. "Get down!" All three fell flat like disciplined soldiers. It was a real bomb. The other children, who were not playing soldier, remained standing, and were killed or wounded. (318)

The sounds of death and suffering throughout *L'espoir* evoke feelings of dread and compassion. Malraux recreates the torture and suffering of the Spanish people through the sounds alone: screaming sirens, dirges, "barbarous litanies," lamentations, the whimpering and screaming of the wounded, howling stray dogs, exploding bombs, roaring guns, crashing window panes and buildings, the cadence of the rain, the silences of dreadful anticipation and bloody aftermaths. As Lopez continues his tour of the city during the bombing attack:

> A building was aflame, a cinematic conflagration. Behind an ornamental facade, still intact, the shattered windows on each floor were transfigured by the flames within, as if the house were inhabited by elemental Fire. Further along a bus stood waiting at a street corner. Suddenly Lopez stopped, breathless for the first time since he came out, and then he frantically started gesturing and shouting, "Get down!" The people in the bus stared at him as though he were one more Madrileño, unbalanced by the war. Lopez dropped flat to the ground—there was an explosion—the bus went up in flame. When he got to his feet again, blood was streaming down walls. (319–20)

Perhaps Malraux's most compelling statement of the psychological effects of the death and destruction wreaked by the rebel bombers on the innocent appears in an anecdote which he related while on his American tour in 1937:

> In Madrid on the first day of January toys which had been sent from every country in the world were distributed to the children. The distribution took place at the center of the great bull ring; the toys were heaped up in little piles, each like a tangled mass of insects. For an hour the children passed in silence among these little piles of toys; and it seemed as if the generosity of all the world was also accumulated there. Then came the sound of the first bomb. A squadron of Junkers was bombarding the city. The bombs fell six hundred meters away; the attack was very short, and the bull ring is very large. By the time the children reached the gates, the Junkers had departed, and the children turned back to get the last toys. When all was over, there remained in the immense empty space one little heap, untouched. I approached to examine it; it was a pile of toy airplanes. It lay where any child could have helped himself. The little boys had preferred anything, even dolls, and had kept away from that pile of toy airplanes, not with fear, but with a sort of mysterious horror. That scene stayed in my memory. We and the Fascists are forever separated by that little heap of abandoned playthings.[3]

Just as the contrast between men and machines is a striking literary device in depicting modern warfare, descriptions of the effects upon children of the aerial bombardments during the Spanish struggle contain even greater impact. Portrayal of the suffering of the children of Madrid is a searing indictment of the fascist concept of total war. Malraux's utter condemnation of the indiscriminate bombing of helpless civilians is expressed in *L'espoir* through the American correspondent Slade who, with a liberal's indignation, protests man's inhumanity:

> Slade had often visited the front, but never before had he experienced this feeling. War was war, but this was something other than war. What he wished to see finished was not so much the aerial torpedoes themselves, as the ghastly slaughter house which they caused. The bombs continued to fall, destroying and maiming with erratic precision. Slade thought of his interviews and his notes, of the uneaten dinners in devastated houses, of the shattered picture glass with the little jet of blood beneath it, of the traveling coat hanging above a suitcase—in preparation for a trip to another world. He thought of a donkey whose hoofs alone had been left, of the long trials of blood left on pavements and walls by the wounded, like the tracks of hunted beasts, of the empty stretchers with a blood stain where each wound had permeated. Would there ever be enough rain to wash all this blood away? (303)

On the one hand, sexual psychopathy may explain the selection of material contained in the broadcasts of rebel General Queipo de Llano in his nightly commentary from Seville; the violation of pregnant women, the rape of children, the burning of living beings were the substance of de Llanos's rantings.[4] On the other hand, Malraux, Hemingway, Regler, Orwell, Bernanos, and Koestler presented the horrors of war as a form of protest. They described the fratricidal carnage during the struggle which they witnessed to enable the readers to understand fully the impact of the war on the Spanish people. They did not resort to atrocity propaganda to cover the political and social implications of the civil war. Nor did they ever indicate, implicitly or explicitly, that one side alone was to blame for the tragedy of the Spanish people caught up in the horrors of modern war. Their descriptions of the devastation wrought during the struggle were not attempts to glorify the deeds of the military heroes with the aim of pandering to the lowest instincts in readers, nor were they attempts to exculpate the Loyalist forces, but rather were a call for an end to the destruction and slaughter of the innocent.

Having established the extent of the revulsion against targetless bombardment and indiscriminate shelling, these novelists, particularly Gustav Regler, registered shock at the refusal of the fascists to abide by the rules of war with regard to treatment of wounded prisoners and immunity from attack accorded medical facilities. Regler mentions ambulances riddled with shrapnel (304) and relates heinous incidents in which captured wounded were slain, on one occasion by the Moors and on another by nuns serving as nurses in hospitals in Loyalist territory. In the first instance the field doctor Werner describes what he witnessed from a distance as the French sections, after they had exhausted their ammunition, were overrun by Moors:

> A shout from the tree drew his attention to the gorge. They were murdering the wounded! . . . "There is a limit to feeling," he said. "As I watched them go from stretcher to stretcher down there, that limit was reached. They did actually go from stretcher to stretcher, the Christian Franco's white-shrouded Africans. They saved their ammunition, they worked with knives, long, triangular, dully shining knives. They stabbed the wounded in the breast or belly. They were unmoved by pleading arms or cries. Besides the cries were too brief and all in French." (261)

And later Albert warns Werner about the nuns serving as nurses:

> And one last word about the nuns in the field hospital at Guadalajara! Throw them out! They'll find time for the Fascist wounded, and suddenly in some corner they'll find a chance to close our boy's eyes and have him sent quickly to the morgue, or they will overlook him, him and several others of ours: they will forget to attend them, "ad majorem dei gloriam." (317)

Regler's charges are confirmed by Bernanos. Bernanos points out that in Majorca the Catalan expedition to take the island was a total failure and that not one prisoner was taken:

> Not a single one of the sick and wounded who was taken prisoner during the military operations in August and September 1936, against the Catalans in Majorca, was spared by the Nationalists. Why should they have been, I ask you? Beyond the law, they

found themselves beyond humanity too, among ferocious animals —*feras*—wild beasts! (227–28)

Later, in *Les grands cimetières sous la lune,* Bernanos expresses his outrage at the actions of certain priests on the island who, under rebel military inspection, offered their ministrations at the mass executions of these prisoners. Nor can he forgive the passivity of that portion of the island's population which might have exerted a moderating influence. After describing the executions, in which priests went from victim to victim offering absolution, Bernanos recounts, in a parody, the pagan aspects of the Catholic ritual, the final atrocity, the burning of the bodies by the rebels:

> With their work finished, the "Crusaders" piled their "sheep" in two mounds—those who had been absolved and those who hadn't. Then they sprinkled gasolene over them. It is quite likely that this purification by fire may have assumed, by reason of the priests officiating, a liturgical significance. Unfortunately I only saw these blackened, charred figures two days later, contorted by the flames, some of them affecting obscene poses in death, which must have greatly disturbed the ladies of Palma and their eminent confessors. (241)

Regler, in *The Great Crusade,* also calls attention to the Insurgents' refusal to honor the procedures of modern warfare which provide for protection of military prisoners against torture and summary executions. In his conversation with Werner, the battalion surgeon, the commissar Albert criticizes the humanitarian code of the doctor. During the battles involving the International Brigades, Werner had risked his life removing dead and wounded from between the lines of combat and had tended the wounded on both sides. Albert tells him of less ethical treatment accorded the Loyalist wounded by the Insurgents:

> You will be surprised when you get nearer to the battlefield. In the hospital of January, where you operated on the Fascist boy, Fascist machine-guns are in every window now. The castle has become Italian. The hospital has been turned into a murderers' cave. Tomorrow they will torture two of our Garibaldis there, beat them with chains. Where two months ago you used your scalpel in those same rooms they will stab the stomachs of cap-

> tured comrades with bayonets. That is the great difference between you and Mussolini, Werner. (316)

The sympathy for the suffering of both sides which Werner felt was not experienced by all Loyalist supporters. Most anti-fascists confined their humanitarian feelings to those fighting and dying for the Loyalist cause; few committed to the Republican cause were inclined to testify to the humanity within the Nationalist ranks. But writers steeped in the humanist tradition, such as Orwell, Bernanos, Koestler, Hemingway, Malraux, and Regler, while venting their indignation at fascist atrocities, nevertheless called for an affirmation of the "fraternity of the suffering" and an end to man's inhumanity to man. These novelists refused to picture all Insurgents as inhuman monsters, although their description of the Moors fighting for the Insurgents are, without exception, almost totally filled with hatred. Rather, these authors insisted on a concept of the enemy's rank and file as men, often conscripts, quite capable of suffering from the same deprivations as the Loyalist soldiers. In this literature the Loyalist fighters are all alike in their hope for victory for their cause, but this does not preclude understanding their adversaries and realizing that these very men who shoot each other could, in different circumstances, have been comrades in arms. In Orwell's *Home to Catalonia,* the author strikes this theme as he humanizes the enemy in relating an incident during the holding war on the Aragon front. At the time desertions were quite common and did much to break the monotony of the military stalemate. Orwell describes his response to one fascist deserter who had recently crossed the lines:

> The chief excitement was the arrival of Fascist deserters, who were brought under guard from the front line. Many of the troops opposite us on this part of the line were not Fascists at all, merely wretched conscripts who had been doing their military service at the time when the war broke out and were only too anxious to escape. . . . These deserters were the first 'real' Fascists I had ever seen. It struck me that they were indistinguishable from ourselves, except that they wore khaki overalls. (16–17)

And in one of his first experiences with the violence of the war, he relates another indication of Republican troops' failure to perform as hardened veterans. Orwell, early in his combat experience, saw a soldier, surprised by a sudden air attack, fleeing from fascist trenches; the soldier was half-dressed and he held up his trousers with both hands as he ran. He was within easy range of Orwell's rifle, but the English author did not fire at him. "I had come here to shoot at 'Fascists'; but a man who is holding up his trousers isn't a 'Fascist,' he is visibly a fellow-creature, similar to yourself, and you don't feel like shooting at him."[5]

Regler's Garibaldi Battalion of the International Brigades, during the battle of Guadalajara, faced Italian conscripts in the field. As the fighting progressed, the Garibaldians attempted to win them over by an appeal to their countrymen, stressing that Mussolini had deceived them. The brigade commissar Albert explains to his troops the purpose of the propaganda leaflets he is circulating across the lines: "Once again the music of humanity was heard in the trenches. Yes, indeed, poor misled peasants were over there. Cowed workers who fought for fear of being shot. It must be explained to them that they had nothing to fear. The leaflets attempted to do so." (333) And Albert explains to his men who are anxious to attack and are impatiently awaiting the impact of the pamphlets on the Italian troops: "Those are proletarians over there, and these are proletarians here. The real enemies sit well out of range in Burgos and Rome. But you can't call proletarians enemies. How do you know how much those men over there may wish they were our friends?" (340)

In both the Hemingway and Regler novels there are similar incidents reminiscent of World War I's *All Quiet on the Western Front.* In each instance, while examining the papers of a slain enemy soldier, the Loyalists find among his personal possessions letters and pictures. The humanizing effect of a concerned mother, wife, or sweetheart, causes the Republican military man to reflect on the inhumanity of war. In *The Great Crusade,* the dead man is an Italian conscript whose letters from his wife accuse Mussolini of having deceived the Italian soldiers. The member of the International Brigades reading the letter expresses his understanding of the dead man's feelings: "Those soldiers went into battle with letters like that in their pockets. Nobody could possibly fight with less true conviction. . . . Had they all fought here under compulsion, and died with a curse for Mussolini on their lips?" (413) And Hemingway's dead Navarrese, a devout Catholic and Carlist, with letters from his sister and sweetheart, appears extremely warm and human; Robert Jordan, upon reading them, can only curse a war which forces him to kill young and innocent men. (302–303)

Hemingway also expounds on the theme of the similarity between the men in the opposing trenches. His peasant Anselmo cannot think in political terms and hate the enemy on ideological grounds. He can only regret that the next day he must kill these same men to whom ideology is equally foreign and who differ very little from himself:

> The fascists are warm, he thought, and they are comfortable, and tomorrow night we will kill them. It is a strange thing and I do not like to think of it. I have watched them all day and they are the same men that we are. I believe that I could walk up to the hill and knock on the door and I would be welcome except that they have orders to challenge all travelers and ask to see their papers. It is only orders that come between us. Those men are not fascists. I call them so, but they are not. They are poor men as we are. They should never be fighting against us. . . . (192–93)

The human qualities of the enemy are seen in their response to their treatment after having been taken prisoner by the Loyalists. Instead of the torture and execution they had anticipated as a result of their propaganda, intended to convince them to fight to the bitter end as capture would mean certain death, they discovered that the Republican forces, particularly the International Brigades, did not shoot prisoners but treated them fairly. In *The Great Crusade,* the Garibaldi Battalion captured a large group of Italians:

> Trembling and with open mouths that were no longer capable even of crying out, the enemy soldiers sat in the village waiting for the "coup de grace." Others fled down the slope of the vast northern valley, pursued more by their own fear than by bullets. "We are brothers," the Garibaldis bellowed at their prisoners. Thereupon the prisoners got up and stood themselves against a wall, resigned to their fate. But the Garibaldis bellowed again, and did not stop bellowing until a smile appeared on the faces of the prisoners. (150)

Hemingway's Anselmo also speaks on a second tangential theme found in all these novelists' work about the Spanish Civil War: the dehumanization of military life and the need to follow orders which conflict with the individual's personal code of morality. The conflict within the individual is never firmly resolved, but in each case presented in the novels in this study, the concept of military necessity dominates moral convictions. In *For Whom the Bell Tolls,* Hemingway contrasts his liberal idealist Robert Jordan and the fascist Lieutenant Berrendo. The religious beliefs of Jordan are challenged by the military mission to which he is assigned:

> Do you think you have the right to kill any one? No. But I have to. How many of those you have killed have been real fascists? Very few. But they are all the enemy to whose force we are opposing force. But you like the people of Navarra better than those of any other part of Spain. Yes. And you kill them. Yes. . . . And you still believe absolutely that your cause is right? Yes. (303–304)

Jordan is compelled to admit his distaste for the violence he is a part of, and he can function only because of his faith in the underlying justice of his cause. Jordan's counterpart, the Navarrese Berrendo, also finds his assignment distasteful and cannot expound social ideology as justification. Nevertheless, after decapitating the dead bodies of El Sordo's band, Berrendo relieves his conscience by asserting he has performed his sworn military duty:

> Lieutenant Berrendo, who was riding at the head of the column, his flankers out, his point pushed well forward, felt no arrogance. He felt only the hollowness that comes after action. He was thinking: taking the heads is barbarous. But proof and identification is necessary. I will have trouble enough about this as it is and who knows? This of the heads may appeal to them. There are those of them who like such things. It is possible they will send them all to Burgos. It is a barbarous business. (326)

This theme of the dehumanizing aspects of war and the introspective protagonist's fight against them recurs throughout *For Whom the Bell Tolls.* On another occasion Jordan experiences serious doubts regarding the human suffering entailed in his mission:

> And that is not the way to think, he told himself, and there is not you, and there are no people that things must not happen to. Neither you nor this old man is anything. You are instruments to do your duty. There are necessary orders that are no fault of yours and there is a bridge and that bridge can be the point on which the future of the human race can turn. (43)

But while Jordan finds some comfort in the knowledge that his mission is of importance in the fight against fascism, he cannot dismiss the thought that many innocent people would have to die before the war was over:

> The first thing was to win the war. If we did not win the war everything was lost. But he noticed, and listened to, and remembered everything. He was serving in a war and he gave absolute loyalty and as complete performance as he could give while he was serving. But nobody owned his mind, nor his faculties for seeing and hearing, and if he were going to form judgments he would form them afterwards. And there would be plenty of material to draw them from. There was plenty already. There was a little too much sometimes. (136)

Koestler, in the "Dialogue with Death" section of *Spanish Testament,* writes of a feeling of comradeship developed with the two civil guards who escorted him on the transfer from the prison in Malaga to the one in Seville. On the first step of his journey he traveled with his guards and other prisoners on their way to be executed, and he drew a fatalistic parallel between the killers and those about to be killed:

> The Civil Guards looked like Andalusian farm labourers or peasants, and the prisoners too looked like Andalusian farm labourers or peasants. There was no hostility between the two groups. We were, rather, like a charabanc party, all the members of which were going on the same excursion for the same purpose, far away from the noise of the big city to some green spot in the countryside. Arrived at our destination, the various roles would be assigned: some would stand up against a wall, the others would send hot leaden projectiles into their flesh. Both groups would, of course, rather be playing football; but that would not do. (257)

But after his arrival in Seville, Koestler realizes that the relationship which had developed between him and his guards could never survive the dehumanizing process of the war. In times of social upheaval, Koestler maintains, the character of the individual involved is dwarfed by the role social pressures force him to play:

> They were not exceptions; they were two out of twenty-five million for the most part kindly Spaniards. Had they been given orders, before we made friends on the journey, to strike me dead or to shoot me, they would have done so with complete sang-froid. Had they been fellow-prisoners, they would have shared their last cigarette with me. . . . I believe that in general we are given to over-estimating the importance of the individual character. Society allows the individual only very restricted scope for the realization of his primitive inclinations. What matters is not what a man is, but what function the social system dictates that he shall fulfil. (264–65)

Koestler's rather cold analysis of the human predicament in a violent social context is echoed by Regler, but in a much more emotional tone. Regler cries out against the pressures of war which do not permit the individual to realize his potential for fraternity with his fellowman:

> Battle of contradictions. For one moment the voice of reason appealed to the friends among the enemy. It shouted across the zone of death from stone wall to stone wall, calling the enemy brother, holding high the white banner of humanity. Then an enemy officer shouted down the appealing voice. . . . Reason sank down gently like a swooning woman. And suddenly all the trenches were deeper again, every yard, every stone a cover against oncoming death. There was nothing more in common. Once more the positions were as far apart as two planets, and the iron cross of hate streamed between them. Oh, it could be crossed, but only for the purpose of annihilating everything encountered, not to seek one's like. (332)

Each of the philosophical humanists involved in this study expresses outrage at the atrocities committed by both sides during the war. Although the irrational violence accompanying the civil war is deplored, a distinction is evidenced between the Loyalist acceptance of such acts as an undesirable consequence resulting from inflamed passions and the fascist glorification of these same atrocities. Only Malraux of the antifascist novelists is at all apprehensive about the general similarities in the irrational acts of individuals on both sides. But Malraux also believes that though the pressures of war are a common denominator which serves to erase ideological distinctions in the behavior of men, the cause for which the Republic is fighting cannot be judged by, or depend upon, the behavior of the individuals engaged in the struggle:

> Either Franco will attempt to adopt our program wherever he conquers, or he will be forced to embark on an endless guerilla war in the territory he occupies. Christ's triumph was only won through Constantine; Napoleon was completely crushed at Waterloo, but the essential points of French liberty defied suppression. One of the things that troubles me most about war is recognizing that each side takes on the characteristics of the enemy, consciously or unconsciously. (429)

Several distinctions may be noted in the treatment by these novelists of the inhumane conduct connected with the Spanish struggle. Notable is a complete absence in their writing of the sexual perverseness, the "pornography of violence," so prevalent in the atrocity literature of the time. In addition, in the novels of Hemingway, Regler, and Malraux, the violence described is one phase of a complex artistic endeavor where the essential purpose certainly transcends the mere presentation of bloated corpses, fetid latrines, and water-filled foxholes for their own sake. Finally, the scenes of atrocities described by these novelists, both in personal narratives and fiction, are realistic in their presentation of the action occurring in hundreds of Spanish communities during the war, and in their vivid descriptions of the realities of war. Each of these writers—contrary to the authors of atrocity literature—attempts to comprehend the psychological basis for such behavior: the causes behind the irrational conduct of men engaged in a passionate civil war. In each case the author attempts to explain—never justify or condone—the evil in the situation, and to reconcile philosophically his ideals with his participation in the horrors of modern war. This is in contrast with the failure of certain authors to exercise personal introspection, a commonplace among the writers who supported the Nationalists and refused to acknowledge any war crimes on the part of the Nationalists.

Perhaps some comment should be made of the public in the democracies. It displayed a fascination with the Spanish Civil War partly, perhaps, because of the gruesome details and morbid nature of the conflict. Such absorption with morbidity did not necessarily preclude a considerable interest in the basic causes of the struggle. At the same time, these novelists' protests of man's inhumanity to man were a part of the humanist tradition. While it is true that the humanitarian indignation against the violence of war was not what led these authors to laud the International Brigades, it is also true that implicit in the themes of their writing was a humanitarian impulse to put an end to the suffering among the innocent on both sides. Perhaps through such a group as the International Brigades victory might be achieved and a lasting peace result. Certainly the fascist threat to all the philosophical beliefs in the human qualities of Western civilization seemed to make that civilization hang in the balance, and a Loyalist victory appeared the only hope for an end to the violence and for man to remain free.

## ▸ NOTES

[1] Gamel Woolsey, *Death's Other Kingdom* (London, 1939), p. 126.

[2] See *Spain,* pp. 496–97.

[3] André Malraux, "Forging Man's Fate in Spain," *The Nation,* CXLIV (March 20, 1937), 316.

[4] See Koestler, *Spanish Testament,* p. 34.

[5] "Looking Back on the Spanish War," *Such Were the Joys,* pp. 135–36.

# ▸ VII

## ▸ The Great Crusade

For the major novelists involved, the Spanish Civil War developed beyond battlefield realities into a true conflict of ideas, thus transcending the concept of the war as a struggle between dictators to wrest power from a progressive, albeit weak, liberal regime. Their works, in essence, affirm a belief in the forces of democracy and social progress, popular government, freedom of worship, separation of church and state, and universal education in the democratic tradition. Although their interpretation of the social, political, and economic issues varied to some extent, as did the degree to which each was misled by communist influence, nevertheless, after examining their writings on the conflict, one must conclude that for each of the novelists in this study the defense of the Loyalists represented a humanitarian cause. Their support was not predicated on Marxist theory or a desire to see revolutionary ideas transformed into action, but rather because they believed in fundamental humanitarian principles and were willing to join with other antifascists to advance their beliefs.

Nor can the motivations which brought these men to Spain be attributed to "communist propaganda." In truth there was a profound moral and ethical justification in their decision to support the Popular Front. The war in Spain raised the destiny of antifascists from a condition of helpless impotence in the face of overwhelming aggression to one of valiant resistance. Motivating these writers were several basic assumptions regarding the nature of the Spanish Republic as a progressive and democratic government and the Insurgents as representative of a reactionary, feudal form of fascism. For the first time they saw the opportunity to defend liberty and advance their own principles, not in the framework of decadent institutions, but in the fiery glare of a dramatic confrontation with the powerful opposing doctrines of fascism. Throughout the conflict, despite internal dissension within the Popular Front, the Republic, for these writers, continued to embody the belief in the power of reason to order life and the desire to improve the social and economic life of the Spanish people. Pervading the novels and personal narratives of these authors is a humanitarian plea for the support of a democratic government motivated by the idea of progress and a repudiation of a movement which appeared both a denial of rationality and a historical retrogression.

Koestler and Regler were communists, and Orwell a socialist fighting with an anarchist unit. Malraux, a leftist, and Bernanos, leaning to the right, were both involved primarily as antifascists. Nevertheless, each of them, including Hemingway, felt he was supporting a government that stood for the disestablishment of the Church, agrarian reform, and universal education which would strike at Spain's feudal heritage of ignorance and superstition. Koestler calls the Republic Spain's great hope of "emerging from the clerical, feudal stage, to the constitutional, material and spiritual level of the great European democracies." (45) And he later repeats that, following the Republican victory during the elections of 1936:

> The way at last seemed clear for the transformation of the semi-feudal, old Spain into a modern democratic State . . . the realisation of those reforms which the middle-classes of the democratic countries of Western Europe had succeeded in obtaining by the second half of the nineteenth century at the latest. (63)

Committed to democratic ideals and appalled by the thought of a fascist takeover of Spain, these writers expressed a faith, less in the actual reform program of the Spanish Republic than in their own conception of the need to fight fascism. Such a view was often myopic in that these dedicated antifascists were in many areas uninformed and on occasion deliberately misinformed. As has been the case throughout history, such men were infinitely more certain of what they were fighting against than what they were fighting for. The principles espoused by the authors were based essentially on a humanistic philosophy, grounded in democratic traditions with no foundation in radical politics and revolutionary ideology. As Hemingway's hero reflects on the nature of his own commitment: "You're not a real Marxist and you know it. You believe in Liberty, Equality and Fraternity. You believe in Life, Liberty and the Pursuit of Happiness. Don't ever kid yourself with too much dialectics. They are for some but not for you." (305) And Malraux's equally politically uncommitted Magnin offers a similar idealized version of what he is fighting for: "Even the wildest dreams of absolute liberty—of power given to the worthiest, and all that goes with it—these concepts are part of what I am here to implement. I want for each man to have a life that isn't determined in terms of what he can exact from others." (105)

The reactionary claim of the pressures of Marxist influence on those authors writing about the Spanish struggle appears exaggerated. Any impulse these writers may have had toward Marxism was overshadowed by their dedication to a vision of a democratic and emerging Spain. Such dedication gave their mission, as expressed in *For Whom the Bell Tolls,* the aura of a crusade:

> That was the only word for it although it was a word that had been so worn and abused that it no longer gave its true meaning. You felt, in spite of all bureaucracy and inefficiency and party strife something that was like the feeling you expected to have and did not have when you made your first communion. It was a feeling of consecration to a duty toward all the oppressed of the world which would be as difficult and embarrassing to speak about as religious experience and yet it was authentic. . . . It gave you a part in something that you could believe in wholly and completely and in which you felt an absolute brotherhood with the others who were engaged in it. (235)

The lack of doctrinaire political commitment in their decision to support the Loyalists is further indicated by Orwell's genuine ignorance in the area of Spanish politics. The thought of treachery within the Republican ranks after the fall of Malaga provided Orwell with his first indication of the complexities within the Spanish struggle—complexities which did not altogether conform with his previous simplified conception of the issues: "It was the first talk I heard of treachery or divided aims. It set up in my mind the first vague doubt about this war in which, hitherto, the rights and wrongs had seemed so beautifully simple." (45) And Orwell later admits that, "I did not realize that there were serious differences between the political parties." (47)

For most of these writers the fight against fascism was sufficient motivation for supporting the Spanish Republic and party politics only served to confuse a rather positive cause. For dedicated antifascists such as the German Regler, already disillusioned with Soviet communism, the defense of the Spanish people possessed an altruistic significance which he would not permit to be beclouded by subjection to the political arena: "But it was not only a question of Germany, not of soil and possessions; it was a question of the decency of the world. A holy war must be fought, and it involved the whole world, for the lie [of fascism] was flooding across the frontiers." (22) And as the war progressed and the Loyalist cause seemed likely to be corrupted by politics, Regler declared: "I'm fighting for an idea, for my idea." (162) In Regler's case his objective was a defensive one—the defeat of fascism—and little thought is expended on the future of Spain in the event of a Loyalist victory. But for such men the hatred of fascism was a sufficient motivation for fighting and dying in Spain, as Hemingway's hero Jordan explains in analyzing his politics: "I am an antifascist." "For a long time?" "Since I have understood fascism." (66) Hemingways conception of Spain's future is only vaguely expressed by Jordan as he reflects on his mission:

> In all the work that they, the "partizans" did, they brought added danger and bad luck to the people that sheltered them and worked with them. For what? So that, eventually, there should be no more danger and so that the country should be a good place to live in. That was true no matter how trite it sounded. If the Republic lost it would be impossible for those who believed in it to live in Spain. But would it? Yes, he knew that it would

be, from the things that happened in the parts the fascists had already taken. (162–63)

Hemingway's faith in the Republic is expressed through the simple nonpolitical peasants in *For Whom the Bell Tolls*. The partisans are essentially "without politics" yet favor a visionary conception of a republic which would permit them to live in peace with dignity. As Pilar articulates this faith: "I put great illusion in the Republic. I believe firmly in the Republic and I have faith. I believe in it with fervor as those who have religious faith believe in the mysteries." (90) And it is the Christian Anselmo who enunciates the goals of such a state: "That we should win this war and shoot nobody. . . . That we should govern justly and that all should participate in the benefits according as they have striven for them. And that those who have fought against us should be educated to see their error." (285)

For these novelists, never scholars of Spain's social and political history, subtleties which tended to cloud the basic issues were often dismissed. For them the Spanish Republic represented a legally and democratically elected constitutional government which, despite its many mistakes, was moving in the direction of progress. Clearly, international law was on the side of the Loyalists, and the declared neutrality of the democracies seemed oppressive. For a lawful government to be refused aid in its own defense against an undemocratic belligerency seemed to these writers an abandonment of traditional principles which the now reluctant France, England, and United States had always defended, and a reversal of practices which these democracies had uniformly followed throughout their modern history. But it was not international law on which these writers predicated their support of the Republic. Traditional beliefs, particularly the concepts of individual freedom and social progress, were the chief philosophical themes found in those works of Hemingway, Malraux, Regler, Koestler, Orwell, and Bernanos which were involved with the struggle of the Spanish people.

The concept of liberty was at the heart of their novels and personal narratives, and their ideal was the emergence of the free individual—freed from a history of economic repression, freed from an authoritarian church, freed from an unrepresentative government. To the monarchist Bernanos the suffering of the Spanish people was a tragedy compounded by their historical capitulation to these forces: "One can even say that the greatest misfortune is submission to injustice, not the suffering of it. 'You submit without understanding,' wrote the elderly Drumont. I believe it to be the only form of damnation in this life." (96) And the communist Regler—right and left seemed meaningless designations once these writers became involved in the cause of the Spanish people—propounds this same desire for justice and individual liberty in the Loyalist fight against submission to repression:

> Tomorrow comes a battle, there will be death, friends must be cared for, and a victory won. Why? So that people may be free. So that a man can speak out what his reason tells him. So that together men may seek the truth. The truth, yes, that's it! The truth and not propaganda. Criticism and not blind obedience. People and not the mass; men not the masses! (198)

The very nature of the anarchists' faith in human nature made the goal of this group the fulfillment of their concept of individual liberty. In the first days after the revolt of the generals, anarchists throughout Spain discovered a freedom which hitherto they had only dreamed of. The descriptions by Orwell of Barcelona during this period are especially meaningful, as is his commentary on the functioning of this libertarianism within the ranks of the anarchist militia units:

> In theory at any rate each militia was a democracy and not a hierarchy. It was understood that orders had to be obeyed, but it was also understood that when you gave an order you gave it as comrade to comrade and not as superior to inferior. There were officers and N.C.O.s, but there was no military rank in the ordinary sense; no titles, no badges, no heel-clicking and saluting. They had attempted to produce within the militias a sort of temporary working model of the classless society. Of course there was not perfect equality, but there was a nearer approach to it than I had ever seen or than I would have thought conceivable in time of war. (27)

This antithesis of the old conception of military order may not have won many battles against mechanized armies, but it did humanize the soldier and permitted him to exercise his own judgment—certainly an innovation in traditional military procedure. Hemingway's Anselmo, not an anarchist but thinking like one, utilizes his prerogative after being ordered to remain at his watch until he is relieved: "But if he does not come soon I must go in spite of all orders for I have a report to make now, and I have much to do in these days, and to freeze here is an exaggeration and without utility." (192) Thus Anselmo asserts his idea of human dignity while conceding the wretchedness of the modern human condition.

These Spaniards, their spirit set free after decades of repression, possessed a religious fervor in their devotion to liberty. Malraux compares them to the first Christians with whom they shared a spirit of devotion to an ideal: "They shared with their religious painters that communion in the darkened catacombs which Christianity long ago had provided, and which today the revolution gave them; they had chosen the same way of life, and were dying the same deaths." (47) And if Hemingway's liberal idealist can devote himself to the Spanish people because "I believe in the people and their right to govern themselves as they wish," (304) Malraux's anarchist Negus can move beyond political considerations in his conception of liberty:

> Even if we are beaten here and at Madrid at least the men will have listened to their hearts, if only for a few days. See what I mean? In spite of hatred. They are free today. Never before have they been. I am not speaking of political freedom, but of another kind. Do you understand me? (175–76)

And by way of explanation of this concept of freedom and its involvement with human dignity, Negus draws an analogy:

> When a man is released from prison, nine times out of ten he cannot look anyone directly in the eye. He has lost his ability to look squarely at people like a man. Among the proletariat, also, there are lots of people afraid to face folks. And that all must be changed, to begin with. (175)

Combined with this spirit of freedom in their writing of the Spanish conflict was a view toward social progress. Although these writers expressed little concern with the specific details of the Republican program, they were unanimous in agreeing that the Republic would, following the war, proceed with effective reforms in the areas of religion, education, and agriculture. Perhaps it is unfair to expect novelists to perform the role of social historians, especially since their attempt to capture the spirit of Loyalist Spain's attitude toward social reform succeeds admirably, whereas an analysis of Republican legislation in this area would be literarily as well as politically unrewarding. Prior to the outbreak of hostilities, the Republic had shown a singular lack of success in implementing its programs in the areas of religious tolerance, universal education, and agrarian reform, all of which were reasons why authors ignored specific accomplishments in favor of concentrating on Spain's future. And, finally, the "hispanicizing" of many of the liberal concepts to suit specific conditions in Spain (ironically the origin for this term is from the Spanish "liberalismo") created differences between the enactment of the ideals envisioned by the novelists and the actual situation in the volatile Spanish Cortes. In any event, the insurrection suspended implementation of all major social reforms while the Republic concentrated on the task of fighting the war.

Nevertheless the six novelists chose to write about the spirit of social progress pervading Republican Spain during the conflict. Malraux recognized that an encomium pointing toward future accomplishments would be misleading, and he and the other authors tempered their praise with the realization that freedom alone would not produce social progress. Rather, as Malraux's Hernandez expressed it, the price of social progress in a country rooted in a history of reactionary feudalism would be extremely costly:

> I have arrived at a simple truth: one expects everything all at once from 'liberty', but for man to progress a bare centimeter, a great many men must die. This street must have looked much as it does now in the days of Charles the Fifth. And yet the world has changed since then because men wanted it to change. . . . Nothing could be more discouraging than fighting here. And still the only thing in the world as important is the help that we can give these fellows. (199)

The spirit of social change, as these novelists communicate it, created a feeling of optimism amongst the people which helped them when experiencing the deprivations as a consequence of the war. Despite shortages of such essentials as food and fuel, the people concentrated on the war effort, hopeful of a new life under a victorious Republic. Orwell, in Barcelona during the first days of the conflict, describes the morale of the people engaged in the process of daily living while attempting to wage war:

> The town had a gaunt untidy look, roads and buildings were in poor repair, the streets at night were dimly lit for fear of air-raids, the shops were mostly shabby and half-empty. . . . Yet so far as one can judge the people were contented and hopeful. There was no unemployment, and the price of living was still extremely low; you saw very few conspicuously destitute people, and no beggars except the gipsies. Above all, there was a belief in the revolution and the future, a feeling of having suddenly emerged into an era of equality and freedom. (5–6)

The peasants were not the only social class affected by the changed economic conditions. According to Malraux, the bourgeoisie also experienced the impact of the government policies enacted in an effort to create a completely new economic structure:

> When I am reliably informed that under the Republic wages have been tripled, and, as a result, the peasants have at last been able to buy themselves shirts; and when I hear that the fascist regime has restored the old wage scale and, as a result, thousands of newly opened shops where they sold their shirts were forced to close—then I understand why the lower middle class in Spain is aligned with the proletariat. (181–82)

An increase in income was not the only economic change under the Republic; the agrarian program also began to take shape. In the rural areas peasants were permitted to farm lands which for years had lain fallow. As the huge estates were subdivided by the peasants, Malraux writes of the dignity displayed by these small farmers; in such context the Spanish Civil War appeared as one more episode in the historical struggle between the tillers of the soil and their hereditary landlords:

> Over Teruel Magnin had glimpsed the walls of the huge estates, with their bulls, lazy or active, scattered among the mountains which the war had claimed; here too he saw, half blurred by snowflakes, the high stone walls which the International and Madrid Brigades were attacking below him. He recalled the

> newly built, squat stone walls which he had seen near Teruel and to the south, almost overpowered by these immense relics of the past. And he remembered the fallow land which the goitrous suffering agricultural workers were not permitted to cultivate. Those infuriated peasants fighting below were struggling to erect those little walls, the first condition of their dignity. And now the pilot observed, across the confused dreams that had so troubled him these last few months, something simple, clear and basic as childbirth, joy, pain and death: the historical struggle of the cultivators of the land against their hereditary oppressors. (419)

Orwell also directs attention to the pre-Republican animosity between peasant laborers and their landlords. While on the Aragon front, Orwell encountered many formerly landless peasants who now farmed their own land. Because of the confusion of life in wartime Spain, he was unable to determine whether the land had been expropriated by the peasants and divided among themselves or whether the new small farms were the result of a government policy of agricultural reform:

> It is typical of the utter vagueness in which the Spanish agrarian revolution is wrapped that I could not even discover for certain whether the land here was collectivized or whether the peasants had simply divided it up among themselves. . . . At any rate the landowners were gone, the fields were being cultivated, and the people seemed satisfied. . . . To some of the older ones the war must have seemed meaningless, visibly it produced a shortage of everything and a dismal dull life for everybody, and at the best of times peasants hate having troops quartered upon them. Yet they were invariably friendly—I suppose reflecting that, however intolerable we might be in other ways, we did stand between them and their one-time landlords. (79)

For Orwell, Republican Spain, particularly the militia units on the Aragon front, represented the first stage in his vision of a socialist society. Besides the atmosphere of equality and freedom which Orwell discovered among these Catalans, he found an elevated moral quality which he believed inconceivable in the social structure of the democracies—England, France, and the United States. Although he recognized that this situation was only temporary and not likely to last under the pressures of the war, nevertheless, it inspired him and confirmed his dedication to a vision of a socialist world. With the eventual dissolution of the militias and the final defeat of the Loyalists, Orwell was neither disillusioned nor discouraged. Rather, the struggle of the Spanish people served to strengthen his socialist convictions:

> Up here in Aragon one was among tens of thousands of people, mainly though not entirely of working-class origin, all living at the same level and mingling on terms of equality. In theory it was perfect equality, and even in practice it was not far from it. There is a sense in which it would be true to say that one was experiencing a foretaste of Socialism, by which I mean that the prevailing mental atmosphere was that of Socialism. Many of the normal motives of civilized life—snobbishness, money-grubbing, fear of the boss, etc.—had simply ceased to exist. The ordinary class-division of society had disappeared. (104)

Nor did the knowledge that such a social structure was susceptible to change through outside pressures affect Orwell's feelings:

> Of course such a state of affairs could not last. It was simply a temporary and local phase in an enormous game that is being played over the whole surface of the earth. But it lasted long enough to have its effect upon anyone who experienced it. However much one cursed at the time, one realized afterwards that one had been in contact with something strange and valuable. One had been in a community where hope was more normal than apathy or cynicism. (104)

The English author acknowledges that the courage and innate decency of the Spanish people were in part responsible for the furtherance of his own political convictions:

> In that community where no one was on the make, where there was a shortage of everything but no privilege and no bootlicking, one got, perhaps, a crude forecast of what the opening stages of Socialism might be like. And, after all, instead of disillusioning me it deeply attracted me. The effect was to make my desire to see Socialism established much more actual than it had been before. Partly, perhaps, this was due to the good luck of being among Spaniards, who, with their innate decency and their ever-present Anarchist tinge, would make even the opening stages of Socialism tolerable if they had the chance. (105)

Orwell was not alone in his vision of life in a new Spain. Regler joins him in a paean to the future in which he ironically contemplates a country achieving a greatness which has been denied it throughout its modern history:

> "Everything you need is here," said Werner, "all that's necessary is to begin. Men, good will, discipline, passion. We'll build sanatoria in the hills and children's homes in the Levante. We'll reforest and change the climate. Springs will be stored up in winter and in summer they'll run out over the country. We'll raise the best mules in the world." Werner interrupted himself with a laugh. "That is, if the army hasn't eaten them all by then." He became serious again. "But it would be nice to work here. Too bad we'll never get the chance." (179)

On a more realistic level, Orwell admits flaws in the politics of the Spanish Republic. The inability of the government to come to terms with Spain's social problems was a historical fact. Nevertheless, as an alternative, fascism seemed not a solution, but a catastrophe. He felt that the idea that an imperfect democracy might be replaced by a feudal social order was sufficient reason to fight for the Loyalists. In the event of a Republican victory, the government, while less than his socialist dream, would still be in a position to institute reforms which would benefit the working-class in Spain:

> Whichever way you took it it was a depressing outlook. But it did not follow that the Government was not worth fighting for as against the more naked and developed Fascism of Franco and Hitler. Whatever faults the post-war Government might have, Franco's régime would certainly be worse. To the workers—the town proletariat—it might in the end make very little difference who won, but Spain is primarily an agricultural country and the peasants would almost certainly benefit by a Government victory. Some at least of the seized lands would remain in their possession, in which case there would also be a distribution of land in the territory that had been Franco's, and the virtual serfdom that had existed in some parts of Spain was not likely to be restored. The Government in control at the end of the war would at any rate be anti-clerical and anti-feudal. It would keep the Church in check, at least for the time being, and would modernize the country—build roads, for instance, and promote education and public health; a certain amount had been done in this direction even during the war. Franco, on the other hand, in so far as he was not merely the puppet of Italy and Germany, was

> tied to the big feudal landlords and stood for a stuffy clerico-military reaction. The Popular Front might be a swindle, but Franco was an anachronism. (181)

It is Malraux, ever the activist, who points out that the course of any representative government can be determined by the people. If the people desire a social change, it is their obligation not only to make their feelings known to the government, but also to participate actively in directing and formulating government policy. For Malraux, in the event of a Republican victory, Spain would be in a state of transition, offering vast opportunities for improvement in human conditions should the people be willing to assume a vital role in determining their destiny. For too many years the masses had been denied an active role in the politics of the country and they could not afford to permit a re-establishment of the previous condition:

> All doors are open to those who are determined to force them. The quality of life is directly related to the quality of mind. The only guarantee of an enlightened policy by a popular government is not to be found in our theorizing but in our presence, here and now. The ethics of our government is dependent on our efforts, on our determination. Enlightenment in Spain will not be the mysterious result of vague aspirations; it will be exactly what we make of it. (339)

Malraux recognized the possibility that without such leadership rooted in the people the new Republic would be no great improvement over the tyranny of previous unrepresentative regimes. Alvear, in *L'espoir,* calls attention to the fact that economic liberation is only a partial solution to Spain's problems; that unless the people are watchful, there is danger that they may be merely exchanging one form of servitude for another:

> But that part of man which war brings into play is not the portion that really is important. What proof is there that the benefits derived from the "economic liberation" will be greater than the losses which will accompany the new order—menaced by all sides, and forced, by fear, to resort to violence, repression, and even treachery? Conceded that economic servitude is a hard life; but if, to eliminate it, the state is obliged to enforce a political, military or religious servitude, what is the importance of choosing sides? (277)

Thus Alvear refutes many of the critics who felt that Malraux was exploiting the novel to present a radical and revolutionary theory:

> There is in man a hope, terrible and profound. For one who has been unjustly condemned, or who has encountered more than his share of ingratitude or baseness or stupidity, the hope of a new order is irresistible. The revolution plays, among other roles, that part once taken by the belief in "eternal life." But if each man would direct even one-third the effort he presently expends on politics towards his own self-improvement, Spain would develop into a truly habitable country. (278)

To this observation Malraux's García introduces a philosophical theme. No state, no social structure, is capable of creating a nobility of character or intellectual qualities within the individual. The individual himself must be responsible for his emergence from the Spanish struggle as a figure reborn. No form of government can do more than provide an environment in which many may strive to develop his fullest potential:

> A revolution is obliged to solve its own problems. The solution to ours depends on ourselves alone. . . . No state, no social structure can create nobility of character, nor intellectual and spiritual qualities; all we can expect from it are propitious conditions. And that's quite a lot! (338)

According to García, to confuse the goals of the revolution with those of the individual can be fatal:

> The man who stakes his life on the revolution is bound to lose. It is a truly disastrous game. Moral perfection, nobility of character, are the concern of the individual, from which the revolution is completely detached. The only relation between the two, for you, I fear, is the prospect that you may be sacrificed for both causes. (187)

Philosophical themes abound in the writings of the Spanish Civil War. Most prominent among them is the concept that the Spanish conflict was a struggle between a liberal and progressive view of Western civilization, which embodied certain traditional and even primitive values, as opposed to the antithetical reactionary and feudal views, which entailed a renunciation of such a concept as human progress and exulted in an aggressive and destructive mechanical order. The anti-intellectualism concomitant with this latter conception leads to a totalitarian rule in which the politician assumes the leading role. Malraux analyzes this trend in Europe since World War I:

> The question raises the whole problem of civilization. For some time the "philosopher" was more or less explicitly regarded as the highest form of European man. The intellectuals were the "clergy" of a world in which the politicians represented the nobility, for better or worse. Their claim to act as spiritual advisers was unquestioned. It was they, not the others—Unamuno and not Alphonso XIII, for that matter Unamuno and not the bishops—who were charged with the responsibility of defining a meaningful life. But today the politicians lay claim to our minds as part of the state: Unamuno against Franco, Thomas Mann against Hitler, Gide against Stalin, Ferrero against Mussolini. In actuality it is all a question of prerogatives. (337)

Koestler, having experienced the horrors of aerial bombardment in Madrid, attacks Franco's concept of total war. The general had deliberately and consciously ordered the slaughter of innocent civilians. Koestler in a more rhetorical vien maintains that the intellectual luxury of objectivity is impossible under such circumstances; that such attacks can never be justified militarily and must be deemed an assault on the basic values of Western civilization:

> This is no political act, it is a challenge to civilization. Anyone who has lived through the hell of Madrid with his eyes, his nerves, his heart, his stomach—and then pretends to be objective, is a liar. If those who have at their command printing machines and printer's ink for the expression of their opinions, remain neutral and objective in the face of such bestiality, then Europe is lost. In that case let us all sit down and bury our heads in the sand and wait until the devil takes us. In that case it is time for Western civilization to say good night. (177)

Thus, for the literary humanists the fight in Spain was a defense of that tradition embodied in the fundamental humanitarian principles of Western civilization. The fascist threat to this vision of a better world striving to improve itself, is expressed by Regler's commissar Albert: "This Fascism is one endless provocation. Not only is it bloody and lying, it lays traps for us, prevents us from distinguishing among men, from following our own better image of the world." (373) This contrast between antithetical philosophies is made clear in Koestler's historical analysis of the war in his *Spanish Testament.* Koestler compares the Carlist wars of the nineteenth century with the Spanish Civil War and concludes that the same historical forces were at work in each:

> In some respects the Carlist wars of the nineteenth century were a prelude, providing many analogies, to the Civil War of 1936. On the one side one finds the Liberal Government of Madrid, a Government all too receptive to illusions; on the other the coldly calculating feudal forces of reaction, in league with the Church and the Army, whose watchwords are "inviolability of the clergy" and "absolute monarchy without parliamentary control." These high-sounding phrases merely serve as a screen to conceal the interest of the reaction in the maintenance of the "status quo" on the land. In both of the Carlist wars the Spanish feudal caste enjoyed the active support of the reactionary European powers, particularly that of Prussia, while the English and French democracies confined themselves largely to platonic expressions of sympathy with the other side. And always with the same melancholy result: democracy bleeds to death, the Middle Ages triumph, and passive observers beyond the Pyrenees raise their hands in pious horror and protest against the atrocities. (46)

Nor will these novelists permit the English and French who wish to remain neutral to use the pretext that the Insurgents represent authority and order while the Loyalists offer anarchy and chaos. They attack the assertion that "if the trains are on time, the country is in good hands." Bernanos refutes the tourists who visit Nationalist-occupied Palma and do little more than comment on the clean roads, punctual trams, and general order of business, and therefore conclude that fascism offers many desirable advantages:

> "What, business as usual, people walking about the streets, and you speak of bloodshed. Nonsense!" They refuse to realize that any shopkeeper who closed down was risking his life. They ignored the fact that the administration had forbidden mourning by the relatives of the executed. How can you expect the exterior appearance of a town to be noticeably changed, just because the staff of its prisons is double, triple, ten or a hundred times what it once was? The discreet slaughter of fifteen or twenty wretched

> people each day will not prevent tramways from running on schedule, cafés from being filled, or churches resounding with "Te Deum." (157)

Koestler also criticizes the foreign visitor to Nationalist Spain who fails to acknowledge the oppressive conditions which remain just below the surface in every village and town, and who instead chooses to delude himself by accepting a superficial form of order:

> He knows all this only too well, this picture of a provincial town under a dictatorship: the trembling townsfolk, the military let loose, the fear of spies, the whispered rumours, the constriction in the throat that affects a whole town, a whole population, like an epidemic, and when, an hour later, he is back on board the steamer and is questioned by the Englishmen in the first class as to his impressions, he replies, in the words used by certain friends of Lord Lothian's to convey their enthusiastic impressions of Berlin: "The city is quiet, the trams are running, and there are no corpses lying about on the pavements." (21)

As Koestler and Bernanos demolish the fascist pretensions toward order, so Malraux attacks the fascist concept of authority. For Malraux, the fascist claim of authority is an illusion created by propaganda, which bears little relation to the facts:

> Actually the inspiration behind three-fourths of all Spanish fascists isn't a concept of authority but rather a desire for a good time. And for the others, the fascists have always regarded their leaders as persons of a superior race. The Germans do not believe in "race" because they are fascists; they are fascists because they believe in "race." A fascist commands by divine right. For that reason the question of loyalty does not pose the problem for them that it does for us. (148–49)

During a devastating air raid over Madrid, an elderly peasant in *L'espoir* expresses Malraux's fervent conviction regarding fascism and its misuse of authority: "I have never meddled in politics. To me they have always appeared beneath contempt. But we cannot let power fall into the hands of people who so abuse it—power which is not even theirs by right—can we?" (328)

The concept that fascism represented a destructive mechanical force became more pronounced as massive shipments of war material reached the Insurgents from Germany and Italy, whereas the nonintervention agreements and embargoes resulted in an effective reduction of such material reaching the Loyalists. These writers were aware of the change in the character of the war that occurred with the impact of foreign intervention, the transformation of the conflict into a vast "machine of violence." As this disparity in the mechanization of opposing forces increased, for these novelists mechanized weapons and their cold destructive power came to symbolize the rebel cause. The Loyalists were viewed in the plight of the poorly equipped troops, primarily those badly armed peasant fighters whose primitive existence left them helpless when attacked by weapons of a highly developed technological order. For these writers the symbols chosen to represent the opposing forces were in keeping with the logistics of the military situation.[1] They were already shocked by the totalitarian conduct of total war and to them the conflict assumed the appearance of a struggle between men and machines, between the warm human qualities of men opposed to the cold inhuman qualities of mechanized weapons of war—mechanical nightmare suppressing the ordered world of nature. With considerable difficulty in the transition, these writers also accepted the Spanish Civil War as a struggle between progress and retrogression, between a belief in society's advance as a basic element of Western civilization and a reactionary return to the Middle Ages. In varying degrees each of the novelists dramatized this symbolic struggle between men and machines in his description of the Spanish Civil War.

Koestler first calls attention to the disparity in armaments early in his *Spanish Testament* when he discusses the relative strength of the opposing forces:

> The chronic lack of man power [for the Insurgents] has been more than compensated for from a strategic point of view by supplies of the most up-to-date war material from abroad. . . . The situation on the Government side was exactly the opposite. Madrid had at its command an infinite supply of men and for a time was numerically twice to three times as strong as the rebels. But these forces were without training, without discipline, without officers and without arms. On the rebel side there were companies with one machine-gun to every four men. On the

Republican side there were companies where four men shared a single rifle. (36–37)

Malraux points out that with little help expected from abroad, the Republic must fight the war and simultaneously attempt to organize its own armament factories. The difficulties involved in setting up a supply system could be overcome with time, but in the interim the militia units must prepare to sacrifice themselves, less to gain victories than to gain time:

> We have hardly any planes left. Hardly any artillery. As for machine-guns, you have seen for yourself, on our right flank there is one for every three companies. In case of attack, they pass it around. The battle isn't between Franco's Moors and our army (we haven't any), but between Franco and the organization of our new army. The militias right now can do little more than get themselves killed so as to gain a little time for us. But this new army, where is it to find rifles, field-guns, planes? It is easier to quickly improvise an army than it is to construct an industry. (152)

Thus Koestler's description of the siege of Malaga appears to verify Malraux's pessimistic prediction: "The rebel cruisers bombarded us and the ships of the Republic did not come. The rebel planes sowed panic and destruction, and the planes of the Republic did not come. The rebels had artillery, armoured cars and tanks, and the arms and war material of the Republic did not come." (216)

In analyzing the efforts of writers to present the struggle waged by the masses to preserve their traditional values, as opposed to those who rejected these values, and preferred the machine and the opposing forces of a destructive and dehumanizing technological order, it is not necessary to rely upon an interpretation of symbolic images. In the works of the major novelists treating the Spanish Civil War, characters express their distaste and, on occasion, their fear of subjugation by these war machines. In *For Whom the Bell Tolls*, Jordan, emerging from a cave, looks at the Heinkels flying overhead and regards them as destroyers of the natural order:

> The bombers were high now in fast, ugly arrow-heads beating the sky apart with the noise of their motors. They *are* shaped like

> sharks, Robert Jordan thought, the wide-finned, sharp-nosed sharks of the Gulf Stream. But these, wide-finned in silver, roaring, the light mist of their propellers in the sun, these do not move like sharks. They move like no thing there has ever been. They move like mechanized doom. (87)

And Pilar is aroused by the appearance of these powerful instruments of destruction: "The sight of those machines does things to one. . . . We are nothing against such machines." (89) But it is the primitive, noble Anselmo who explicitly states the theme which permeates the liberal writing of the Spanish Civil War: "We must teach them. We must take away their planes, their automatic weapons, their tanks, their artillery and teach them dignity." (328)

Malraux shares Hemingway's belief in tanks and bombers as omens of doom. But in the Hemingway novel there is no sense of human agency behind these mechanized weapons, merely a sense of impotent humanity confronted by mechanized authoritarianism. In *L'espoir,* however, Malraux recognizes the need for the Republic to acquire and use such instruments in its own defense: "This war is going to be a mechanized war, and right now we are conducting it as if noble sentiments were all that counted." (103) To the realist García, any sentimentality which encourages martyrdom by suicidal attempts to resist the fire power of modern weapons is a senseless anachronism:

> We are aided but nevertheless handicapped by two or three dangerous myths. First, the French fallacy that the People brought off the French Revolution. Even though it is true, the fact that a hundred Frenchmen armed with clubs could knock off some inefficient muskets doesn't indicate that one hundred shotguns can confront a modern warplane. Second, the fallacy of the Russian Revolution has compounded the confusion. Although politically it was the first revolution of the twentieth century, militarily it was the last of the nineteenth. The Czarists had neither tanks nor planes and the revolutionaries could use barricades—barricades to battle the imperial cavalry since peasants never have horses. Today Spain is covered with barricades—to oppose Franco's air force! (104)

The adoption of the machine as an appropriate symbol for the terrible realities of the Spanish Civil War prevails throughout the literature of the conflict. For the most part the Loyalists, as was actually the case, possessed neither the guns nor the planes in the quantity and quality to successfully oppose the Insurgents. The resistance of the militias in the early stages of the war to any major rebel advances is a tribute to their courage. For the Spanish peasant, the mechanization of the Insurgent forces was contrary to his nature and foreign to Spain's chivalrous tradition. Malraux describes their heroism in the defense of Estremadura:

> Without leaders, without arms, the militia in the Estremadura struggled to resist. From Medellín a force composed of café workers, field laborers, innkeepers, and a mixture of thousands of the downtrodden people of Spain set forth carrying a few hunting rifles to battle against the machine-guns of Franco's African Brigade and Moorish infantry. (90)

But Malraux also recognizes that such courage cannot withstand the massive assaults of a modern army:

> Mass courage in the field cannot possibly resist fighter planes and machine-guns. The truth is that if the militias were well trained and sufficiently armed, they are brave enough to stand up to any force. Unorganized, they cut and run. With enough "milicianos" we could form enough columns to build an army. Courage in this case is actually a problem of organization. (181)

In his introduction to Luis Quintanilla's realistic sketches of the war, Hemingway refers to Spain's battlefields "where men with rifles, hand grenades and bundled sticks of dynamite faced tanks, artillery, and planes, and died so that their country might be free."[2] These "dinamiteros" were former miners from the Asturias who have handled dynamite and who use it principally as a defense against tanks. To Malraux, the actions of these miners seem the final effort in this century for men to successfully withstand the mechanized weapons of war:

> In this valley, watching for the approach of the tanks, the men exchanged tales of prior battles, some heroic and the others trivial. Without a doubt, "dinamiteros" are the last body of men who can face machines on equal terms. The presence of the Catalonians was pure chance but the Asturians were fulfilling a tradition.

> They were the original *Jacquerie* of Spain, and now at last were organized; perhaps the only men for whom the golden legend of the total revolution was being implemented by actual war experience, instead of being disintegrated by it. (201)

In the development of the Hemingway, Regler, and Malraux novels, the conditions of the conflict between men and machines are gradually reversed. No longer are the Loyalists represented by the traditional peasants and the Insurgents by the machines of war. As the plots evolve, the Loyalists gradually assume the role of the force of the future, while the Nationalists assume the role of the force of reaction and of the past. In Regler's *The Great Crusade,* the Moors are depicted as remnants of "the forest primeval," as "bestial Africans with the knife between their teeth." (257) The Moors are not repelled and they overwhelm the French, swarming over the wounded like animals. But as they advance, the Moors encounter the Loyalists' tanks, they are halted, and "now the tanks came wobbling in from both sides of the ravine in front of the line of Poles. Their guns felt out their targets for a moment, then as the machines rumbled slowly forward, the blue explosion burst." (271) Thus the African invasion is repulsed.

In Malraux's *L'espoir,* early praise of the peasant in his natural environment is eventually tempered by the realities of war. As the acts of individual heroism accomplish little against the mechanized units of fascist violence, the necessity for organized collective action becomes apparent. Thus for Malraux the conflict between men and machines assumes lesser importance as Russian equipment arrives. Descriptions of the valiant struggle against a mechanized enemy are transformed into accounts of victory for those who forsook the land to fight steel with steel. "Manuel began to realize that to wage war successfully, it was necessary to riddle living flesh with fragments of steel." (84) In the air squadron supporting the International Brigades, the obsolete planes are gradually replaced by more formidable modern aircraft, and Russian planes defend Madrid after the city had been subjected to weeks of incessant bombing. In the French novelist's account of the victory at Guadalajara, the discipline imposed by the International Brigades is the decisive factor; a second theme introduces an extraordinary dramatic episode—that of the primitive and voluntary action of peasants in their rescue of survivors of an airplane wrecked on a mountainside. However, Malraux's central concern is with the "organization of the Apocalypse," with the implicit goal of a modernized Spain.

Although Regler's view, with its elements of Marxian socialism, envisions man living in a classless society in which technology is employed for the benefit of mankind, and Malraux's conception only hints at his own version of a modernized and industrialized Spain, Hemingway's conversion to the acceptance of the machine as an instrument of war has no political or social implications. The American author sees the machine as aiding the Loyalist cause and now gladly extols those machines which he had formerly designated as "mechanized doom":

> His eyes, watching the planes coming, were very proud. He saw red wing markings now and he watched their steady, stately roaring advance. This was how it could be. These were our planes. They had come, crated on ships, from the Black Sea through the Straits of Marmora, through the Dardanelles, through the Mediterranean and to here, unloaded lovingly at Alicante, assembled ably, tested and found perfect and now flown in lovely hammering precision, the V's tight and pure as they came now high and silver in the morning sun to blast those ridges across there and blow them roaring high so that we can go through. (429)

Nevertheless, to say that these novelists were willing to accept the advantages of mechanization when it was offered in the service of the Republic, cannot be reconciled with a subsidiary theme in their works. Implicit in their writing is an underlying fear of mechanized authoritarianism and its dehumanizing qualities. Thus the Spanish Civil War served to dramatize yet another conflict in the life of twentieth-century man—the issue between men and machines, the dilemma and paradox of primitive values, and a dehumanized mechanized progress. Spain's desire to preserve the spontaneous, organic, archaic relationship between man and nature, as typified by Don Quixote, Sancho Panza, and Rosinante, and the specter of an urbanized, industrialized, mechanized, and regimented world represented by the socialization of industry to provide the Loyalists with war materiel, confronts these writers with an insoluble dilemma. With the realization that modern warfare requires these same mechanized weapons in defense of all values, human, unmechanized, and even primitive, they were forced to accept the new values, but were unable to satisfactorily resolve the conflict in their own minds.

In face of the horrors of mechanized destruction, these authors called for an all-inclusive concept of social equality. They asked more than equality for all men before the law—they sounded a call for universal brotherhood. Feelings of fraternity—comradeship in the struggle for survival—were manifested in the works of all of them. Malraux describes the Loyalists' foreign volunteers singing the "Internationale," and the spirit of fraternity is embodied in his description of the International Brigades. His paean to the diversity and unity in the formation of this fighting unit is both symbolic and factual:

> Still in civilian clothes but wearing military boots, with their determined communist faces or the pale pallor of the intellectual, old Polish veterans with their Nietzschean mustaches, young boys whose faces recalled Soviet films, Germans with shaved heads, Algerians, Italians who resemble Spaniards that had strayed into the International fold, florid Englishmen, Frenchmen on the lines of Maurice Thorez or Maurice Chevalier, all were tramping down the narrow street which resounded beneath their tread; and all were inspired, not with the young Madrid recruits' eagerness to learn, but by memories of military service or of actual fighting against each other. They were nearing their barracks and broke into song. For the first time in history, the strains of the "Internationale" were rising from men of every nation united in a mutual cause. (241)

This element of fraternity was part of their Western tradition. The impulse which motivated these novelists was linked to the natural instinct that is a vital part of the humanism embodied in their basic philosophy. Malraux uses a peasant to draw a comparison between the democratic and reactionary aristocratic attitudes towards humanity and the brotherhood of man:

> When I was still a farmer, before moving to Perpignan, the Marquis once came out to the field to have a look at us. He was talking about us to the people who had accompanied him: "Did you ever see such peasants! Why they think more about humanity in

> general than they do their own families!" The scorn in his voice set me thinking. After a while I realized that when we—our people, I mean—try to do something for humanity, we are *also* working for our own families. It's one and the same thing. But those others, they pick and choose. (88–89)

Thus for Malraux's peasants, the goal of humanity is not equality but, rather, fraternity: "And let me tell you, the opposite of what you call 'humiliation' isn't equality. You know that slogan the French inscribed on all their buildings, 'Liberté, Égalité, Fraternité.' Those French realized what 'fraternity' really means: the opposite of being badgered." (89) Thus in their drive toward a vision of a free and equal society, courage was not the only factor required to maintain their enthusiasm. Hemingway's Pilar recognizes the need to share their hopes and dreams with others involved in the struggle: "Every one needs to talk to some one. . . . Before we had religion and other nonsense. Now for every one there should be some one to whom one can speak frankly, for all the valor that one could have one becomes very alone." (89)

The most common expression of this sharing of hopes and fears sustained men under the pressures of combat. Malraux's pilot Magnin, severed from political ties by his own ideals, and from close friends by responsibilities of rank, experiences a feeling of loneliness as he watches his men working together in a united effort to repair their planes. "For the first time he was profoundly conscious of the loneliness of war, as he trudged across the dry field toward the hangar where his men were busy repairing the old machines—men united in a spirit of fraternity." (40) For most men the violence of the war drew them closer spiritually. Orwell describes a soldier, badly wounded during an attack, whom he thought he would never see again, only later to meet him at the field hospital: "He recovered, I am glad to say. Later he told me that he had worked his way some distance lying on his back, then had clutched hold of a wounded Spaniard and they had helped one another in." (100) Malraux's International Brigade troops instinctively respond to their mutual dependence on one another under attack: "The shells were falling nearer. Half-unconsciously, many of the soldiers were touching each other—a leg or a shoulder—as if the physical nearness of comrades was the chief defense against death." (285) Such incidents illustrating the spiritual fraternity in the Loyalist ranks are common in the novels and personal narratives of the Spanish Civil War.

The feeling of comradeship in arms is a prevailing theme in the literature of most wars, but the international overtones of such references in the writings of the Spanish conflict are exceptional. In Regler's *The Great Crusade,* the members of the International Brigade are under attack by the Moors in the Jarama valley. An Englishman, a Frenchman, and a German, all exiled from their homeland for political reasons, are making a valiant stand; and in the moments before the crucial charge, Regler writes of their feelings: "They're all together, that helps them forget how isolated they are. . . . No matter if the boys were isolated and abandoned, they would help one another as long as a man was alive." (256–57)

This comradeship or fraternity among men at war also occurs in Malraux's *L'espoir* in a political context. During the military uprising, while storming the barracks in Madrid, the antifascist Jaime translates this brotherhood into a faith in the Popular Front:

> For Jaime, who was twenty-six, the Popular Front meant fraternity in life and in death. The hope he drew from the workers' organizations was intensified by the despair he felt over the corruption of the Spanish kings of the last few centuries. His acquaintances in Spanish left-wing groups were those dedicated, uncompromising militants, always ambitious for change, embodiment of the new spirit of devotion to a modern Spain. And now, in the blazing sunlight and beneath Falangist bullets, with a full heart they pushed the massive battering ram toward the door. (40)

And, later, in the retreat from Toledo, the workers are the ones who organize a delaying action to slow the Insurgents' advance. When presenting their plan of action to Manuel, the government's military representative, the Loyalist leader joyfully envisions a brotherhood of the working class expressing itself in action for the first time:

> Behind the speaker his three comrades in overalls stood against the white background of the cell; that was the formation adopted by the workers' delegations. These men were conscious that they were representing their own men, their lives, their faults, their responsibilities, before one of their own kind. It was as if the

> revolution itself, in its simplest, most significant form, was personified in this action. For the spokesman the revolution meant just such a right to speak out. Manuel embraced him as a Spaniard, and said nothing. For the first time he was in the presence of a fraternity which expressed itself in action. (236–37)

But to Malraux the concept of activism—praise of the man of action—is not without its defects. In his Manichean universe, all attempts at decisive action of necessity must contain some degree of injustice. In a world comprised of good and evil forces, the theoretician must compromise or be reconciled to failure and disillusionment:

> For the man who thinks, the revolution is tragic. But for such a man, life, too, is tragic. . . . Some writer once said: "I am as crowded in by corpses as an old graveyard." . . . All of us have been oppressed by corpses. The road that leads from moral ethics to political activism is strewn with our dead selves. The conflict between the man who acts and the conditions of his action—that which he must assume to win, not that which will lose all that we value—is ever-present. It is a problem of commitment and, one might say, not a subject for discussion. (339)

Thus for Malraux the true intellectual is a tragic figure, by nature anti-Manichean, yet constrained to a course of action for survival in a universe suspicious thereof:

> The true intellectual is a man of nuances, of degrees, of fine shadings, of evaluations; he is concerned with the complexity and relativity of truth. He is, by definition, "antimanichean." But all forms of action are manichean, because *all action is manichean.* The manichean element is most intense when masses are involved. Thus every true revolutionary is a born manichean, and the same is true of those who devote themselves to politics. (335)

Bernanos conceives of the influence of a Manichean universe on the nature of man, and derides theologians who support the romantic concept that man is born pure and good only to be corrupted by a profane world. To the devout French Catholic novelist, the existence of good and evil in the world can only be explained by the existence of God and a devil, in perpetual combat for man's soul:

> It is absurd to believe with Rousseau that man is born good. He is born with a capacity for good and evil far beyond the imagination of the moralists, for he was not created in their image, but in the image of God. And his corruptor is not only the disturbing influences he carries within him—instinct, desire, call it what you like. His corruptor is the greatest of the angels fallen from heaven's highest peak. (94)

To Malraux's American journalist, the baroque quality of the art of the Spaniards provides a symbolic manifestation of this spirit of man torn by these forces engaged in mortal conflict for his soul:

> Slade had little faith in the artistic theories which become affixed to the revolutions; he was familiar with the work on the Mexican painters, and the huge barbaric frescoes, drawn by Lopez—so typically Spanish, bristling with horns and claws—vivid symbols of man engaged in mortal combat. (45)

All of which may help to explain Hemingway's comment on the nature of the Spaniard: "They are wonderful when they are good, he thought. There is no people like them when they are good and when they go bad there is no people that is worse." (16)

Although the Manichean element is present in the works of these novelists, it does not dominate their philosophy. The dominant theme in their conception of the individual during the conflict is of a transcendental nature. For them the Spanish figures of Don Quixote and Sancho Panza represent a truly organic society in which a nobility of character is evident on all social levels. These humanists recognized in Spain the suspension of rigid class distinctions which had served to separate one man from another and which had perpetuated an already decadent European tradition. At least one aspect of their engagement in the Spanish Civil War was their desire to see these distinctions eliminated—prejudices which had turned men into peasants and clerks, but not into whole human beings. To Orwell, the Spaniard emerging during the conflict represented the complete man, uncorrupted by the dehumanizing elements so common to twentieth-century civilization:

> I have the most evil memories of Spain, but I have very few bad memories of Spaniards. I only twice remember even being seri-

> ously angry with a Spaniard, and on each occasion, when I look back, I believe I was in the wrong myself. They have, there is no doubt, a generosity, a species of nobility, that do not really belong to the twentieth century. (223)

This ability to maintain an individuality in face of pressures and the worst of circumstances, according to Orwell, is the Spaniard's and his country's chief hope for survival: "It is this that makes one hope that in Spain even Fascism may take a comparatively loose and bearable form. Few Spaniards possess the damnable efficiency and consistency that a modern totalitarian state needs." (223)

Whether the social divisions of Spanish life under the Republic were truly less distinguishable from the structure of the rest of European society is a moot point. But it was obvious to these literary intellectuals that the leaders in the Spanish Republican government were making an effort to improve the conditions of the masses. It also appeared true that the primitive conditions in much of Spain helped considerably to protect the people from the many divisive strains of more industrialized countries. The very primitiveness of the country made the efforts of the Republic all the more dramatic. Thus, the violence of the war served to turn the attention of the novelists to the plight of the Spanish people with whom they sympathized. Spain appeared in flames and these writers sensed in the outcome of the struggle their own destinies.

For these "engaged" writers, the Spanish Civil War became a decisive moment in their lives. As Bernanos first sensed this importance: "Within one lifetime there are very few decisive crises, but it is these moments which give existence significance." (219) And thus the cause of the Spanish people became their cause. It was, according to Malraux, as if history had designated their role, and their responsibility lay in fulfilling it: "Don't forget that we are under observation. History is watching us, judging us, and such circumstances call for that kind of courage which creates victory, not that kind which consoles." (146) No longer was their writing alone sufficient to provide meaning to their lives: these men were now forced by their consciences to actively commit themselves to the struggle of defending their vision of Western civilization. That the war gave their lives new meaning is attested by Malraux: "I truly believe another life started for me with this war." (422) Behind this meaning was the French writer's satisfaction in the fulfillment of Donne's altruistic philosophy implied in the title of the Hemingway novel: "Never again as at this moment was he to know all it can mean to be a man." (205)

In the final moments of Robert Jordan's life, the Hemingway hero speaks for all those intellectuals who had adopted the cause of the Spanish people as their own and had sacrificed their lives in this cause: "I hate to leave it very much and I hope I have done some good in it. I have tried with what talent I had. . . . I have fought for what I believed in for a year now. If we win here we will win everywhere. The world is a fine place and worth the fighting for." (467) The idea that their efforts might help to change the course of history and assist in defeating fascism, while preserving the positive aspects of their humanist tradition, inspired these writers. Too pragmatic and hardened by the realities of modern war to be classed as utopians, nevertheless each possessed a vision of a new and better world which they explicitly expressed in their novels. Regler's political refugee promulgates this inspired belief in a new world: "The world of tomorrow can be born and have a right to live only if we are strong enough." (200) The politics of the war seem no longer to be important. Their vision is not of a particular social or political state, but rather a simple concept of life in a climate free from tyranny and repression. As Robert Jordan articulates this feeling:

> You did the thing there was to do and knew that you were right. You learned the dry-mouthed, fear-purged, purging ecstasy of battle and you fought that summer and that fall for all the poor in the world, against all tyranny, for all the things that you believed in and for the new world you had been educated into. . . . It was in those days, he thought, that you had a deep and sound and selfless pride. (236)

If this conception of the new world is apolitical in the novels of Regler and Hemingway, in Malraux's *L'espoir* the vision is even more abstract: "The only hope that the new Spain has of preserving that which we all have been fighting for . . . is to maintain that quality which year after year has remained constant: the human element, the dignity of men." (280)

Faith in the cause of the Spanish Republic inspired these writers. The excitement of the time and the proximity to death shared with the Spanish people moved them to impart to their writing extremely human qualities. Acts of heroism by the Loyalist troops were described by the novelists and interpreted within a philosophical context. To Regler the battalion doctor's courage under fire could be explained by his faith in the justice of his cause: "If Madrid fell, his life would not be worth living. This gave him a calm that impressed everyone. He went about like the living embodiment of faith in a surprise salvation." (14) The faith of the individual communicated itself to the group in Werner's case; he gained the admiration of, and became a model for, the volunteers of the International Brigades. Malraux writes of the heights to which men can aspire when they experience a common faith in the justice of their cause: "Men who are united, bound together in a common hope—a shared quest—have, like men whom love unites, access to regions they could never gain by themselves alone." (279).

Such faith inspires men to the greatest sacrifices. There is a disregard of self-interest and a desire to see action in terms of its effect on the human condition. Thus Hemingway's Christian peasant Anselmo can berate the selfish interests of Pablo who desires to live in peace and not be involved in the guerrilla action proposed by Jordan: "Art thou a brute? Yes. Art thou a beast? Yes, many times. Hast thou a brain? Nay. None. Now we come for something of consummate importance and thee, with thy dwelling place to be undisturbed, puts thy fox-hole before the interests of humanity. Before the interests of thy people." (11) Paralleling this theme, in the ashes of a prostrate Madrid, Malraux projects the creation of a new world, predicated on the dreams, aspirations, and self-sacrifice of the Spanish people:

> And in this silent phantasmagoria the old Madrid was dying; for the first time, behind the drama of individual lives, of personal dreams and aspirations, beyond the lesser hopes and fears that tend to divide people, a spirit commensurate with the collective

soul of new Madrid was emerging in the fogbound dusk of the beleaguered city. (268)

Thus, these writers were stirred by the Spanish Civil War, by the thought that Spain was about to emerge as an organic society of complete men in a purposeful community. The beginning of a new era seemed possible on Spanish soil. In spite of the Republic's eventual reliance on the weapons of modern warfare, Hemingway, Malraux, and Regler could still envision a return to a simpler life, embraced instinctively by the Spanish peasants. They shared the feelings which led them to praise the "whole" culture of Spain and to glorify the land and the peasant who worked the land. In no other European country could the culture and the historic action of the nation have sprung so clearly from the human soil. Hence it was not difficult for them to view the conflict as one between man vis-à-vis machine. The Spanish conflict inspired them and moved their conscience as men. They found themselves on the side of democracy and social justice, even defending civilization itself. And their primary interest was not confined during the struggle to the choice of opposing ideologies or to the purely political side of the war. Rather their interest in Spain centered on philosophical considerations, on the will of the Spanish people to maintain, under the most inhuman conditions, a sense of human dignity. Defending freedom in Spain seemed tantamount to defending it in their own country, and the issues involved transcended national boundaries.

## ▸ NOTES

[1] Guttmann in his *Wound in the Heart,* Chap. VII, examines this theme with particular reference to Hemingway's *For Whom the Bell Tolls.*

[2] Ernest Hemingway, Preface to *All the Brave,* by Luis Quintanilla (New York, 1939), p. 7.

# VIII

# Epilogue and Conclusions

The major influence of the Spanish Civil War on literature in Europe and the United States is that, for many writers, it destroyed, almost entirely, the means by which they had tried to establish order in a chaotic and violent world.[1] In earlier periods religion and the liberal concepts of democracy—freedom and the quest for equality and fraternity—had served such ends. But by the time of the military rebellion in Spain, these philosophical concepts either had been disregarded, because of the events in Europe, or were obliterated in the bloodshed of the Spanish conflict. The war revealed, in the case of fascism, a capacity for evil in human beings that negated certain optimistic psychological assumptions and destroyed the basic political arguments advanced in the democracies by right-wing defenders of "national socialism." It also cast doubt upon the potential for survival of a democratic culture grounded in the traditions of a humanistic Renaissance and Enlightenment. Often the individual conscience was numbed, and acquiescence to nihilism as a result of the loss of human identity was the immediate consequence. No longer were authors convinced that the violence and destruction of war were justified in order to improve the human condition.

With the defeat of the Spanish Republic, the accompanying disillusionment impelled many writers to reject politics completely. Such disillusionment brought with it a tired and disheartened bitterness. Faith in political movements and their parties had proven treacherous for young authors who had been politically inexperienced and who had adopted the cause of the Spanish people as their own. The insoluble paradox contained within this most political of wars—the discovery that the ideal and the means employed to achieve this ideal contradicted each other hopelessly, one often defeating the other—was a devastating realization. To adhere to the ideals for which they were fighting and lose the battle against fascism, or to sacrifice many of these ideals in order to wage a successful campaign, made the objective of the defense more and more of an abstraction. Writers, politically innocent at the start of the struggle, sustained permanent scars in the process of their subsequent maturation. The abstract tenets on which they had based their faith had crumbled under the shock of violence and treachery, and all wars and visions of a better world were regarded cynically. Idealists who had hailed the heroic struggle of the Spanish people and had envisioned it as a noble cause were shown to be unprepared for the horrors of modern warfare.

Their general suspicion of political ideology was the natural result of their Spanish experience. Failure to achieve any of their ideological goals caused many intellectuals to regard war as totally irrational with all the combatants as victims. This reaction to the horrors of the conflict probably accounts for the contrast in their literary treatment of the Spanish Civil War and that of World War II. The literature of this enlarged study of violence and man's inhumanity differs drastically from that written about the Spanish struggle. In the books of World War II there is remarkably little discussion of war aims and aspirations. Thus, literary intellectuals came to see war as incomprehensible and meaningless, inevitably leading to the corruption of man. Any attempt to maintain ethical standards, should he have any to begin with, would only hamper man's effectiveness as a combat soldier. In much of the literature of the global war the enemy is no longer the dictator and the black figures of fascism; rather, it is the war itself that is the enemy.

For those writers who had been under the influence of Marxism in the 1930s, the Spanish Civil War proved a bitter disappointment. The intellectuals who embraced the Marxian doctrines or its variants with such fervor had been motivated by despair. The traditional democratic virtues had appeared hopeless before the rising power of the fascist dictators and their plans for world domination. That this Marxist appeal was almost entirely dispelled by 1940 in the literature of Europe and the United States can be attributed largely to the result of the Spanish Civil War. Spain provided the opportunity to study at first hand a violent situation in which, according to Marx, Lenin, and their disciples, the forces of history were working to produce a dictatorship of the proletariat which would be the first phase of the evolution toward a workers' paradise. Because of the communist policies during the war and the conflict among the communists and anarchists and the Republican government in general, these writers now had reason to believe that a Loyalist victory in Spain could have conceivably resulted in a dictatorship of secret police and Soviet military rather than that of the Spanish proletariat. It was apparent that the Spaniards, having first rid their country of German and Italian invaders, would then have been faced with the problem of liberating themselves from the attempted Soviet domination of the Negrín government.

The reactions to this realization struck individual writers with varying impact. The defeat of the Spanish Republic and the subsequent signing of the Stalin-Hitler Pact signaled the end of the effectiveness of Marxist literature outside Russia, which formerly had nourished socially-conscious idealists of the noncommunist left as well as party members. The responses of the less mature writers took one of two courses: they either produced polemics in which the Marxist ideals were propounded with increasingly desperate intensity, or they fashioned a literature from which ideals had completely disappeared. In almost every instance, once the ideology was abandoned, political interests were forsaken as well. At one end of this radical spectrum were the political diehards who refused to acknowledge that the war in Spain had changed anything; at the other end were writers who were convinced that politics had no meaning or was simply incomprehensible. Authors were no longer concerned with idealistic causes or the reform of institutions and men. What they now saw only too clearly was a justification for the cynicism which others had earlier cultivated as an indispensable condition for survival.

Essentially a historical phenomena, the war novel involving revolutionary aspirations, as well as most fiction propounding social radicalism, appeared by the end of the 1930s, either lacking in contemporary relevance or totally meaningless. The cultural life now surrounding the writer, a product of its own historical accumulations and internal tensions, was marked by incoherence and uncertainty. He was compelled to examine the possibilities for literature in a world of fragmented beliefs, where a sense of philosophic nihilism had replaced a unified social and political orientation. This fragmentation of ideals did not take place in the 1940s, but the decade of World War II was heir to it, heir to the failure of so many revolutionary social, economic, and political theories by which man had hoped to live. The variety of ways in which intellectuals responded to the Second World War—their pervasive sense of nihilism, their withdrawal from society and politics—may be at least partially attributed to their Spanish experience. The decade following the Spanish Civil War could offer these young and intellectually maimed writers neither an ideology nor a faith to which they might adhere.

For the more radical of these writers, the Marxist ideology had been destroyed by the treachery of the communists, first in Spain and then by the Stalin-Hitler Pact, and the process of disenchantment with political philosophy quickly followed. This disengagement from politics was to mark much of the creative work of the next ten years.[2] Social revolution could no longer appeal to writers who saw that their efforts in Spain to change the world for the better had provided little more than a choice between forms of totalitarian regimentation. In sum, the radical disunity that marked these writers' lives had created a spiritual and intellectual turmoil. Confronted by the realigned power relations among nations, a situation in which could be envisioned the possible destruction of the Western world and the humanistic ideals which were embodied in it, many of these authors chose to withdraw from the political scene, and as artists turned their attention to nonsocial themes.

More mature literary intellectuals withdrew from the struggle with the knowledge that a worthy cause could not be victorious without having to resort to dehumanizing and corruptive methods, which ultimately would only frustrate its purposes. For these writers, withdrawal was in no sense a surrender, nor an admission that fascism could no longer be contained. It was done partly with the hope of gaining some perspective toward a situation in which they were passionately involved, holding to beliefs which might have grown firmer as a result of their Spanish experiences. The writers in this study who withdrew from party politics in no way indicated that they were abandoning their beliefs in the cause for which the Republic had been fighting. The result for these more politically mature intellectuals was that a close-up view of political life had led to the shedding of some ideological illusions. The ruthlessness, dishonesty, and opportunism of the political factions engaged in the Spanish struggle proved too bitter a potion for them to accept, and they consequently were forced to revaluate how their beliefs in social progress might best be effected. The creative imagination of these novelists retreated from the frontiers of social revolution, though not from social meliorism, and they began the painful process of redefining prerogatives. From their experiences in the Spanish Civil War they became aware of Russia's true role in the struggle for political ideals; they now recognized the totalitarian threat from the left as well as from the right. They then revised their political ideas, curbed any revolutionary inclinations, and in the face of a more terrifying challenge, asserted a new antifascist philosophy grounded in the spirit of humanism.

After examining thc works of Hemingway, Malraux, Regler, Orwell, Koestler, and Bernanos and their treatment of the Spanish Civil War, for one to conclude that the conflict produced a group of disillusioned idealists would be extremely misleading. These writers were too knowledgeable for us to conclude that they were docile pawns in a power struggle, that they were duped by cynical politicians, or that their ideals proved too illusory. These charges may be validly leveled at lesser literary figures, at men who placed their faith in political movements above their personal convictions. It is true that after the defeat—intellectuals tend to exaggerate both defeats and victories assuming an unjustifiable finality—many writers left their souls dead on the soil of Spain and never again were able to face the realities of life. There were also some who faced the Spanish realities with such resoluteness that they left their bodies on that soil too—first proof to encroaching fascism that heroic men were willing to die for a cause. They proclaimed, however briefly, that a moment comes when actions have to bear some relation to beliefs. But some critics examining Spanish Civil War literature conclude, in retrospect, that even the more sophisticated writers were ineffectual in their efforts to alter existing conditions. Notwithstanding the foresight, concern, and sacrifices of the novelists in this study, the Spanish Republic was defeated, and six months later the Second World War, which each had predicted, began. But they had been more than Cassandras haranguing the self-interested democracies.

This study has made clear that the reasons for the defeat of the Spanish Republic lay outside the sphere of influence of these writers. International and national politics and power structures moved relentlessly through the war, and once set in motion could not be halted. If the burden of guilt for the Loyalist defeat must be assigned, the democracies as well as Russia should not escape censure. Despite the loss of the Spanish Republic and the failure of these authors to influence the course of the war, it would be entirely unfair to dismiss them as writers who had betrayed their function as artists, or who had abjured their responsibilities as men. The defeat of their cause does not in any way lessen the generous idealism, hope, and purpose they put into their literary efforts. Such writers during this period were, in a sense, the conscience-keepers of the intellectual elite of Europe and America. In discussing the efforts of all men who committed themselves to the defense of the Loyalist cause, Hugh Ford reflects, "To scorn their defense of the Republic is to mock their belief in humanity at a time when it was above all needed."[3]

At the conclusion of the Spanish Civil War, these novelists were scattered in various parts of the globe. Gustav Regler, as a German refugee and then truly a man without a country, resided in Paris during the latter part of 1939. Stalin had signed his pact with Hitler, and France had made hurried preparations to protect its borders from what now seemed an inevitable onslaught. Regler by this time, as a result of old dissatisfactions with the Communist Party and the allying of Stalin with Hitler, had decided to sever relations with the party. He was arrested by the French police as an alleged communist and was interned in a prisoner-of-war camp in the south of France. At this point the paths of Regler and Arthur Koestler again crossed, and both were to suffer under the wretched conditions of the French concentration camp. Ironically, Regler, ever the antifascist, had volunteered for the French army moments before his detention.

Because of the intercession on his behalf by such liberals as Hemingway, Eleanor Roosevelt, and Felix Frankfurter, Regler was released. He and his wife migrated temporarily to the United States, and finally to Mexico. While he was in Mexico, the communists chose to launch an invidious attack against him, charging that Regler was now a fascist in the pay of the Nazis.[4] Although the libel against a man who had dedicated his life to the fight against fascism was incredible, the communists succeeded in so defaming his reputation that he and his wife, both in extremely poor health as a result of their many vicissitudes in Europe, were refused visas to settle in the United States.[5]

It should be stressed that Regler's decision to break with the Communist Party was not a result of his Spanish Civil War experiences. The ultimate break, although made while in Mexico, had been planned years before, during his trip to Russia and while he was engaged in undercover activities in Germany. The Spanish conflict had merely served to prolong his political alignment. The hardships imposed by the war, Regler's admission that only the communists were capable of organizing a Spanish army which might contain and perhaps even defeat the forces of reaction and fascism, sustained his belief in the need for communist affiliation. To conclude that the Spanish Civil War played a primary role in his decision to abandon party activities would be erroneous. His dissatisfaction with the totalitarian aspects of party policy and the Stalin-Hitler Pact contributed more to his decision than any experiences in Spain. Not once in *The Great Crusade* does Regler imply a betrayal of the Spanish people by the Communist Party or Russia. His charges of betrayal are consistently directed against noncommunist factions in the Republican government:

> Aren't there moments when treason comes so thick and fast that you can't help thinking our leaders don't want a victory? No, I'm not talking about the Communists, not about Negrín, but about

> all the useless baggage sitting around in the Ministries and Staffs, and selling out us and these splendid peasant lads. (427)

Only after the defeat of the Republic did Regler again feel free to follow his convictions which had been suppressed for the duration of the war and which were basically incompatible with communist dogma. Even then he gave no evidence of bitterness on his part in his break with the party. At the French concentration camp he describes the communist cell which seemed almost schizophrenic in its attempt to maintain a hold over the internees:

> It was impossible not to admire the fantasy which sustained them in the depths of defeat. Basically they were only five, a political leader, an administrative leader, a treasurer, a controller of propaganda and agitation, and—the fifth man, representing all the rank and file, the masses: truly the fifth wheel of the wagon! They were Quixotes enacting a daily chapter of their romance of chivalry, and their Sancho Panza was the battered proletariat of the twentieth century. They flattered the masses and did not allow them to follow their own inclinations; as the possessors of the Book of Wisdom they knew what was good for them. They tilted indefatigably against windmills. What they lacked, to be true Quixotes, was the charm and gallantry and gentleness of heart of that Castilian knight.[6]

Regler's separation from politics and his subsequent interest in the primitive art of Mexico seem a natural response to his experiences in Spain. In his case a stereotype label of disillusioned idealist seems inconsistent. Regler had fought in Spain for a set of ideals, and his disassociation from politics was not the result of a sudden awareness of the duplicity involved in the machinations of a political organization. Rather, Regler, a humanist, had become disillusioned with radical politics. As a consequence of his experiences, in his last days, he chose to abandon revolutionary causes in favor of the study of man through art. In a manner, he was expressing those liberal values which were inherent in his philosophy, but which had been suppressed by Communist Party discipline.

Arthur Koestler's experiences in Spain more directly contributed to his renunciation of communism, but not necessarily of politics generally. His months of confinement in a Nationalist prison cell, followed by further internment in a French concentration camp, had profoundly altered his perspective. The fear and pity he experienced during his incarceration produced a complete change in his political and philosophical beliefs:

> The lesson taught by this type of experience, when put into words, always appears under the dowdy guise of perennial commonplaces: that man is a reality, mankind an abstraction; that men cannot be treated as units in operations of political arithmetic because they behave like the symbols for zero and the infinite, which dislocate all mathematical operations; that the end justifies the means only within very narrow limits; that ethics is not a function of social utility, and charity not a petty-bourgeois sentiment but the gravitational force which keeps civilization in its orbit. Nothing can sound more flat-footed than such verbalizations of a knowledge which is not of a verbal nature; yet every single one of these trivial statements was incompatible with the Communist faith which I held.[7]

These convictions, followed by the signing of the Stalin-Hitler Pact, precipitated Koestler's final break with the Communist Party. Orwell asserts that Koestler [as did Regler] "from 1933 onwards . . . wanted to be anti-Fascist without being anti-totalitarian. In 1937 Koestler already knew this, but did not feel free to say so."[8]

How much Koestler's role in the Spanish conflict played in his decision to reorient his political thinking appears less clear. The intensity of the impact on the man is reflected in his assertion: "Other wars consist of a succession of battles; this one is a succession of tragedies." (187) As it had Regler, the Spanish Civil War caused Koestler to examine his political and philosophical convictions, with the inevitable conclusion that they were incompatible with party policies. Yet his final decision, after many last-minute vacillations, was not reached until some time after the war ended. In the interim Koestler had assumed an assignment with the *News Chronicle,* reporting on turbulent political crises in Greece, Palestine, and the Middle East. Although during this period he no longer considered himself a communist, Koestler continued his career as a political writer, advocating partition in Palestine and the creation of a homeland for the remnants of Jewish refugees throughout Europe. In an understandable parallel, Regler also had concerned himself with the humane problem of Spanish refugees seeking asylum in Mexico. The final Stalin purges played a crucial role in Koestler's political disaffection, and his writing at this time was highly critical of all aspects of Marxist theory and the Soviet Union. His condemnation of all totalitarian states expanded to include Russia, and his novel *Darkness at Noon,* which found its nucleus in the author's experiences in a Spanish prison cell, established him as one of the leading opponents of political tyranny.

It is therefore difficult to label either Koestler or Regler, as a result of the Spanish Civil War, a disillusioned idealist. During the conflict each had acknowledged that the Loyalists had been able to prolong their defense only because of Russian intervention. Both were too experienced to be shocked by the operations of the O.G.P.U. in Spain and too sophisticated not to expect the communists to infiltrate important military and political positions in the Republican government. Neither writer seriously objected to the treatment of uncooperative factions, such as the suppression of the P.O.U.M. in Catalonia. And neither Koestler nor Regler was willing to concede in his writings on the Spanish conflict that the Soviet Union had betrayed the Loyalists.

What is true is that each had felt a personal betrayal by the Communist Party and each was subjected to abuse by party-directed critics in future years. Nevertheless, the Spanish Civil War was not the direct cause for their decision to sever relations with the communists. Their disaffection with the Communist Party has been documented in their respective autobiographies and can be traced to a period preceding 1936. From the earlier review of their political commitments, it is evident that the Spanish Civil War was instrumental in continuing their membership in the party organization. Without their involvement in Spain, it is likely that each would have renounced the Communist Party in 1936 rather than delaying until 1940. Their feeling of betrayal was the result of political demands in conflict with their personal convictions and not because of their encounter with the violence of the Spanish Civil War. In the end, Koestler, like Regler, once freed of political ties, has developed into a philosophical humanist forsaking concern with the revolutionary masses in order to concentrate on the nature of man.

Perhaps George Orwell may be considered the only truly disillusioned idealist among the novelists involved in this study. Certainly his feelings upon returning from the internecine strife in Catalonia were bitter and grim. In England, while the war was still being fought, Orwell was able to write:

> I suppose there is no one who spent more than a few weeks in Spain without being in some degree disillusioned. . . . No one in his senses supposed that there was any hope of democracy, even as we understand it in England or France, in a country so divided and exhausted as Spain would be when the war was over. It would have to be a dictatorship, and it was clear that the chance of a working-class dictatorship had passed. (180–81)

At the same time there is ample evidence that his experiences in Spain had not appreciably altered either his faith in humanity or his political beliefs in the benefits of socialism. His exposure to the treachery of political parties, particularly during the P.O.U.M. repression and purge, appears to have done more toward developing his political convictions than disillusioning him. Although he had become contemptuous of communist claims of "fighting for democracy," Orwell recognized the need to turn the tide against fascism, and was willing to accept a possible future struggle in Spain between the Spaniards and the communist infiltrators within the Republic as the price for a fascist defeat:

> Moreover, there was the question of the international prestige of Fascism, which for a year or two past had been haunting me like a nightmare. Since 1930 the Fascists had won all the victories; it was time they got a beating, it hardly mattered from whom. If we could drive Franco and his foreign mercenaries into the sea it might make an immense improvement in the world situation, even if Spain itself emerged with a stifling dictatorship and all its best men in jail. For that alone the war would have been worth winning. (182)

His decision to continue to espouse the cause of socialism, or to continue actively in politics at all, is evidence that Orwell does not conform to the stereotype pattern of a disenchanted idealist. What he learned from his painful experiences in Spain caused him to revise his political thinking, but it did not destroy his faith in mankind, nor weaken his political impulse, nor change its direction. There was no feeling of guilt or self-recrimination. No longer, however, could Orwell maintain his position as an antifascist without, like Koestler, also attacking the totalitarian similarities to be found in a communist regime. Some time afterwards, in his essay, "Looking Back on the Spanish War," he was able to write, "I remember saying once to Arthur Koestler, 'History stopped in 1936,' at which he nodded in immediate understanding. We were both thinking of totalitarianism in general, but more particularly of the Spanish Civil War."[9] His later works, particularly *Animal Farm* and *1984*, significantly parallel Koestler's *Darkness at Noon* in expressing both contempt and fear at the encroachment of totalitarian states across Europe.

With regard to the Spanish Civil War, Orwell's response differs significantly from that of Koestler and Regler in his contention that Russia betrayed both the Spanish people and the proletarian revolution. Throughout *Homage to Catalonia,* Orwell maintains that Spain was headed in the direction of such a revolution and only the Communist Party, wielding its power through Soviet aid, thwarted the inevitable. And if, as Orwell contended, during the war the best qualities of those who were doing the fighting emerged, he also maintained that the war often exposed the worst in those behind the front lines who were attempting to establish political policies. In many ways these treacherous political experiences influenced his thinking years later. Orwell, in his *Animal Farm,* expresses the belief that all revolutions are likely to be betrayed, from within as well as from without. In his involvement with the politics of the Spanish struggle, Orwell failed to touch on the contemporary theme of man's fear of being subjugated by a soulless mechanical totalitarianism. But in later years, when Orwell became less the revolutionary and more the liberal humanist, possibly as a delayed reaction to his Spanish Civil War experiences, he devoted his novel *1984* to this theme. No doubt his experiences in Barcelona in 1937 contributed importantly to his preoccupation with the theme of the falsification of history which he developed so elaborately in *1984*. The assumption that the themes of these two fine novels, the betrayal of revolutionary causes and the dehumanizing aspects of mechanization, found their inspiration in Orwell's adventures in Spain, is not without foundation.

Of importance, before labeling Orwell a disillusioned idealist, is recognition of the fact that, unlike Regler and Koestler, his rejection of communism did not alter his previous faith in socialism. Actually what he rejected was the use of communism as a device for achieving a socialist state. Awareness of the communists' ruthlessness during the Spanish struggle would not permit him in good conscience to accept an alliance with them, however temporary, as a means to an end. To achieve a victory on communist terms might have been acceptable in the fight against fascism, but in terms of a social revolution it appeared to him a sacrifice of human decency, justice, and equality in the process. Thus his disillusionment, as a result of his involvement in Spain, did not concern his faith in mankind or his political beliefs in the desirability of a socialist state. Rather, his misconceptions had been concerned with party politics, particularly those of the Communist Party, and the exigencies of the war compelled a revaluation of his own political views. No longer could he consider communism, with its powerful political and propaganda machinery, an ally of the individual in the achievement of a socialist society.

If at the close of the Spanish Civil War Regler abandoned radical politics and Koestler and Orwell became leading anticommunists, the reasons involved in their reactions cannot be glibly ascribed to their disillusionment with the party because of their Spanish Civil War experiences. The role played by the Soviet Union during the conflict merited both severe criticism (mostly by Orwell) and some degree of admiration (mostly by Regler and Koestler). Without Russian assistance, even Orwell is forced to concede that the Republic could never have withstood the combined assault of the rebel military with the covert and overt assistance of the fascist powers. At the same time the generally totalitarian tactics of the communists served to negate their contribution, at least in the eyes of a writer like Orwell. To attempt to classify either Orwell, Koestler, or Regler in the category of "disillusioned idealist," based on their experiences in Spain from 1936 to 1939, would prove extremely misleading. The politics of each, particularly their antitotalitarian beliefs, were undoubtedly influenced by their stay in Spain, but in the case of Regler and Koestler, their response to communist policies in Spain was the opposite of Orwell's. If the latter rejected the communists because of their role in the Spanish Civil War, the former two continued their support of the communists for this very reason.

Georges Bernanos' response to the Loyalist defeat differed considerably from that of the three left-oriented authors just discussed. His decision to leave France shortly after returning from Majorca in 1938 may be partially attributed to his pessimism over the developing European political situation, the attitude in his own country toward the Spanish Civil War, and the factionalism splitting France:

> I left Spain in 1937 to return to France. The surrender of the individual conscience was a forecast of the eventual capitulation to foreign armies. I discovered that the triple corruption—Nazi, fascist and Marxist—had left my own country devoid of that which I most love and respect in her. I departed from France as soon as possible. It was no longer possible for a free man to write, or even to breathe there.[10]

If Bernanos, like Orwell, can be termed an embittered idealist, his discouragement may be attributed to a faith which this Christian humanist had vested in an unsympathetic and reactionary Church. To an independent philosopher such as Bernanos, it appeared that Western civilization was deteriorating rapidly and that most of the Christian values in Europe, which he cherished, were declining with it:

> Perhaps the truly great causes for which one would be willing to "faire son droit" have passed from the world. But I refuse to accept as a substitute the cynical and careless exploitation of the tenets and princes I am no longer capable of honoring. Europe owes its greatness to Christianity, and if Christianity is dead, Europe must perish with it. (193)

He interpreted the Church's partisanship during the Spanish conflict as a betrayal of its traditional theological doctrines. Europe's only hope for salvation was to be found in the hidden resources of its old Christian traditions.

Bernanos' other disappointment dealt with semifascist political elements in France. These reactionaries insisted that Russia was France's real enemy. Bernanos' warnings on the true nature of fascism and the actual belligerency of the Axis powers did not alter their position. It should not be assumed, however, that Bernanos favored the communists over the fascists. To him revolutions, either fascist or communist, resulted in a totalitarian state, with little noticeable distinction. Thus, the former French monarchist, believed by many in his early days to be a dedicated rightist, supported his humanist inclinations by expressing his contempt for any totalitarian regime or form of government which would inhibit the natural freedom of its citizens:

> I have always believed the truth behind revolutions, fascist or communist, is rather deceptive. Hitler, Stalin or Mussolini were well aware that only a totalitarian dictatorship could suppress the avarice of the bourgeoisie. . . . It is not the use of force on their part which seems so iniquitous, but its inherent mystique: the religion of Force at the service of a totalitarian state or dictatorship, not as a means, but as an end in itself. (128–29)

It appeared to the embittered Bernanos that Europe had failed in its effort to institute any form of democracy, and he attributed this failure to the corruption, injustice and lack of stature of the democratic leaders. Instead of producing great men, such a society relied on modern technology to direct the destinies of its citizens:

> Social democracy has exploited the ideal of justice, and has kept none of its promises, except that of compulsory military service and the nation in arms. Parliamentary democracy dissipates any chance of national grandeur. Military democracy places infants in uniform, and prostitutes both heroism and honor. Authoritarian democracies today are submerging even the memory of a free Christian monarchy. (193–94)

What he had seen in Spain alarmed him. All the mistakes of European politics seemed embodied in the agonizing struggle of the Spanish people. Bernanos' words are those of a man of goodwill who has lost faith because of the perfidy of those in whom he had once believed:

> The war in Spain is a charnel-house. It is a charnel-house of real and false principles, of good intentions and bad. . . . There is no more pathetic sight than these wretched men—republicans, democrats, fascist or antifascists, Catholics or anticlericals—desperately unhappy human beings. (192–93)

Although Bernanos' reception after returning from Spain did much to alienate him from his former right-wing friends, especially following their severe attacks on *Les grands cimetières sous la lune,* nevertheless his love for France never waned. The Spanish Civil War had clarified the issues which were to plague his own country for years to come, and his disappointment resulted from a sense of frustration at his inability to convince his countrymen of their errors and have them heed his warnings of the impending disaster:

> The Spanish tragedy, prefiguration of the universal tragedy, is undeniable evidence of the unhappy condition of men of good will in modern society—a society which gradually eliminates them as an unusable byproduct. A man of good will can no longer commit himself to a political party, and before long I am wondering if he will be able to maintain allegiance to a country. (288)

In the seven years Bernanos remained in Brazil, his faith in France never wavered. His writings expressed his hopes for his country following World War II, his distaste for fascism, and the menace of dictatorships. Like Orwell, his leftist counterpart, he expressed his fear of the more subtle tyrannies of the "robot mentality" and mechanized authoritarianism. These themes prevail in his later writings, especially in his condemnation of the Vichy regime and fascist elements within France. In Bernanos' vision of his country's greatness, all elements in France which he believed to be irresponsible and mediocre merited condemnation. Bernanos referred specifically to the sycophantic "political realists" of occupied France, dupes of their own self-assurance, and lack of vision and personal courage.

Thus the Spanish Civil War had served to enlighten Bernanos as to the future political situation in France. Although a politically "engaged" writer, he was not one in the sense of a party adherent and the Spanish conflict did little to alter his attitude toward a desirable society. As a humanist and philosopher, Bernanos cared little for the factionalism splitting the right and left. By placing himself above the conspiratorial machinations of political parties, he was in a better position than more politically committed writers to interpret the defeat of the Loyalists in the context of its effect on the human condition. His severe criticism of the tacit consent of the Church for the crimes perpetrated by the Nationalists in Majorca during the Spanish struggle was in accord with his personal convictions and was essentially apolitical in nature. The triumph of the Nationalists in Spain concerned Bernanos less from a political standpoint than from its possible philosophical implications. For him there was little qualitative difference between a fascist dictatorship and the bourgeois-capitalist system, since he believed each sought to exploit man for its selfish ends. The doctrines of both governmental systems included an ordering of the human elements within a nation by utilizing the machines of modern technology. For Bernanos, any attempt to inhibit the freedom of the individual was tantamount to tyranny. His support of the Loyalists had been predicated on a belief that cruelty and inhumanity were more commonly the tool of fascism and that a democratic republic, whether or not he agreed with its political and economic structure, was infinitely to be preferred to the former. Thus the Loyalists' defeat could never truly affect his own philosophical convictions, which were based on a faith in the nobility of man and the inevitable triumph of free men. "No, it is not you whom we fear most, Herr Hitler. We shall triumph over you and your followers, if we have the ability to preserve our souls." (433) To the noble Bernanos the problems of the world were neither economic nor social, but moral. In a world populated by men of honor, the difficulties which now seemed insurmountable, might easily be resolved:

> Political alignments are of slight interest. The world is in need of honor; it is a sense of honor the world lacks. The world has all that it requires, and rejoices in nothing, because without honor it has lost all its self-esteem. And no sensible man would attempt to recover it by studying Machiavelli or Lenin, or, for that matter, the Casuists. Honor is an Absolute, and has nothing in common with doctrinaires of the Relative. (128)

Following the defeat of the Loyalists and his intensive effort at composing *For Whom the Bell Tolls,* Ernest Hemingway plunged into the turmoil of World War II. Between 1940 and 1946 he wrote little fiction, choosing to postpone literary projects for the duration of the war. The Spanish conflict, in light of his subsequent actions, was the initial step in his personal fight against fascism. "We're in for fifty years of undeclared wars," he maintained in *The Fifth Column,* "and I've signed up for the duration." Dedicating himself to the struggle, Hemingway accompanied elements of the American First Army through France and into Germany in the final offensive of 1944–1945. Earlier in the war he had been active as a volunteer in the antisubmarine cordon in Florida and Cuban coastal waters, and before the fighting ended had participated in bombing missions over Germany in British and American aircraft.[11]

The Spanish Civil War was only the beginning of the offensive which Hemingway had urged against the fascist dictators. The political treachery experienced during the Spanish conflict, the tragic sense of betrayal implicit in *For Whom the Bell Tolls,* did little to discourage his zeal. As a war correspondent he had become friendly with the Loyalist leaders who permitted him access to confidential information concerning the military campaigns and the complexities of the internal political situation. This knowledge distinguishes Hemingway's novel from the other works in this study, with the exception of Malraux's *L'espoir.* For all its realism and consideration of the violence and corruption in Republican Spain, *For Whom the Bell Tolls* derives its peculiar strength from a recognition of the generous idealism that governed the action of so many men. Hemingway, while he hated war ["Qué puta es la guerra"], is passionately interested in everything connected with the fighting. And in the case of the war in Spain, he indulged this interest with a good conscience, since he was so certain that what was here at issue was nothing less than the freeing of an oppressed people from intolerable tyranny.[12] Because of the apolitical attitude of the novelist, his refusal to be personally involved in the political machinations of the feuding factions supporting the Republic, and his shrewd understanding of the seamy side of revolutionary politics, he cannot possibly be characterized as a disillusioned victim of the war in Spain. No other writer of the conflict was more convincingly apolitical than Hemingway, yet none had pleaded more urgently for a militant struggle against the forces of fascism. He continued this effort even after the fighting in Spain had ceased. Like Bernanos', Hemingway's ideals transcended the failings in the political factionalism which so greatly influenced Orwell. To the American novelist the Spanish tragedy had settled nothing, and this attitude permitted him to remain faithful to his earlier convictions regarding the evils of fascism and the justice of the Loyalist cause.

Hemingway's subsequent rejection by radical critics in the United States[13] was provoked by his scathing description of the fanatical communist André Marty and his attempt in *For Whom the Bell Tolls* to make the Spanish Civil War appear a test of personal courage for his hero, with only slight socio-economic implications. These critics accused him of misrepresenting the Republican cause, of maligning the communist contribution, and presenting it in a sinister and reprehensible manner, and treating the rebels too sympathetically. These very critics now dismissed his impressive contribution on behalf of the Loyalists and "what they wrote expressed the frustrated awareness that they were dealing with no convert, but essentially the same man, whether he had been raising money for ambulances in 1937 or condemning André Marty in 1940."[14] What particularly angered them was that at the conclusion of the Spanish War, in which he had displayed a deep personal interest in the cause of the Spanish people, Hemingway chose to reject the code of collective action [Harry Morgan's dying words in *To Have and Have Not,* "A man alone ain't got no bloody———chance."] in favor of a system which stressed the independence of the individual. While left-wing critics had made much of the possible conversion of Hemingway as a result of *To Have and Have Not* and his work on behalf of the Popular Front during the Spanish conflict, they were bitterly disappointed in *For Whom the Bell Tolls.*

Hemingway's code for the individual had been given expression earlier in his *Green Hills of Africa:*

> If you serve time for society, democracy, and the other things quite young, and declining any further enlistment make yourself responsible only to yourself, you exchange the pleasant, comforting stench of comrades for something you can never feel in any other way than by yourself. (148)

This philosophy is explicit in *For Whom the Bell Tolls;* throughout the novel his concern is with the actions of individuals rather than the political or collective elements in the war effort. Perhaps the nonpolitical nature of the novel can be traced to the fact that Hemingway could devote himself to the cause of the Spanish people without reservation, but the political forces supporting the Spanish Republic could not command more than his partial allegiance. His hero Robert Jordan several times expressed the necessity of subordinating political and intellectual opinions in order to devote himself to the greater cause. Thus, his hero's apolitical antifascism possessed the same determined qualities of Hemingway's own ideals.

Not politics but Hemingway's familiarity with Spain and the Spanish people had conditioned him for the experiences he underwent during the conflict. As he states in his motives for writing the novel: "It wasn't just the civil war I put into it . . . it was everything I had learned about Spain for eighteen years."[15] He was well acquainted with the country and its people, their folkways and speech, and was fascinated by the paradoxes and contradictions in their national character: the cruelty and tenderness, cowardice and courage, and the treachery and loyalty:

> Well . . . it is part of one's education. It will be quite an education when it's finished. . . . He was lucky that he had lived parts of ten years in Spain before the war. They trusted you on the language, principally. They trusted you on understanding the language completely and speaking it idiomatically and having a knowledge of the different places. A Spaniard was only really loyal to his village in the end. First Spain of course, then his own tribe, then his province, then his village, his family and finally his trade. If you knew Spanish he was prejudiced in your favor, if you knew his province it was that much better, but if you knew his village and his trade you were in as far as any foreigner ever could be. (135)

Thus, in the novel Hemingway attempted to provide a Spanish interpretation of the civil strife. The extent to which he succeeded is questionable, but there is little doubt that he was trying to present what he felt were the underlying immutable truths in the struggle of the Spanish people.[16] In order to accomplish this goal it was necessary for him to go beyond the political sphere of the conflict; the only political theme in *For Whom the Bell Tolls* is the need for all factions to unite to rid Spain and the rest of Europe of the growing menace of fascism. Hence, he was able to reiterate this theme at the close of the war, confirming the constancy of his ideals which had not changed in the intense heat of the crucible that was the Spanish Civil War:

> Our dead live in the hearts and minds of the Spanish peasants, of the Spanish workers, of all the good simple honest people who believed in and fought for the Spanish Republic. . . . The Fascists may spread over the land blasting their way with weight of metal bought from other countries. They may advance aided by traitors and by cowards. They may destroy cities and villages and try to hold the people in slavery. But you cannot hold any people in slavery.[17]

The complexity of *For Whom the Bell Tolls* may be attributed to the many diverse forces affecting Hemingway at the time. All the emotions felt by Hemingway from 1936 to 1939 were fused into the novel, which he wrote immediately after the fighting ended. So too was the realization that the battle against the forces which were determined to destroy his liberal ideals had only just begun: the overthrow of the author's nonpolitical attitude in the face of a pressing need for action, his hatred of fascism and sympathy for the Loyalist Republic, his romantic love of old Spain, and the enthusiasm and anxiety for the future of the world which might be determined in this decisive crusade for liberty.[18]

Following the Spanish Civil War Malraux, like the more doctrinaire Regler and Koestler, decided to sever relations with the communists. The Moscow trials and the Stalin-Hitler Pact provided the final justification for withdrawing his support, were such justification necessary. But the pragmatic Malraux had supported the Communist Party only when its actions had helped to further his ideals. With the defeat of the Spanish Loyalists, the French novelist no longer shared a common purpose with the communists. Malraux's attitude during this period may best be defined negatively: he was with the communists because he was against fascism. Fascism was the greater danger, but if graver danger threatened more immediately from another quarter, Malraux could justifiably alter his political orientation. The focus of his loyalty was not vested in political parties, but in a set of values which—according to the moment—one party or another appeared best able to protect.[19] Or, as Malraux in his depiction of Negus expresses it:

> For more than a month he had ceased believing in the revolution. The apocalypse was over, but there remained the struggle against fascism. . . . Negus had fought for so long against the bourgeoisie, had found meaning in the struggle, that it was not difficult to continue on in the battle against fascism; negative emotions had always been his driving force. (354)

As early as 1937, Malraux, in *L'espoir,* had implied that the purpose behind the communists' involvement in Spain differed from their publicly proclaimed one:

> The communists have all the virtues of action and no others. . . . Are you certain that among your men the dedicated communist, who at first went to his death crying, "Long live the Proletariat!" or "Long live Communism!" doesn't declaim today, in the same circumstances, "Long live the Party!" (427)

If his relations with the Party members had been strained during the Spanish Civil War, the Stalin-Hitler Pact strengthened Malraux's determination to withdraw his support from a political organization with which he no longer shared common ideals.

Malraux's antagonism to fascism, however, like that of Hemingway's, was just beginning. As he had predicted in *L'espoir,* the cruelest and most inhuman threat to humanitarian ideals had been developing in Europe; and immediately following the Spanish struggle, like a tidal wave, it had inundated his own France. No novelist of Malraux's generation had been so closely associated with the raw violence of contemporary events, and he now chose to fight for his country in its struggle against his old political and ideological enemies. Malraux joined the French tank corps as a private, was captured in June 1940 after the fall of France, escaped from a prisoner-of-war camp after five months, and made contact with the Resistance. His adventures in occupied France during the ensuing period are of such heroic proportions that any attempt at description would appear like romantic fiction.[20] Among the deeds which have been documented is a record of Malraux's efforts in the allied état-major operations in eastern France and his commission as "chef du Maquis" and commander of 1500 men in the Lot, Dordogne, and the Corrèze regions of

France. Malraux eventually participated in the liberation of France, although before this was accomplished, he had once more been wounded and captured.

The eventual coalition between Malraux and de Gaulle was extremely controversial. Paris intellectual and political circles could not explain the basis for the alliance between the leftist author and the conservative general. The revolutionary Malraux of the Escadre España had not really changed; he was still "un homme engagé," motivated by patriotism, who would neither accept the direction in which his country was moving nor consider international communism as a viable solution to France's problems. Like the characters in *L'espoir,* Malraux had entered the battle against fascism, with its innate economic and social injustices, but at the same time he had continued his philosophical struggle against the limitations of life and man's destiny; within the context of the latter conflict, Malraux had sufficiently altered his perspective by the end of World War II to consider communism a threat to his personal convictions, as well as to the security of western Europe. It is difficult to ascertain the extent to which his experiences in the Spanish Civil War influenced this transition. The conversion of Malraux was a slow process and, typical of the man, he did not choose to publicize his growing disaffection. Unlike Koestler and Regler, Malraux's withdrawal provoked no immediate scandal or vilification. As it had for the characters in his novels, history had provided the test of ideas at times when human experiences were most strained and in places where they had become most decisively engaged.

Malraux's association with the communists had been the pragmatic relationship of an activist who recognized the threat to elemental values in the emergence of the fascist powers in Europe and the necessity for joining with the strongest forces to oppose that threat. During the Spanish Civil War the personal conflict between his developing doubts regarding the future of communism and the necessity for a well-organized resistance to the fascists is reflected as a major theme in *L'espoir*. Although the communists are accepted as the most expedient instrumentality in the defense of the Spanish Republic, in the novel Malraux softens such acceptance in discussion after discussion of the ethics behind the party's activities in Spain. At one point in the novel, a communist makes the observation, totally unacceptable to the independent Malraux, "Unfortunately you will only too soon discover that your own sense of morality has almost no value in political action." (179) Much of *L'espoir* contents concern the tragic dialectic between means and ends inherent in all organized political violence, even when, as in Spain, the violence is a necessary and justifiable defense of liberty and human dignity. Thus, the necessity to violate the dignity of the individual to preserve that of the group, for Malraux, is part of the tragedy of human existence. And the tragedy is intensified by the knowledge that there is no absolute guide in choosing the course of action. Even Manuel, the young communist destined to assume a major command in the Republican army, is forced to concede: "Every move I have made towards greater efficiency, towards becoming a better officer, has estranged me more and more from my fellow-men. Each day I grow a little less human." (347)

The less doctrinaire characters in the novel express the conviction that neither political ideology nor economic theory is of avail in the violence of modern war. The philosophical issue of any man's right to destroy another assumes paramount importance. Malraux comments that to the condemned prisoners, politics affords little comfort:

> In prison they speak of just about anything but politics. If anyone had said: "I have defended what I though was just, I have lost, and now I am willing to pay," he would have stood alone. When a man dies, he dies alone. (217–18)

Even literature, philosophy and art seem of little consequence in the face of death: "Neither writers nor philosophers have any meaningful message on this night. . . . People who are concerned with life are unavailing in the face of death. . . . Art is of little value where there is great suffering and no picture can retain its import when confronted by pools of blood." (276–77) Malraux argues that romantic dreams of revolution cannot overcome the violence of modern war ("C'est pas la guerre! . . . C'est la chaude-pisse! Ça finiera plus!"), and the only meaning emerging from the bloodshed in Spain is not found in political ideology but rather in the patience, sorrow, and humble dignity of the Spanish people who are the instruments and the victims of violence: "And now he was alone in the abandoned palace, confronted by a polluted and suffocating world. Whichever way the war finally ends, he thought, after such bitter hatreds what sort of peace is possible here? And what has this war made of me?' (264)

Malraux, like Regler and Koestler, felt an intense anti-Sovietism engendered by a sense of personal betrayal at the hands of the Communist Party. He considered the Stalin-Hitler Pact, irrespective of its justification from the Soviet point of view, to be a betrayal of the universal common man. From that point on Malraux joined with Bernanos as a dedicated Frenchman, his dream of internationalism suspended indefinitely.[21] His participation in the defense and eventual liberation of France only served to strengthen this devotion to his country and provided him with the direction for future channeling of his seemingly limitless energies.

Regarding his Spanish Civil War experience, in retrospect it is clear that he could not, as had Koestler and Regler, merely sublimate his personal convictions in deference to the struggle against fascism; nor could be assume an apolitical stand similar to that of Hemingway's. Malraux was too much the military realist, however, to emulate Orwell's uncomplicated course and denounce the communists, thereby sacrificing the cohesion of the Popular Front in favor of pursuing a strong personal revolutionary vision. Rather he was forced by his knowledge of the complexity of the issues to avoid any definitive conclusion in the dialectic between ethics and politics until the war ended. Although such an unresolved position was the only course for the French novelist in 1937, one critic has noted that "the whole treatment of the matter shows a tendency to avoid a head-on collision with a problem admitting of no satisfactory solution, a hesitancy raised to the level of anguish by the absolute necessity for resistance against fascism."[22]

As the war drew to a close, Malraux felt free to conclude that the violation of his own ethical code need no longer be excused as a military expediency, and his renunciation of the communists and revolutionary politics in general may be attributed to a large extent to his experiences in Spain. The arbitrary and totalitarian tactics of the communists had rid him of any reservations he might have had regarding the future of a Europe under Soviet domination. His withdrawal of support for the party was the result of its failure to agree with his own code of social and political ethics. By 1939 he had suddenly found himself, under the impact of political, economic, and diplomatic events, in total opposition to communist policy.[23] Malraux's experiences in Spain were mainly responsible for his change in attitude toward revolutionary politics as well. The French novelist, much like Orwell, recognized the inevitable corruption of revolutionary causes, from within as well as from without: If revolution still appeared to him as the myth of the modern world, he was prepared to acknowledge the usual aftermath—one tyranny replaced by another, perhaps worse. No revolution can be effected without a dynamic "apocalypse." But no revolution can survive without developing organization and order resulting in the crystallization, or perhaps the strangulation, of the revolutionary impetus.[24] Much in Malraux's *L'espoir* parallels Orwell's *Animal Farm:* the themes involving the corruptive influences of power, the knowledge that most revolutions end in the establishment of an even stronger centralized authority, a more repressive police, and rigid bureaucracy than had existed under the previous regime. The choice in a revolution between a glorious but short-lived anarchy and a reactionary tyranny resulting from military necessity is a tragic one.

In a natural transition, Malraux the active revolutionary has become Malraux the dedicated humanist. His concern for the history of mankind, as reflected in art, parallels the study by Regler of primitive Mexican art, except that Malraux's endeavors have been on a higher intellectual and scholarly level. In the nature and function of art, Malraux envisions a means of elevating the human condition and achieving freedom from outside oppressive forces of history. And in this area he has achieved his maximum understanding of the nature of man, possibly because of his shift from the limited realm of political action. Thus he has been able to clarify his own conception of man's fate. His change of focus from the revolutionary concept of masses to the humanist study of man also recalls Koestler's most recent studies. Both Koestler and Malraux have protested the inhumanity engendered in the name of ideology and the attempt of totalitarian states to create a tyranny of the mind. Malraux's irremediable solitude, his obligation to assume the burden of freedom by staking his life for his values, his defiance of death as an ultimate affirmation of "authentic" existence—all these themes find expression in *L'espoir* long before they became fashionable intellectual catchwords or tedious artistic platitudes of the existentialists.[25] "The European heritage," Malraux resignedly stated in 1946, "is tragic humanism."

In a sense Spain was a sacrifice, but it cannot be said that the war was fought in vain. Although the issues were somewhat confused, it is true that the totalitarian evil, for the first time, was confronted there. The conflict also had a positive meaning which, with the passage of time, has transcended the suffering and destruction which were its immediate consequences. It presented mankind with the tragic dilemma: at times men have no choice between submission to tyranny and a war which in all likelihood would destroy many of the institutions they were determined to defend. In Spain a humanitarian cause was defeated, but it was not humiliated. By their sacrifice the Loyalists delayed the fascist advance immeasurably. The three years in which Spain was tortured and lacerated may have saved all Europe and might have provided the delay which was essential for the awakening of the democracies.

Perhaps nowhere more than in Spain, the decade ending with the Second World War resulted in a profound disillusionment. There remains a mysterious afterglow of the passions that once burned so fiercely. Writing in 1946, Albert Camus said of the Spanish struggle:

> It is now nine years that men of my generation have had Spain within their hearts. Nine years that they have carried it with them like an evil wound. It was in Spain that men learned that one can be right and yet be beaten, that force can vanquish spirit, that there are times when courage is not its own recompense. It is this, doubtless, which explains why so many men, the world over, regard the Spanish drama as a personal tragedy.[26]

This study has attempted to consider only those literary intellectuals who were active participants in the Spanish Civil War. Of all the men who participated and suffered, these writers were perhaps best equipped to testify as truly honest and articulate witnesses to the horrors and moments of courage, as well as the complex social and political issues concerned in this war on the peninsula. Shortly thereafter these very issues were to plunge the rest of Europe into a bloody battlefield. Of the writings produced by foreign witnesses in Spain, the novels and personal narratives in this study alone seem to survive as both literature and literary history, recording the message behind the struggle of the Spanish people. Considered collectively, such writings complement each other and illuminate the various perspectives of the cataclysm which the literary imagination found possible.

These memorable works by the European and American authors are the product of the vanquished rather than the victors, although in theme and tone there would probably have been little difference had the Loyalists eventually triumphed. Rather than have their work depend on the immediate victory or defeat of their side in the Spanish conflict, these writers chose to give a definitive and lasting expression to their experience by justifying their cause in philosophical and moral terms. As writers they wished to register their convictions that the struggle had meaning far beyond the victories and defeats of the actual fighting in Spain. There can be little doubt that the stark reproduction of the inhumanity of the war should have deeply influenced the conscience of Western man.

The immense wave of interest that the Spanish conflict has aroused in the last few years has produced several studies of military and political history, and some revival of the old controversies. Many families are still marked by its destruction of lives; witness the Spanish Refugee Aid organization, sponsored by Salvador de Madariaga and Pablo Casals, which still accepts the responsibility for caring for the families forced to exist in southern France, having fled there during the closing days of the war. In the cinema there has been produced an outstanding documentary of the war, "To Die in Madrid." In the perspective acquired by the thirty-year interim since it began, it is clear that the struggle in Spain had a decisive impact on literature. In the works of many writers still fascinated by events on the peninsula from 1936 to 1939, there are attempts even at this late date to return to that violent time of social upheaval, as if somehow it contained mysteries yet to be revealed. Partial explanation may be found in the fact that many of the issues of the conflict are the same which continue to divide the world today. Because of the imposition of the major ideologies of the twentieth century on the war of the

Spanish people, the events in Spain will continue to exert an intense attraction for those who lived through it and for those who know it only as a historical event. Thus the war has lost little of its emotional appeal: the drama of human passion and compassion, of idealism, hope, sacrifice, and despair reflecting Western civilization's highest virtues and greatest shortcomings.

In the context of literary history, the six novelists in this study avoided certain tendencies of World War I writers to infuse into war literature a decided element of adventurous romance. Rather, they patterned their work, consciously or unconsciously, on the great literature of earlier wars. They returned to the tradition of the major nineteenth-century novels—Stendhal's *The Charterhouse of Parma,* Tolstoy's *War and Peace* and *Sevastopol Sketches,* Zola's *Débâcle,* and Crane's *Red Badge of Courage*—which cut incisively into the realities of their conflicts. Much of the material produced as a result of combat experience in the Spanish Civil War reflects the shock ensuing from this first encounter with the intense brutality and large-scale waste of modern warfare. At their best moments these novelists were capable of depicting the horrors of their experiences and blending their emotions with literary technique. If there is a shift in perspective from the great nineteenth-century war novels to those in this study, at least part of it may be attributed to the distance between these modern novelists and their materials. The significance in the fact that these writers on the Spanish War were active participants and their work had an immediate impact on the events of the time, cannot be underestimated. The results of this personal involvement must have influenced both the political focus and literary subtlety of their writing, unlike the feeling of isolated comfort which affected their literary predecessors. As Irving Howe expresses their predicament: "They *are* in their tragedies, their blood and hope are ground into the defeated revolutions which they mourn."[27]

## ▸ NOTES

[1] Muste's major contention in his study, *Say That We Saw Spain Die.*

[2] See Chester E. Eisinger, *Fiction of the Forties* (Chicago, 1963), for a perceptive analysis of this trend.

[3] *Poets' War,* p. 255.

[4] The psychology behind the party's need to castigate any members who chose to break with it has been fully treated by Koestler in his contribution to *The God that Failed.*

[5] This contention is expressed by Regler in his *Owl of Minerva;* the possibility is at least as likely, considering the activities of the Dies Committee in the United States during this period, that he was refused entry because of his communist background.

[6] *Owl of Minerva,* pp. 334–35.

[7] *God that Failed,* p. 68.

[8] George Orwell, "Arthur Koestler," *Dickens, Dali and Others* (New York, 1946), p. 189.

[9] *Such Were the Joys,* p. 139.

[10] "Autobiography," *La nef,* p. 5.

[11] See Malcolm Cowley's "A Portrait of Mister Papa," *Life,* January 10, 1949, for a detailed account of Hemingway's adventures in World War II.

[12] See Joseph Warren Beach's, "How Do You Like It Now, Gentlemen?" *Sewanee Review,* LIX (Spring 1951).

[13] See Alvah Bessie's review of *For Whom the Bell Tolls, New Masses,* XXXVII (November 5, 1940), 25–29, and Burgum's caustic analysis of the novel in his *Novel and the World's Dilemma,* pp. 184–204.

[14] David Sanders, "Ernest Hemingway's Spanish Civil War Experience," *American Quarterly,* XII (Summer 1960), 133.

[15] Quoted in Cowley's "A Portrait of Mister Papa."

[16] See Arturo Barea, "Not Spain but Hemingway," *Horizon,* III (May 1941), for a Spanish rebuttal to many aspects of Hemingway's book.

[17] Ernest Hemingway, "On the American Dead in Spain," *New Masses,* XXX (February 14, 1939), 3.

[18] See Nemi D'Agostino, "The Later Hemingway," *Sewanee Review,* LXVIII (Summer 1960).

[19] Frohock, *André Malraux and the Tragic Imagination,* p. 164.

[20] See Flanner's "The Human Condition" in *Men and Monuments,* p. 44, for a more detailed record of Malraux's personal heroism during the major war: "There were a good many outstanding French writers in the Resistance, but of them all Malraux was the most influential."

[21] Blend, *André Malraux: Tragic Humanist,* p. 36. Malraux had only to point out that the Stalin-Hitler Pact had violated the communist concept of revolutionary continuity.

[22] Blend, *André Malraux: Tragic Humanist,* p. 115.

[23] See Gaetan Picon's "Interrogation à Malraux," *Esprit,* 149 (October 1948), p. 456.

[24] Henri Peyre, *The Contemporary French Novel,* p. 186.

[25] See Joseph Frank, "Malraux's Image of Man," *The Widening Gyre* (New Brunswick, N. J., 1963).

[26] Preface to "L'Espagne libre" (1946), included in *Essais* (Paris, 1965), 1604.

[27] *Politics and the Novel,* p. 207.

# Appendix

# Chronology of the Spanish Civil War

## 1936

| | |
|---|---|
| 17 July | Military pronunciamiento in Morocco |
| 18 July | Military risings in Andalusia; Seville captured by Rebel General Queipo de Llano; Cádiz, Jerez, Algeciras, La Linea in Rebel hands as units arrive from Africa; all Morocco falls to Rebels; Majorca, Ibiza, and the Canary Islands in Rebel hands, but Minorca remains Republican |
| 19 July | Rebel uprising quelled in Barcelona; General Goded surrenders; Asturias with exception of Oviedo in Republican hands; in Basque provinces, Álava to Rebels, Vizcaya and Guipúzcoa with Loyalists; Rebels capture Burgos, Segovia, Ávila, Valladolid in Castille, Huesca, Saragossa, Jaca, and Teruel in Aragón, Pamplona, and all of Navarre; much of Estremadura falls to Rebels but Badajoz remains Republican |
| 20 July | Republican cabinet under Giral formed; arms distributed to trade unions in Madrid; Mon- |

| | |
|---|---|
| | taña Barracks stormed by Loyalists and Rebel uprising in capital crushed; Granada and Córdoba surrender to Rebels; Galicia falls to Rebels; General Sanjurjo killed in plane crash on flight to Burgos; Republic appeals to France for aid |
| 21 July | Insurgents send emissaries to Italy and Germany for aid |
| 23 July | Anarchist columns leave Barcelona for Saragossa and Huesca siege; Alcazar in Toledo besieged by militias |
| 23–25 July | Insurgents capture Alto de León and Somosierra Pass, but remainder of Guadarrama held by Republic |
| 25–27 July | Military barracks at San Sebastián and Albacete subdued |
| 28–30 July | Italian and German planes arrive in Seville and Morocco; obsolete French aircraft dispatched to Madrid |
| 29 July-5 August | Germans airlift Franco's army of Africa |
| 1–7 August | Republican offensives in Aragón and Sierras stall |
| 8 August | French border closed; unilateral start of Nonintervention |
| 9 August-3 September | Republican Balearic expedition fails |
| 11 August-5 September | Insurgent offensive in north; Irun falls, city burned by retreating anarchists |
| 14 August | Insurgents' capture of Badajoz followed by mass executions; Portuguese border sealed off from Loyalists |
| 15 August | British accept Nonintervention; prohibit exports of war materiels to Spain |
| 16 August | Garrison besieged as Gijón destroyed; Oviedo holds out |

| | |
|---|---|
| 20 August-3 September | Insurgents drive from south towards Madrid; Talavera falls |
| 20 August | Loyalist attack on Córdoba repulsed by Moroccans |
| 23 August | Massacre at model prison in Madrid |
| 24 August | Italy, Germany, Portugal accept Nonintervention "in principle" |
| 28 August | Russia accepts Nonintervention agreement |
| 4 September | Giral government falls under pressure; Republican cabinet under Largo Caballero formed |
| 7 September | Basque government formed |
| 9 September | Nonintervention Committee first meets in London |
| 12 September | Basques surrender San Sebastián; Franco assumes unified Nationalist command |
| 24 September | Álvarez del Vayo, Republican minister, addresses League of Nations |
| 27 September | Generalitat government formed in Barcelona with Esquerra, P.S.U.C., P.O.U.M., anarchist participation |
| 28 September | Nationalists take Toledo, siege of Alcazar lifted; Nonintervention Committee refuses to hear charges against Portugal |
| 1 October | Cortes passes Basque Statute; Franco named Generalissimo |
| 6 October | Soviets declare they will not be more bound by Nonintervention than Portugal-Germany-Italy; Nationalists resume Madrid offensive as militia units retreat |
| 14 October | First units of International Brigades arrive in Albacete; Russian military supplies reach Spain |
| 16 October | Nationalists relieve garrison at Oviedo |

| | |
|---|---|
| 17 October | Nationalists capture Illescas on road to Madrid |
| 25 October | Spanish gold reserves shipped from Cartagena to Odessa |
| 29 October | Russian tanks and planes arrive in Madrid; German and Italian bombers over capital |
| 2 November | Nationalists drive into Manzanares valley |
| 4 November | Anarchists join Caballero government |
| 6 November | Republic transfers capital to Valencia; General Miaja named head of Madrid Defense Junta; Condor Legion assembled in Seville |
| 8 November | Nationalists attempt all-out assault on Madrid; arrival of International Brigades to defend city |
| 9–12 November | Fierce fighting in Carabanchel suburb of Madrid |
| 15–23 November | International Brigades halt Nationalists at University City sector; Nationalists increase aerial bombardment of Madrid |
| 18 November | Germany and Italy recognize Nationalist government in Burgos |
| 19 November | José Antonio Primo de Rivera, Falangist leader, tried and executed at Alicante |
| 30 November | Basques attack Álava unsuccessfully |
| 10 December | Álvarez del Vayo asks League of Nations to condemn intervention by Germany and Italy |
| 13–15 December | Nationalists turned back at Boadilla in attempt to reach Madrid-Corunna road |
| 18 December | Italian infantry divisions leave Naples for Spain |
| 31 December | Unamuno dies after denouncing fascism |

## ▸ 1937

| | |
|---|---|
| 4 January | Bilbao bombed and prisoners executed in retaliation |

| | |
|---|---|
| 3–15 January | Fierce fighting as Nationalists resume attack on Madrid-Corunna road |
| 17 January–10 February | Nationalists take Málaga with aid of Italian planes and tanks; refugees slaughtered fleeing city |
| 6–15 February | Battle of the Jarama; Nationalists cross river; Russian fighter planes prove superior to German bombers; both sides suffer tremendous losses |
| 8–18 March | Battle of Guadalajara; Italian divisions routed; Republican morale reaches peak |
| 31 March–4 April | Nationalist Navarre units launch offensive in north under General Mola; Condor Legion bombs Basque villages |
| 6–22 April | British accept blockade of Bilbao |
| 16 April | Reorganization of Barcelona government; tension between anarchists and P.O.U.M. in opposition to Esquerra and P.S.U.C. mounts |
| 19 April | Merger of Falange and Carlists under Franco; Nonintervention land and sea patrols inaugurated |
| 20 April | Nationalists advance on Vizcaya |
| 26 April | Heavy bombing of Basque village of Guernica; Basque defense collapses |
| 1 May | Loyalists capture Santa María de la Cabeza |
| 3–8 May | Barcelona civil war; Valencia Asaltos restore order |
| 17 May | Caballero ousted by communists; Republican cabinet under Negrín formed |
| 24 May | Italian cruiser Barletta hit during bombing raid on Majorca |
| 26 May | German battleship Deutschland bombed at Ibiza |
| 31 May | German ships shell Almería in retaliation |

| | |
|---|---|
| 31 May | Republicans attack Huesca and Segovia to draw Nationalists from Bilbao |
| 3 June | Death of General Mola in airplane accident |
| 11–19 June | Nationalists break through Basque "ring of iron" protecting Bilbao |
| 16 June | P.O.U.M. leaders arrested in Barcelona |
| 23 June | Germany and Italy withdraw from Nonintervention naval patrol |
| 30 June | Portugal ends Nonintervention frontier patrol |
| 1 July | Collective letter of Spanish bishops on behalf of the Nationalists |
| 6–13 July | Republic launches battle of Brunete; Loyalists capture as far as Boadilla |
| 12 July | France ends Nonintervention frontier patrol |
| 18–25 July | Nationalists counterattack at Brunete; Loyalist losses heavy |
| 6 August-3 September | Italian submarines and planes attack shipping in the Mediterranean |
| 14–23 August | Nationalists capture Santander |
| 24 August-6 September | Loyalist offensive on Aragón front; Belchite and Quinto captured |
| 28 August | Vatican recognizes Burgos as official Spanish government |
| 14–30 September | Nyon Conference on piracy in the Mediterranean |
| 22–30 September | Republican offensive in Aragón stalls |
| 1 October | Caballero ousted from U.G.T. leadership |
| 7 October | Papal nuncio arrives in Salamanca |
| 21 October | Gijón surrenders; Nationalists end war in the north |
| 31 October | Republican government transferred to Barcelona |
| 15 December | Loyalists begin Teruel offensive; weather delays Nationalist counterattack |

▸ 1938

| | |
|---|---|
| 22 February | Nationalist counterattack captures Teruel |
| 6 March | Cruiser Baleares sunk in naval battle with Loyalists |
| 9 March | Nationalist offensive in Aragón; Loyalists in full retreat |
| 11 March | Hitler occupies Austria |
| 16–19 March | Italians bomb Barcelona heavily |
| 17 March | French open frontier |
| 25 March | Nationalists gain control of Aragón; drive into Catalonia |
| April | Burgos laws repealing divorce, Catalan autonomy, agrarian reform |
| 5 April | Negrín cabinet reorganized; Prieto dismissed because of defeatism |
| 15 April | Nationalists reach Mediterranean and split Barcelona from Valencia |
| 16 April | Anglo-Italian Mediterranean Pact agrees to withdrawal of Italian troops after war is ended |
| 18 April | Italians capture Tortosa |
| 1 May | Negrín lists 13 points for peace negotiations |
| 13 June | Daladier under pressure from Britain closes French border |
| 5–23 July | Republicans delay Nationalist drive toward Valencia |
| 24 July-2 August | Battle of the Ebro launched as diversionary attack from Valencia |
| 6 August-3 September | Nationalist counterattack only partially successful along the Ebro; Loyalists defenseless against air attack |
| 9 September | Negrín conducts fruitless peace talks with the Duke of Alba |

| | |
|---|---|
| 14 September | Franco declares Spain neutral in event of European war |
| 30 September | Munich conference decides fate of Czechoslovakia |
| 25 October | Barcelona trial of P.O.U.M. leaders absolves them |
| 30 October-18 November | Nationalist offensive pushes to Ebro; Loyalists withdraw International Brigades; Republican losses extremely heavy |
| 20 November | 10,000 Italians withdrawn from Spain in accord with Anglo-Italian Agreement |
| 20 November | Burgos gives Germany mine concessions in return for arms build-up |
| 23 December | Nationalists' total forces begin drive in Catalonia |

▸ 1939

| | |
|---|---|
| 15 January | Nationalists overwhelm Loyalists, capture Tarragona |
| 25 January | Barcelona occupied; mass flight of refugees into France |
| 27 January-10 February | 500,000 refugees cross into France, including most of the Republican army |
| 9 February | Nationalists occupy all of Catalonia; Minorca surrenders |
| 13 February | Nationalist Law of Political Responsibilities; Franco demands unconditional surrender |
| 27 February | Franco-British recognition of Burgos government; resignation of Azaña |
| 2 March | Negrín reorganizes military; pledges war to continue |
| 5 March | Pronunciamiento of Casado in Madrid designed to end war; Negrín cabinet flies to France |

| | |
|---|---|
| 7–11 March | Civil strife in Madrid; communists oppose Casado and Miaja unsuccessfully |
| 23–26 March | Unsuccessful peace negotiation efforts of Casado junta |
| 28–30 March | Nationalists occupy Madrid and Valencia |
| 1 April | Surrender of Republican armies completed |
| May–June | Repatriation of German and Italian troops |

# A Selected Bibliography

## I. HISTORICAL BACKGROUND AND SOCIAL CONDITIONS LEADING TO THE SPANISH CIVIL WAR

Alba, Victor, *Histoire des républiques Espagnoles.* Vincennes, 1948.

Altamira y Crevea, Rafael, *A History of Spain.* New York, 1949.

Blasco Ibáñez, Vicente, *La Bodega.* Madrid, 1904.

Brenan, Gerald, *The Face of Spain.* London, 1950.

——— *The Spanish Labyrinth.* Third Edition. Cambridge, Eng., 1950.

Castillejo y Duarte, José, *War of Ideas in Spain.* London, 1937.

Ellis, Havelock, *The Soul of Spain.* Boston, 1937.

Madariaga, Salvador de, *Spain: A Modern History.* New York, 1958.

Marvaud, Angel, *L'Espagne au xxième siècle.* Paris, 1915.

Marx, Karl, and Frederick Engels, *Revolution in Spain.* London, 1939.

Ortega y Gasset, José, *España Invertebrada.* Madrid, 1921.

Peers, E. Allison, ed., *Bulletin of Spanish Studies.* Liverpool, 1923–1940.

Pritchett, V. S., *The Spanish Temper.* New York, 1954.

Ramos Oliveira, Antonio, *Politics, Economics and Men of Modern Spain.* London, 1946.

Smith, Rhea March, *The Day of the Liberals in Spain.* Philadelphia, 1938.

Souchère, Elena de la, *An Explanation of Spain.* New York, 1964.

Trend, J. B., *The Origins of Modern Spain.* Cambridge, Eng., 1934.

——— *A Picture of Modern Spain.* London, 1921.

Unamuno, Miguel de, *En Torno al Casticismo.* Madrid, 1916.

Vicens Vives, Jaime, *Approximación a la Historia de España.* Barcelona, 1952.

Vilar, Pierre, *Histoire de l'Espagne.* Paris, 1947.

## ▸ II. HISTORICAL ACCOUNTS OF THE SPANISH CIVIL WAR INCLUDING ARTICLES, PERSONAL NARRATIVES, AND MEMOIRS

Acier, Marcel, ed., *From Spanish Trenches.* New York, 1937.

Aguirre [y Lecube], José Antonio, *Freedom Was Flesh and Blood.* London, 1945.

Álvarez del Vayo, Julio, *Freedom's Battle.* New York, 1940.

——— *The Last Optimist.* New York, 1949.

Aragon, Louis, "Ne rêvez plus qu'à l'Espagne." *Europe* (November 15, 1936).

Araquistain, Luis, "Communism and the War in Spain." *Spain* (July 6, 1939).

Atholl, Katherine, Duchess of, *Searchlight on Spain.* London, 1938.

Attlee, C. R., "What I Learnt in Spain." *Left News,* No. 21 (January 1938).

Aznar, Manuel, *Historia Militar de la Guerra de España (1936–1939).* Madrid, 1940.

Bahamonde, Antonio, *Memoirs of a Spanish Nationalist.* London, 1939.

Barea, Arturo, *The Forging of a Rebel.* New York, 1946.

——— *Struggle for the Spanish Soul.* London, 1941.

——— and Ilsa Barea, *Spain in the Post-War World.* London, 1945.

Baroja, Pío, "What Underlies Marxism." *Spain,* No. 18 (February 1, 1938).

Bates, Ralph, "Castilian Drama." *New Republic,* No. 92 (October 20, 1937).

Beccari, Gilberto, ed., *Scrittori di guerra Spagnoli, 1936–1939*. Milan, 1941.

Bell, Julian, "No Quiet in Spain." *English Review*, No. 62 (May, 1936).

Belloc, H., "The Issue in Spain." *Spain*, No. 44 (July, 1938).

Bernanos, Georges, "Autobiography." *La nef* (August, 1948).

——— *Les grands cimetières sous le lune*. Paris, 1938.

Bessie, Alvah, *Men in Battle*. New York, 1939.

Bloch, Jean-Richard. "Espagne! Espagne!" *Europe* (August-November, 1936).

Bolloten, Burnett, *The Grand Camouflage*. London, 1961.

Borkenau, Franz, *The Spanish Cockpit*. London, 1937.

——— *European Communism*. London, 1953.

——— *World Communism*. Ann Arbor, 1962.

Bowers, Claude, *My Mission to Spain*. New York, 1954.

Brasillach, Robert, and Maurice Bardèche, *Histoire de la guerre d'Espagne*. Paris, 1939.

Brereton, Geoffrey, *Inside Spain*. London, 1938.

Brooks, Van Wyck, and R. L. Duffus, "An Attack on Democracy." *Commonweal*, XXV (April 9, 1937).

Broué, Pierre, and Emile Témime, *La revolution et la guerre d'Espagne*. Paris, 1961.

Browder, Earl, and Bill Lawrence, *Next Steps to Win the War in Spain*. New York, 1938.

Buckley, Henry, *Life and Death of the Spanish Republic*. London, 1940.

Campbell, Roy, "Flowering Rifles." *New Statesman and Nation*, XVII (April 8, 1939).

Casado, Segismundo, *The Last Days of Madrid*. London, 1939.

Cassou, Jean, *La mémoire courte*. Paris, 1953.

*Catholics and the Civil War in Spain*. London, 1936.

*Catholics Speak for Spain*. New York, 1937.

Cattell, David T., *Communism and the Spanish Civil War*. Berkeley, 1955.

——— *Soviet Diplomacy and the Spanish Civil War*. Berkeley, 1957.

Caute, David, *Communism and the French Intellectuals, 1914–1960*. New York, 1964.

Chamson, André, *Devenir ce qu'on est*. Paris, 1959.

——— *Rien qu'un témoignage.* Paris, 1937.

——— *Retour d'Espagne.* Paris, 1937.

Churchill, Winston, *Arms and the Covenant.* London, 1938.

——— *The Gathering Storm.* Boston, 1948.

Ciano, Count Galeazzo, *Ciano's Hidden Diary, 1937–1938,* ed. Malcolm Muggeridge. London, 1948.

Cleugh, James, *Spanish Fury: The Story of a Civil War.* London, 1962.

Cockburn, Claud, *In Time of Trouble.* London, 1956.

[Cockburn, Claud] "Frank Pitcairn," *Reporter in Spain* (London, 1936).

*Collective Letter of the Spanish Bishops on the War in Spain.* London, 1937.

Colodny, Robert G., *The Struggle for Madrid.* New York, 1958.

*Communist Atrocities in Southern Spain, A Preliminary Report on.* London, 1936–1937.

Connolly, Cyril, *The Condemned Playground.* London, 1945.

——— "The Future of Spain." *New Statesman and Nation,* XII (December 26, 1936).

——— "Spanish Diary." *New Statesman and Nation,* XIII (February 20, 1937).

Conze, Edward, *Spain Today.* London, 1936.

Cot, Pierre, *The Triumph of Treason.* New York, 1944.

Cox, Geoffrey, *The Defense of Madrid.* London, 1937.

Delaprée, Louis, *Le martyre de Madrid.* Madrid, 1937.

——— *Mort en Espagne.* Paris, 1937.

Dimitrov, Georgi, *Spain and the People's Front.* New York, 1937.

Dos Passos, John, "The Communist Party and the War Spirit." *Common Sense,* VI (December, 1937).

——— *Journeys Between Wars.* New York, 1938.

——— "The Road to Madrid." *Esquire, VIII* (December, 1937).

——— "Room and Bath at the Hotel Florida." *Esquire,* IX (January, 1938).

——— *The Theme Is Freedom.* New York, 1956.

——— *The Villages Are the Heart of Spain.* Chicago, 1937.

Dreiser, Theodore, "Barcelona in August." *Direction,* I (November-December, 1938).

——— *Letters of Theodore Dreiser.* Philadelphia, 1959.

Dzelepy, E. N., *Britain in Spain.* London, 1939.

Eden, Anthony, *Facing the Dictators,* Volume II of *Memoirs of Anthony Eden.* Boston, 1962.

Ehrenburg, Ilya, *Memoirs: 1921–1941.* Cleveland, 1964.

——— "Spain's Tempering." *International Literature,* III (March, 1938).

——— "Volunteers for Murder." *Living Age,* No. 354 (August, 1938).

——— and Michael Kol'tsov and others. *Guadalajara: Eine Niederlage des Fashismus.* Strasbourg, 1937.

*Encyclical on Spain. . . .* New York, 1937.

[Estelrich, Juan], *La pérsecution religieuse en Espagne.* Paris, 1937.

Farmborough, Florence, *Life and People in National Spain.* London, 1938.

Fast, Howard, *Spain and Peace.* New York, 1952.

Fischer, Louis, *Men and Politics.* New York, 1941.

——— *The War in Spain.* New York, 1937.

——— *Why Spain Fights On.* London, 1938.

Fitts, Dudley, "What Spanish Children See." *Saturday Review of Literature,* XIX (November 19, 1938).

Foltz, Charles, Jr., *The Masquerade in Spain.* Boston, 1948.

*Foreign Journalists Under Franco's Terror.* London, 1937.

Foss, William, and Cecil Gerahty, *The Spanish Arena.* London, 1938.

Fox, Ralph, *A Writer in Arms,* John Lehmann, and C. Day Lewis, eds. London, 1937.

Frank, Waldo, "Viva España Libre! . . ." *New Masses,* XX (August 18, 1936).

Gannes, Harry, and Theodore Repard, *Spain in Revolt.* London, 1936.

*Garibaldini in Spagna.* Madrid, 1936.

Gerahty, Cecil, *The Road to Madrid.* London, 1937.

Gellhorn, Martha, *The Face of War.* London, 1959.

*General Cause: Red Domination in Spain.* Mass lawsuit brought by the Spanish Nationalist Government. Madrid, 1953.

Goldman, Emma, "Enemy Within." *Man!,* V (December 1936–January 1937).

——— "P.O.U.M. Frame-Up Fails," *Vanguard,* IV (February 1939).

Gollancz, Victor, "Spain." *Left News*, No. 21 (January, 1938).

Gonzáles, Valentin ["El Campesino"], *Listen Comrades!* London, 1952.

Graves, Robert, and Alan Hodge, *The Long Week-End.* London, 1940.

Gunther, John, *Inside Europe.* New York, 1938.

Guttmann, Allen, ed., *American Neutrality and the Spanish Civil War.* Boston, 1963.

Hamilton, Thomas J., *Appeasement's Child.* New York, 1943.

Hanighen, Frank, ed., *Nothing But Danger.* New York, 1939.

Hellman, Lillian, "Day in Spain." *New Republic,* No. 94 (April 13, 1938).

Hemingway, Ernest, "On the American Dead in Spain." *New Masses,* XXX (February 14, 1939).

——— "The Spanish War." *Fact* (July, 1938).

Herbst, Josephine, "Spanish Village." *The Nation,* CXLV (August 14, 1937).

Héricourt, Pierre, *Pourquoi Franco vaincra.* Paris, 1936.

Hicks, Granville, "A Writer in Arms." *Communist,* XVII (January, 1938).

"Hispanicus." *Foreign Intervention in Spain.* London, 1937.

Hook, Sidney, "The Anatomy of the Popular Front." *Partisan Review,* VI (Spring, 1939).

*How Mussolini Provoked the Spanish Civil War.* London, 1938.

Hughes, Langston, "Laughter in Madrid." *The Nation,* CXLVI (January 29, 1938).

——— "Negroes in Spain." *Volunteer for Liberty* (September 13, 1937).

Hull, Cordell, *Memoirs.* New York, 1948.

Humphries, Rolfe, "Cultural Heritage." *Fight,* V (April, 1938).

Huxley, J. S., "The Spanish News: A Quantitative Analysis." *New Statesman and Nation,* XII (August 8, 1936).

Ibarruri, Dolores, *Speeches and Articles, 1936–1938.* London, 1938.

Jackson, Gabriel, *The Spanish Republic and the Civil War, 1931–1939.* Princeton, 1965.

Jellinek, Frank, *The Civil War in Spain.* London, 1938.

Jerrold, Douglas, *Georgian Adventure.* London, 1937.

Joll, James, *Three Intellectuals in Politics.* New York, 1960.

Junod, Marcel, *Warrior Without Weapons*. New York, 1951.
Kaminski, Hans Erich, *Ceux de Barcelone*. Paris, 1938.
Kempton, Murray, *Part of Our Time: Some Monuments and Ruins of the Thirties*. New York, 1955.
Knoblaugh, H. E., *Correspondent in Spain*. London, 1937.
Koestler, Arthur, *The Invisible Writing*. London, 1954.
——— *Spanish Testament*. London, 1937.
Kol'tsov, Michael, "Spanish Diary." Serialized in *International Literature*, VII–VIII (July-August 1938).
Krivitsky, Walter G., *In Stalin's Secret Service*. New York, 1939.
Langdon-Davies, John, *Behind the Spanish Barricades*. London, 1936.
——— *The Spanish Church and Politics*. New York, 1938.
Last, Jef, *The Spanish Tragedy*. London, 1939.
Lehmann, John, *The Whispering Gallery*. London, 1955.
Lewis, C. D., *We're Not Going To Do Nothing*. London, 1936.
Lewis, Sinclair, "Glorious Dirt." *Newsweek*, X (October 18, 1937).
Lewis, Wyndham, *Count Your Dead: They Are Alive!* London, 1937.
Longo, Luigi, *Le brigate internationali in Spagna*. Rome, 1956.
Lunn, Arnold, *Spain and the Christian Front*. New York, N.D.
——— *Spanish Rehearsal*. London, 1937.
Macdonald, Dwight, "Reading from Left to Right." *New International*, V (February, 1939).
Machado, Antonio, *Madrid 1936–37*. Madrid, 1937.
MacLeish, Archibald, "The War Is Ours." *New Masses*, XXIII (June 22, 1937).
MacNeice, Louis, "Today in Barcelona." *Spectator*, No. 162 (January 10, 1939).
Malraux, André, *The Fascist Threat to Culture*. Harvard Student Union, 1937.
——— "Forging Man's Fate in Spain." *The Nation*, CXLIV (March 20, 1937).
——— "Men in Spain." *New Republic*, No. 96 (October 12, 1938).
Mann, H., "Spain and Culture." *Life and Letters Today*, No. 17 (Autumn, 1937).

Mann, Thomas, "Epilogue to Spain." *Life and Letters Today,* No. 16 (Summer, 1937).

——— "I Stand with the Spanish People." *The Nation,* CXLIV (April 17, 1937).

Marañón, Gregario, *Liberalism and Communism.* London, N.D.

Maritain, Jacques, *Rebeldes Españoles No Hacen una 'Guerra Santa.'* Paris, 1937.

Marty, André, *En Espagne . . . où se joue le destin de l'Europe.* Paris, 1937.

——— *Volontaires d'Espagne.* Paris, 1938.

Massis, Henri, and Robert Brasillach, *Les cadets de l'Alcazar.* Paris, 1937.

Matthews, Herbert, *Two Wars and More To Come.* New York, 1938.

——— *The Yoke and the Arrows.* New York, 1957.

Maurras, Charles, *Vers l'Espagne de Franco.* Paris, 1943.

McGovern, John, *Terror in Spain.* London, 1937.

Mendizábal Villalba, Alfredo, *The Martyrdom of Spain.* New York, 1938.

Merin, Peter, *Spain between Death and Birth.* New York, 1938.

Mitchell, Mairin, *Storm Over Spain.* London, 1937.

Mitchell, Sir Peter Chalmers, *My House in Malaga.* London, 1938.

Mora, Constancia de la, *In Place of Splendor.* New York, 1939.

Moreno, Antonio Montero, *Historia de la Persecución Religiosa en España, 1936–1939.* Madrid, 1961.

Morrow, Felix, *The Civil War in Spain.* New York, 1936.

Muggeridge, Malcolm, *The Thirties: 1930–1940 in Great Britain.* London, 1940.

Mumford, Lewis, "Good Will Must Act." *Fight,* VI (February, 1939).

*Nazi Conspiracy in Spain.* London, 1937.

Nehru, Jawāhir-Lāl, *Spain, Why?* London, 1937.

Niebuhr, Reinhold, "Arrogance in the name of Christ." *Christian Century,* LIII (September 2, 1936).

Nelson, Steve, *The Volunteers.* New York, 1953.

Nenni, Pietro, *Spagna.* Rome, 1958.

Noel-Baker, Francis, *Spanish Summary.* London, 1948.

Nolte, Ernst, *Three Faces of Fascism.* New York, 1966.

North, Joseph, *No Men Are Strangers.* New York, 1958.

O'Duffy, Eoin, *Crusade in Spain*. Dublin, 1938.
Orwell, George, *Homage to Catalonia*. London, 1938.
——— *Such, Such Were the Joys*. New York, 1953.
Pacciardi, Randolfo, *Il battaglione Garibaldi*. Lugano, 1948.
Padelford, Norman, *International Law and Diplomacy in the Spanish Civil Strife*. New York, 1939.
Palencia, Isabel de, *Smouldering Freedom*. New York, 1945.
Parker, Dorothy, "Incredible, Fantastic . . . and True." *New Masses*, XXV (November 23, 1937).
——— "Not Enough." *New Masses*, XXXI (March 14, 1939).
Paul, Elliot, *The Life and Death of a Spanish Town*. New York, 1937.
Paul-Boncour, Joseph, *Entre deux guerres, 1935–1940*. Paris, 1946.
Payne, Robert, ed., *The Civil War in Spain*. New York, 1962.
Payne, Stanley G., *Falange: A History of Spanish Fascism*. Stanford, California, 1961.
Peers, E. Allison, *Catalonia Infelix*. London, 1937.
——— *Spain, Church and the Orders*. London, 1939.
——— *Spain in Eclipse, 1937–1943*. London, 1943.
——— *The Spanish Tragedy*. London, 1936.
Penrose, R., *Picasso: His Life and Work*. London, 1958.
Pierats, José, *La CNT en la Revolución Española*. Toulouse, 1951–1953.
Plenn, Abel, *Wind in the Olive Trees*. New York, 1946.
Pollitt, Harry, *Arms for Spain*. London, 1936.
——— "Building the People's Front." *Left Review*, II (December, 1936).
——— *Selected Articles and Speeches*. London, 1954.
Priestley, J. B., and Rebecca West, *Spain and Us*. London, 1937.
Pritchett, V. S., "Ebb and Flow in Spain." *Spectator*, No. 158 (May 21, 1937).
——— "Spain and the Future." *Spectator*, No. 157 (September 4, 1936).
Puzzo, Dante A., *Spain and the Great Powers, 1936–1941*. New York, 1962.
Rahv, Philip, "Twilight of the Thirties." *Partisan Review*, V (Summer, 1939).
Regler, Gustav, *The Owl of Minerva*. New York, 1960.

Renn, Ludwig, *Der Spanische Krieg*. Berlin, 1956.

——— *Warfare*. London, 1939.

Richards, V., *Lessons of the Spanish Revolution*. London, 1953.

Riesenfeld, Janet, *Dancer in Madrid*. New York, 1938.

Roethke, Theodore, "Facing the Guns." *Poetry*, LII (April, 1938).

Rolfe, Edwin, *The Lincoln Battalion*. New York, 1939.

Rolland, Romain, "Humanité appellé à toi." *Unité*, III (April, 1938).

Romilly, Esmond, *Boadilla*. London, 1937.

Rosselli, Carlo, *Oggi in Spagna, domani in Italia. Paris*, 1938.

Ruiz Vilaplana, Antonio, *Burgos Justice*. New York, 1938.

Rukeyser, Muriel, "Barcelona, 1936." *Life and Letters Today*, XV (Autumn, 1936).

——— "Barcelona on the Barricades." *New Masses*, XX (September 1, 1936).

Saint-Exupéry, Antoine de, Reports on Spanish Civil War, in *L'intransigeant*, August 16 and 19, 1936; *Paris soir*, June 27, July 3, August 3, 1937.

Sánchez, José M., *Reform and Reaction: The Politico-Religious Background of the Spanish Civil War*. Chapel Hill, 1962.

Sanjuan, José Pemartin, *Los Origenes del Movimiento*. Burgos, 1938.

Sedwick, Frank, *The Tragedy of Manuel Azaña*. Ohio State, 1963.

Sencourt, Robert, *Spain's Ordeal*. London, 1938.

Sender, Ramón, *Counter-Attack in Spain*. Boston, 1937.

——— "The First Steel Battalion." *International Literature*, VII (July, 1937).

——— *The War in Spain*. London, 1937.

Sheean, Vincent, *Not Peace But a Sword*. New York, 1939.

Siegel, Janet, *French Opinion on the Spanish Civil War* (M.A. Thesis), New York University, 1943.

Simon, Yves, *The Road to Vichy*. London, 1942.

Sinclair, Upton, "The Haves and Have Nots." *American Guardian*, XIX (October 23, 1936).

Rust, William, *Britons in Spain*. London, 1939.

Sloan, Pat, ed., *John Cornford: A Memoir*. London, 1938.

*Somebody Had to Do Something*. Los Angeles, 1939.

Sommerfield, John, "From a Spanish Diary." *Left Review*, III (March, 1937).

——— *Volunteer in Spain*. New York, 1937.
*Spain's War of Independence*. Washington, D.C., 1938.
*Spanish Liberals Speak on the Counter-Revolution in Spain*. San Francisco, 1937.
Spender, Stephen, "An Open Letter to Aldous Huxley on his Case for Constructive Peace." *Left Review*, II (August, 1936).
——— "Heroes in Spain." *New Statesman and Nation*, XIII (May 1, 1937).
——— *World within World*. New York, 1948.
Steer, G. L., *The Tree of Gernika*. London, 1938.
Taylor, F. J., *The United States and the Spanish Civil War, 1936–1939*. New York, 1956.
Téry, Simone, *Front de la liberté: Espagne, 1937–1938*. Paris, 1938.
Tharaud, Jean, and Jerome, *Cruelle Espagne*. Paris, 1937.
Thomas, Hugh, "The International Brigades in Spain." *History Today*, II (May, 1961).
——— *The Spanish Civil War*. New York, 1961.
Thomas, Norman, "In Defense of a Free Spain." *New Masses*, XX (September 8, 1936).
——— "Spain: A Socialist View." *The Nation*, CXLIV (June 19, 1937).
[Togliatti, Palmiro], "Ercoli, M." *The Spanish Revolution*. New York, 1936.
Toller, E., "Madrid-Washington." *New Statesman and Nation*, XV (October 8, 1938).
Toynbee, Arnold, with V. M. Boulter, and Katherine Duff, eds., *Survey of International Affairs, 1937*, Vol. II, London, 1938; and *1938*, Vol. I, London, 1940.
Trotsky, Leon, *The Lesson of Spain, the Last Warning*. London, 1938.
Untermeyer, Louis, "Viva España Libre! . . ." *New Masses*, XX (August 18, 1936).
Van Paassen, Pierre, *Days of Our Years*. New York, 1939.
Watkins, K. W., *Britain Divided: The Effect of the Spanish Civil War on British Political Opinion*. London, 1963.
*We Saw In Spain*. Articles by C. R. Atlee, Ellen Wilkinson, Philip Noel-Baker, and John Dugdale. London, 1937.
Wintringham, Tom, *English Captain*. London, 1939.

Wood, Neal, *Communism and British Intellectuals.* New York, 1959.

Woolsey, Gamel, *Death's Other Kingdom.* London, 1939.

Ydeville, Charles d', *Interlude in Spain.* London, 1945.

Yeats-Brown, Francis, *European Jungle.* Philadelphia, 1939.

Zayas, Marqués de, *Historia de la Vieja Guardia de Baleares.* Madrid, 1955.

Zugazagoitia, Julián, *Historia de la Guerra en España.* Buenos Aires, 1940.

## ▸ III. FICTION, PLAYS, POETRY, AND ART CONCERNED WITH THE SPANISH CIVIL WAR

Alberti, Rafael, *Poesias.* Buenos Aires, 1940.

——— *Entre el Clavel y la Espada.* Buenos Aires, 1941.

Anderson, Maxwell, *Key Largo.* Washington, D.C., 1939.

Andres, Stefan, *Wir Sind Utopia.* Berlin, 1943.

Aub, Max, *Campo Abierto.* Mexico, 1951.

——— *Campo Cerrado.* Mexico, 1943.

——— *Campo de Sangre.* Mexico, 1945.

Auden, W. H., *Spain.* London, 1938.

Ayala, Francisco, *La Cabeza del Cordero.* Buenos Aires, 1950.

Barea, Arturo, *La Raíz Rota.* Buenos Aires, 1955.

——— *Valor y Miedo.* Barcelona, 1939.

Barker, George, *Elegy on Spain.* London, 1939.

——— *Collected Poems.* London, 1957.

Bates, Ralph, *The Miraculous Horde.* London, 1939.

——— *Sirocco and Other Stories.* New York, 1939.

Bell, Quentin, ed., *Julian Bell: Essays, Poems, and Letters.* London, 1938.

Benét, William Rose, "Catalonia." *New Masses,* XXVII (May 31, 1938).

Bernardete, M. J., and Rolfe Humphries, eds., *And Spain Sings.* New York, 1937.

Bessie, Alvah, ed., *The Heart of Spain.* New York, 1952.

——— *The Un-Americans.* London, 1957.

Blankfort, Michael, *The Brave and the Blind* [novel]. Indianapolis, 1940.

——— *The Brave and the Blind* [play]. New York, 1937.

Botella, Pastor, V. *Así Cayeron los Dados.* Mexico, 1959.

——— *Por Qué Callaron las Campañas*. Mexico, 1953.
Brecht, Bertolt, *Señora Carrara's Rifles* in *Theatre Workshop*. New York, 1938.
Bredel, Willi, *Vom Ebro zur Volga*. Berlin, 1954.
Calmer, Alan, ed., *Salud!* New York, 1938.
Campbell, Roy, *Collected Poems*. London, 1957.
——— *Flowering Rifles*. London, 1939.
——— *Light on a Dark Horse*. London, 1951.
*Canciones de las Brigades Internacionales*. Barcelona, 1938.
Capa, Robert, *Death in the Making*. New York, 1938.
Caudwell, Christopher, *Poems*. London, 1939.
Cela, Camilo José, *La Colmena*. Buenos Aires, 1953.
Claudel, Paul, "Aux martyrs Espagnols." *Oeuvre poétique*. Paris, 1957.
Conchon, Georges, *La corrida de la victoire*. Paris, 1960.
Davidson, Jo, *Spanish Portraits*. New York, 1938.
Del Castillo, Michel, *The Disinherited*. New York, 1960.
Dos Passos, John, *Adventures of a Young Man*. New York, 1938.
Eluard, Paul, *Poemes politiques*. Paris, 1948.
Fernández de la Reguera, Ricardo, *Cuerpo a Tierra*. Barcelona, 1954.
Freemantle, Anne, "Davos-Parsenn." *New Statesman and Nation*, XVII (March 4, 1939).
Funaroff, S., "To Federico García Lorca." *Poetry*, LII (July, 1938).
Gellhorn, Martha, "Visit to the Wounded." *Story*, XI (October, 1937).
Ginsburg, Louis, "Bombs on Barcelona." *New Masses*, XXVIII (August 2, 1938).
Gironella, José María, *Los Cipreses Creen en Dios*. Barcelona, 1953.
——— *Un Millón de Muertos*. Barcelona, 1961.
Girri, Alberto, and William Shand, eds., *Poesia Inglesa de la Guerra Española*. Buenos Aires, 1947.
Greene, Graham, *The Confidential Agent*. New York, 1939.
Hellman, Lillian, "A Bleached Lady." *New Masses*, XXIX (October 11, 1938).
Hemingway, Ernest, "The Butterfly and the Tank." *Esquire*, X (December, 1938).

——— "The Denunciation." *Esquire,* X (November, 1938).
——— *For Whom the Bell Tolls.* New York, 1940.
——— "Night Before Battle." *Esquire,* XI (February, 1939).
——— "Nobody Ever Dies." *Cosmopolitan, CVI* (March 1939).
——— *The Short Stories of Ernest Hemingway: The First Forty-Nine Stories and the Play, The Fifth Column.* New York, 1938.
——— *The Spanish Earth.* Cleveland, 1938.
——— "Under the Ridge." *Cosmopolitan,* CVII (October 1939).
Hernández, Miguel, *El Rayo Que No Cesa.* Madrid, 1936.
——— *Viento del Pueblo.* Valencia, 1937.
Hewett, Peter, ed., *Poets of Tomorrow.* London, 1939.
*Homenaje de Despedida a las Brigadas Internacionales.* Palabras de Antonio Machado; versos de Rafael Alberti, Manuel Altolaguirre, Pedro Garfias y otros. Madrid, 1938.
Hughes, Langston, "Air Raid: Barcelona." *Esquire,* X (October, 1938).
——— "Madrid." *Fight,* V (July, 1938).
——— "October 16th." *Volunteer for Liberty* (April 9, 1938).
——— "Post Card from Spain." *Volunteer for Liberty* (April 9, 1938).
Humphries, Rolfe, "A Gay People." *New Republic,* XCVIII (April 12, 1938).
Huxley, Aldous, ed., *They Still Draw Pictures.* New York, 1939.
Jarrell, Randall, *The Rage for the Lost Penny* in *Five Young American Poets,* ed. James Laughlin. Norfolk, Conn., 1940.
Kesten, Hermann, *Die Kinder von Guernika.* Amsterdam, 1939.
Keyes, Francis Parkinson, *The Great Tradition.* New York, 1939.
Lawson, John Howard, *Blockade.* Hollywood, 1938.
Lee, Laurie, *The Sun My Monument.* London, 1944.
Lehmann, John, ed., *Poems from New Writing, 1936–1946.* London, 1946.
Lewis, C. Day, *Child of Misfortune.* London, 1938.
——— *Noah and the Waters.* London, 1936.
——— *Overtures to Death and Other Poems.* London, 1938.
——— *Starting Point.* London, 1938.
Lucas Phillips, C. E., *The Spanish Pimpernel.* London, 1960.
MacDiarmid, Hugh, *Collected Poems.* New York, 1962.
——— *Speaking for Scotland.* Baltimore, 1946.

Machado, Antonio, *Vida y Obra.* New York, 1951.
MacLeish, Archibald, *Air Raid.* New York, 1938.
MacNeice, Louis, *Autumn Journal.* London, 1939.
——— *I Crossed the Minch.* London, 1938.
Malraux, André, *L'espoir.* Paris, 1937.
Maulvault, Lucien, *Glaieul noir.* Paris, 1939.
——— *El requeté.* Paris, 1938.
McCarthy, Mary, *The Company She Keeps.* New York, 1939.
Millay, Edna St. Vincent, "Say That We Saw Spain Die." *Harper's,* CLXXVII (October, 1938).
Milne, Ewart, *Letter from Ireland.* Dublin, 1940.
Miqualarena, Jacinto, *El Otro Mundo.* Burgos, 1938.
Neruda, Pablo, *España en el Corazón.* Santiago, Chile, 1938.
——— *Poemas Últimas.* Buenos Aires, 1945.
Norman, James, *The Fell of Dark.* London, 1960.
[Ormsbee, David] Stephen Longstreet, *Chico Goes to the Wars.* New York, 1943.
Paoli, Roberto, *Antologia di poeti spagnoli d'oggi in Il verri,* October, 1958.
Parker, Dorothy, "Soldiers of the Republic." *New Yorker,* XIII (February 5, 1938).
Payne, Robert, *The Song of the Peasant.* London, 1939.
Pereda, Prudencio de, "The Bullfighter." *New Masses,* XII (March 16, 1937).
——— "Fascist Lament." *New Masses,* XXXI (February 18, 1939).
——— "The Spaniard." *Story,* X (March, 1937).
Prokosch, Frederic, "Peninsula." *New Masses,* XXV (October 19, 1937).
Quintanilla, Luis, *All the Brave.* New York, 1939.
——— *Franco's Black Spain.* New York, 1946.
Read, Herbert, *Thirty-Five Poems.* London, 1940.
Regler, Gustav, *The Great Crusade.* London, 1940.
Rexroth, Kenneth, "Requiem for the Dead in Spain." *New Republic,* XC (March 24, 1937).
Rolfe, Edwin, *First Love and Other Poems.* Los Angeles, 1951.
Rollins, William, Jr., *The Wall of Men.* New York, 1938.
*Romancero de los Voluntarios de la Libertád.* Madrid, 1937.
*Romancero General de la Guerra de España.* Madrid, 1957.

Rosten, Norman, *The Fourth Decade and Other Poems.* New York, 1942.

Rukeyser, Muriel, "Mediterranean." *New Masses,* XXIV (September 14, 1937).

——— *A Turning Wind.* New York, 1939.

Saint-Exupéry, Antoine de, *La terre des hommes.* Paris, 1939.

Sartre, Jean-Paul, *Le mur.* Paris, 1939.

Sender, Ramón, *Los Cinco Libros de Ariadna.* New York, 1957.

——— *El Rey y la Reina.* Buenos Aires, 1947.

——— *Siete Domingos Rojos.* Barcelona, 1932.

Serrano Poncela, Segundo, *La Venda.* Buenos Aires, 1956.

Sheean, Vincent, "Four Verses." *New Masses,* XXIX (October 4, 1938).

Sinclair, Upton, *No Pasarán!* Pasadena, California, 1937.

Slater, Humphrey, *The Heretics.* New York, 1947.

Spender, Stephen, and John Lehmann, eds., *Poems for Spain.* London, 1939.

Téry, Simone, *La porte du soleil.* Paris, 1939.

Teweleit, Horst L., ed., *Na Pasaran!: Romanzero aus dem Freiheitskampf des Spanischen Volkes, 1936–1939.* Berlin, 1959.

Todrin, Boris, *At the Gates.* Prairie City, 1944.

——— *Seven Men.* New York, 1938.

Villalonga, José Luis de, *L'homme de sang.* Paris, 1959.

Vittorini, Elio, *Il garofano rosso.* Verona, 1948.

*Volunteer For Liberty.* New York, 1949.

Warner, Rex, *Poems.* New York, 1938.

——— *Return of the Traveler.* New York, 1944.

Westerman, Percy F., *Under Fire in Spain.* Glasgow, 1937.

Zglinitzki, Baroness de [Helen Nicholson], *The Painted Bed.* New York, 1938.

## ▸ IV. LITERARY CRITICISM PERTINENT TO *WRITERS IN ARMS*

Aaron, Daniel, *Writers on the Left.* New York, 1961.

Aron, Raymond, *The Opium of the Intellectuals.* London, 1957.

Atkins, John, *Arthur Koestler.* London, 1956.

——— *George Orwell: A Literary Study.* London, 1954.

*Authors Take Sides.* London, 1937.

Baker, Carlos, ed., *Ernest Hemingway: Critiques of Four Major Novels.* New York, 1962.

——— ed., *Hemingway and His Critics: An International Anthology.* New York, 1961.

——— *Hemingway: The Writer as Artist.* Third Edition. Princeton, N. J., 1963.

Balthasar, Hans Urs von, *Le Chrétien Bernanos.* Paris, 1956.

Barea, Arturo, "Not Spain but Hemingway." *Horizon,* III (May, 1941).

Beach, Joseph Warren, "How Do You Like It Now, Gentlemen?" *Sewanee Review,* LIX (Spring, 1951).

Béguin, Albert, *Bernanos par lui-même.* Paris, 1954.

Bessie, Alvah, Review of *For Whom the Bell Tolls, New Masses,* XXXVII (November 5, 1940).

Blend, Charles D., *André Malraux: Tragic Humanist.* Ohio State, 1963.

Blotner, Joseph, *The Political Novel.* Garden City, N.Y., 1955.

Brander, Laurence, *George Orwell.* London, 1954.

Brée, Germaine, and Margaret Guiton, *The French Novel from Gide to Camus.* New York, 1962.

*Bulletin de la Société des Amis de Bernanos.* 1949–1961.

Burgum, Edwin Berry, *The Novel and the World's Dilemma.* New York, 1947.

Caudwell, Christopher, *Illusion and Reality.* London, 1937.

Connolly, Cyril, *Enemies of Promise.* London, 1938.

Cowley, Malcolm, "A Congress in Madrid." *New Masses,* XXIV (August 10, 1937).

——— "A Portrait of Mister Papa." *Life* (January 10, 1949).

——— "Spanish War Posters." *New Republic,* XCII (September 8, 1937).

——— "Spender, Auden and After." *New Republic,* No. 107 (October 5, 1942).

Crossman, Richard, ed., *The God That Failed.* New York, 1949.

Cruickshank, John, ed., *The Novelist as Philosopher.* New York, 1962.

Cunard, Nancy, "Three Negro Poets." *Left Review,* III (October, 1937).

D'Agostino, Nemi, "The Later Hemingway." *Sewanee Review,* LXVIII (Summer, 1960).

Dupee, F. W., "André Malraux." *Partisan Review*, IV (March, 1938).

Eisinger, Chester E., *Fiction of the Forties*. Chicago, 1963.

Estang, Luc, *Présence de Bernanos*. Paris, 1947.

Flanner, Janet, *Men and Monuments*. New York, 1947.

Flores, Angel, and Ben Ossa, "The Role of the Artist in Spain." *Art Front*, II (September-October, 1936).

Ford, Hugh Douglas, *A Poets' War: British Poets and the Spanish Civil War*. New York, 1965.

Fox, Ralph, *The Novel and the People*. London, 1937.

Frank, Joseph, *The Widening Gyre*. New Brunswick, N.J., 1963.

Frohock, Wilbur M., *André Malraux and the Tragic Imagination*. Stanford, 1952.

——— *The Novel of Violence in America, 1920–1950*. Dallas, 1950.

Gannon, Edward, *The Honor of Being a Man: The World of André Malraux*. Chicago, 1957.

Garosci, Aldo, *Gli intellettuali e la guerra di Spagna*. Turin, 1959.

Gollancz, Victor, "The Left Book Club, the People's Front, and Communism." *Left News*, No. 15 (July, 1937).

Graves, Robert, "A Life Bang-Full of Kicks and Shocks." *New York Times Book Review* (January 5, 1958).

Guttmann, Allen, *The Wound in the Heart: America and the Spanish Civil War*. New York, 1962.

Hart, Henry, ed., *The Writer in a Changing World*. New York, 1937.

Hemingway, Ernest, *Green Hills of Africa*. New York, 1935.

Hoffman, Frederick J., *The Modern Novel in America*. Chicago, 1951.

Hollis, Christopher, *A Study of George Orwell: The Man and his Works*. London, 1956.

Hopkinson, Henry Thomas, *George Orwell*. London, 1953.

Howe, Irving, *Politics and the Novel*. New York, 1957.

Humphries, Rolfe, "The Balladry of the Civil War." *International Literature*, III (March, 1937).

"Interrogation à Malraux." *Esprit*, No. 149 (October, 1948).

Kazin, Alfred, "Modern Men on the Battlefield." *New York Herald Tribune Books* (November 13, 1938).

Kelyin, F. V., "Heroism in Spanish Literature." *International Literature*, III (March, 1937).

——— "Fascist Kultur in Spain." *International Literature,* XI (November, 1937).

——— "Recent Spanish Literature." *International Literature,* II (February, 1937).

Lehmann, John, "Should Writers Keep to Their Art?" *Left Review,* II (January, 1937).

Lewis, C. Day, "English Writers and a People's Front." *Left Review,* II (October, 1936).

——— *A Hope for Poetry.* London, 1934.

——— "Labour and Fascism, the Writer's Task." *Left Review,* II (November, 1936).

——— "Sword and Pen." *Left Review,* II (December, 1936).

——— "Poetry To-Day." *Left Review,* II (January, 1937).

Lewis, R. W. B., ed., *Malraux: A Collection of Critical Essays.* Englewood Cliffs, N.J., 1964.

Lewis, Wyndham, *Men Without Art.* London, 1934.

——— *The Writer and the Absolute.* London, 1952.

Malraux, André, "L'art est une conquète." *Commune* (September-October, 1934).

——— L'attitude de l'artiste." *Commune* (November, 1934).

Mander, John, *Writer and Commitment.* London, 1961.

Mauriac, Claude, *Malraux ou le mal du héros.* Paris, 1946.

McCaffery, John K. M., ed., *Ernest Hemingway: the Man and His Work.* Cleveland, 1950.

Molnar, Thomas, *Bernanos: His Political Thought and Prophecy.* New York, 1960.

Muggeridge, Malcolm, "Exploding Bombs and Poets." *Time and Tide,* No. 42 (May 11, 1961).

Muste, John M., *Say That We Saw Spain Die.* Seattle, 1966.

Orwell, George, *Dickens, Dali and Others.* New York, 1946.

——— *The Road to Wigan Pier.* London, 1937.

"Passion and the Intellect: or André Malraux." *Yale French Studies,* No. 18 (New Haven, 1957).

Peyre, Henri, *The Contemporary French Novel.* New York, 1955.

Picon, Gaetan, *Georges Bernanos.* Paris, 1948.

——— *Malraux par lui-même.* Paris, 1953.

——— "Poetry, the Voice of the New Spain." *Spain,* XV (January 8, 1938).

——— "The Poetry of the Nationalist Movement." *Spain,* VII (April 20, 1939).

Pritchett, V. S., *Books in General*. New York, 1953.

Read, Herbert, "Poetry in My Time." *Texas Quarterly,* I (February, 1958).

Rees, Sir Richard, *George Orwell, Fugitive from the Camp of Victory*. London, 1961.

Rickword, Edgell, "In Defense of Culture." *Left Review,* III (August, 1937).

——— "Writers in Spain." *Left Review,* III (September, 1937).

Rideout, Walter B., *The Radical Novel in the United States, 1900–1954*. Cambridge, Mass., 1956.

Rousseau, André, Introduction to Georges Bernanos' *Français, si vous saviez*. Paris, 1961

Rumbold, Richard, *The Winged Life: A Portrait of Antoine de Saint-Exupéry, Poet and Airman*. London, 1953.

Sanders, David, "Ernest Hemingway's Spanish Civil War Experience." *American Quarterly,* XII (Summer, 1960).

Sartre, Jean-Paul, *Situations, II*. Paris, 1948.

Savane, Marcel, *André Malraux*. Paris, 1946.

Spender, Stephen, "Spain Invites the World's Writers." *New Writing,* I (Autumn, 1937).

Stephane, Roger, *Portrait de l'aventurier*. Paris, 1950.

Symons, Julian, "The Betrayed Idealists." *Sunday Times,* XXI (July 23, 1961)

——— *The Thirties*. London, 1960.

Trilling, Lionel, *The Opposing Self*. New York, 1955.

Trevor, D., "Poets of the Spanish War." *Left Review,* III (September, 1937).

Vorhees, Richard Joseph, *The Paradox of George Orwell*. Purdue University, 1961.

Weeks, Robert P., ed., *Hemingway: A Collection of Critical Essays*. Englewood Cliffs, N.J., 1962

Wellek, René, and Austin Warren, *Theory of Literature*. New York, 1941.

Wilson, Edmund, "Hemingway and the Wars." *The Nation,* CXLVII (December 10, 1938).

——— *The Triple Thinkers*. New York, 1948.

Woodcock, George. *The Writer and Politics*. London, 1947.

"Writers-in-Arms with the Spanish Republican Forces." *International Literature,* XII (December, 1937).

*Writers Take Sides.* New York, 1938.
Young, Philip, *Ernest Hemingway.* New York, 1952.

### V. CRITICAL STUDIES OF THE IMPACT OF THE SPANISH CIVIL WAR ON SPANISH LITERATURE

Alborg, Juan Luis, *Hora Actual de la Novela Española.* Madrid, 1958.
Aub, Max, *Discurso de la Novela Española Contemporánea.* Mexico, 1945.
Baquero Goyanes, M., "La Guerra Española en Nuestra Novela." *Ateneo,* III (March 1, 1952).
Cernuda, Luis, *Estudios sobre Poesia Española Contemporánea.* Madrid, 1958
Chabás, Juan, *Literatura Española Contemporánea.* Havana, 1952.
Fernández Cañedo, J. A., "La Joven Novela Española: 1936–1947." *Revista de la Universidad de Oviedo,* XLIX–L (1948).
Flóres, Angel, ed., *Spanish Writers in Exile.* Sausalito, California, N.D.
López Aranguren, José Luis, "La Evolución Espiritual de los Intelectuales Españoles en la Emigración." *Cuadernos Hispanoamericanos,* No. 38 (February, 1953).
Marañón, Gregorio, *Españoles Fuera de España.* Buenos Aires, 1947
Marra-López, José R., *Narrativa Española Fuera de España.* Madrid, 1963.
Nora, Eugénio de, *La Novela Española Contemporánea.* Madrid, 1958–1962.
Perez Minik, Domingo, *Novelistas Españoles de los Siglos XIX y XX.*
Serrano Poncela, Segundo, "La Novela Española Contemporánea." *La Torre,* II (April-June, 1953).
Torre, G. de, "Afirmación y Negación de la Novela Española Contemporánea." *Ficcion,* II (Buenos Aires, 1956).
Torrente Ballester, G., *Panorama de la Literatura Española Contemporánea.* Second Edition. Madrid, 1961
Vila Selma, José, *Tres Ensayos sobre la Literatura y Nuestra Guerra.* Madrid, 1956.

# Index

*Figures in boldface indicate pages upon which important references occur.*

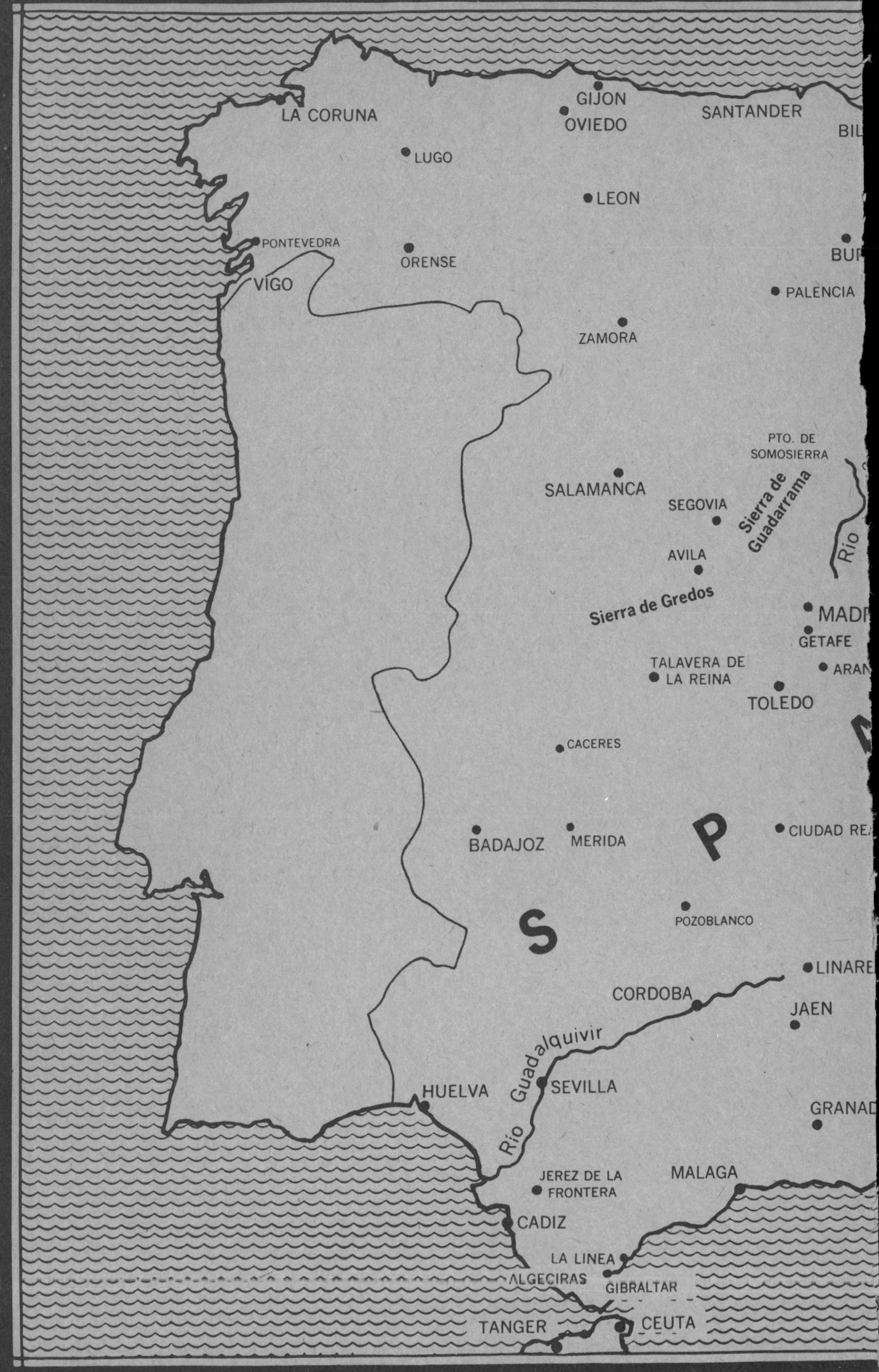
LA CORUNA
GIJON
OVIEDO
SANTANDER
LUGO
LEON
PONTEVEDRA
ORENSE
VIGO
PALENCIA
ZAMORA
PTO. DE SOMOSIERRA
SALAMANCA
SEGOVIA
Sierra de Guadarrama
Rio
AVILA
Sierra de Gredos
GETAFE
TALAVERA DE LA REINA
TOLEDO
CACERES
BADAJOZ
MERIDA
P
S
POZOBLANCO
CORDOBA
JAEN
Rio Guadalquivir
HUELVA
SEVILLA
JEREZ DE LA FRONTERA
MALAGA
CADIZ
LA LINEA
ALGECIRAS
GIBRALTAR
TANGER
CEUTA